# TOTAL QUALITY MANAGEMENT AND RELIABILITY

**2ND EDITION**

**PROF. M.P. POONIA**
VICE CHAIRMAN
All India Council for Technical Education (AICTE)

**S.C. SHARMA**
Former General Manager
THDC India Limited.

**KHANNA BOOK PUBLISHING CO. (P) LTD.**
Publisher of Engineering and Computer Books
4C/4344, Ansari Road, Darya Ganj, New Delhi-110002
**Phone** : 011-23244447-48 **Mobile:** +91-9910909320
**E-mail** : contact@khannabooks.com
**Website** : www.khannabooks.com

Dear Readers,

To prevent the piracy, this book is secured with HIGH SECURITY HOLOGRAM on the front title cover. In case you don't find the hologram on the front cover title, please write us to at contact@khannabooks.com or whatsapp us at +91-99109 09320 and avail special gift voucher for yourself.

Specimen of Hologram on front Cover title:

Moreover, there is a SPECIAL DISCOUNT COUPON for you with EVERY HOLOGRAM.

How to avail this SPECIAL DISCOUNT:

Step 1: Scratch the hologram
Step 2: Under the scratch area, your "coupon code" is available
Step 3: Logon to www.khannabooks.com
Step 4: Use your "coupon code" in the shopping cart and get your copy at a special discount
Step 5: Enjoy your reading!

Thanks,
Khanna Publishing House

**ISBN:** 978-93-91505-22-6

**TOTAL QUALITY MANAGEMENT AND RELIABILITY**
*by* **Prof. M.P. Poonia and S.C. Sharma**

**First Edition:** 2018
**Second Edition:** 2024
**Reprint: 2026**

To view complete list of books, please scan the QR Code:

*Published by:*
**Khanna Book Publishing Co. (P) Ltd.**
*CIN: U22110DL1998PTC095547*

*Visit us at:* www.khannabooks.com
*Write us at:* contact@khannabooks.com

*Printed in Bharat.*

# PREFACE

Total Quality Management, is an integrated approach in satisfying customer needs in totality on a continuing basis, through involvement of each and every employee in the organisation, making continuous improvement on one side and an appropriate cost effective technology on the other side. It is a management philosophy for professional excellence that too through customer orientation.

With the rapid advancement in technology and awareness, the users (customers) have become highly quality conscious and demands quality, reliability and safety in product and service. In view of this, industries need to upgrade their quality continuously.

Product and service quality requires managerial, technological and statistical concepts throughout all the major functions of an organisation. The concepts like strategic management, competitive benchmarking, self–managing teams, getting it right first time, zero defects, employee empowerment are important as a move towards Total Quality Management (TQM).

This book provides a fundamental and comprehensive coverage of Total Quality Management (TQM) in simple and easy to understand language. The book is divided in to two parts, Part–I covers the principles and practices of TQM, while part–II covers the tools and technology of TQM.

The book covers the syllabii of various university and therefore, should serve the needs of students of MBA and those of engineering, technology, and related disciplines. The professionals too will find this book to be a valuable reference in the field.

**Prof. M.P. Poonia**

**S.C. Sharma**

## CONTENTS

# Quality Concept

## 1.1 HISTORICAL BACKGROUND

The quality of goods produced has been monitored, either directly or indirectly, since beginning. During the Middle Ages and upto the nineteenth century, the production of goods was confined to a single person or a small group of persons. The groups generally owned businesses and the responsibility for controlling the quality lay with that person or the group.

The concept of specialization of labour was introduced during the Industrial Revolution. Then, a worker no longer made the entire product, he is responsible for producing only a portion of the product. This change resulted a decline in workmanship since most products manufactured during this early period were not complicated, the quality was not affected much. But since productivity improved, there was a decrease in cost which resulted in lowering customer expectations. When products become more complicated and jobs become more specialised inspection of products after manufacture became essential.

Till early 1950s "Inspection" was treated as the only method for controlling quality. Inspection was used as a process of sorting good items from a lot and rejecting below standard materials and products. Thus, the inspection was the process of measuring the quality of a product or service in terms of established standards. Attaining quality through inspection involved high costs which included the cost of preventing poor quality, rectification of quality, high wastages of material, labour and overheads on manufacture of products which later on found defective, besides the cost of inspection of each item at different stages of manufacture. Later on, concept of sampling inspection was added, as automation increases.

Later on quality control concept became popular, which is concerned with making things right rather than discovering and rejecting those made wrong. On the basis of this, emphasis was given to manufacture products of uniform acceptable quality. In this, variables resulted from the application of materials, men, machines and manufacturing conditions are regulated. Later on concept of Acceptance, Sampling and Statistical Quality Control (SQC) was introduced.

In the next phase, when quality awareness was increased in customers, concept of Quality Assurance came. In Quality Assurance (QA) phase, the focus shifted from quality through inspection to procedure compliance and product conformity to specification through production and operations management using statistical process control as a tracking tool.

In early 1950s, Dr. W. Edwards Deming, an American statistician to whom Americans did not listen, advocated his philosophy for widespread use of statistical ideas in Japan, where top managers took strong initiative in building quality into all products, processes and services. His philosophy requires the minimisation (through statistical, techniques) of variability, which always lead to less wastage, errors, reworking and costs resulting in high reliability, productivity, reputation, market share and in turn profit. This shifted quality improvement efforts from mass inspection to process control.

Dr. Genichi Taguchi then took the further step back from production to design. Efforts of Deming and Taguchi convinced the professionals that for attaining the excellence managers/ engineers and statisticians has to understand each other's language.

As a consequent to the above Total Quality Control phase started, which attempted to expand QA philosophy from manufacturing and production shops to other areas of the organisation so as to create awareness of quality and participation of total staff in this. Thus, focus shifted from reduction in direct cost to the quality through the elimination of waste and non-value added procedures and assuring continuous improvement.

The Quality is no longer a technical issue now, it has become a business issue. The customers want to have the best quality at a lower cost. With the application of contributions of Deming, Juran, Crossby, Kaizen and Taguchi, an approach of managing the total quality of managing for effectiveness and competitiveness, involving each and every activity and persons of all levels in the organisation, is now being followed. This is the Total Quality Management (TQM) approach—an approach which demand a total transformation of the existing management culture. This is a culture, advocating a total commitment to customer satisfaction through continuous improvement and innovation in all aspects of the business.

There is always a recipient of the output from every process, activity, operation action, single task or decision that is taking place. This makes everyone a customer of, and a supplier to someone else, with quality inputs and outputs demanded and expected at every part of the chain. Due to this definition of a customer, the actions required for the achievement of customer satisfaction become the everyday duties of every individual or division within the organisation.

The new ideas of various quality gurus were introduced in this TQM approach, under different names, such as : continuous quality improvement, statistical process control, reliability engineering, quality cost analysis, zero defects, six–sigma concept, quality circles, quality audit etc.

## 1.2 EVOLUTION OF QUALITY MANAGEMENT

Quality management is a recent phenomenon. Advanced civilizations that supported the arts and crafts, allowed clients to choose goods meeting higher quality standards than normal goods.

The importance of craftsmen diminished as mass production and repetitive work practices were instituted. The aim was to produce large numbers of the same goods. The first proponent in the US for this approach was Eli Whitney, who proposed (interchangeable) producing the identical components.

The next step forward was promoted by several people including Frederick Winslow Tylor, a mechanical engineer who sought to improve industrial efficiency. He was one of the intellectual leaders of the Efficiency Movement and part of his approach laid a further foundation for quality management, including aspects like standaradization and adopting improved practices.

Walter A. Shewhart made a major step in the evolution towards quality management by creating a method for quality control for production, using statistical methods, first proposed in 1924. W. Edwards Deming later applied statistical process control methods in the United States during World War II.

After the Second World War, Japan decided to make quality improvement a national imperative as a part of rebuilding their economy, and sought the help of Shewhart, Deming and Juran, amongst others. W. Edwards Deming championed Shewhart's ideas in Japan from 1950 ownwards. He is probably best known for his management philosophy establishing quality, productivity and competitive position. He has formulated 14 points of attention for managers, which are a high level abstraction of many of his deep insights. They should be interpreted by learning and understanding the deeper insights.

These 14 points include key concepts, such as:

- Break down barriers between departments
- Management should learn their responsibilities, and take on leadership
- Supervision should be to help people and machines and gadgets to do a better job
- Improve constantly and forever the system of production and service
- Institute a vigorous program of education and self-improvement

In the 1950s and 1960s, Japanese goods were synonymous with cheapness and low qulity, but over time their quality initiatives began to be successful, with Japan achieving very high levels of quality in products from the 1970s onward. For example, Japanese cars regularly top the customer satisfaction ratings. In the 1980s. Deming was asked by Ford Motor Company to start a quality initiative after they realized that they were falling behind Japanese manufacturers. These methods are now adopted by the same western countries that decades earlier derided Japanese methods.

Customers recognize that quality is an important attribute in products and services. Suppliers recognize that quality can be important differentiator between their own offerings and those of competitors (quality differentiation is also called the quality gap). In the past two decades, this quality gap has been greatly reduced between competitive products and services. This is partly due to the contracting (also called outsourcing) of manufacture to countries like India and China, as well as internationalization of trade and competition. These countries, amongst many others, have raised their own standards of quality in order to meet international standards and customer demands. The ISO 9000 series of standards are probably the best known international standards for quality management.

The influence of quality thinking has spread to non-traditional applications beyond the manufacturing, extending into service sectors and into areas, such as sales, marketing and customer service.

## 1.3. IMPORTANT TERMS AND DEFINITIONS

**1. Quality**

Quality is closely allied to cost and customer needs. 'Quality' may simply be defined as fitness for the purpose at lowest cost.

"Quality" of any product or service is regarded as the degree to which it fulfills the requirements of the customer. Quality means degree of perfection. It can also be defined as the degree to which a specific product conforms to the design or specification.

Quality is not absolute but it can only be judged or realized by comparing with standards. It can be determined by some characteristics, namely design, size, materials, chemical composition, mechanical functioning, workmanship, finish and other properties.

While some of the attributes which contribute to the poor quality are measurable, some like appearance, are not measurable. The advantages by maintaining good quality are :

(*a*) Retaining existing customers and gaining new ones.

(*b*) Enhanced prestige and reputation.

As per International Organisation for Standardization (ISO), 'Quality' can be defined as the totality of features and characteristics of a product or service that bear on its ability to satisfy stated or implied needs.

### Definitions of Quality

In current quality control theory and practice, the meaning of "Quality" is closely allied to cost and customer needs. "Quality" may simply be defined as, "fitness for purpose at lowest cost".

"Quality"of any product is regarded as the degree to which it fulfills the requirements of the customer. "Quality" means degree of perfection. Quality is not absolute but it can only be judged or realized by comparing with standards. It can be determined by some characteristics, namely design, size, material, chemical composition, mechanical functioning, workmanship, finish and other properties.

As per ISO-8702:1994 Standard, Quality can defined as the totality of features and characteristics of a product or services that can bear on its ability to satisfy stated or implied needs.

As per Crossby, quality is conformance to requirements of specifications.

Quality is the defect free production through prevention rather than detection.

In many instances, needs can change with time. This simples periodic revision of specifications. Needs are usually translated into features and characteristics with specified criteria. Needs may include aspects of:

– Usability –Safety
– Availability – Reliability
– Maintainability – Economics, and
– Environment.

The work quality is expressed, usually, in terms of an excellent product or service that fulfills or exceeds the expectations. These expectations are based on the intended use and selling price. The quality can be quantified as;

$$Q = \frac{P}{E}$$

where,

$Q$ = quality

$P$ = performance

$E$ = expectations

When Q is greater than 1, the customer has a good feeling about the product or service

Some of the other definitions of quality, as given by quality gurus are as under:

– Quality is fitness for use ....(Juran)

– Quality is conformance to requirements or specifications. ....(Crossby)

**2. Quality Control**

Quality of a product depends upon the application of materials, men, machines and manufacturing conditions. The systematic control of these factors is the quality control. The quality of a product differs greatly due to these factors. For example, a skilled worker will produce products of better quality and a less skilled worker will produce poor quality products. Similarly, better machines and better materials with satisfactory manufacturing conditions produce a better quality product. Therefore, in order to control the quality of product, various factors responsible for quality are required to be controlled properly.

In the words of Alford and Beatly, "quality control" may be broadly defined as "that industrial management technique by means of which products of uniform acceptable quality are manufactured". Quality control is concerned with making things right rather than discovering and rejecting those made wrong.

Quality control may also be defined as the function or collection of duties which must be performed throughout the organisation in order to achieve its quality objective. In other words, "Quality" is everybody's business and not the duty of the only inspection staff.

In short, we can say that quality control is a technique of management for achieving required standard of products.

Quality control, in its simplest term, is the control of quality during manufacturing. Both quality control and inspection are used to assure quality. Inspection is a determining function which determines whether raw materials, supplies, parts or finished products etc. are acceptable or unacceptable. As control becomes effective, the need for inspection decreases. Quality control determines the cause for variations in the characteristics of products and gives solution, by which these variations can be controlled. It is economical in its purpose, objective in its procedure, dynamic in its operation and helpful in its treatment.

Since variation in raw materials have large effects on the quality of in-process materials, quality control includes statistical sampling and testing before acceptance. It also includes the examination of quality characteristics in finished products so as to assure satisfactory outgoing material.

**3. Inspection**

The reputation and success of any industrial concern largely depends upon quality of its products. Inspection does not create quality but it helps to control it. The aim is to prevent defects by finding and eliminating the causes of trouble. Inspection sorts out below standard materials and products.

According to W.R. Spriegel, "Inspection is the process of measuring the quality of a product or service in terms of established standards." As per definition given by 'Kimball', "Inspection is the art of comparing materials, products or performance with established standards."

Inspection department performs the following functions :

1. Inspection of raw materials
2. Metallurgical inspection
3. Inspection of purchased parts
4. Work-in-process inspection
5. Inspection of tools
6. Periodic inspection of gauges and other measuring instruments
7. Suggest improvement in design and manufacturing methods
8. Inspection of finished products
9. Re–working of defective items/salvaging
10. Attending complaints.

**4. Other Definitions**

1. **Customer.** A customer is anyone who is impacted by the product or process.
   - **(*a*) External Customers.** These are not only the ultimate users but also intermediate processors as well as merchants.
   - **(*b*) Internal Customers.** These are not only the other divisions of a company providing components for assembly but also others that are affected.
2. **Product.** A product is the output of any process. This may be (*a*) goods, (*b*) software, or (*c*) service. Services include support activities within company *e.g.* plant maintenance, secretarial support, caretaking and other services like banking, insurance, transportation etc.

3. **Quality Assurance.** All those planned and systematic actions necessary to provide adequate confidence that a product or service will satisfy the given requirements for quality.
4. **Quality Policy.** Overall quality intentions and directions of an organisation as regards quality, as formally expressed by top management.
5. **Quality Management.** It is that aspect of the overall management function that determines and implement the quality policy.
6. **Quality Control.** These are the operational techniques and activities that are used to fulfill requirements for quality, which are aimed both at monitoring a process and at eliminating causes of unsatisfactory performance at relevant stages in order to result in economic effectiveness.
7. **Quality System.** It is an organisation structure, responsibilities, procedures, processes, resources for implementing quality management. The quality system should only be as comprehensive as needed to meet the quality objectives.
8. **Quality System Reveiw.** A formal evaluation by top management of the status and adequacy of the quality system in relation to quality policy and new objectives, resulting from changing circumstances.
9. **Quality Plan.** This is a document setting out the specific quality practices, resources and sequence of activities relevant to a particular product, service, contract or project.
10. **Quality Audit.** A systematic and independent examination to determine whether quality activities and related results comply with planned arrangements and whether these arrangements are implemented effectively and suitable to achieve objectives. The purpose of quality audit is to evaluate the need for improvement or corrective action.
11. **Reliability.** The ability of an item to perform a required function under stated conditions for a stated period of time. The term 'reliability' is also used as a reliability characteristic, denoting a probability of success or a success ratio.
12. **Non-conformity.** It is the non-fulfillment of specified requirements, and covers the departure or absence of one or more quality characteristics or quality system elements from specified requirements.
13. **Defect.** It is the non-fulfillment of intended usage requirements, and covers the departure or absence of one or more quality characteristics from intended usage requirements.
14. **Specification.** It is the document that prescribes the requirements with which the product or service has to conform. A specification refers to include drawings, patterns or other relevant documents and should also indicate the means and the criteria, whereby conformity can be checked.
15. **Total Quality Control.** An effective system for integrating the quality development, quality maintenance and quality improvement efforts of various groups in an organisation so as to enable production and service as the most economical, which allow for full customer satisfaction.

**5. Difference between Inspection, Quality Control and Quality Assurance**

**Inspection** is a process of sorting good from a lot, whereas 'quality control' is aimed at prevention of defects at the very source, relies on effective feedback system, and procedure for corrective action. In quality control programme, inspection data are used to take prompt corrective action to check defects. For this purpose,detailed studies are conducted to find out that from where the defect is originating and how to prevent it, may it be at manufacturing design, purchase of materials, storage or dispatch stage.

The quality control can be defined as the assurance of conformity of the manufactured products or the processes to establish specifications by systematic observations, inspections or tests and by regulation of materials, workmanship or other influences.

Quality assurance means to provide the necessary confidence to the customer as well as to top management that all concerned are carrying out their job effectively and that the product quality is as per customer's satisfaction with economy.

Difference between 'quality control' and 'quality assurance' is that while 'quality control' is related to actual inspection or test so as to determine whether a particular component or process is acceptable or not; whereas 'quality assurance' encompasses numerous activities, such as planning the required actions, establishing acceptance criteria, assigning qualified personnel for the process as well as for the inspection etc.

## 1.4. QUALITY IN CHANGING BUSINESS SCENARIO

In the age of competition, customer wants products and services of best quality with lowest possible cost. The business conditions of yesteryear did not hold good, when product inspection to control quality was adopted and internal costs of poor quality were included in the selling price. In today's everchanging scenario and in the current worldwide competition scenario, following four requirements are necessary to be fulfilled :

(*a*) To understand the wants of the customer and provide it immediately on demand at lowest cost.

(*b*) To provide products and services of high quality and reliability consistency.

(*c*) To keep pace with the developments in the fields of technology, social, legal, environmental etc.

(*d*) To predict and plan for customer's needs in advance.

As explained earlier, customer in the TQM culture is not only the final recipient of the end product or service, but also every individual or department within the organisation.

Actions required for the achievement of customer satisfaction and continuous improvement in the present day condition is the everyday duty of every individual or the division within the organisation. In these circumstances, the top managers should themselves be advocated of change, as no improvement can ever materialise without a change in attitude of the management.

Following are the reasons for changing the business conditions :

(*i*) **Competition.** In the age of competition, customer wants high quality and low prices simultaneously. Therefore, it is not sufficient to have a "good quality image", if the internal cost of achieving this image (sorting inspection, rework, scrap etc.) is high. In that case, the company will lose the sales because of higher prices needed to cover the cost of poor quality.

(*ii*) **New companies entering in the market.** New companies entering in the industrial or consumer market try to capture the market. New units, due to new technologies, may have the advantage of better quality and competitive cost due to lesser wastage and mass production.

(*iii*) Changing product mix

(*iv*) Higher levels of customer expectations

As discussed earlier, quality products and services ensure not only retention of the old customers, but also fewer complaints and lower warranty costs, higher profits, improved reputation and hence, increased market share. Continuous process improvement ultimately work towards 'zero defects' expectation. This saves not only scrap but also overheads i.e. workings hours, energy etc. This ultimately leads to higher productivity. This improvement in quality ultimately leads to setting of competitive prices of the end product or service.

## 1.5. PHASES OF QUALITY REVOLUTION

**1. Inspection**

In the pre-industrialisation era, product inspection was performed by the workman himself or the master of the small shop. When large industries came up, the inspection was performed either by the foreman of the shop or by those workmen who were asked to perform this function by the foreman. With the further complexity of the products, the time and skill needed for product inspection extended beyond the capacity of shop floor. This brought the concept of inspection by the inspectors. During this period, emphasis was on the productivity improvement and incentive systems were also introduced for increasing the quantity of production. This necessitated need for independent inspection department.

**2. Quality Control**

Independent Inspection Department led to Quality Control phase. But after some time, it was felt that system of quality control was not so effective, as it was under attack due to strained relationship between production and inspection, as manufacturing was no longer responsible for quality and paying attention only on increasing production, whereas Quality Control department was returning the defective items after their production.

Even when it was realised that production and quality control departments had strained relations, it was not possible at that point of time to re–allocate function of quality control to the production because of high degree of sophistication in product inspection, such as non–destructive examination, measurement of surface finish, measurement of electrical characteristics etc. requiring special skills and training. Further the costly equipment that is needed for checks cannot be provided in large numbers to all the production men. Also, various supporting services for inspection, such as gauges and instruments were required to be under the control of one agency. Hence, quality control function remained under a separate entity. Meantime, statistical quality control techniques were adopted for checking the quality of products.

**3. Quality Assurance (QA)**

In this phase, the process control approach that followed in 1950s, introduced statistical methods to monitor trends and to ensure that only such products which fall within the specified tolerance limits are produced. Later on stress was shifted from "quality of manufacture" to "quality of design". Quality Assurance movement then recognised that quality function cannot be the responsibility of the inspection or quality control department alone, but also the departments who have anything to do with the product or service have to contribute.

Quality Assurance focuses on procedure compliance and product conformity to specifications through production and operation management. QA emphasised that quality is the everyone's responsibility. The QA has moved towards the area of "prevention" from sorting defectives during inspection ; compliance with "customer requirements", and "doing right the first time". It relies on a comprehensive system of planning, documentation, statistical process control.

**4. Total Quality Control (TQC)**

In this phase, philosophy adopted are continuous improvement, managing through systems and procedures instead controlling through inspection and quality control, and finally quality aspects moved to the quality culture in the organisation.

In total quality control, the purpose of problem analysis is to develop the long term solutions rather than responding to short term variations.

**5. Total Quality Management (TQM)**

TQM means meeting the requirements of the internal/external customer consistently by continuous improvement in the quality of work of all employees. Thus, TQM is an integrated management approach in satisfying customer needs in totality on a continuing basis through involvement of each and every employee in the organisation, making continuous improvement by adopting appropriate cost effective technology. Management must think strategies to empower and involve workers, as the only way to tackle the complexities and problems of modern processes is through the involvement of people and inculcating team spirit.

**Old and New Quality Concepts**

| ***Old Philosophy*** | ***New Philosophy*** |
|---|---|
| – Believes in **technological** solutions | – Believes in **strategic** solutions. |
| – Concentrate about **products** | – Concentrate about **organisations** |
| – Quality activities are led by **experts** | – Quality activities are led by **management**. |
| – Quality is the responsibility of **inspectors** | – It is the responsibility of **everyone**. |

| – Quality is of **high grade**. | – Quality is of **appropriate grade** |
|---|---|
| – Emphasis is on **control** | – Emphasis is on **improvement**. |
| – Concentrate on meeting the **specifications** | – Concentrate on **customer satisfaction**. |

## 1.6. QUALITY MOVEMENT IN INDIA

Before independence, the quality was practiced in an informal way. Importance of formal quality management was realised only in post – independence era. Though, the Indian Statistical Institute was founded in the year 1931, but this gained the status of National importance by an Act of Parliament in 1959. Its offices are located in various cities. These offices are primarily engaged in projects and consultancy in Statistical Quality Control and Operation Research.

Dr Walter Schewhart visited India in 1947–48 and toured to various places to hold conferences and created interest in Statistical Quality Control among industrialists.

Department of Space, Department of Atomic energy and later followed by BHEL (Bharat Heavy Electricals Limited), and SAIL (Steel Authority of India Limited) in the 1960s initiated formal quality measures.

Quality movement was further consolidated in 1980s with the efforts of CII (Confederation of Indian Industries. Large scale of quality tools in private industry sector was encouraged through other industry associations like FICCI (Federation of Indian Chambers of Commerce and Industry) and ASSOCHAM (Associated Chambers of Commerce and Industry of India).

Professor Ishikawa, another quality guru and founder of the quality movement in Japan was invited by CII (Confederation of Indian Industries) in 1986, when he addressed the first National conference for top management on TQC (Total Quality Control). A similar address was also made by Dr Juran (another important quality guru) in 1987.

The IS0-9000 standards were introduced in 1987, and several organisations adopted these standards in their business strategies in 1990s. The use of TQM spread over the service and technology sector at a very fast rate.

Quality Council of India (QCI), an organisation jointly set up by Government of India with Indian industry, in 1997 as an autonomous body, to establish and operate the National Accreditation Structure for conformity assessment body. Besides accreditation structure, it also promotes the adoption of quality standards, relating to quality management systems (1S0.14001 Series), Food Safety Management System (1S0.22000 Series).

After 2000 Indian manufacturing companies have imbibed world class practices in manufacturing management. At the end of the first decade of the 21st century, Indian manufacturing companies are at par with the best in the world from a quality perspective. India has the largest number of companies, outside Japan that have been recognised for excellence in quality, 21 companies have been awarded the Deming Excellence Award and 153 companies have bagged the TPM Exellence.

Award for the Total Productivity Management Practices from the JIPM (Japan Institute of Plant Maintenance). As many as 165 companies have been recognised for the CII (Confederation of Indian Industries) – Exim Bank Award for Business Excellence.

## 1.7. INTRODUCTION TO QUALITY CONTROL

Quality control in its simplest term is the control of quality during manufacturing. Both, quality control and inspection are used to assure quality. Inspection is a determining function which determines raw materials, supplies, parts or finished products etc. as acceptable or unacceptable. As control becomes effective, the need for inspection decreases. Quality control determines the cause for variations in the characteristics of products and gives solution by which these variations can be controlled. It is economic in its purpose, objective in its procedure dynamic in its operation and helpful in its treatment.

Since variations in raw materials have large effects on the quality on in-process materials, quality control includes statistical sampling and testing before acceptance. It also includes the examination of quality characteristics in finished products so as to assure satisfactory outgoing quality.

Co-operation between the quality control group and other departments, such as production, planning and inspection is of vital importance. With proper managerial support and co-operation, the quality control programme will be more successful.

Quality control is a very important function as even a single defect may result in economic loss and also commercial damage due to loss of image. Such situations can be avoided, if quality control function is pre-planned where responsibilities are worked out and implemented with a commitment for quality satisfaction best to the customer requirement. The objective of quality control function at operators level, foreman level, inspectors level or managers level is to involve with operational techniques and activities carried both, at monitoring a process and at eliminating causes of unsatisfactory performance.

The development of Quality Control has taken place over the entire century with changes in approach to quality control. The four quality control concept changes took place from operators quality control to Foremen quality control to Inspectors quality Control to Managers quality control is that it provides sampling inspection rather than 100% inspection. The data, so obtained through sampling inspection, can be used to identify variations and to take appropriate action in order to achieve and maintain state of statistical control (Pre–determined upper and lower limits of control charts) and to improve the capability of the process. Now-a-days emphasis is on Total Quality Control and Total Quality Management.

Various aspects of quality control have been discussed in detail in other chapters.

Quality of a product depends upon the application of materials, men, machines and manufacturing conditions. The systematic control of these factors is the quality control. The quality of a product differs greatly due to these factors. For example, a skilled worker will produce products of better quality and a less skilled worker will produce poor quality products. Similarly, better machines and better materials with satisfactory manufacturing conditions produce a better quality product. Thus, it is clear that to control the quality of product various factors which are responsible for quality are required to be controlled properly.

## Factors Affecting Quality

In addition to men, materials, machines and manufacturing conditions, there are some other factors which affect the product quality.

These are :

(*i*) Market *i.e.* demand of product.

(*ii*) Money *i.e.* capability to invest.

(*iii*) Management *i.e.* Management policies for quality level.

(*iv*) Production methods and product design.

(*v*) Information system.

(*vi*) Motivation of employees.

Apart from these, poor packing, inappropriate transportation and poor after-sales-service are the areas which can cause damage to a company's quality image. There are cases where goods of acceptable quality before transportation were downgraded on receipt by the retailer just because they had been damaged in transportation.

Modern quality control begins with an evaluation of the costomer's requirements and has a part to play at every stage from goods manufactured right through the sales to a customer, who remains satisfied.

## Objectives of Quality Control

Following are the important objects of quality control:

1. To decide about the standard of quality of a product that is easily acceptable to the customer and at the same time this, standard should be economical to maintain.
2. If quality of product is falling down during manufacturing, then different steps should be taken to check this deviation.
3. To take necessary steps so that the products which are below standard should not reach to the customers.
4. Evaluation of quality standards of incoming material, product during manufacture, and of outgoing product.
5. Developing quality consciouness both, within and outside the organisation.
6. To take different measures to improve the standard of quality of product.

## Functions of Quality Control Department

Quality control department has the following important functions to perform :

1. Only the products of uniform and standard quality are allowed to be manufactured and sold.
2. To suggest methods and ways to prevent the manufacturing difficulties.
3. To reject the defective goods so that the products of poor quality may not reach to the customers.
4. To find out the points where the control is breaking down and investigate the causes of it.
5. To correct the rejected goods, if it is possible. This procedure is known as rehabilitation of defective goods.
6. The necessary material specifications and any specific requirements be attached to the raw material purchase order to assure that the purchased material is capable of meeting any special requirement of the customer.
7. Perform and document inspection, tests and verification of purchased material, as specified in procedures. Also, maintain documentation about corrective actions.
8. Perform in-process tests, final inspections, tests and verifications, as required by quality control procedures.
9. Ensure calibration of all equipment and tools in accordance with requirements, as laid down in quality manual.

## Advantages of Quality Control

There are many advantages by controlling the product quality. Some of them are listed below :

1. Quality of product is improved which in turn increases sales.
2. Scrap, rejection and rework are minimised thus, reducing wastage. The cost of manufacturing is, therefore, reduced.
3. Good quality product improves reputation.
4. Inspection cost reduces to a great extent.
5. Uniformity in quality can be achieved.
6. Improvement in manufacturer and consumer relations.
7. Improvement in technical knowledge and engineering data for process development and manufacturing design.

## 1.8. FACETS OF QUALITY (QUALITY REQUIREMENTS)

Quality characteristics, as discussed in earlier chapters, can be grouped into following categories :

1. **Quality of Design :**
   (*a*) The designer must meet all the qualities desired by the customer, for which he should be aware of their requirements.

(*b*) Designer should aim to make product competitive.

(*c*) Designer should take into account the question of appearance, reliability and maintainability of the product.

2. **Quality of Conformance :**

Quality of conformance means the degree or extent to which a product actually conforms in accordance with the specifications and drawings.

3. **Availability :**

This includes such characteristics as reliability, maintainability and length of life. These indicate as to what extent the product will be available for use. Here, reliability of a product means the extent to which it can give continuous service. If a product breaks down frequently, it is not reliable, and during the period of break down, the product is not available for use. Maintainability of a product means it should lend itself of easy maintenance within the least possible time. Life of the product in real life should not be less than that it was expected.

4. **Customer Service :**

This is after-sales function, and indicates the extent to which the customer get assistance from the manufacturer in keeping the product in continuous use. The customer service include (*a*) replacement of defective component, conveying sufficient know-how for maintenance through maintenance manual, leaflets etc., deputing experts to customers' place for commissioning and attending to breakdowns, training the customers' staff for proper maintenance of the product etc.

### Other Quality Requirements

From the definition of quality, it should be seen that a product should have certain abilities to perform satisfactorily in a stated application. These abilities in addition to those mentioned above, are:

(*i*) Suitability
(*ii*) Durability
(*iii*) Dependability/reliability,
(*iv*) Safe workability
(*v*) Affordability, and
(*vi*) Applicability

A product is said to have a good quality, if all the above mentioned abilities are balanced while designing and producing it.

## 1.9. QUALITY CHARACTERISTICS (DIMENSIONS) FOR PRODUCTS AND SERVICES

As already discussed, quality is the "fitness for the purpose at lowest cost". Further I.S.O. has defined the quality as "the totality of features and characteristics of a product or service that bear on its ability to satisfy stated or implied needs". Here, the issue arises about the 'purpose' or 'stated or implied needs', which is required to be specified precisely so that quality can be measured or controlled accordingly. For this, characteristics about the products or services need to be specified. Therefore, we are discussing the characteristics of the products or services in the following paragraphs:

*Gravin* divided the characteristics of quality into five categories:

(*i*) transcendent,
(*ii*) product-based,
(*iii*) user-based
(*iv*) manufacturing based, and
(*v*) value-based.

He further identified **eight attributes** (dimensions) that may be used to define quality:

(*i*) performance,
(*ii*) features,
(*iii*) reliability (consistency of performance over time),
(*iv*) conformance (meeting specifications or standards),
(*v*) durability (useful life),
(*vi*) serviceability (resolving problems, complaints and ease of repair),
(*vii*) aesthetics (sensory characteristics),
(*viii*) perceived quality.

Other notable pioneers have further added different characteristics, comprehensive list of characteristics have been discussed in the following paragraphs with regards to manufactured products and services.

Thus, we have seen that one or more elements define the intended quality level of a product or service. These elements (known as quality characteristics), can be categorised in to following groups:

(*i*) **Structural characterises.** These include the length, weight, strength, viscosity etc.
(*ii*) **Sensory characteristics.** These include the taste of food, smell, beauty etc.
(*iii*) **Time–oriented characteristics.** These include warranty, guarantee, reliability, maintainability etc.
(*iv*) **Ethical characteristics.** These include honesty, courtesy, friendliness etc.

**1. Product Quality**

A product may be either (*a*) goods like machines, appliances, components, consumer goods etc. or (*b*) processed materials like steel, cement, sugar, chemical, textile, petroleum, fertilizer etc. Quality of a product is specified by the characteristics it has. Product characteristics refer to the quality of design. Increasing the quality of the design generally leads to higher costs.

The quality of a product comprises several engineering and manufacturing characteristics, which meet the ultimate performance expectations of the designer and customer.

**Quality characteristics of a product can be expressed by :**

– Performance
– Features
– Reliability
– Chemical properties
– Durability
– Metallurgical properties
– Serviceability
– Aesthetics
– Sensory properties
– Availability of options and expandability
– Maintainability
– Safety aspect
– Perceived quality
– Structural aspects like size, shape, strength, stability etc.
– Warranty
– After-sales service and customer training.

**2. Quality For Services**

As we know that for service organisations, it is essential for achieving the quality (*a*) to properly understand and meet the customer needs, (*b*) commitment to quality at all levels of organisation; and (*c*) establish a quality management system for continuous review and improvement of quality based on customer's feedback and their perception of the service provided.

Here, it is clarified that service is the result generated by activities at the interface between the service provider and the customer and by service provider internal activities to meet customer needs. The requirements of a service need to be clearly defined in terms of characteristics that are observable and subject to customer evaluation against defined standards of acceptability.

**Major service characteristics are :**

– Responsiveness,
– Credibility
– Reliability
– Service facilities
– Accuracy in service and billing
– Timeliness
– Completeness
– Warranty

– Courtesy and friendliness
– Security, safety and hygiene
– Aesthetics/appearance
– Knowledge of server and competence
– Access
– Waiting time
– Cleanliness
– Comfort
– Communication
– Reputation
– Customer's perception.

## 1.10. PROBLEMS RELATED TO QUALITY ASPECTS

Quality control activities are mainly related to the evaluation, maintenance and improving quality economically. The broad areas of applications are incoming material control, process control, and product control. Problems related to quality aspects can be classified into following three categories:

1. **Engineering Aspects:**
   (*a*) Creation and development of a product.
   (*b*) The development of quality evaluation through improved inspection procedures,
   (*c*) The knowledge of the causes of defects and sub-standard products and their rectification.
2. **Statistical Aspects:**
   Building an information system to satisfy the concepts of 'prevention' and 'control' and improving upon product quality.
3. **Managerial Aspects:**
   (*a*) Effective use of the engineering and statistical technology.
   (*b*) Creation of a climate for quality consciousness in the organisation.
   (*c*) The effective co-ordination of the quality control functions with those of the others.

## 1.11. QUALITY STATEMENTS

Quality statements include the vision statement, mission statement, and quality policy statement once these are developed, they remain for long period of time and are only occasionally reviewed and updated. Small organisations may use only the quality policy statement. Most organisations have a vision of what quality is and how to attain it.

## Vision Statement

The vision statement is a short declaration of what an organisation aspires to be tomorrow. A company's vision comprises its values and beliefs. Their vision is what they want to be and it is a message that every employee should believe. Visions are about the future, and should be simple and inspirational. Successful visions provide guideline for decision–making. Employees should understand the vision and connect their work with the well-being of the organisation.

## Mission Statement

A mission statement emanates from a vision. The mission statement for the organisation is more specific and goal oriented. The mission statement is usually one paragraph in length and easy to understand and describes the function of the organization. It provides a clear statement of purpose for employees, customers, and suppliers.

Mission deseribes the company's overall reason for existence. Mission refers to be broad purpose that society expects the organisation to serve.

## Quality Policy Statement

A quality policy is the company's road map and is prepared by the senior management. The quality is a guide for everybody in the organization as to how they should provide products and services to the customers.

Quality policy is an overall quality intentions and directions of an organization as regards quality, as formally expressed by top management. Quality policy should be expressed in an easily understandable language and should be relevant to organisations policies. The management should be committed to implement its quality policy.

**Quality policy should include:**

– Grade of quality to be provided,
– Image and reputation for quality,
– Objectives for quality,
– Approach to be adopted to achieve quality objectives
– Role of company personnel responsible for implementation of quality policy.

**Common characteristics of quality policy are:**

- Meet the needs of the internal and external customers.
- Equal or exceed the competition.
- Continually improve the quality.
- Quality is first among equals.
- Include best practices for business and production
- Effective utilization of entire work-force.

## 1.12. QUALITY AWARENESS

For the purpose of creating and maintaining quality awareness, it is necessary to start with creating and disseminating information on the current status of quality. This helps in knowing the serious quality problems, and hence, need for presenting a programme of action. To create awareness, it is necessary to present information in different languages for different people in the organisation.

For upper management, usually General Manager and the top management team, quality awareness is created in the language of money, highlighting threats to sales income or opportunities for cost reduction. A study on existing quality culture will help to identify some of the obstacles to inspiring action. The presentation of this current status should be accompanied by an explanation of the 'benefits' expected from new approach to quality.

For middle and lower management levels, the impact of quality can be translated into the language of job security. The results can be dramatic, if this is explained through data.

Maintaining awareness of quality is more important, and therefore, the message on quality must be sustained through continuous reinforcement through quality measurement. Quality measurement is usually adopted for major functional activities *viz*. product development, purchasing, manufacturing, marketing and customer service etc. These measurements provide data to the people to facilitate them to perform their tasks in addition to maintain a continuing awareness of quality, employees must also be provided with continuous feedback showing the overall quality story. The reports and score—boards of quality measurements are highly effective. These must recognise the management-controllable as well as worker-controllable causes. In cases of worker-controllable problems, publishing or posting of data must accompany the steps which workers must personally take to improve their quality of output.

Other measures taken for maintaining an awareness of quality can be quality newsletters, quality items on all meeting agendas, announcements about quality by key executives, company conferences on quality etc.

## 1.13. FACTORS AFFECTING QUALITY

In addition to men, materials, machines and manufacturing conditions, there are some other factors which affect the product quality. These are :

(*a*) Market research *i.e*. demands of customers.

(*b*) Capability to invest.

(*c*) Management policies for quality.

(*d*) Production methods and product design.

(*e*) Target group of customers.

Apart from these, packaging, transport system, and after sales service also affects the company's quality image. There are many cases where goods of acceptable quality before transportation were downgraded, on receipt by the retailer just because they had been damaged in transportation.

Modern quality control performs an evaluation of the customer's requirement and has a part to play at every stage from goods manufactured right through sales to a customer who remain satisfied.

## 1.14. CAUSES OF QUALITY FAILURES

Quality failures occur due to various causes, most of them are because of lack of involvement of men concerned with the quality. Studies have indicated that more than 50% of quality failures are due to human errors at various levels, such as understanding of customer's requirements, manufacturing, inspection, testing, packing, design etc.

Errors affecting quality can be classified into following categories:

(*a*) **Error due to inadvertence.** These are due to lack of knowledge of the product, and continues due to lack of information about quality deficiency. Such mistakes can be controlled, if a system for feedback is developed in which quality performance results are analysed in a regular and timely manner.

(*b*) **Errors due to lack of technique.** These errors are due to lack of knowledge, skill, technique, etc. In such cases, performance of 'better' operation are compared with those of 'poor' or 'defect prone' operators, and the process adopted by them are studied and reasons for errors are investigated.

(*c*) **Willful errors.** Sometimes quality is compromised due to early delivery schedules, reduction in cost, safety etc. Different types of errors have been discussed in details in earlier chapters.

### Reduction of Errors by Improved Motivation

Quality motivational programmes are developed for getting quality product from the line staff so that they take interest in improving the quality. Motivational programmes are designed after identifying the sources/reasons of failures. Operators are motivated by designing a campaign to secure alertness, awareness and new actions and by observing the managers for their behaviour or reactions on any quality problem. Campaign can be launched through mass meetings, quality posters, exhibition of quality deficiencies etc. Campaign may also invite operators to participate in analysing the cause of defects or the failure on the part of operation and/or systems. Training are very helpful in making the operators aware of the technological do's and don'ts and the purpose behind each operation.

### 1.14.1 Types of Errors

(1) **Inadvertent Errors.**

These are those errors which workers are unable to avoid because of human inability to maintain attention. The features of these errors are :

- These are unintentional.
- These are unnoticeable.
- These are unpredictable.

**Remedial approaches of these inadvertent errors are :**

(*a*) Reducing the extent to dependence on human attention.

(*b*) Making it easier to remain attentive by reducing fatigue and monotony.

2. **Technique Errors.**

These errors arise due to lack of essential technique, skill, or knowledge of worker needed to prevent the error. The features of these errors are :

– These are unintentional.
– These are unique to certain types of errors.
– These are consistent.
– The inferior workers are unable to match the performance of superior workers.

**The steps to identify, analyze, and remedy these technique errors are :**

(*a*) Create and collect data necessary to disclose any significant differences between workers.

(*b*) Analyze the data to discover whether there is any consistency.

(*c*) Identify consistently best and consistently worst performers.

(*d*) Study the work methods used by the best and worst performers : to identify their differences in technique.

(*e*) Study these differences further and discover the beneficial way of doing and negative way of doing.

(*f*) Bring everyone upto the level of the best through training, changing the technology and error-proofing the process.

3. **Conscious Errors :**

The features of these errors are :

– these are intentional.
– worker who makes the error usually intends to keep it up.
– worker is aware at the time of making these errors.

These errors exhibit consistency. Sometimes to meet cost, delivery and productivity standards management is interested in conscious violation of one standard in order to meet another. This generally happens in seller's market. Sometimes workers, to get their revenge with their boss or company, do it to show their resentment. Sometimes such errors although seems to be worker initiated but they have their origin in inadequate communication by management.

**Possible remedies to such errors are :**

– Establishing individual accountability.
– Explaining the impact of the error on internal customers.
– Providing a balance between quality and productivity.
– Improving communication on quality issues.
– Creating competition and incentives.
– Re-assigning the work.

## 1.15. AREAS OF APPLICATION OF QUALITY CONTROL

As already mentioned, broad areas of application of quality control are :

1. Incoming Material Control
2. Process Control
3. Product Control.

1. **Incoming Material Control.** Incoming material control, means procuring and stocking materials best suited for producing the established quality standards. Right quality of incoming material is essential, for getting product of right quality. In any manufacture, acceptable quality standards have to be evaluated and maintained in all the stages of manufacture. Incoming materials include, materials, parts, assemblies etc. moving from one department to another. Poor quality material, if accepted, will not only affect the quality, but also production due to increased rejections, downtime on machines, idle time for men and longer processing time.

2. **Process Control.** Process control refers to the procedure 'adopted to evaluate, maintain and improve quality standards during various stages of manufacture so as to build the desired quality in the finished product. The success of process control is evaluated in terms of scrap, rejections, rework etc. The objectives of process control are :

   (*a*) To ensure that items produced conform to the specifications, as the manufacturing is continuing.

   (*b*) Deviations, if any, must be found out as quickly as possible, so that immediate corrective action can be taken.

   (*c*) To build up an efficient information system so that trouble is timely found out.

3. **Product Control.** Product control refers to the procedure adopted for evaluating the quality of the out-going product including finished products in stores and warehouses, feedback mechanism, quality audit, complaints redressal system, analysis, life test studies, reliability studies, opinion surveys etc.

## 1.16. ECONOMICS OF QUALITY (QUALITY COST)

Good economic performance is most essential for survival and growth of any organisation in the highly competitive environment. Therefore, one of the most common objectives of every organisation is to attain excellence in its economic performance. The single most important factor which leads to good economic performance is the 'quality' of its products or services.

In order to achieve economy, quality management system must contribute towards the establishment of customer – oriented quality discipline in the marketing, design engineering, procurement, production, inspection, testing and other related servicing functions. Everybody in the organisation must be involved in the production and delivery of quality product or services, consistently to meet the customer needs and satisfaction.

**Various components of quality costs are:**

- achievement of requirements identified by product or service conformance or non-conformance.
- prevention costs.
- cost components of appraisal and failure costs.

In other words, we can say that the quality costs may be interpreted as the difference between the actual cost and the reduced cost, if products and services were all conforming. Major categories of quality costs are discussed in this section.

As discussed earlier, quality means freedom from deficiencies (*i.e.*, errors). Freedom from deficiencies of an organisation lead to higher quality which enables companies to;

(*i*) reduce rework,
(*ii*) reduce error rates,
(*iii*) reduce field failures,
(*iv*) warranty charges,
(*v*) reduce time to put new products to the market,
(*vi*) increase yields/capacity,
(*vii*) improve delivery performance, and
(*viii*) increase customer satisfaction.

Therefore, poor quality adversely effect income as well as cost. In many markets, products with superior features are able to secure superior income, while product deficiencies have an adverse effect on income. The customer who encounters a deficiency have an adverse effect on income. The customers who encounters a deficiency may take action which require. Further cost e.g., file a compliant, return the product, make a claim or file a suit.

## Quality and Cost

Studies have indicated that any reduction in quality results in a reduced level of satisfaction and decrease in customer goodwill towards the producer. This will lead to reduction in return on investment in the long run. Following are the general principles of quality and cost relationship:

(*i*) Costs of poor quality are far larger than that had been recognized.
(*ii*) Appraisal costs are reduced by focussing on preventing errors at the source.
(*iii*) System be established for reducing the cost rather than reducing the quality.
(*iv*) By focussing on quality improvement, overall performance of the firm can be improved.
(*v*) Focus of quality improvement be shifted from product attributes to operational procedure.

## Quality Cost (or Costs associated with quality)

Costs associated with the improvement of product/services refer to quality cost. Quality cost can be classified into following categories :

**1. Failure Costs**

(*A*) *Internal Failure Costs:*

These are the costs associated with the defects detected before the despatch of the product to the customer :

(*i*) Scrap and re-work cost.
(*ii*) Costs involved in testing, inspecting and sorting for down-gradation.
(*iii*) Losses due to avoidable processing.
(*iv*) Expenditure on failure analysis.

(*B*) *External Failure Costs :*

These are the costs associated with the defects detected after the product is shifted to the customer :

(*i*) Warranty charges
(*ii*) Redressal of complaints
(*iii*) Loss of future sale
(*iv*) Other expenses on return of materials, failure analysis etc.

(*C*) *Hidden Costs of Poor Quality*

Hidden costs of poor quality include:

(*i*) Lost sale due to poor quality
(*ii*) Costs of re-design due to quality reasons
(*iii*) Costs of changing manufacturing processes including cost of corresponding software changes.
(*iv*) Extra manufacturing costs due to defects. This include overtime to correct errors, delays.
(*v*) Excess process costs.
(*vi*) Loss of goodwill.
(*vii*) Extra process costs and extra inventory.

**2. Appraisal/Detection Costs.**

These are the costs incurred in determining the degree of conformance to quality requirements:

(*i*) Test and inspection of purchased materials, in process materials, and final product
(*ii*) Quality audits
(*iii*) Equipment calibrations
(*iv*) Evaluation of performance
(*v*) Evaluation of customer satisfaction.

**3. Prevention Costs.**

These are the costs incurred in keeping failure and appraised costs to a minimum:

(*i*) Quality planning (*ii*) New product review

(*iii*) Process control (*iv*) Training and education

(*v*) Process quality planning.

**4. Cost of Inefficient Processes.**

Examples of these costs are:

(*i*) Variability of product characteristics.

(*ii*) Unplanned downtime of equipment resulting into loss of production.

(*iii*) Inventory shrinkage *i.e.* loss due to difference between actual and recorded inventory amounts.

(*iv*) Variation of process characteristics.

(*v*) Non-value added activities, A value added activity increases the utility of a product customer, whereas non-value added activity does not add any utility.

**5. Cost of Lost Opportunities For Sales Revenue.**

Examples of these costs are :

(*i*) Customer defection.

(*ii*) New customer lost *i.e.* profit on potential customers lost.

(*iii*) Lack of capability to meet customer needs.

For the purpose of reducing the cost, when internal and external failure costs are cut down, the appraisal cost and preventive cost may slightly go up. Therefore, it is necessary for optimum balance to reduce failure cost with slightly increase in appraisal and preventive cost, with the aim of substantial reduction in total quality cost without compromising with the quality.

Efforts for reducing quality cost must be continuous. The cost reduction programme must be followed in following stages :

(*i*) Identification of quality cost items.

(*ii*) Structuring of quality cost reporting, including related analysis and control, and

(*iii*) Maintenance of programme to ensure the objectives of higher quality at lower cost.

Quality control and quality cost must be directed in such a way so as to provide the firm with major added busines value and cutomer satisfaction.

## Quality Cost Evaluation

Total quality costs are related to other business figures of the firm with which managers are familiar. This relationship have the great impact on top management. Some of the common relationships are:

(*i*) Quality costs as a percentage of sales.

(*ii*) Quality costs compared to profit.

(*iii*) Quality costs as a percentage of total manufacturing costs.

The relationship in terms of money is an universal language which convey its significance to the upper management.

### Objectives of Quality Cost Evaluation

Companies estimate the quality costs due to following reasons:

(*a*) Quantification of the size of the quality problem in terms of money for effectively communicating the problem by middle managers to the top managers.

(*b*) To identify major opportunities for cost reduction. It helps in identifying the vital few segments which account for bulk of the costs of poor quality. (Discussed in detail under heading "The Pareto Principle").

(*c*) To identify the opportunities for reducing customers, dissatisfaction. This also helps in detecting the associated threats to product salability like product failures which may take place after sale.

### Quality Loss

(*a*) *Loss due to scrap :* Loss of material, labour and overheads on the manufacture of defective product.

(*b*) *Loss due to repair and rework :* Labour for repairing/rework and overheads on it.

(c) *Other losses :*

(*i*) Losses due to discount on second grade quality,

(*ii*) Excess inspection costs,

(*iii*) Charges on quality guarantee/free replacement,

(*iv*) Losses due to delays, stoppages, loss of goodwill of customers.

## 1.17. QUALITY GURUS (PIONEERS)

Different pioneers (also known as '*gurus*') of quality philosophy have produced their doctrines from the lands of America, Japan and United Kingdom. The most widely known quality gurus from America and Japan are given below:

**American Quality Gurus.**

(*i*) W. Edwards Deming.

(*ii*) Dr. Joseph M. Juran.

(*iii*) Philip B. Crosby.

**Japanese Quality Gurus.**

(*i*) Kaoru Ishikawa.

(*ii*) Massaki Imai.

(*iii*) William E. Conway.

(*iv*) Genichi Taguchi

## 1. W. Edwards Deming.

Born in 1900, he was awarded his Ph.D in mathematical physics in 1928. He then worked in the US Government service for many years, particularly in statistical sampling techniques. After Second World War, he was sent to Japan as an adviser to the Japanese Census. There, he involved with the union of Japanese scientists and engineers (JUSE) after its formation in 1946. In Japan, he taught Japanese managers methodically about quality. In Japan, he taught statistical process control.

Deming's work in Japan has been identified as putting Japan on the road to leadership in international business and industry. Deming is the best known quality expert in the world.

His prescription for improved quality, productivity, and competitive position was based on his 14 points (These 14 points are different from crossbyes 14 points). These 14 points are explained later on in the book.

According to Deming, interpreting quality in terms of reliability, dependability, predictability and consistency of product and service, it is clear that quality improvement is analogous to reduction of variation, *i.e.*

**"Quality and productivity increases as variability decreases".**

**Reduce Variation.** Deming's philosophy can be summarized in just two words: "Reduce variation". These two words are fundamental to the principle of (*i*) continuous improvement, and (*ii*) the achievement of consistency, reliability and uniformity. In other words, this "reduce variation" means trust worthiness, competitive position and success.

Deming has authored a number of books including "out of the crisis and quality, productivity, and competitive position" as well as 161 scholarly studies.

## 2. Dr Josph M. Juran.

Born in America in 1904, Juran worked at Western Electric Company from 1924 to 1941. He travelled to Japan in 1954 to teach quality management and conducted seminars for top and middle level executives. His lectures focused on planning, organisational issues, management, responsibility for quality, and the need to set goals and targets for improvement. He emphasised that quality control should be conducted as an integral part of management control. Juran expressed his essential message to managers through the three basic quality related processes: quality planning, quality control and quality improvement which is known as the *Juran trilogy*.

According to Juran, there are 3 types of errors, namely; inadvertent errors, technique errors, and willful errors (already discussed).

Jurans work emphasises the need for specialist knowledge and tools for successful conduct of quality functions. He also emphasised the need for continuous awareness of the customer in all functions. He believes that the majority of quality problems are the fault of poor management, rather than poor workmanship on the shop floor. According to him, management controllable defects account for over 80% of the total quality problems. He further believes that quality happens only through projects "quality improvement projects", established in every part of the company.

## Deming v/s Juran

It has been noted that teachings of Deming and Juran are most of the time complementary, though sometimes are different, but many of their fundamental principles are basically the same. The background of both of them is similar, as they both studied under *Schewart*, they were both invited to teach the Japanese in the early 1950s, they both are world authorities in the field of quality. Deming in his approach is concerned with education and training, whereas Juran is more concerned with actual implementation. In general, Deming provides the philosophy, whereas Juran provides the specific structure which can help in the materialization of these principles.

**Similarities.**

**The similarities in the fundamental principles are:**

(*a*) ***The role of top management.*** The main responsibility for guidance towards quality lies with the senior management, as they are mainly responsible for most of the company problems (Juran put these problems as 80%, while Deming's latest revised estimate for management controllable errors to 94%.

(*b*) The importance of the customers.

(*c*) ***The necessity of quality.*** Juran refers to the habit of quality, while Deming to an obsession with quality, in order to satisfy the customer and survive in the competitive world market.

(*d*) The importance of continuous improvement.

(*e*) The need for scientific knowledge.

(*f*) ***Distinction of the causes of problems.*** Deming's special and common causes while Juran's sporadic and chronic causes.

(*g*) Training as an investment for future.

**Dissimilarities**

1. Deming strongly recommends a total transformation of current management practices as the only solution to the current crisis. Juran prefers to take existing management culture as a starting point and emphasized on improving management performance rather than transforming management.
2. Both uses different terminology and stresses different aspects. Deming's main issues on quality are : variation, continuous improvement, optimization of the total system. Juran concentrates on the quality triology (planning, improvement and control), goal setting approach towards increased conformance, quaided by the quality costs.
3. Deming emphasized on the management of the process rather than on the outcome, unlike Juran who focuses on the results, but with an emphasis on feedback loops as a model for managerial control.

## 3. Philip B. Crosby

Crosby prefers to target his training on managers rather than on quality control people. He cited his zero defects goal as something practical, reasonable and achievable. He listed the following four **essentials of quality management**. He calls them **'the absolutes'**:

1. Quality is defined as conformance to requirements, not as goodness.
2. Quality is achieved by prevention not appraisal.
3. The quality performance standard is zero defect.
4. Quality is measured by the price of non-conformance not by indexes.

He authored his first book, 'Quality is Free', in 1979, which was translated in 15 languages. It sold 1.5 million copies. It helped in changing the way management looked at quality. He was of the opinion that, "doing it right the first time" is less expensive than the costs of detecting and correcting non-conformities. In 1984, he wrote a book, quality without tears," which contained hs four absolutes of quality management.

## 4. Dr. Kaoru Ishikawa

Professor Ishikawa was born in 1915 and graduated in 1939, in Engineering from Tokyo University and later obtained his Doctorate of engineering. He adopted Total Quality Control concept for the Japanese. He also authored Statistical Process Control texts in Japanese and in English. He is best known for the development of the "Cause and effect diagram', sometimes also called as Ishikawa diagram.

He is known as 'Father of Quality Circles' and is known for his role in launching Japan's quality movement in the 1960s.

According to him, seven basic tools were 'indispensable for quality control'. These tools are :

(*i*) Pareto analysis.
(*ii*) Fishbone diagrams.
(*iii*) Stratification.
(*iv*) Tally charts.
(*v*) Histograms.
(*vi*) Scatter diagrams.
(*vii*) Control charts.

With these tools, Ishikawa argued, managers and staff could tackle and solve the quality problems facing them.

Ishikawa also associated with the company wide quality control movement, which started in Japan in the years following the visits of Deming and Juran, and was concerned with company-wide participation for the quality and its control, from top-management to lower ranking employees. Efforts were concerned with controlling and improving the quality not only of the final product, but also of the management, the after-sales service and the company itself.

## 5. Massaki Imai

Imai has brought together the management philosophies, theories and tools that have been popular in Japan, as a single concept—known as Kaizen. The views of the Imai have been discussed in detail in the chapter on "Quality Improvement".

## 6. William E. Conway

Conway defines quality as a result of quality management is 'the development, manufacture, administration and distribution of consistent low-cost products and services that customers want and need'. He targets three categories of waste in a company: time, capital and material, with time being his priority, excessive inventory comes second which requires space with all the associated costs.

Conway recommended following six tools for continuous improvement :

1. ***Human Relations Shills :*** Motivate and train all employees at all Heyels of the company.
2. ***Statistical Surveys :*** Collection of data about internal and external customers, employees, technology and equipment.
3. ***Simple Statistical Techniques :*** Charts and diagrams should be used to identify problems.
4. ***Statistical Process Control :*** These are used to reduce variation
5. ***Imagining for Problem Solving :*** Technique encourages creativity when linked to 'vision statements' and 'brainstorming'.
6. ***Industrial Engineering :*** To use workstudy including pacing, work simplification, method analysis, plant layout and material handling to make improvement.

## 7. Genichi Taguchi

Genichi Taguchi, Ph.D a, mechanical engineer developed his loss function concept that combines cost, target and variation into one metric (*i.e.*, measurable unit) with specification being of secondary importance.

Taguchi devised a quality improvement technique that uses experimental design methods for efficient characterisation of a product or process, combined with a statistical analysis of its variability. He divided the behaviour of a product or process in terms of factors (parameters or variables) as follows :

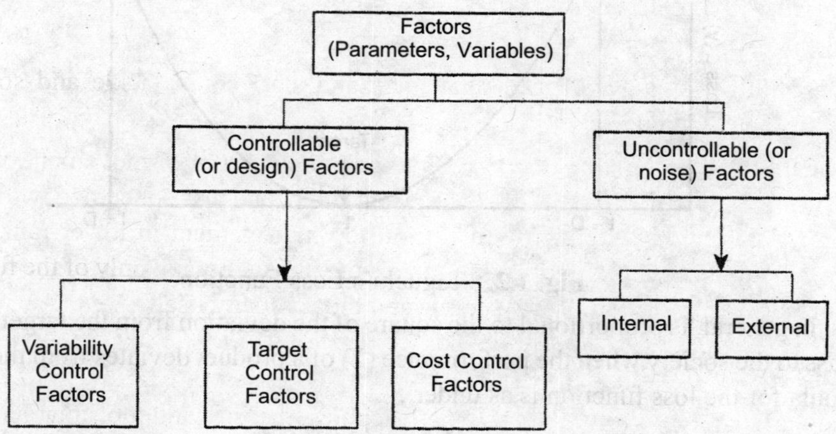


**Fig. 1.1** Behaviour of a product in terms of Factors.

Principal idea in the Taguchi philosophy is that statistical testing of a product should be carried out at the design stage in order to make the product and the process robust to variations in the manufacturing and use environment.

Taguchi suggested that following steps should be taken for carrying out statistical studies (also known as experimental studies):

1. Define the problem.
2. Determine the objectives.
3. Conduct a brainstorming session.
4. Design the experiment.
5. Conduct the experiment.
6. Analyse the data.
7. Interpret the results.
8. Run a confirmatory experiment.

These steps have been discussed in detail in the chapter "Quality Improvement".

**Taguchi Loss Function.**

Taguchi defines quality in a negative way as, "the loss imparted to society from the time the product is shipped." This loss include: (*a*) the cost of customer dissatisfaction which may lead to a loss of reputation and goodwill for the company, (*b*) direct loss to the company arising from warranty and service costs, (*c*) indirect loss due to market share loss, and (*d*) increase marketing efforts needed to overcome lack of competitiveness.

According to Taguchi, the main objective of any quality improvement programme should be the minimisation of the variation of product performance about its target value. The smaller the performance variation, the better the quality. The larger the deviation from the target, the larger is the society's (producer's and consumer's) loss. This loss can be approximately evaluated by Taguchi's loss function, which unites the financial loss with the function specification.

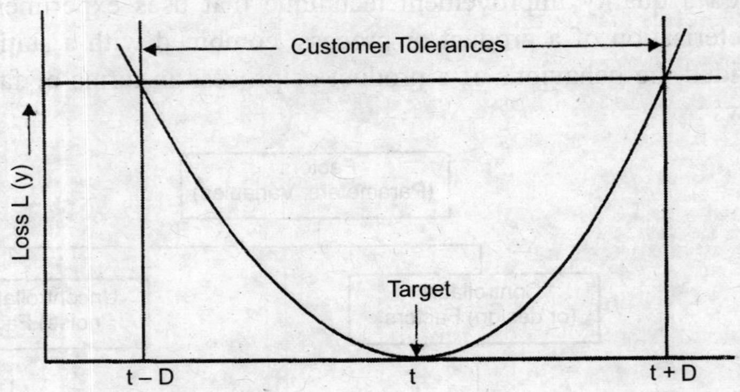


**Fig. 1.2.** Taguchi's Loss Function.

The loss, in general, is proportional to the square of the deviation from the target. Loss function $L(Y)$ is the loss to the society when the performance ($Y$) of a product deviates from the desired target ($t$). The formula for the loss function is as under :

$$L(y) = \frac{M}{D^2}(y - t)^2$$

where, $M$ = Producer's loss (in monetary terms) when the customer's tolerance $D$ is exceeded. Graphical representation of the loss to society is represented by the Fig. 1.2.

## Deming v/s Taguchi

Deming advocates the implementation of a statistical quality management approach. He considers it essential that the top managers acquire knowledge, or at least a clear appreciation, of the usefulness of statistical tools for achieving enhanced quality and increased productivity.

Deming provides a road map which can lead to the satisfaction of the customer, the creation of a happy working environment for the employee (through co-operation, job satisfaction, breaking down of barriers, elimination of fear), the safeguarding of jobs, the creation of more jobs etc.

Taguchi's main objective lies in his definition of quality (or non-quality) i.e., "Quality is the amount of damage incurred to society from the moment the product has left the factory". By 'society' he means the customer as well as the employees of the company, because if the customer suffers, the whole company will eventually suffers through re-work, guarantee costs, loss of reputation, market share, and ultimately loss of jobs. Thus, service of the society is also Taguchi's aim.

Deming strongly recommends consistency of purpose for continuous improvement of product and service. Statistically speaking, the problem of establishing and maintaining consistency of purpose can be related to Taguchi's problem of achieving the mean (target) and minimizing dispersion (variability around the mean.)

Deming advocates for major transformation in current practices to solve problems. He suggests that a basis for this transformation is provided in his fourteen points. Deming's fourteen points and Taguchi's main principles are important for a never-ending effort towards variation reduction. Evaluating and predicting the damage that this variation causes, is the basis of Taguchi's efforts.

Deming's main achievement to convince companies to shift quality improvement from inspection to statistical control of production process. While Taguchi has made further step back from production to design, so as to make the design robust against variability downstream in both, production and the user environment. This is in complete agreement with Deming's belief that reducing variation is the key to improving quality, to decreasing quality costs, and therefore, for surviving in this new economic age of worldwide competition.

Thus, Deming's and Taguchi's methods are complementary. Deming mainly concentrates on a theory of management, while Taguchi provides some important techniques that management can use to solve chronic problems.

## 1.18. DEVELOPMENT OF FITNESSES FOR QUALITY

Following are the four levels of fitnesses for the development of quality:

1. Fitness for standard.
2. Fitness for use.
3. Fitness for market.
4. Fitness for latent requirements

## 1. Fitness for Standard

Inspection and test are used to determine the conformance to a standard. The terms 'inspection' and 'test' usually refer to manufacturing industries. This concept also applies to service industries. In service sector different terms are used, e.g., review, examination, checking etc. These terms are used to determine whether product (or service) conforms to standard, and thereby whether the product should be accepted.

**Need for Inspection:** Man had always used inspection for determining the fitness of anything made by him. But industrial inspection is of recent origin *i.e.* after industrialisation when mass production necessitated interchangeability of parts and has scientific approach. In large scale production, any part is required to fit properly into any other mating component part so that each assembly functions properly. In modern production technology, each component part becomes independent process and various parts from various shops are brought to assemble together in the assembly shop. Even some parts may be manufactured in other factories and are bought for assembly.

Therefore, in order to ensure that the dimensions of the component parts are confined within prescribed limits so as to permit the assembly with a pre-determined fit. Hence, industrial inspection assumed its importance for ensuring suitability of mating components manufactured separately. For checking the dimensional accuracy, gauges were used in mass production to save time, without measuring actual dimensions. This allows the variations within the prescribed limits, as we are interested only in interchangeability of parts suitable for pre-determined fit. High precision inspection instruments are used, where high accuracy and precision is required.

The product acceptance involves different important decisions, such as:

(*i*) *Conformance.* Judging whether the product (or service) conforms to specification.

(*ii*) *Fitness for use.* Deciding whether the product is fit for use.

(*iii*) *Communication.* Deciding what to communicate to insiders or outsiders. This aspect is being discussed under the heading 'fitness for market' and 'fitness for latent requirements.

For conformance decisions, the work is organised so that inspectors or production workers themselves can make these decisions. For this purpose, they are trained to understand the products, the standards and the instruments.

## 2. Fitness for Use.

In the case of non-conforming products, a decision should be taken whether this product is fit or unfit for use. Where the non-conformance is severe the product is clearly unfit, it is scrapped or if economically repairable, bring it to the state of conformance. In most cases, where fitness for use is not very clear, a study is made to determine whether it is fit for use or not. Such a decision is taken based on the following:

(*i*) **How will this product be used ?** In many cases, specifications are broad enough to cover a large variety of possible uses. Where such products have no problem in use, these may be declared fit for use.

(*ii*) **Is there any risk to safety ?** Where there is chance of hazard from this product, it should be declared as unfit for use.

(*iii*) **Urgency.** Where customer cannot wait and there is no risk for failure, it may be delivered, and can be repaired or replaced later on, if required.

(*iv*) **What is the user's measure of fitness for use ?** If this product is fit to use from client's point of view, the product can be declared fit for use.

If the investigation conclude that the lot should not be shipped, following alternatives are considered :

(*a*) Repairing the item

(*b*) Downgrading the item and sold as 'seconds'

(*c*) Scrapped, etc.

For non-conforming products, disposal is not the only solution, in such cases corrective action is necessary. The reasons must be found out and remedial actions are taken. In case, the non-conformance is of repetitive nature, a serious thought is required to be given at higher managerial level and decision is taken to find a permanent solution.

One of the elements of fitness for use is availability. Availability is a function of reliability and maintainability. An adequate field maintenance programme requires that product problems are solved correctly and in a timely manner.

## 3. Fitness for Market.

This include the quality related activities, when the product is made available to potential customers. This means the activities in marketing, distribution, installation, use, product safety, customer service, processing of complaints, and field feedback,

It is important to examine the factors that influence customer perception of quality, and include the matters related to: (*a*) before purchase, (*b*) at point of purchase, and (*c*) after purchase.

A seller provides a warranty in the form of assurance that the product is fit for use or failing this, the user will receive a some kind of compensation. In this way a warranty constitutes a system for reducing user costs of poor quality,

Following manufacturing and before customer use of the product, a number of pre-use phases take place, such as: packing, shipping, receiving, and storage. Finally, there are the use phases: installation, checkout, operation and maintenance. These field factors cause 20–30 percent of problems concerning fitness for use on long life products of moderate to high complexity.

All the above aspects must help in achieving for low cost. Hence, this aspect is also known as Fitness for cost.

## 4. Fitness for Latent Requirements

Fitness for latest requirement can be analyzed by listening to the voice of the customers. The uncovering latent requirement add value to the product which need continuous innovation.

A product (or service) should have following abilities to perform satisfactorily in a stated application:

(*i*) Suitability.
(*ii*) Durability.
(*iii*) Dependability.
(*iv*) Sale workability.
(*v*) Affordability.
(*vi*) Applicability.

A product can be said to have a good quality, if all the above abilities are balanced while designing and manufacturing it.

Field complaints are not a fool–proof measure of product performance, because some users complain despite the fact that a product is fit for use, while others do not complain even if a product is not fit for use. Whether or not a complaint is made, depends on several factors, such as economic climate, seriousness of the defect as seen by the user, unit price of the product.

Thus, a low complaint rate is not proof of customer satisfaction. However, a high complaint rate is proof of dis-satisfaction, and therefore, the complaint rate should be measured and watched closely. Therefore, a field survey is a reliable method for assessing the fitness for latent requirements.

## QUESTIONS

**1.** (*a*) Define 'Quality' and 'Quality Control'. (*b*) Elaborate historical background of quality concept.
**2.** Explain the advantages by maintaining good quality.
**3.** "Quality Control is a system of inspection, analysis and action applied to a manufacturing process". Discuss this with examples.
**4.** (*a*) Explain the difference between 'Inspection' and 'Quality Control'.
(*b*) How does quality control relates to inspection?
**5.** (*a*) State the principle and purposes of 'quality control'.
(*b*) State the important objectives of 'quality control'.
**6.** (*a*) Explain the factors affecting the quality of product.
(*b*) Differentiate between internal and external customers.
**7.** Describe the different types of causes of quality failures.
**8.** How will you classify the errors affecting quality ? Explain them.
**9.** Explain the different types of quality characteristics.
**10.** State the areas where quality control can be applied.
**11.** Differentiate between inspection, quality control and quality assurance.
**12.** Write an essay on "Economics of Quality".

13. Explain the term 'quality cost'. Illustrate the different types of quality costs.
14. What is 'quality loss'? Explain in detail.
15. (*a*) Write a short note on 'prevention cost'.
    (*b*) Write a short note on 'appraisal/detection cost.'
16. What is Japanese Quality Management ? What are the important aspects of their approach ?
17. Explain KAIZEN philosophy.
18. Explain in detail about the phases of quality revolution.
19. "Customer satisfaction can be achieved through two components, viz. product features and freedom from deficiencies". Elaborate the statement.
20. Write a detailed note on historical background on Quality.
21. Write a detailed note on 'quality movement in India'.
22. What are the factors which affects the quality in an organisation?
23. Explain the objectives of quality control.
24. What are the causes of quality failures? How the errors can be reduced by improving the motivation?
25. Explain the different types of quality characteristics.
26. Explain the different types of quality requirements.
27. Explain the following:
    (*a*) Quality statement.
    (*b*) Quality awareness.
28. Discuss the areas where quality control can be applied,
29. Explain in brief about the famous 'gurus' (pioneers) of quality.
30. Discuss the various fitnesses for quality.

# 2 Total Quality Management Concept (TQM Concept)

## 2.1. INTRODUCTION

In order to capture increased market share, quality had been the main concern of every manufacturer since old days. Started with the inspection concept moved to the quality control concept, when it was realised that making the inspection department also responsible for quality of the product would be counter productive. Concept of quality control emphasises self-inspection and appropriate systems to ensure quality by indentifying defectives and eliminating them. Help of statistical quality control and sample analysis were also undertaken.

Then arose the concept of quality assurance. But the quality movement did not stop with this, and the attempt is to continuously improve the quality and assure higher standards of quality, offer better products to the consumer, ensure better and longer service, and improve the utility of the product. It was felt that quality is not the job of quality control department only but other departments like sales, procurement, material handling, accounting, industrial relations, design, production, forecasting, marketing, stores, after sales service have also to contribute substantially. Thus, quality is the responsibility of all the employees. The workers should run the system, managers should design and improve the systems, while top management should provide leadership and team spirit.

In a "Total Quality Management" (T.Q.M.) concept, the word 'quality' has a wider meaning, it means quality of output of every department and by every employee, cleanliness, orderliness, punctuality, customer service, standardization of works and continuous efforts for their improvement are also part of T.Q.M. In this, needs of the customer are constantly monitored to improve the products and processes to meet their requirements.

In Total Quality Management programme, voluntary participation of work people is sought for the quality of the task. Effective T.Q.M. results in greater customer satisfaction, fewer defects, less waste, reduced costs, improved profitability and increased productivity. For the effectiveness of T.Q.M. programme a careful analysis of the customer's needs and an assessment of the extent to which these needs are currently met, and a suitable plan to fill up the gap between the current level and the expectation is necessary.

For the success of T.Q.M., top managers must provide vision, reinforce values emphasizing quality, set quality goals and deploy necessary resources for these quality programmes. For this purpose, training and development and free flow of information is essential. The top managers must continuously monitor, evaluate, get feedback about the T.Q.M. programme and take necessary steps for its improvement.

Customer satisfaction is the most important aspect of T.Q.M. The customer may be external to the organisation or may be inside the organisation. Meeting the needs of outside customers depend on meeting the needs of the inside customers. Inside customer is an individual or department, receiving the output of another individual or department of the concern.

From the above, we can say that the T.Q.M. involves effective decision-making, problem solving and integration of Quality Planning, Quality Implementation and Quality improvement strategies of all the departments of an organisation, committed and involved employees, lower costs, higher revenue and high profits for the organisation.

In the case of T.Q.M., the quality is embedded within and is driven by the culture of the organisation. T.Q.M. has emerged as the most integrated form of organisation development. ISO - 9000 standards on quality system provide a sound base for T.Q.M. It must be management led, companywide in implementation and dedicated to continuous improvement. T.Q.M. provides an opportunity to all the employees to directly participate in their work and take decisions concerning their job. The function of T.Q.M. is to improve the quality of work of all the people at all the functional areas of the organisation. Implementing T.Q.M. calls for a complete change in the behaviour of people working in the organisation.

It is a detailed approach to quality and relates to every facet of the business. T.Q.M. is an approach of managing for total quality, of managing for effectiveness and competitiveness, and involving each and every activity and person at all levels in the organisation. The approach is called 'total' because it includes everything that company does. This approach aims at continuous improvement.

T.Q.M. message empowered the Japanese managers and gave them the quality vehicle with which they established global trade supremacy. With the implementation of T.Q.M. concept, Japanese measure defects in 'parts per million' rather than the traditional Western percentages. In addition to marketing advantages and financial savings, T.Q.M. programmes increase customer satisfaction producing a tidal wave of goodwill and additional business.

The keywords and phrases used in T.Q.M. concept are : getting it right first time, zero defects, internal customer, customer benchmarking, cost of quality, synergy in teamwork, self-management, self-inspection etc. TQM is not a management tool, it is a style of work. TQM means to satisfy the customer at the first time and all the times. It means train the people to solve the problems and avoid waste. Remember that TQM is the result of using solid background like ISO-9000, TPM, Quality circles, management commitment, peoples involvement and other tools and techniques until TQM is obtained.

T.Q.M. concept, although discussed throughout in preceding chapters, here we shall discuss about only salient points.

### TQM as a New Culture

In the age of worldwide competition,following ability characteristics are demanded from any company:

(a) To understand what customer wants and to provide it immediately on demand, at the lowest cost,

(*b*) To provide products/services of high quality and reliability consistently.

(*c*) To keep up with the pace of change, may it be technical, social or political.

(*d*) To predict what the customer will want in near future.

TQM culture advocates a total commitment to customer satisfaction through continuous improvement and innovation in all aspects of the business. The continuous improvement and innovation are the objectives and is a non-static, updating and never-ending process. It is an objective without a completion date, because nothing can ever be immune from further improvement, new technologies, methods and attitudes or the presence of innovators and supporters of change. Major achievements resulting from TQM culture include cost reduction and corporate success. It must be noted that removal of waste, reduction of costs, improvement of reputation and increased market share are not the objectives. They are simply the natural consequences.

TQM provides an environment where fear is eliminated, where all the employees take pride in their work, where they feel respected and accepted, where they feel part of same team, and where they strive not only for their own interests, but also for the interests of the whole organisation. TQM culture needs the establishment of the following three fundamental characteristics:

1. Commitment (to never-ending quality improvement and innovation)
2. Scientific knowledge (of the proper tools and techniques for the 'technical' change).
3. Involvement (all in one team, for the social change).

All these three characteristics will be discussed under the heading TQM Axioms.

## 2.2. DEFINITIONS

Definitions related to the various terms used in Quality Systems have been standardized by International Organisation for Standardization (I.S.O.) vide their I.S.O. 8402 : 1986 'Quality-Vocabulary'. Bureau of Indian Standards has adopted the same vide its I.S. 13999 : 1988. Here, some definitions are being given for various terms, used in the field of quality as applied to products, and services:

1. **Product or Service** may be either (*a*) the result of activities or processes (tangible product; intangible product, such as a service, a computer programme, a design, direction for use) or (*b*) an activity or process (such as the provision of a service or the execution of a production process).
2. **Quality:** The totality of features and characteristics of a product or service that bear on its ability to satisfy stated or implied needs.

3. **Quality Policy:** The overall quality intentions and direction of an organisation as regards quality, as formally expressed by the top management.
4. **Quality Management:** It is that aspect of the overall management function that determines and implements the quality policy.
5. **Quality Assurance :** All those planned and systematic actions necessary to provide adequate confidence that a product or service will satisfy the given requirements for quality.
6. **Quality Control:** The operational techniques and activities that are used to fulfill requirements for quality. The quality control involves operational techniques and activities aimed at both monitoring a process and eliminating causes of unsatisfactory performance at relevant stages in order to result in economic effectiveness.
7. **Quality System:** The organisational structure, responsibilities, procedures, processes and resources for implementing quality management. The quality system should only be as comprehensive as needed to meet the quality objectives.
8. **Quality Plan :** A document setting out the specific quality practices, resources and sequence of activities relevant to a particular product, service, contract or project.
9. **Quality Audit:** A systematic and independent examination to determine whether quality activities and related results comply with planned arrangements and whether these arrangements are implemented effectively and are suitable to achieve objectives.

   The purpose of a quality audit is to evaluate the need for improvement or corrective action.
10. **Quality System Review:** A formal evaluation by the top management of the status and adequacy of the quality system in relation to quality policy and new objectives resulting from changing circumstances.
11. **Design Review :** A formal documented, comprehensive and systematic examination of a design to evaluate the design requirements and the capacity of the design to meet these requirements and to identify problems and propose solutions.
12. **Inspection:** Activities, such as measuring, examining, testing, gauging one or more characteristics of a product or service and comparing these with specified requirements to determine conformity.
13. **Reliability :** The ability of an item to perform a required function under stated conditions for a stated period of time.

    The term 'reliability' is also used as a reliability characteristic denoting a probability of success or a success ratio.
14. **Non-conformity :** The non-fulfillment of specified requirements, covers the departure or absence of one or more quality characteristics or quality system elements from specified requirements.
15. **Defect:** The non-fulfillment of intended usage requirements, covers the departure or absence of one or more quality characteristics from intended usage requirements.
16. **Specification :** The document that prescribes the requirements with which the product or service has to conform.

A specification should refer to or include drawings, patterns or other relevant documents and should also indicate the means and the criteria, whereby conformity can be checked.

17. **Total Quality Management.** Total quality Management (TQM) is the system of activities directed at achieving delighted customers, empowered employees, higher revenues and lower costs.

Thus, TQM is an enhancement to the traditional way of doing the business. This system changes the actions of the management to transform the culture and actions of entire organisation. The meaning of the three words of TQM can be analysed as under:

*Total* → whole

*Quality* → degree of excellence provided to the product or service

*Management* → Art, act or manner of implementing (handling), controlling, directing etc.

Thus, we can say that **TQM is an art of managing the whole to achieve excellence.**

## 2.3. TQM AND JAPANESE SUCCESS

After the World War II, as Japan, under American occupation, began to attempt to re-construct its industry. Problems that Japan faced are mainly as under:

1. Shortage of raw materials.
2. Destroyed plants.
3. Disillusioned labour force.
4. Shortage of foreign currency.
5. Poor quality reputation in western markets.

The USA was anxious for Japan's economic recovery to safeguard it against communism. Consequently much American aid and consultancy was supplied for setting up new plants. This resulted the Japanese businessmen to become conscious of the wastage and inflexibility associated with American–style of mass production. Prior to the World War II, Japanese culture had taylorism and craftsmanship in their attitude. Therefore, anything which could waste precious raw materials was a serious objection.

Therefore, Japanese adopt western methods in a way which suits to Japanese strategy of :

1. Economy in the use of raw material
2. Recognising that Japanese people are significant resource.
3. Purchasing the resources Japan did not possess (e.g., oil,minerals etc.) from overseas using the revenue from selling Japanese finished products into the western markets.

At this time two industrial experts, Daming and Juran, were sent out to Japan by the US Government. As explained in the previous chapter, their teachings had an enormous impact. Earlier Quality was missing in Japan's policy, now the quality enabled Japanese products to gain acceptance by making the best use of their scarce resources and compete on price.

The most distinctive policies of large Japanese companies in their own country are:

1. Lifetime employment.
2. Pay increases based on length of service.
3. Company based on trade unions.
4. Emphasis on training throughout a worker's career.
5. Wide range of welfare benefits.
6. Consensus style of decision–making.
7. Important and prestigious role given to the first – line supervisor.
8. *Kaizen* (continuous improvement.)

As Japanese companies are challenging the companies throughout the world and their growing success in capturing the market share, even western countries are giving attention to the Japanese way of quality management. Japanese, after the World War II, learned some important lessons from western industry, and have developed some unique manufacturing strengths, Some important aspects of their approach are:

1. Employee involvement (including Quality Circles)
2. Japanese Management Principles.
3. Just-in-time (JIT) system. (kanban).
4. Stockless production
5. Total Quality Control (TQC)
6. Eliminating wastage:
   (*i*) waste of overproduction
   (*ii*) waste of waiting
   (*iii*) waste of movement
   (*iv*) waste of stock
   (*v*) waste of motion
   (*vi*) waste of making defective product
   (*vii*) waste of processing.
7. Value added manufacturing
8. Application of SQC methods
9. Quality Control Audit
10. Quality education and training.

## 2.4. ELEMENTS OF TOTAL QUALITY MANAGEMENT (TQM)

1. Customer's Satisfaction.

2. Employee's involvement,
3. Morale of empolyees.
4. Quality Control Circles and suggestion system.
5. Higher revenue.
6. Lower cost.
7. Quality control.
8. Control of Production.
9. Quality planning.
10. Quality Improvement.
11. Quality Implementation.
12. Quality Assurance System.
13. Vendor control and quality in procurement.
14. Customer relationship management.
15. Total organisation involvement.
16. Measurement information analysis.
17. Quality education and training.
18. Strategic quality management.
19. Leadership.

**1. Requirements of T.Q.M.**

(*i*) **Sound Foundation :** Philosophy, Policy , Culture, Leadership and Commitment.

(*ii*) **Sound Infrastructure :** Organisation, Systems, Procedures, Manuals, Customer involvement, Suppliers involvement, Training and Education and Total Employee's Involvement.

(*iii*) **Use of Specific Tools and Techniques**

**2. Aims of T.Q.M.**

(*i*) Conformance to customer requirements.

(*ii*) Prevention of producing bad quality.

(*iii*) Measurement of cost of quality.

(*iv*) Provide products and services of high quality and reliability consistently.

(*v*) To keep up with pace of change, technological as well as political and social.

(*vi*) To predict what the customer will want after one year or five years from now.

**3. Ways for T.Q.M.**

(*i*) Adopt new philosophy of 'not to allow defects to occur'.

(*ii*) Create consistency of purpose for improvement.

(*iii*) Improving production and service quality, should be a continuous process.

(*iv*) Cease dependence on mass inspection. Adopt statistical Quality Control.

(*v*) Insist quantifiable evidence from the suppliers about the quality of their product.

(*vi*) All empolyees should be trained, re-trained and refresher courses be arranged.

(*vii*) Provide proper tools to all the employees.

(*viii*) Adopt proper communication system.

(*ix*) Encourage productivity.

(*x*) Encourage co-ordination between departments.

(*xi*) Permanent commitment of top management to quality.

(*xii*) Respect towards 'work' and 'humanity'.

(*xiii*) Adopt consumer orientation and not the product orientation.

(*xiv*) Objective should be 'Quality first, and not the short term profits'.

(*xv*) Use facts and data.

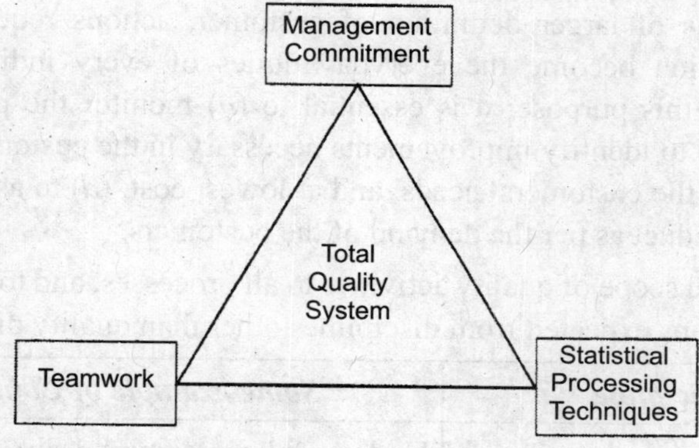


**Fig 2.1.** The T. Q.M. Model.

## 2.5. "LITTLE-Q" (TRADITIONAL QUALITY) AND "BIG-Q" (MODERN QUALITY)

As discussed earlier, traditional quality activities were concentrated on manufacturing only, which has been termed here as "little-Q" ; whereas, modern quality activities include all activities in all functions of the organisation.

In order to attain quality, it requires the performance of wide variety of quality activities which may be mainline activities or administrative and support activities, such as finance, warehousing, data processing or human resources. There are certain activities which are performed even outside the manufacturing or service companies e.g., by suppliers, merchants etc. Thus, we achieve the objective of "fitness for use" through entire collection of activities, no matter where these activities are performed.

| *Scope of "Little-Q"* | *Scope of "Big-Q"* |
|---|---|
| – Manufactured goods | – All products, goods and services whether for sales or not |
| – Proceses directly related manufacture of goods | – All processes, manufacturing support, business etc. |
| – Manufacturing industries | – All industries |

Though, modern "Big-Q" *i.e.* TQM culture vary from company to company and division to division of the same company. Major achievements of this culture include cost reduction and corporate success. But removal of waste, reduction of costs, improvement of reputation and increased market shares are simply the natural consequences of 'Big-Q' or TQM culture, and not the objectives. Continuous improvement and innovation are the real objectives. This means further improvement, new technologies, methods and attitudes or the continuous efforts of innovators and advocates of gradual change is the non-static and never-ending process.

Having as a basis of larger definition of customer, actions required for the achievement of customer satisfaction become the everyday duties of every individual or division within the organisation. For this purpose, it is essential to (*a*) monitor the performance and customer satisfaction levels, (*b*) to identify improvements necessary in the customer interface, (*c*) to deliver improved products to the customers' needs, and at lowest cost, (*d*) to assess the customers' needs, and (*e*) to produce product as per the demand of the customers.

With the expanded scope of quality activities to all processes, and to both, external and internal customers, contributions expected from disciplines other than quality disciplines are :

| *Dicipline* | *Some example of Contribution* |
|---|---|
| – Market Research. | Understand customers' desire, quality of competitors' products. |
| – Strategic Planning. | Quality as a means of achieving a competitive advantage. |
| – Systems Engineering | Translating customer needs into product features. |
| – Industrial Engineering | Design of integrated systems, measurement, problem solving, work analysis. |
| – Operations Management | Management of integrated systems, Satisfying needs of both external and internal customers. |
| – Organisational Behaviour | Understanding and contributing towards quality culture. |

| – Value Engineering | Analysis of essential functions needed by customers. |
|---|---|
| – Finance | Measuring the cost of poor quality. |

Based on the 'Little-Q' and 'Big-Q', there are two views of quality : the conventional internal view and the modern external view. Some of the examples of both these views are illustrated hereunder :

| *Conventional internal view* | *Modern external view* |
|---|---|
| – Compare product to specification | – Compare with the products of competitors |
| – Get product accepted at inspection | – Provide satisfaction over product life. |
| – Prevent defects during manufacture and transport | – Meet customer needs. |
| – Concentrate on manufacturing | – Cover all the activities of all the functions. |
| – Use companies quality measures | – Use customer based quality measures |
| – Quality is considered as a technical issue. | – Consider Quality as a business issue. |
| – Responsibility of quality is solely of quality manager | – Quality efforts are directed by senior management. |

## 2.6. BENEFITS OF T.Q.M.

The main benefits of TQM are as under:

- Improved quality of product and services.
- Good working relationships.
- Customer satisfaction.
- Employee satisfaction.
- Employee participation.
- Team work.
- Improved productivity.
- Improved market share.
- Improved financial performance.

## 2.7. BARRIERS (OBSTACLES) TO TQM IMPLEMENTATION

Many organisations, especially small ones, generally feel comfortable with their current state. They are satisfied with the amount of work being performed, profits earned. They also perceive that the customers are also satisfied.

The common obstacles felt by the organisations in successful implementation of TQM are mentioned hereunder:

1. **Lack of Management Commitment.** For the success of any organisation, there must be substantial management commitment of management time and organisational resources.
2. **Inability to Change Organisational Culture.**

   It is difficult to change an organisation, as individuals resist change because they are accustomed to doing a particular precess in their way. For the purpose of change in the organisational culture, management should consider:

   (*i*) Spending more time in planning for implementation of a TQM programme, as it improves the chances of success,

   (*ii*) People change when they want to meet their own needs.

   (*iii*) The people never change their behaviour unless they are convinced.

   (*iv*) The people accept the change only when they move from a state of fear to the state of trust.

The slogans, campaigns speeches etc. are effective only for a short period of time.

3. **Improper Planning.** For TQM implementation, all the sections of the organisation must be involved in the development of the implementation plan. Participation of all personnel and two – way communication of ideas are important during the development of the plan and its implementation.
4. **Lack of Continuous Training and Education.** Training and education should be an ongoing process for every body in the organisation. Training needs for TQM should be determined, and plan should be developed to achieve these needs.
5. **Incompatible Organisation Structure.** The organisation structure must be responsive to customer needs. Differences between departments and individuals create implementation problems. Such problems can be sorted out by using the multi-functional teams.
6. **Ineffective Performance Measurement Techniques.** Key performance (characteristics) of the organisation should be measured correctly so that effective decisions can be made. This is necessary to improve processes.
7. **Inadequate Attention to Internal and External Customers.** It is necessary that organisations should understand the changing needs and expectations of the customers. This is possible by adopting effective feedback mechanism, which provide data for decision–making.
8. **Inadequate Empowerment and Teamwork.** It is necessary that teams should have the proper training. Further, in the beginning a facilitator should also be provided for the team. Teams recommendations, related to the improvement of efficiency of the process and also regarding customer satisfaction should be followed.
9. **Failure to Continually Improve.** A lack of continuous improvement of the processes, product and / or service harm the spirit of the TQM. In order to continue to address culture, staff and service issues also, continuously improvement in all spheres is necessary.

## 2.8. TOTAL QUALITY CONTROL (TQC) AND ITS IMPLEMENTATION

Total quality control (TQC) may be defined as "an effective system for integrating the quality development, quality maintenance and quality improvement efforts of the various groups in an organization so as to enable production and service at the most economical levels which allow for full customer satisfaction". TQC requires participation of all divisions.

### Characteristics of Total Quality Control

1. Quality Control is the responsibility of all the workers and all the divisions.
2. Total Quality Control is a group activity and cannot be done by individuals.
3. It calls for team work.
4. Quality Control Circle (also known as Quality Circle) activities are part of the T.Q.C.
5. It adopts the philosophy of refusing to allow any defect.
6. It relies the Sampling (S.Q.C.) rather than cent-per-cent inspection.
7. Continuous process for improving quality of products and services.
8. All employees are provided with proper tools and proper training to do the quality job.
9. It clearly defines top management's permanent commitment to quality.

### Integrated Quality Control

In affecting integrated quality control, control of quality is central, but at the same time cost control (profit control and price control), quantity control (amount of production, of sales, of stock), and control of delivery date to be promoted. This method is based on the fundamental assumption of QC that a manufacturer must develop, produce and sell commodities that satisfy the needs of consumers. This extends the term, quality, to the quality of work in the offices, in the service related industries and in the banks etc.

### EFFECTIVE IMPLEMENTATION OF TQC

1. Quality Implementation ensures that a process continuously produce the quality that was planned into it. **Effective Implementation includes :**
   (*i*) A clearly stated policy.
   (*ii*) Development of Resources of men, machine and others to specific tasks involved, identifying the departments/individuals to do the specific tasks.
   (*iii*) Proper selection of Control factors, with details of when, where, who, what, how and why they are to be done.
   (*iv*) Establishing self-control for all those who run the process.

(*v*) Personnel Leadership from the Manager in motivating, training and recognising the work of his people. Creation of a healthy culture.

(*vi*) Existence of an established Quality Assurance System.

(*vii*) Total Organisational Involvement, both, formal and informal, such as Quality circles.

(*viii*) Informations needed about deficiencies in the goods and processes, and cost of poor quality, with analysis of their causes.

(*ix*) Measurable Standards are to be established for having a benchmark for Quality Implementation purposes.

2. **A feed-back loop** measures an output from a process, compares them with the established standards and takes the necessary action. Control standards are established, based on the actual performance of the process. CONTROL CHARTS are the tools for establishing control standards and testing the actuals against standards.

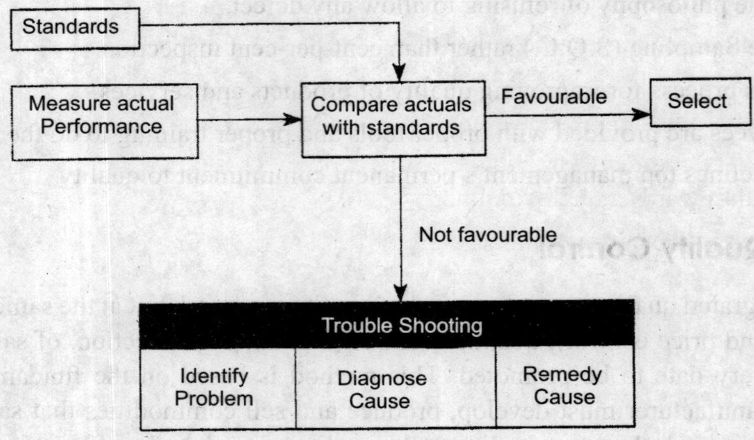


**Fig. 2.2.** Quality Control Feedback Loop

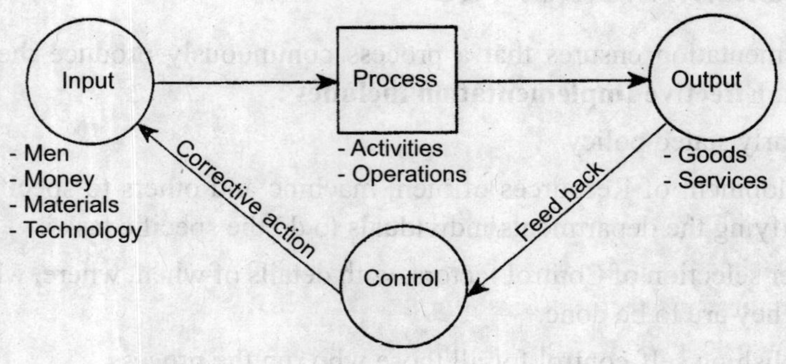


**Fig. 2.3.** Quality Control System

## 2.9. QUALITY CULTURE

Quality culture means opinions, beliefs, traditions and practices concerning quality in the organisation. To gain an understanding of the quality culture is an important step towards the company assessment of quality. For this purpose, following actions are generally taken :

(*a*) discussions with different groups of employees are arranged, and

(*b*) written questionnaire is used.

This helps in understanding the following :

(*i*) Attitudes, perceptions and activities within the organisation at different levels towards the quality.

(*ii*) Perceived user attitudes about the quality of products.

(*iii*) How the 'quality tools' are understood by the employees. Here, 'quality tools' means process control concepts, statistical tools, sampling practices etc.

For any organisation, to become superior in quality, it is necessary to adopt following two courses of action:

1. Develop technologies to meet customer needs.
2. Develop 'quality culture' throughout the organisation. Various approaches must be adopted to provide a path towards a quality culture.

Quality culture is a pattern of human habits, beliefs and behaviour concerning quality. The quality culture issues apply to all levels *i.e.* upper management, middle management, supervisors, technical specialists, business specialists and the workforce.

**Various quality culture approaches are :**

1. Motivation Theories (already discussed).
2. Quality awareness
3. Leadership
4. Self-development
5. Participation
6. Recognition and awards.

## 2.10. THREE T.Q.M. AXIOMS (SELF-EVIDENT TRUTHS)

For achieving sustainable, long term competitive advantage, continuous efforts should be made for improvement. The essence of the strategy should be the establishment of a TQM culture, which should be based on its three principles: Commitment, involvement and scientific knowledge. These three principles are inter-dependent. Considering these principles, TQM can be defined as follows :

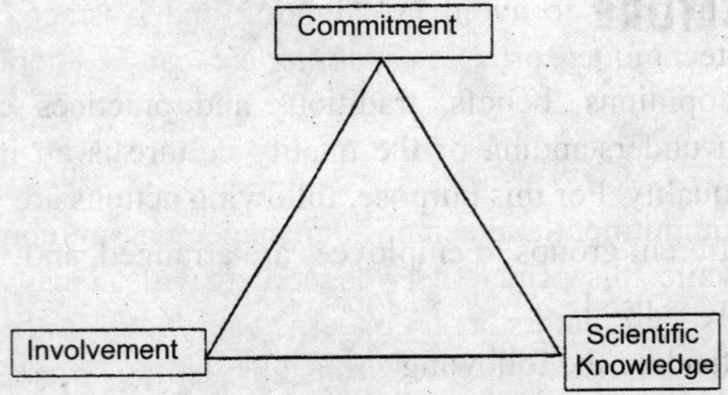


**Fig. 2.4.** The T.Q.M. Triangle

Total quality management is a culture , inherent in this culture is a total commitment to quality and an attitude expressed by everybody's involvement in the process of continuous improvement of products and services, through the use of innovative scientific methods.

The three TQM axioms are discussed hereunder :

## 1. Commitment.

A management commitment to continually improving the quality of products and services is most essential, but it needs a total cultural transformation in the company. Management participation and demonstration by example are the best ways of convincing the workforce that the managers are serious about quality and that the same should be expected of everybody. Commitment should be demonstrated by actions and not just words and declarations.

Change in attitudes and culture can be achieved by :

- Proper working conditions.
- Adequate education and training.
- Good communication and co-operation.
- Modern leadership.
- Good incoming materials.
- Good equipment.
- Appropriate tools of good quality.
- Job satisfaction etc.

From this, it can be seen that such a change is not possible by quality department alone. In this, top management is responsible to plant the seed of quality tree (through quality policy and demonstration of commitment) and to provide appropriate soil and environmental conditions, middle management is responsible to ensure that the quality tree is continuously nourished and strengthened (by spreading TQM principles to maintain TQM culture so as to bring results).

## 2. Scientific Knowledge

The role of a TQM quality department should be that of co-ordination, education and support of scientific quality tools throughout the organisation, and continuous research on and development of innovative methods. In order to avoid fire–fighting and wastage, 'preventive' methods like predictability, statistical techniques, process capability etc. can be adopted.

### 3. Involvement

Principles 1 and 2 *i.e.* commitment and scientific management are concerned with structural and technological aspects, while this principle is concerned with social aspects. TQM culture can only be brought through social factors, as it concerns everybody in the organisation and requires a new social attitude and new network of relationships. Unless workforce is motivated enough, commitment and scientific knowledge will not help much.

It has been experienced that higher salaries and monetary rewards can motivate only for a short duration, real motivators for the long term are : pride in one's work and being involved in the achievement of excellence are the real motivators.

## 2.11. FOCUS ON CUSTOMER

Total quality management focuses on the requirements of the customers. Following facts should be recognised about the customers :

(*i*) Customers are the most important people in any business.

(*ii*) They are not dependent on us, rather we are dependent on them.

(*iii*) They are doing a favour when they are coming to us.

(*iv*) They are part of our business.

(*v*) They are human beings with feelings and emotions.

(*vi*) People come to us with their needs and wants, and it is our job to fulfill them.

(*vii*) They deserve most courteous and attentive treatment.

(*viii*) Without them we would have to close our business.

Consumers are now-a-days becoming stronger and well-organised. Consumer forums are becoming popular. In some countries consumer reports are published by them in respect of large number of products. Most manufacturing concerns concentrate on 'getting' the new customers rather then 'retaining' them. Marketing relationship must, therefore, be given more importance.

In TQM, quality involves 5 dimensions for the customer to be satisfied. Quality measurements of these should be decided through questionnaire asked from the customers. These elements are :

1. **Specifications.** Customers must be asked as to what he expects from the product or service, during the survey to ascertain the customer requirements.
2. **Conformance.** Whether the product fulfills his expectations ?
3. **Reliability.** Does it continue to do, what was expected ?
4. **Cost (Value).** How much customer expects to pay ?
5. **Delivery.** When customer expects to have it ?

Considering above factors, quality can be defined as : fully satisfying agreed customer requirements at the lowest internal cost.

To meet the customers' requirements means to listen to the customer and to respond to what he wants and to what is agreed. Customers may be:

(*a*) external to the company *i.e.* the people outside who are the end-users of firm's products, and

(*b*) internal customers *i.e.* the person within the company who ' receives the work of another and then adds his contribution to the product before passing it onto someone else. In manufacturing, the internal customer is the next person down the line who builds the product. If the internal customers' requirements are agreed and met, a chain of quality is made.

Some of the routine **duties of every individual or division within the organisation**, for the achievement of customer satisfaction could be as follows:

1. To monitor performance and customer satisfaction levels.
2. To identify improvement necessary in the customer interface.
3. To deliver improved customer products at the lower cost.
4. To assess and agree the customer's requirements.
5. Output should be as per customer's demand.

## 2.12. CONCEPTS OF TQM

### 2.12.1 Basic Concepts

Following are the basic concepts of TQM:

1. Committed and involved management.
2. Focus on the customer.
3. Effective involvement and utilisation of the workforce.
4. Continuous improvement of the business and production process.
5. Treating suppliers as partners.
6. Establish performance measures for the processes.

### 2.12.2. Other Main Concepts of TQM

#### 1. Quality for Profit.

Quality improvement in product and services, business processes and people is profitable. Quality is the single largest factor in achieving market success for any company. Actual quality improvement also increases sales by generating customer demand.

Fig. 2.5. indicates that to gain increase in profit $P$ through increased sales would require a significant increase in operating costs $A$ (sales personnel, promotion, inventories etc.), while the same profit *P* can be increased through quality improvement by reducing operating costs *B*, which also diminishes through time.

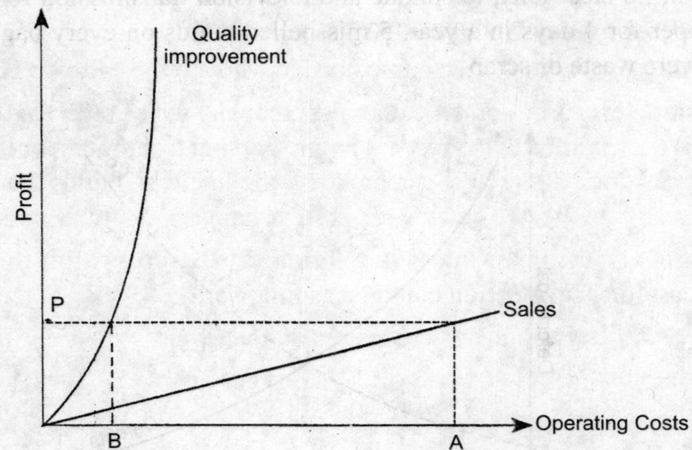


**Fig. 2.5.** Quality improvement reduces cost

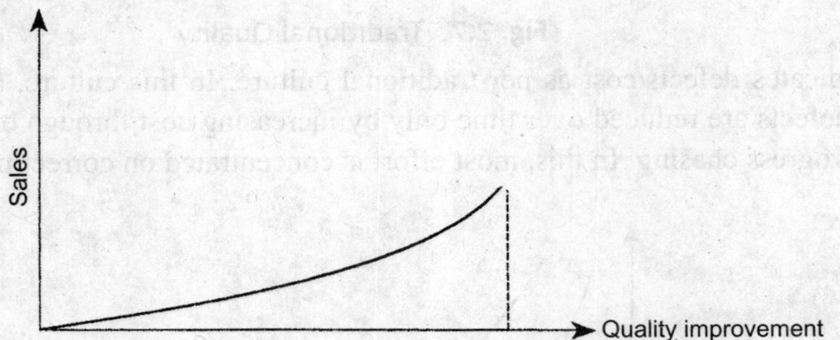


**Fig. 2.6.** Quality itself increases sales

Fig. 2.6 indicates more quality improves, faster will be increase in sales because customer satisfaction carries its own acceleration. 'Quality reputation' when grows, it acts as a major element in advertising and reduce the money required on advertisement.

## 2. Right First Time or Zero Defect

Main aim of TQM is the conviction that it is possible to achieve defect-free work most of the time. This can be phrased as : right first time or zero defects. The idea is to strive for perfection in the work. Right first time is the result of an emphasis on prevention; and the use of measurement, process control and the data-driven elimination of waste and error, continuous improvement. Planned and systematic action, such as documentation work processes, or quality audits, quality assurance etc. prevents quality problems.

Importance of zero defect can be visualised from the fact that if one sets an acceptable quality level of 99 percent, the results will be: 10,000 wrong prescriptions in a hospital, treating one million patients in a year, no electricity, telephone and television transmission for about 15 minutes each day, no newspaper for 4 days in a year, 5 misspelled words on every page of a book. It means 1 percent goods were waste or scrap.

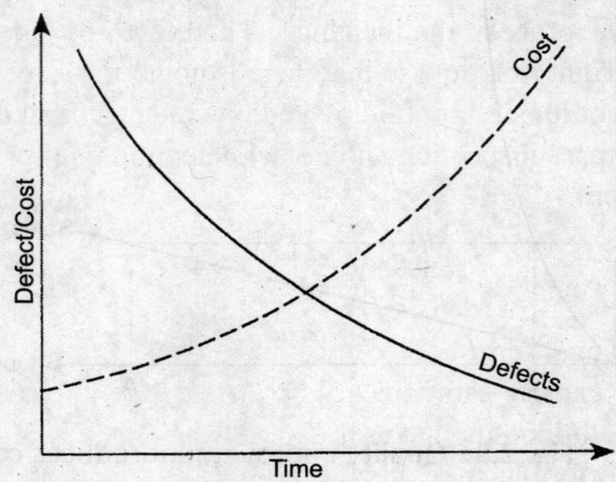


**Fig. 2.7.** Traditional Quality

Fig. 2.7 indicates defects/cost as per traditional culture. In this culture, achieving quality is expensive *i.e.* defects are reduced over time only by increasing cost through extensive inspection, checking and progress chasing. In this, most effort is concentrated on correcting failure.

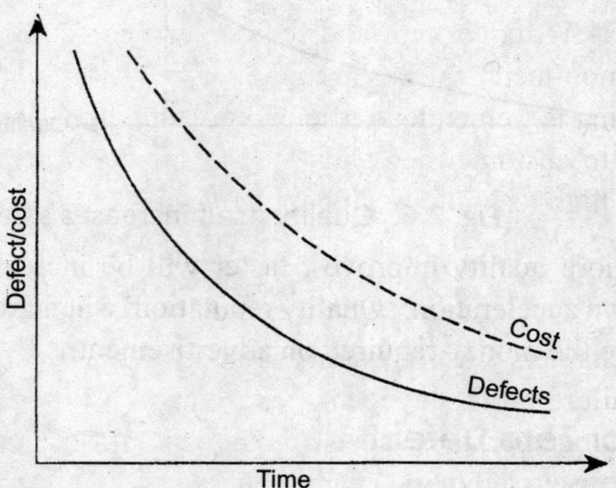


**Fig. 2.8** Total Quality Concept

**Fig. 2.8.** indicates that by adopting TQM management, after certain time defects and costs, both will be minimal.

Basically, 'zero defect concept' is an approach for securing a high level of error-free work performance. Under this approach, in fact, the slogan, used to motivate employees, is 'Do it right the first time'. Proper planning is required for the concept of ZD (Zero Defect) to become properly embedded in the company culture. It will have to start with a zero defect commitment on the part of top management, as this is the only way that the concept will be taken seriously.

As we have seen, mass inspection cannot compensate for below standard incoming materials, bad design and ineffective process maintenance. Therefore, by adopting zero defect culture, everything has to be made right first time so that there is no need for rectification later. It should not be just a slogan, rather it should be supported by genuine management efforts. Thus, there is a need to replace the practices of mass inspection and defect detection with practices of defect prevention and continuous improvement.

## Six–Sigma Concept

Six-Sigma (6 σ) is a statistical term coined by Phillip Crosby used to describe the state of zero defects or as close as the experts estimate, it is possible to come to perfection. Six-Sigma is a rigorous and disciplined methodology that uses data and statistical analysis to measure and improve a company's operational performance by identifying and eliminating defects in manufacturing and service related processes. Six-Sigma translates to 3.4 defects per million or 99.99976% perfection. Six-Sigma quality is not just product quality, it also means getting everything right throughout the organisation. Thus, Six-Sigma is a culture, according to which improvement will occur because the elimination of defects at the source of the defects within the design stage rather than adjusting the machinery after detecting the defects. To succeed at a Six-Sigma level, the suppliers also must be encouraged to follow along the same quality lines.

For adopting the Six-Sigma concept and for implementing this culture, training is essential to technical as well as non-technical groups. The costs of training and changing the corporate culture to adopt Six-Sigma is tremendous resource, as they translate into substantial cost savings and increased sales due to customer demands of high quality. Such companies will be poised to succeed in the emerging high technology global markets.

## 3. Cost of Quality

As discussed in earlier chapters, cost of quality include prevention costs, appraisal costs, internal failure costs, external failure costs, the cost of exceeding customer requirements and the cost of lost opportunities. Taken together, these costs amounts to 20-30 percent of its revenue. The cost of quality has already been discussed in the chapter on 'Quality Concept'.

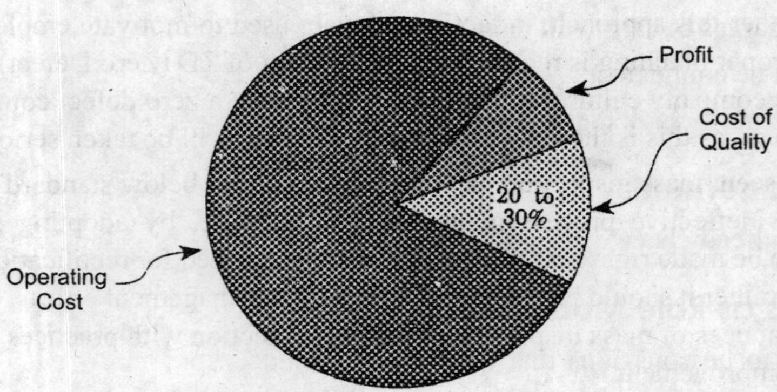


**Fig. 2.9.** Cost of Quality as a proportion of revenue

## 4. Competitive Benchmarking

Competitive benchmarking is a continuous process that helps firms to assess their competition. In this case, to strive to be better than the best competitor is the target. The means to achieve this aim are :

(*a*) benchmarking the products and services delivered to external and internal customers,

(*b*) benchmarking the business processes in all departments and functions, and

(*c*) benchmarking the organisation, business culture and calibre of people.

Benchmarking process has the following steps :

1. Decide what is going to be benchmarked.
2. Select the competitors who are the best in terms of products and services, business processes and people, and aspects that one's firm wants to measure.
3. Decide the most appropriate measurements.
4. Determine competitor's strengths against own company.
5. Develop an action plan.

## 5. Involving Everybody

This aspect has already been discussed in this chapter.

## 6. Synergy in Teamwork

Synergy means harmony in working, and is the result of team work in which output is greater than each of the inputs taken separately and also greater than the sum total of the inputs. As theoretical knowledge of engineers as well as practical knowledge of workers are essential for progress, both of them acts as partners for effective management.

Main points for the success of teamwork are :

(*i*) Team members be valued as individual.

(*ii*) Individuals feel integrated within a team.

(*iii*) Team-in-charges be fair to all team members.

(*iv*) Team must be confident.

(*v*) Individuals must enjoy themselves.

## 7. Self-management

This aspect has already been discussed.

## 8. Managers as Role Models

Managers need to be conscious that they are role models for total quality. It is very important that what they say and do about total quality. The best TQM programme has a system of management feedback so that managers get some idea on how they are doing as role models for quality. Performance feedback is most important to enable managers at all levels to improve their contribution.

Feedback should be on general management areas : leadership, teamwork, motivating, people development and commitment to the total quality process.

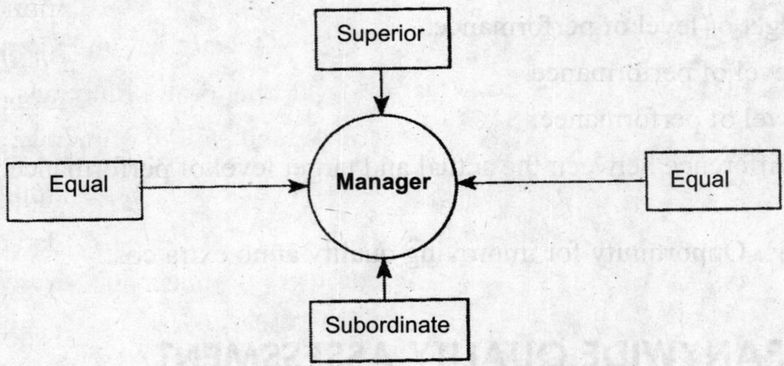


**Fig. 2.10.** Directions of managerial feedback

## 9. Recognition and Rewards

This concept has already been discussed in the preceding chapters.

## 10. Quality Delivery Process

It is the name given to the implementation of new systems. This is necessary for quality improvement which is a continuous process.

**Following steps are taken for quality delivery process:**

(*i*) Create mission statement.

(*ii*) Determine the outputs of the workgroup.

(*iii*) Identify both, internal and external customers.

(*iv*) Define agreed customer requirements for each output.
(*v*) Develop specifications for each output of workgroup.
(*vi*) Determine the group's work processes.
(*vii*) Identify the measurements of each output.
(*viii*) Identify any problem/opportunity for achieving target.
(*ix*) Establish a project team to solve the identified problem.
(*x*) Measure customer satisfaction against the agreed customer requirements.

### Quality Measurements

The ways in which the quality of outputs can be measured are :

1. Defects
2. Re-work
3. Scrap
4. Lost items
5. Work behind schedule
6. Late deliveries
7. Surplus items.

Key measurements for the output are :

1. ***Target:*** budget or level of performance.
2. ***Forecast:*** level of performance.
3. ***Actuals :*** level of performance.
4. ***Problem :*** difference between the actual and target level of performance, where actual is less than target.
5. ***Opportunity :*** Opportunity for improving quality at no extra cost.

## 2.13. COMPANYWIDE QUALITY ASSESSMENT

As we have already discussed in the chapter on "Quality Planning", for total quality mangement, companywide participation from top management to all levels of employees of all the departments is essential. Participation by not only departments of technology, design, research and manufacturing but also by sales, materials, marketing, electrical and other management departments like planning, finance, personnel, business development etc. Similarly, in the total quality management, quality control concept is used not only for incoming materials, production process, new product design but also for checking whether quality policies of the management are being implemented.
Companywide assessment of quality comprises of the following major elements:

1. Cost of poor quality.
2. Standing in the market place.
3. Quality culture in the organisation.
4. Operation of the company quality system.

**1. Cost of Poor Quality**

This aspect has already been discussed in detail in the chapter on "Quality Concept". This assessment of cost of poor quality is essential for quantifying the size of the quality problem in the language of money, as this can be easily understood by the upper management and middle management.

This assessment or analysis identifies major opportunities for cost reduction. The vital few segments so identified, accounts for the bulk of the costs, are tackled through "the Pareto Principle" as discussed later in the book. This also identifies the opportunities for reducing the customer dissatisfaction and associated threats to product salability.

**2. Standing in the Market Place**

Although it is essential to estimate the cost of poor quality, but it is also necessary to understand where the company stands in the marketplace as regards to quality relative to the competition. This component of assesment is very important in increasing sales income by identifying opportunities and threats.

Such market studies should be conducted by a team involving members from marketing, product development, quality, manufacturing and other areas, as needed. The questionnaie, should include the questions which enable to understand customer needs. The market study report, based on the answers to such questions, is prepared considering them as inputs from customers. This study helps in understanding the company's standing in the market.

**3. Quality Culture in the Organisation**

Quality Culture in the organisation is judged by the employees' opinions, beliefs, traditions and practices regarding the quality. For this, if required, a detailed survey can be got conducted, which may also include the aspects related to the attitudes of employees and management in this regard.

**4. Operation of Company Quality System**

The assesment of this aspect is carried out by evaluating the current quality related activities in the company.

## 2.14. TEN MANTRAS FOR TQM

1. Quality is always the will to produce a quality product and is the result of continuous and intellegent efforts.
2. Quality never comes out without hardwork and devotion.
3. Quality is everybody's business.
4. Quality begins with the cleanliness of the workplace.
5. Take care of quality, quantity (productivity) will take care of itself.
6. Make it right for first time and all times.
7. Quality is achieved through teamwork.

8. Document is dependable and not the memory.
9. Quality begins and ends with education (includes knowledge).
10. Quality is the attribute that a customer uses to evaluate products or services.

## 2.15. TOOLS AND TECHNIQUES FOR TQM

Commonly used tools and techniques for analysing quality process and then utilising for quality improvement are :

1. Histograms
2. Block diagrams
3. Bar charts
4. Line graphs
5. Control
6. Pareto analysis
7. Brainstorming
8. Scatter diagram
9. Break-even analysis
10. Quality circles
11. Statistical tools
12. OC curves
13. Risk analysis
14. Quality Function Deployment (QFD)
15. Kaizen
16. Poka Yoke
17. Kanban system
18. 5-S compaign (Principle of House-keeping).
19. Just-In-Time (JIT) philosophy
20. Cause and effect diagram (Fishbone diagram) or Ishikawa diagram.

Tools and techniques mentioned at serial numbers from 1 to 8 are also known as basic analytical tools.

### 2.15.1 Uses of Techniques/Tools of TQM

| *Tool/Technique* | *Main use* |
|---|---|
| Histograms | Plotting the shape of a distribution and comparing it with specifications. |
| Control Charts | Checking whether a process is in control. |
| Pareto analysis | Singling out the really serious problems from among all the lesser serious ones. |
| Scatter diagrams | Finding correlation between paired sets of data. |
| Graphs and Charts | Making data visual. |

| | |
|---|---|
| Cause and Effect diagram | Picking up and then arranging all possible causes without any omissions. |
| Checksheets | Simplifying data collection and ensuring that no items are omitted. |
| Correlation analysis | Investigating correlation between variables. |
| Regression analysis | Investigating functional relations between variables. |
| Affinity diagram | Unearthing problems by organising data on chaotic situations. |
| Inter-relationship diagram | Elucidating complex problems by identifying logical connections. |
| Tree diagrams (Systematic diagrams) | Systematically searching for the most effective means of accomplishing given objectives. |
| Matrix diagrams | Clarifying problems through multi-dimensional thinking. |
| Matrix data analysis | Arranging data in matrix form for easy visualisation and comprehension. |
| Progress decision program charts. | Determining the process to be used to achieve the desired results. |
| Arrow diagrams | Controlling schedules by expressing relationships among tasks in the form of a network. |

## 2.16. COMPREHENSIVE LIST OF MEASURES FOR TQM

Here, attempts have been taken to list out maximum possible measures which are taken for implementing Total Quality Mangement.

**1. Focus on 'Competitive Quality'**

1. Assessment of current performance
2. Continuous improvement of processes
3. Techniques for improving competitive quality
4. Manufacturing best practices
5. Achieving service and quality
6. *Kaizen* implementation
7. PDCA for core and support processes
8. Reliability improvement techniques
9. Failure analysis for manufacturing quality
10. Accuracy and precision through 6-sigma

**2. Implementing Management Techniques**

1. Removal of root causes of low productivity.
2. Five'S, for workplace.
3. Just-in-Time concept in production.
4. *Kanban* Systems.
5. Supplier best practices.
6. Methods of supplier quality improvement.
7. Reduction in non-value added activities.
8. Product design checklist.
9. *Taguchi* Methods and robust designing
10. Achieving zero defects through Total Productive Maintenance.
11. Value engineering
12. Ergonomics
13. Management tools
14. Quality Function Deployment

**3. Achieving Cost Efficiency**

1. Quality, Maintainability and Cost.
2. Reducing cost of quality.
3. Zero defect manufacturing.
4. A low cost approach.
5. Analysis of variation and their controlling.
6. *Pokayoke* (to avoid unintentional errors).
7. Functionwise Quality Cost.
8. Waste assessment.
9. Types of wastes and their reduction.

**4. Reduce Time-to-Market**

1. Time based competition
2. Product innovation techniques
3. Product Development Cycle
4. Risk (hazard) analysis
5. Risk abatement

**5. Exceed Customer Expectations**

1. Strategies for gaining competitive edge
2. Customer Supplier Mode
3. Improving chain of internal customers

4. Quality and its attributes
5. Quality MIS for detecting major trends
6. Quality Management Principles
7. Customer Satisfaction Measurement
8. Methods of gaining customer loyalty
9. Customer practices of global leaders
10. Customer survey forms
11. Launching successful products

**6. Having a Global Perspective**

1. International Marketing
2. Shingo Prize Parameters of Manufacturing Excellence
3. Registration for ISO-9000.

## QUESTIONS

**1.** Explain the term TQM (Total Quality Management).

**2.** (*a*) Enumerate the elements of TQM.
(*b*) Explain the aims of TQM.

**3.** Enumerate the ways for total quality management.

**4.** (*a*) What are the characteristics of Total Quality Control ?
(*b*) How total quality can be effectively implemented ?

**5.** What are the three fundamental characteristics of Total Quality Management ? Explain them.

**6.** While conducting a survey to know about the customer's satisfaction, what are the 5 dimensions which should be enquired from them?

**7.** Write a note on 'focus on customer' with reference to TQM.

**8.** Write short notes on :
(*a*) Quality of profit (*b*) Right first time
(*c*) Cost of quality (*d*) Competitive benchmarking
(*e*) Synergy in teamwork.

**9.** Explain the ways in which the quality of outputs can be measured.

**10.** Name any three most important pioneers of total quality movement and explain their views.

**11.** Write short notes on :
(*a*) Zero defect concept (*b*) Ten Mantras for TQM
(*c*) Pareto Analysis (*d*) Kaizen

**12.** Write an essay on "Companywide Quality Assessment".

**13.** Explain the different types of tools and techniques for TQM.

# Quality Planning

## 3.1. INTRODUCTION

As already explained in the chapter on "Quality Concepts", short definitions of quality are :

– Quality is customer satisfaction.

– Quality is fitness for use.

To understand first and most popular definition, we must first discuss the keyword 'customer.' Customer may be either 'external customer' or 'internal customer.' External customers include intermediate processors as well as merchants in addition to ultimate users. Internal customers include other sections or divisions of a company that are provided with components for an assembly and all others who are affected.

Thus, customer is anyone who is impacted by the product or process. A ***'product'*** may be :

(*a*) Goods, also known as hardware product – machines, appliances, components etc.

(*b*) Processed materials like – steel, cement, sugar, chemical, textile, petroleum, fertilizer etc.

(*c*) *Service e.g.*, technical, professional, banking, health, transportation, communication, government, hospitability etc.

In other words, we can say that 'quality' of any product or service is regarded as the degree to which it fulfills the requirements of customer.

The primary objective of any company is, therefore, to produce a quality product or service which meet the well-defined needs, satisfy customer expectations, conforms to applicable standards, available at competitive price and provide good profit to the company.

A quality management system must organise overall activities of the company in such a way that the technical, administrative and human factors affecting the quality of its products or services under control. The system is 'required to meet the inter-related needs of company as well as of customer.

Here,

(*a*) ***Company needs*** are to attain and maintain Quality at optimum cost, by efficient utilization of its technological, human and material resources.

(*b*) ***Customer needs*** are to have confidence in the capability of the company to deliver the desired quality product at competitive cost and maintaining the same consistently.

Keeping above in view, 'quality planning' is done and a comprehensive quality plan is prepared for implementation in the company. 'Quality plan' is a document setting out the specific quality practices, resources and activities relevant to a particular product, process, services, contract or project.

## 3.2 QUALITY PLANNING

**Quality planning** is a systematic process for:

(*i*) establish quality goals,

(*ii*) indentifying customers,

(*iii*) discovering the customer's needs,

(*iv*) designing the responsive products,

(*v*) developing the process for creating and delivering the products,

(*vi*) transferring the process and its contents to those who will perform the product or service,

(*vii*) establish process control.

An **integrated planning** helps in:

(*i*) reducing the overall time, effort and cost for entire product cycle,

(*ii*) higher customer satisfaction, and

(*iii*) reducing the deficiencies in the product and processes.

### Planning Concept

Planning is the main function of management. Other functions, which follow the planning function are: organizing, staffing, directing and controlling. Planning deals with what has to be done today to be ready for tomorrow. Planning is a mental process requiring the use of intellectual faculties, imagination, foresight, sound judgement etc., to decide in advance as to what is to be done, how and where it is to be done, who will do it and how the results are to be evaluated. Planning means to assess the future and make provisions for it. In planning, a manager reaches for the alternative courses open to him, and then selects to these alternatives to determine general and specific objectives and detailed means for achieving them.

For the purpose of planning, following steps are required to be taken:

(*i*) Recognition of the need for planning.

(*ii*) Establishing objectives.

(*iii*) Building the premises for planning. In this step, collection and dissemination of the facts and figures necessary for planning are done. Inferences drawn from the known facts and figures helps in planning.

(*iv*) Indentifying alternative courses of action.

(*v*) Evaluating alternative courses.

(*vi*) Selecting a course of action.

**Objectives of Planning**

Planning is done to attain objectives :

(*i*) To offset change and uncertainty.

(*ii*) To focus attention on objectives.

(*iii*) To secure economy in operation.

(*iv*) To facilitate in effective controlling.

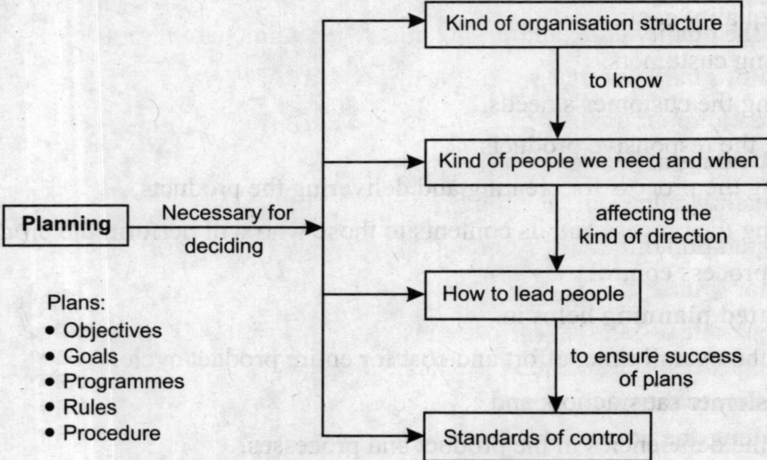


**Fig. 3.1.** Types of plans and necessity of planning

## 3.3. QUALITY MANAGEMENT

'Quality Management involves functions of:

1. Quality Planning.
2. Quality Control.
3. Quality Improvement.

These three functions are known as "three aspects of quality" or **"Juran's Quality Trilogy".**

**Quality management** is the process of identifying and administering the activities needed to achieve the quality objectives of an organisation. These three processes of the quality trilogy are inter-related. This chapter and later chapters will develop further details of these three aspects.

The Quality is always required to be planned, for which customers and their needs are to be identified, these needs are then translated into design and development of product, operating conditions are then established, optimized and put to operation.

After planning for quality, the production process and product should be controlled for quality. Control is the process of detecting and correcting adverse change as soon as they occur. Conforming to quality specifications and adhering to standards and procedures requires prompt corrective action of any problem, so that the status quo is restored. It has been observed that majority of quality problems can be controlled through management action on the system itself.

A quality breakthrough (an improvement which takes us to an unprecedented level of performance) is needed to reduce substantially the chronic waste and achieve a new improved zone of quality control.

## 3.4 ASSESSMENT OF QUALITY

In order to meet the challenges of the customer due to rapid growth on quality front, a companywide review of the status of quality is carried out for 'quality assessment.' This is a starting point of quality planning and helps in understanding:

(*a*) the size of the quality issue,and (*b*) the areas demanding attention.

**Assessment of quality** comprises following elements :

1. Cost of poor quality
2. Standing in the market place
3. Quality culture in the organization
4. Operation of quality system in the company.

**1. Cost of Poor Quality:**

This is the result of failures of materials, systems, activities, equipments, human elements, procedures, processes etc. For every organisation, it is very important to bring down the cost of poor quality to the minimum possible level, in order to improve its quality and profitability. For controlling the cost of poor quality, it is essential to classify the quality cost elements, conduct cost studies and take appropriate measures to control the cost of poor quality. Elements of poor quality cost are :

**(*a*) *Internal Failure Cost :*** These are the costs associated with defects that are found before the product is transferred to the customer. These may be :

(*i*) scrap and re-work cost,

(*ii*) costs involved in testing, inspecting and sorting for down gradation,

(*iii*) losses due to avoidable processing,

(*iv*) expenditure in failure analysis etc.

**(*b*) *External Failure Cost :*** These are the costs associated with defects that are found after the product is shipped to the customer. Examples of these costs are :

(*i*) warranty charges,

(*ii*) redressal of complaints,

(*iii*) loss of future sales,

(*iv*) other expenses on return of materials, failure analysis and concessions offered to the customer.

**(c) *Hidden Quality Costs :*** These hidden costs include :

(*i*) potential lost sales,

(*ii*) cancellation of orders,

(*iii*) costs of redesign,

(*iv*) costs of changing manufacturing processes,

(*v*) costs of software changes,

(*vi*) additional costs for space, inventory charges, overtime charges etc.,

(*vii*) loss of goodwill,

(*viii*) additional paper work,

(*ix*) Delays.

***Relating the Quality Costs to Business Measures:*** The quality costs are required to be related to other business measures with which managers are familiar. This helps in interpretation and analysis. Some examples of such relationships are :

(*i*) Quality costs as a percentage of sales.

(*ii*) Quality costs compared to profit.

(*iii*) Quality costs as a percentage of cost of goods sold.

(*iv*) Quality costs as a percentage of total manufacturing costs.

(*v*) Effect of quality costs on the break-even point.

The objectives of determining these relationships is to help in evaluation. These datas are used for :

(*i*) Quantifying the size of the quality problem in the language of money, which can be easily understood at higher level of management.

(*ii*) Help in tracing to the specific cause.

(*iii*) Providing opportunities for reducing customer dissatisfaction. Associated threats to product stability can also be identified.

**2. Standing in the Marketplace:**

In order to increase sales income, after evaluating the cost of poor quality, next step should be to know as to where the company stands on quality in the marketplace as compared to other competitors. For this purpose, 'marketing research study' is conducted to know its marketplace and also to identify opportunities and threats.

Marketing research studies should be planned by a team involving members from marketing, product development, quality, manufacturing and other concerned departments. This team design the objectives of the study, questionnaire to be answered by the customers. This aspect is being dealt separately in detail in this chapter.

**3. Operation of Current Quality System:**

Fourth element of assessment is the evaluation of current quality related system in the organisation. For this assessment, questions are addressed considering:

(*i*) companywide issues of quality management

(*ii*) matters related to functional areas.

For the purpose of assessment of current quality activities, generally the questions that address company wide issues of quality management are:

(*i*) Have quality objectives been established?

(*ii*) Have quality objectives been linked to business objectives?

(*iii*) Whether quality will be competitive in the market place, after the policies and plans regarding quality are followed?

(*iv*) Whether the organisation is following quality approach through line management rather than through staff?

(*v*) Does it cover by *Q* process fully?

(*vi*) Whether the system is effective for providing early warning of potential quality problems?

Following questions should be asked regarding functional areas:

(*i*) What measures are used to judge output quality?

(*ii*) What is the company's performance, as reflected in these measures?

(*iii*) Whether the resources spent in detecting and correcting quality-related responsiblities have been estimated?

(*iv*) Whether the quality related responsibilities have been properly understood by the concerned personnel?

(*v*) Whether the personnel have been trained to desired level in quality disciplines?

(*vi*) Does the data system fulfill the needs of the personnel?

## 3.5. QUALITY PLANNING TO GENERATE SALES INCOME

As discussed earlier, for achieving the customer satisfaction, quality of product must consider two components, namely product features and freedom from deficiencies. Both these components have been discussed in detail in section discussing "customer satisfaction". These aspects should be identified, planned and excecuted in designing a specific product or service. Customer input must be taken into account, when defining specific characteristics. Emphasis on understanding customer needs is a prerequisite to meeting sales goals.

Juran has suggested following steps as a quality planning road map for salability of products:

1. Establish quality goals.
2. Identify those impacted–the customers.
3. Discover customer's needs.

4. Develop product features.
5. Develop process features.
6. Establish process controls and transfer to operations.

**Contribution of quality to sales income occurs through following :**

(*i*) Increasing market share.
(*ii*) Securing premium prices.
(*iii*) Achieving economics of scale through increased production.
(*iv*) Achieving competitive advantages.

Here, it is important to mention that following are the main at tributes which represent quality in broad sense which help in generating sales income:

1. Consistent quality.
2. Dependable delivery.
3. High performance.
4. Timely deliveries.
5. Offer low prices.
6. Introduce new products quickly.
7. Offer a broad product line.
8. Effective publicity.
9. Wide base distribution.
10. Rapid volume change.
11. After-sales service.

**Competitive Benchmarking:**

A benchmark is a point of reference by which performance is judged or measured.

The possible benchmarks are :

1. The specifications.
2. Customer desires/expectations.
3. Competition.
4. Best in industry.

If benchmarking is done correctly, it provides hard facts needed to plan and execute effective business strategies that fully satisfy agreed customer requirements. Competitive benchmarking process has following steps:

1. Decide what should be the benchmark.
2. Select the competitors to compare themselves in terms of products and services, business processes and people.
3. Decide the appropriate measurements which should be used to define the performance levels in the competitor's business and in one's own company.
4. Determine one's competitors' strengths and weaknesses as compared to one's own company.
5. Develop an action plan, using the analysed data and set goals to gain or maintain superiority.

## 3.6. PLANNING FOR INSTALLATION OF QUALITY SYSTEM

The installation process of a quality system can be carried out in the following phases :

1. Preparation for quality system.
2. Implementation of quality system.

Time required for installation of quality system varies from 6 months to even 5 to 7 years depending upon :

(*i*) Existing level of quality management.

(*ii*) The will of management and personnel engaged to adopt the quality system.

(*iii*) Complexity of the process.

(*iv*) Characteristics of the product and competence of the employees.

### 1. Preparations for Quality System

Preparation for installation of quality system is done in the following steps:

**Step 1:** Management's commitment. It can be demonstrated by :

(*a*) Making the organization's people to understand and implement the quality policy.

(*b*) Taking appropriate action for establishment and implementation of a quality system.

(*c*) Not permitting any deviation in quality activities.

(*d*) Involvement of top management in planning implementation and review activities of quality system.

**Step 2:** Set up an implementation committee. This committee may have 4 to 6 members selected from various disciplines. One co-ordinator is also appointed to co-ordinate all quality system activities under the leadership of top management.

**Step 3 :** Start-awareness campaign. Awareness programmes are conducted to communicate the employees of all levels to make them understand the purpose of introduction of quality system, its advantages to the employees and customers.

**Step 4 :** Conduct Status Review and prepare an Action Plan. This includes the following:

(*a*) List out as to what is needed to install the quality system ?

(*b*) Review the existing set up against what is needed.

(*c*) What actions are to be taken to meet the requirements of quality system ? It should be clarified:

What is to be done ?

Who will do it ?

By what time it shall be done ?

**Step 5:** Develop an organisation structure for quality management. This aspect has already been discussed in detail in the chapter on 'Organising the Quality'.

**Step 6 :** Develop Quality System Documentation. **Quality** system is normally documented by means of;

Quality Manuals.

Quality Procedures.

Work instructions, and

Quality records.

**Step 7 :** Prepare the resource system to meet the requirements of standards. For design, development, production and supply of the products or services, various resources, such as machineries, facilities, know-how, testing and measuring equipments, material handling equipments etc. are required. Right type of process technology, and right type of processing and control equipments are required for effective implementation of quality system.

## 2. Implementation of Quality System

Quality system can be implemented only after preparation phase, as explained above, is complete. Main steps involved in the implementation phase are:

**Step 8 :** *Implement the documented quality system :* In this step, quality related activities are performed as per the quality policies, procedures, work instructions, as defined in quality manual and other quality system documentation.

**Step 9 :** *Establish internal quality audit system :* An internal auditors team is formed, who are trained by professional agency. They should conduct a planned and documented periodical audit of all quality related activities of the quality system. In initial stages, it helps various departments to continuously improve their performance.

**Step 10:** *Monitor and stabilize the quality system:* Implementation of quality system should be continuously monitored to ensure that all activities are being performed as planned, any deviation found is corrected. The observations of monitoring should be reported to the management and concerned persons.

# 3.7. QUALITY BY DESIGN

Quality by design is the practice of using a multi-disciplinary team to conduct conceptual thinking, product design, and production planning all at one time. It is also known as simultaneous engineering, Concurrent or parallel engineering. The team is composed of specialist from business, engineering, production and the customers base. Suppliers of process equipment, purchased parts, and services are also included on the team at appropriate times.

There are number of tools for successful implementation, such as TQM, quality function deployment (QFD), computer network, computer aided drafting and designing, failure mode and effects analysis (FMEA), Design by six-sigma, designing for reliability and statistical tools.

Quality by design is more effective when combined with production tools, such as robotics, computer aided manufacturing, just-in-time etc. Various tools have been discussed in the book at relevant places.

The main benefits of implementing quality by design techniques are:

(*i*) Significant decrease in time to market.

(*ii*) Faster product development.

(*iii*) Better quality.

(*iv*) Better reliability.

(*v*) Less work-in-progress.

(*vi*) Increased productivity.

(*vii*) Reduce engineering changes afterwards.

(*viii*) Less re-work and significant reduction in direct labour costs.

The purpose of design function is the translation of customer needs from product brief into specifications for materials, processes and products. The perfect product design provides customer satisfaction at an acceptable price. The specifications and design should be such that the product is producible, verifiable, controllable under proposed production, installation and operational conditions. This activity of translating the customer needs into a set of product design requirements for manufacturing is called product development, research and development, engineering or product design.

During design and development, essential quality aspects, such as safety, performance and reliability of a product are established. Design should include schedule, verification points and activities, performance evaluation plan, organisational and technical interfaces etc.

**Phases of New Product Design**

1. Concept and feasibility study.
2. ***Portotype design :*** For design review, reliability and maintainability prediction, failure mode, effect and criticality analysis, safety analysis, value engineering.
3. ***Proto type construction :*** Proto type test, environmental test, overstressing.
4. ***Preproduction :*** Pilot production lots, evaluation of tolerance.
5. ***Early full-scale production :*** In-house testing, use in limited marketing area.
6. ***Full scale production, marketing and use:*** Prompt feedback.

**Phases in Designing**

1. ***Designing for Basic Functional Requirements:*** In this phase, customer expectations for functional requirements are translated into specific engineering and quality characteristics. The necessary characteristics should be identified for raw materials, parts, assemblies and processes.
2. ***Designing for Reliability:*** A product should have a long service life with few failures. As products become more complex, failures increase with operating time. To prevent these failures, help of reliability engineering is taken. Reliability is the ability of a product to perform a required function under stated conditions for a stated period of time.

3. ***Availability:*** This is one of the important parameters of 'fitness for use'. Availability is the ability of a product, when used under given conditions, to perform satisfactorily, when called upon. The proportion of time that a product is available for use depends on: (*a*) freedom from failures *i.e.* reliability, and (*b*) the ease with which service can be re-stored after a failure *i.e.* maintainability.
4. ***Designing for safety :*** This is done through hazard analysis, fault tree analysis etc.
5. ***Design for manufacturability :*** This aim is to simplify a product design to facilitate manufacture. Tolerance affects on cost of manufacture and productivity on one side, and quality on other side.
6. ***Value Engineering:*** This technique analyses design to achieve an optimum balance between performance and cost.

### 3.7.1 Implementation

Quality by design mainly considers the reliability improvement with a consideration of economy. The designer should understand the engineering principles involved in the design. He should take the help of Reliability Engineer for;

(*i*) defining areas needing improvement, and
(*ii*) assisting in the development of alternatives.

Following steps are generally required to be taken by the Design Engineer for improving a design:

1. Review the users, needs
2. Consider trade-offs of reliability for other parameters. Here, customers' real needs are required to be better served by such a trade-off.
3. Use redundancy.
4. Use standard parts whose reliability has been proven by actual field usage.
5. Ensure that stresses applied to the parts are lower than the stresses withstand by the parts.
6. The product should enable to handle unexpected environments.
7. Specify replacement schedule for low-reliability parts before they reach the wear-out stage.

Another major consideration for the designer is the **availability**. Availability means, the 'ability of a product, when used under given conditions, to perform satisfactorily when called upon'.

The proportion of time that a product is available for use depends on;

(*i*) reliability *i.e.*, freedom from failures, and
(*ii*) maintainability *i.e.*, the ease with which service can be restored after a failure.

**Designing for safety** is also an important consideration for a designer. Various tools considered for safety analysis include, hazard quantification (hazard frequency and hazard severity), designation of safety-oriented characteristics and components, fault-tree analysis, fail safe concepts, and field testing.

Other factors for design are related to the **manufacturability**: These factors are:

1. Product costs.
2. Economics of quality.
3. Selection of tolerances. The tolerances affects:

   (*a*) fitness for use,
   (*b*) tooling
   (*c*) productivity
   (*d*) equipment
   (*e*) inspection
   (*f*) scrap and rework
   (*g*) selection of material etc.

Quality by design takes help of **teams** to take advantage of experience, quick high-quality decisions, feedback constrants, and efficient management of risk. These teams include experts from product development, research and development, design, production, testing labs, and logistics along with project management etc. For working concurrently, all the members of the team must share ideas and work towards a common goal.

A good design can be achieved through better interaction between design team members. This process begins when the members from testing, design, production etc provide input during the final revision of the product proposal from the marketing.

### Design for Six Sigma (DFSS)

In the recent past, a refinement of the quality by design has been evolved and is used by some organisations world-wide. This refinement is known as "Design for Six Sigma". Its road-map is described as under:

1. Define the project goals and customer deliverables.
2. Measure and determine customer needs and specifications.
3. Generate innovative concepts, and evaluate and then select the best concept for the design.
4. Design details, optimise the design, and plan for design verification and validation. If required simulation is carried out.
5. Verify and validate the design reliability and capability to meet customer requirements.

This design can result in reduced defects, reduced cycle time, better reliability, availability and maintainability, higher customer satisfaction, market share and profit.

## 3.7.2 Design Review

Design review is a comprehensive and systematic examination of a design to evaluate the design requirements and the capability of the design to meet these requirements and to identify problems and propose solutions.

For achieving an optimum design, design engineers should have specialized knowledge in reliability, maintainability, safety, productibility etc.: For modern products, design reviews are based on the following:

1. Design reviews are necessary so as to ascertain whether it meets the customers demand.
2. Design reviews are conducted by a team consisting mainly of specialists who are not directly associated with the development of the design.
3. Design reviews should be formal and documented. Review meetings should have recorded minutes of meetings.
4. Design reviews cover all quality related parameters alongwith others. These parameters should include reliability, maintainability, safety, productibility, weight, packaging, appearance, cost, etc.
5. Design reviews are made based on defined criteria, such as customer requirements, internal goals and experience with previous products.
6. Design reviews should be made at several levels of product hierarchy, such as system and subsystem.

## 3.8. PRODUCTION PLANNING FOR QUALITY

Quality in production can be achieved by planning and implementing the production operations under controlled conditions. These controlled conditions include control of:

1. Materials.
2. Production Equipments.
3. Processes.
4. Personnel.
5. Utilities and environment.
6. Supplies.
7. Measurement control.
8. Control of non-conformance.
9. Documentation.

To ensure right quality of material and product, the **product verification** is conducted at three main stages of production process, namely:

(*a*) Incoming materials and parts.
(*b*) In-process inspection, and
(*c*) Completed product verification

Appropriate methods for inspection and testing of incoming material, semi-finished, and finished products should be applied to verify conformity.

The production activity involves the use of manufacturing processes to change the physical raw materials into product. A quality product can be produced only when the 'process is capable' and production operation are performed under 'controlled conditions'.

Under *process capability*, production process should be verified as capable of producing in accordance with product specifications. The critical operations of the process, which are of significant importance from quality point of view should be identified, and if required, suitably modified to ensure that these characteristics remain within specifications.

## 1. Integrate Quality in Manufacture Planning

Integrate quality in manufacture planning with following objectives :

1. to prevent defects
2. to minimise variability.

For the purpose of preventing the defects, product design as well as process design should be reviewed. The concept of designing the process to be error free through **'error-proofing'**. The idea is the design of machines and tools so as to make human error improbable. In error-proofing care is taken for redundancy *i.e.* requiring multiple improbable events to occur simultaneously before a defect can be created or can escape. The **objectives of error-proofing are :**

1. Eliminating the possibility of error
2. Substituting a more reliable process for the worker
3. Making the work easier to perform
4. Detecting the error before further processing
5. Minimising the effect of the error.

## 2. Controllability Concept

(*a*) **Worker-controllable defects:**

- Failure to check work.
- Improper operation of machine.

(*b*) Management-controllable defects:

- Inadequate training
- Inadequate machine
- Inadequate machine maintenance
- Problems related to process
- Material handling problems
- Wrong material
- Tool, fixture and gauge maintenance problems.

**Self-inspection**

Under this concept, all inspection and conformance decisions, both on the process and on the product, are made by the production worker. However, independent audit of these decisions is also required. Quality department inspects a random sample to ensure that the decision-making process, used by production workers, regarding to accept or reject a product is valid.

The self-inspection system should be instituted in a well-planned manner, and for this, a quality culture should be developed in the production department.

In the self-inspection concept, it was thought that the operator who is producing should also inspect his work and segregate defectives. Later on it was felt that self-inspection activity can not survive by merely transferring inspection responsibility from inspector to operator by providing him a measuring instrument.

Subsequently, the concept of self-control was adopted, in which the people are provided with :

(*a*) Knowledge of what they are supposed to do, such as operating instructions, quality instructions, trouble shooting instructions, (*b*) Feedback on their performance for which know-how to monitor 'The quality of his job/process is essential. This can be achieved through : first piece inspection, sampling inspection, control charts or 100% inspection.

(*c*) Know-how to correct the process, if defectives are produced. This can be done by using trouble shooting charts or process sheet.

(*d*) Know-how for repairing the defectives on their detection, where possible, otherwise reject as scrap.

With the development of "Total Quality Management" concept, the self-inspection system has moved towards throughout the organisation and to all employees for taking care of quality aspects at each level. This not only requires procedures and work-instructions but also maintenance of records to demonstrate effectiveness of the system.

### 3. Automated Manufacturing

(*a*) ***Computer-integrated Manufacturing.*** This is a process of applying a computer in a planned manner from design through manufacturing and shipping.

(*b*) ***Computer-aided Manufacturing.*** This is the process in which a computer is used to plan and control the work of specific equipment.

Automation with proper planning can benefit product quality in following ways :

(*i*) It eliminates some of the monotony or fatigue tasks.

(*ii*) Automatic monitoring and continuous adjustments can reduce the process variations.

(*iii*) Immediate feedback displayed by the automatic machines can provide an early warning.

### 4. Overall Review of Manufacturing Planning and Quality Audits

Manufacturing planning review is most effectively accomplished through preproduction trials and runs, which provide the ultimate evaluation by manufacturing real product.

A quality audit is an independent evaluation of various aspects of quality performance. These audits should be performed for :

(*a*) 'systems quality audit', which includes any activity that can affect final product quality. This audit is usually made on a specific activity.

(*b*) 'product audit', which involves the re-inspection of product to verify the adequacy of acceptance or rejection decisions. Such audits can take place at each inspection station for the product or after final assembly and packing.

## 3.9. STRATEGIC QUALITY MANAGEMENT

Strategic quality management is the process of establishing long range quality goals and defining the approach for meeting these goals.

This strategic quality management is developed and implemented by higher management.

For strategic quality management, following elements are considered :

1. Focus on customer needs
2. Develop quality goals and strategies under the leadership of higher management.
3. Translation of strategies into annual business plans.
4. Implementation of actions by line departments instead of solely depending on quality department

Strategic Quality Management (SQM) framework is decided after considering the following widely accepted elements:

(*a*) Carry out SWOT analysis *i.e.* analyze the opportunities and threats, and strengths and weaknesses of the organisation.

(*b*) Select a strategy after identifying and evaluating the alternative strategies.

(*c*) Prepare detailed short range plans and then translate these plans into budgets.

(*d*) Monitor performance.

***Application of General Management Principles***

General management principles when applied to quality, following elements emerges :

1. Quality policies
2. Quality goals
3. Plans to meet goals
4. Organizational structure.
5. Resources
6. Measurement feedback
7. Review
8. Rewards based on performance
9. Training.

## 3.9.1. Quality Policy

Quality policy is the overall quality intention and direction of an organisation as regards quality as formally expressed by top management. The quality policy should be expressed in an easily understandable language and should be relevant to organizational policies. The quality objectives should be both, ambitious and achievable. The management should be committed to implement its quality policy. Quality policy should be developed and documented related to the following:

(*i*) level of clientele constitutes the company's market.

(*ii*) whether the company strive for quality leadership, competitiveness, or adequacy.

(*iii*) grade of quality to be provided.

(*iv*) objective for quality.

(*v*) approach to be adopted to achieve quality objectives.

(*vi*) role of company personnel responsible for implementation of quality policy.

(*vii*) whether the company to market its products on the basis of high reliability at higher price or lower reliability at lower price.

(*viii*) should the reliability, maintainability etc. be quantified.

(*iv*) should top management actively participate in quality planning and assurance or should it delegate this to someone else?

Most commonly documents related to Quality policy, Quality manual, Quality and Quality records.

### 3.9.2 Quality Goals

A goal is a statement of the desired result to be achieved within a specified time. These goals form the basis of detailed planning of quality activities. Tactical goals are short range (say 1 year), and strategic goals are long range (say 5 years).

Goals are set either for breakthrough or for control. There are several reasons for setting goals for achieving breakthrough, some of them are :

(*i*) To attain or hold quality leadership.

(*ii*) To increase market share by creating competitiveness.

(*iii*) To identify opportunities to improve income through superior fitness for use.

(*iv*) To reduce too many field troubles and to cut the external costs resulting from guarantee charges, investigation and repair or replacement costs.

(*v*) To identify the activities for either internal cost reduction opportunities or for improving process yield and reduction of scrap, re-work, inspection or testing.

(*vi*) To improve the image with customers, suppliers or general public.

**Criteria used for defining quality goals are:**

- Past performance.
- Engineering analysis.
- Competition in the market place.

## QUESTIONS

1. 'Quality of any product or service is regarded as the degree to which it fulfills the requirement of customers'. Discuss this statement.
2. 'Quality management system is required to meet the inter-related needs of company as well as of customer'. Discuss.
3. What are the steps which should be taken while planning for quality ?
4. What is planning? Explain the objectives of planning.
5. Name the types of plans. Explain why planning is necessary?
6. Write short notes on:

   (*a*) Product features for manufacturing industries

   (*b*) Product features for service industries

(*c*) Functions of quality management

(*d*) Elements of quality planning.

**7.** Explain as to how assessment of quality is done?

**8.** Explain the term 'cost of poor quality' in detail.

**9.** What is a quality culture in an organisation? How it should be assessed?

**10.** How the quality planning is done with the aim to generate sales income?

**11.** Write short notes on:

(*a*) Competitive benchmarking.

(*b*) Assessment to company's standing in the market place.

(*c*) Hidden quality costs.

(*d*) Internal failure costs.

(*e*) External failure costs.

**12.** What are the service characteristics ? How they effect service quality?

**13.** What is the management responsibility for planning, development and maintenance of quality system and customer satisfaction? How the management can accomplish this responsibility?

**14.** Write short notes on:

(*a*) Quality policy. (*b*) Quality manual.

(*c*) Quality system structure.

**15.** How will you plan quality aspects in design?

**16.** How production planning is done for quality?

**17.** Write short notes on:

(*a*) Integrated quality in manufacture planning.

(*b*) Worker-controllable defects.

(*c*) Management-controllable defects.

(*d*) Quality loop.

**18.** How will you integrated the quality in manufacture planning? Explain in detail.

**19.** Explain the term 'strategic quality managements'.

**20.** How will you apply general management principles?

**21.** Write an essay on Quality Management.

**22.** How will you plan for installing a quality system? Explain.

**23.** Write short notes on:

(*a*) Quality policy (*b*) Quality goals

(*c*) Automated manufacturing (*d*) Self-control

(*e*) Self-inspection

# 4 Organising (Leadership) for Quality

## 4.1. ORGANISING CONCEPT

Organising is an important function of management by which it combines the human power with other resources to give desired output. Organising includes formation of structure of authority and responsibility among the people to achieve the objectives of the organisation.

Organisational structure must be designed and maintained for people to work together in carrying out plans and fulfilling the objectives. Organising involves grouping of tasks necessary to carry out plans, assigning activities to departments and making provisions for co-ordination through delegation of authority.

Organisation structure means the systematic arrangement of the people working for the organisation, their positions and the relationships between positions. The organisation varies with the organisations and the functions to be performed and depends upon the goals and objectives established, the resources available, the communications and the working relationships of the individuals, motivational and other factors.

**Guidelines for Good Organising**

1. Allotment of work.
2. Clarify relationship.
3. Proper delegation of authority.
4. Sufficient flexibility to permit slight alterations and expansions, whenever needed.
5. Distribution of working in different departments avoid conflicts.
6. Co-ordination among different departments.
7. Organisation should be able to avoid wastage of labour, money and materials.

**Leadership**

Leadership can be defined as follows:

- Leadership means to inspire confidence and trust so that there is maximum co-operation from the employees within the control of a manager.

- Leadership is the ability to persuade others to seek defined objectives enthusiastically.

Success of a leader depends upon his qualities and characteristics.

**How to do Organising ?**

First of all, organisation is roughly made from several perspectives, and then attempt to weld these systems into a unified concept. Thereafter, it is refined until it becomes fit for implementation.

**Phases of organising are :**

- Develop a classical hierarchical organisation structure, based on the traditional methods for departmentation. The departments can be based on functions, products, territary (zones), process, project or services.
- Start with total company objectives and develop a hierarchy or network of systems required. This is done by considering span of control, chain of command, unity of command. Determine the work activities, job description, organise people into groups and assign them to supervisors, establish objectives, and determine standards of performance.
- Matrix is developed by involving experts. Analysis of decision and information requirements must also be done during the process.
- Organising will be complete only after we introduce the behavioural aspects and information concepts in the system.

**Sub-systems of Organisation System**

1. ***Organisational System.*** This defines the level of authority and responsibility, tasks, positions and methods of operation.
2. ***Individual as a System.*** Co-operation, behaviour of people, interactions of those around individual affect the values, attitudes and behaviour of the individual.
3. ***Organisational Communication System.*** This is the fornix and informal procedure established by the management, and is dependent on the management information system.
4. ***Management Information System.*** This is a means of gathering and transmitting informations to the major decision-makers to control present and future activities.
5. ***Functional Systems.*** In order to meet customers' needs, sequence of activities take place starting from purchase of raw material and then converting it to finished goods till their distribution. These activities or functions are the sub-systems and include purchasing, engineering, production, marketing, finance etc.

**Staffing**

Staffing function is a function of management, and in most cases, it is considered as a part of the organising function. Staffing function comprises the activities essential to manage and keep manned the positions created by the organising structure.

For an on-going enterprise, staffing is a continuous process for new jobs or to fill up the vacancies created by retirement or leaving by employees.

Staffing can be identified as that managerial function which involves selection, training, promotion and retirement of personnel.

**Organisational Hierarchy and Management Skills**

In an organisational hierarchy, various levels require varying degree of managerial skills, namely technical, human and conceptual skills. Technical skills are of maximum importance at supervisory level. Conceptual skills are of maximum use for top level of management, as shown in Fig. 4.2.

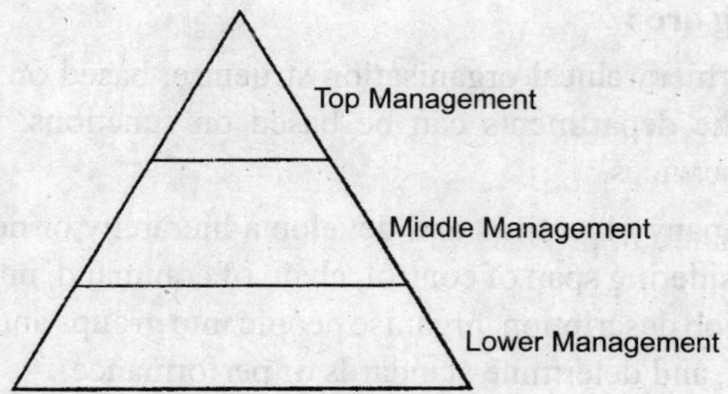


**Fig. 4.1.** Hierarchy of Management

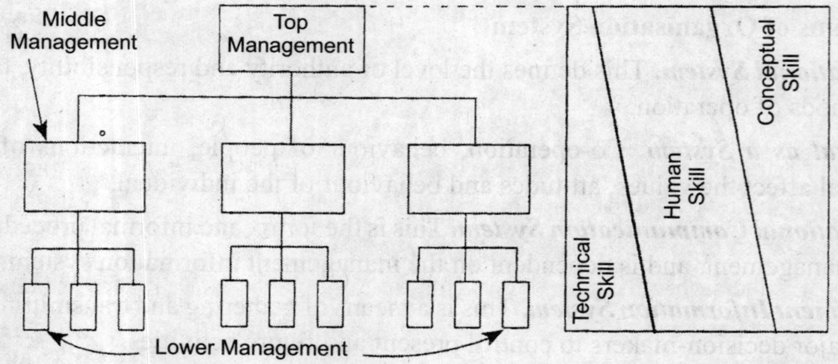


**Fig. 4.2.** Organisational hierarchy and managerial skills

## 4.2. EVOLUTION OF ORGANISATION FOR QUALITY

Many industrial organisations are assigning quality related activities to the department known as "Quality Department". During the last 2-3 decades, the names and the scope of activities have changed—Inspection, quality control to statistical quality control, reliability engineering, total quality control, total quality management, quality assurance etc.

Over the years, the status of the quality control organization has changed from a function merely responsible for detecting inferior or standard material to a function that establishes what are termed as preventive programmes. These programmes are designed to detect quality problems in the design stage or at any point in the manufacturing process and to follow up on corrective action. Immediate responsibility for quality products rest with the manufacturing departments. All the activities, concerning product quality are usually brought together in the organisation which may be known as inspection, quality control, quality assurance department or any other similar name.

Quality control is a staff activity for assisting the line or production department in managing quality. Since the quality control function has authority delegated by management to evaluate the quality of material produced by the manufacturing department, it would not be in a position to control or dictate to the quality activity.

The quality control department depending upon the type of product, and method of quality control should be sufficient enough to carry out following activities:

1. Inspection of raw material, product or processes.
2. Salvage inspection to determine rejected part and assembly disposition.
3. Records and reports maintenance.
4. Statistical quality control.
5. Gauges for inspection.
6. Design for quality control and inspection.
7. Quality control system maintenance and development.

During the last about two decades, following major **trends in organizing for quality** are emerging:

1. Quality management tasks are assigned to functional line departments rather than the quality department.
2. The scope of quality management is broadened from operations only to all activities and from external customers to external and internal customers.
3. Quality teams are being formed and extensively used.
4. Authority for decision-making is delegated to lower levels through 'self-managing teams'.

In order to meet the quality objectives and implementation of quality policy an organisation for quality is required to be designed and developed in such a way that the technical, human and administrative factors affecting the quality remain under control. The designing of an organisation structure means defining the tasks to be performed and the hierarchical responsibility and relationship of doing it. The **designing of structure** can be done in the following steps :

(*i*) Identify the activities to be performed.

(*ii*) Assign responsibilities for performing these activities.

(*iii*) Divide the groups of activities in a logical manner into jobs.

(*iv*) Define the responsibilities and authorities associated with each job.

(*v*) Define relationship of each job with other jobs. This includes the chain of command, communication and co-ordination pattern so as to carry out the inter-departmental activities.

(*vi*) Integrate the work of internal departments and external agencies so as to achieve the quality objectives in an optimal manner.

Organisation structure can then be developed into three tiers, namely top level, middle level and lower level (or front line) managers. Top level managers are responsible for overall planning, implementation and effective functioning of the system. Middle level managers (mostly heads of functional departments) are responsible for designing and implementation of quality related activities in their areas so as to achieve the desired product or service quality. The lower level managers (supervisory personnel) directly monitor and control the quality related activities during various stages of processing.

The organisation for quality management should be adequately staffed and equipped with sufficient resources. Head of the quality, generally known as quality director or chief of quality, should directly report to the top management.

The quality organisation should develop, establish, document, implement and maintain a quality system as a means, by which stated policies and objectives can be accomplished.

## 4.3 ROLE OF THE QUALITY HEAD

Quality Director or Chief of Quality has two primary roles : administering the quality department and assisting top management with strategic quality management.

**(*A*) *Functions of the Quality Department:***

Juran has given the list of functions as under :

- Companywide quality planning.
- Producing executive reports on quality.
- Auditing out-going quality.
- Auditing quality practices.
- Co-ordination and assisting with improvement projects.
- Training for quality.
- Consulting for quality.
- Developing new quality methodologies.
- Transferring quality activities to line departments.

**(*B*) *Assisting Top Management with Strategic Quality Management***

- Assessing quality
- Formulating goals
- Formulating policies
- Developing strategies
- Delegating responsibilities
- Carrying out reward and recognition
- Reviewing progress

- Integrating
- Integrating quality during strategic business planning cycle.

**Requisites of a Quality Head**

Quality Director/Chief of Quality department should have following requisites/qualifications:

(*i*) Knowledge of complete production system.

(*ii*) Ability to conceive or understand the system.

(*iii*) A knowledge of technical and cost aspects of the product/ services and the system.

(*iv*) Knowledge of computer application in the quality system.

(*v*) A good experience of major functional disciplines of the organisation.

## 4.4. ROLE OF TOP MANAGEMENT

Main roles of the top management are :

1. Establish a quality council.
2. Establish quality policies.
3. Establish quality goals.
4. Provide the resources.
5. Provide problem-oriented training.
6. Serve on quality improvement teams which address chronic problems.
7. Stimulate improvement.
8. Provide for reward and recognition.

The top management is required to: (*a*) develop strategies for quality, and (*b*) provide leadership for implementation of these strategies.

**1. Quality Council**

Quality council is a group of senior level managers, both, line and staff, who develop the quality strategy, and guide and support their implementation. Councils may be established at corporate level, division level and plant level. The chairperson of a council is the person who is head at that level *e.g.*, Chairman/President at corporate council, and Chief of the division or plant for their levels. One member of the council is the quality director or chief of quality.

**Functions of the council** may be as follows :

– Formulating quality policy.
– Estimating major dimensions of the quality problem.
– Establishing the infrastructure.
– Planning for training for all levels.
– Establishing support for teams.
– Providing for co-ordination.
– Establishing new measures for progress review.

- Revising the merit rating approach.
- Designing a plan for recognition.
- Establishing a plan for publicity of quality related activities.

The aim of constituting the quality council is to give a focus on seriousness and complexity of the quality issues. One or more full time staff people should be deployed to assist the council.

**2. Quality Policies**

As we know, a policy is a broad guide to action, and is a statement of principles, subject matter of quality policies must be tailor-made for each company, however, there are some fundamental matters for any company. Some of these fundamental topics are :

- What level of clientele constitute the company's market ?
- Is the company to strive for quality leadership, competitiveness, or adequacy ?
- Is the company to market its products on the basis of high reliability at higher initial price or lower reliability at lower initial price?
- Should the effort be to optimize user's costs or manufacturers' costs ?
- Should the reliability and maintainability etc. be quantified?
- Should the company rely for its control on systems or on people?
- Should quality planning be done by staff or line people ?
- Should the supplier be put onto the team ?

The policies may be corporate policy and divisional policies. The corporate policy applies companywide, and mentions the lists of the subjects that are to be contained in the policies created by each division.

The policies of some organisations also include 'vision statements' e.g.

- Definition of quality.
- Scope of quality effort.
- Quality linked to business goals.
- Long range and short range goals.
- Focus on customers-internal and external.
- Involvement of employees.
- Implementation by line organisation.

**3. Quality Goals**

A goal or objective is a statement of the desired result to be achieved within a specified time. These goals form the basis of detailed planning of activities. Tactical goals are for short range (say, for 1 year), and strategic goals are for long range (say for 5 years). Under the concept of management by objectives (MBO), managers participate in establishing objectives, which are then reduced to writing and become the basis of planning for objectives. The goals are created for the purpose of planning and then control.

Criteria used for defining quality goals are :

- Past performance
- Engineering analysis
- Competition in the market place.

**4. Resources for Quality Activities**

Quality activities require an investment of time and resources throughout the entire organisation. Higher management is required to take decision regarding providing of resources for quality activities. In the times of high competition, it is difficult to add resources, time and resources can be found only by changing the priorities of both, line and staff. This means some work must be eliminated or delayed. Resources for quality project teams are made available, only if the pilot teams demonstrate benefits by achieving tangible results.

**5. Training for Quality**

The training should be given for the persons who need it and at the time, when it is needed. The training should be problem and result oriented. A trainee should be able to apply the concepts during the training process. Training on following subjects should be imparted to the groups who need them :

- Quality awareness.
- Quality concepts.
- Strategic quality management.
- Quality roles of personnel.
- Quality processes.
- Problem solving methods.
- Statistics.
- Motivation for quality.
- Quality in functional areas.

ISO standards require training needs to be carefully identified and procedures to be established for the systematic training of all personnel performing activities affecting quality. Therefore, every department is required to assess its traning needs as well as the scope and level of training required. Departmental heads should identify the personnel to be trained. Particular attention should be paid to the training of newly recruited workers and personnel at higher levels.

Workers and their supervisors should be trained in the skills required for their tasks. They should have skill in operating machinery, tools and instruments. They should be able to read and understand specifications, drawings and other documents on quality related activities.

**6. Serve on Quality Improvement Teams**

Management leadership is expected to serve on upper management quality improvement teams which address chronic problems of an upper management nature. Each team, consisting solely of upper management members, addresses a problem which requires attention at its level. The visibility of upper management taking quality training and then conducting such products sets an example for other levels to follow. Upper management should take dramatic action to demonstrate its commitment to quality, whenever any opportunity arises. Such dramatic actions, even though they are rare, are inspiring for a long period of time.

7. **Provide Recognition and Rewards**

"Recognition" is a public acknowledgement of superior performance of specific activities. Recognition can be provided at several levels—individuals, teams, and business units. "Rewards" are benefits which are conferred for superior performance against goals. These play an important role in inspiring people on quality. More important is the positive internal feeling of the people, when: (*a*) their job has been designed to focus on self-development and (*b*) they are given opportunities to participate in planning and decision-making. This conveys to the employees that their skills, their judgement, and their integrity are trusted.

Forms of recognition range from a simple verbal message for a job well done to modest or token awards. Token awards may be tangible (like a savings bond, time off, a dinner etc.) or intangible (like letter of appreciation, sending the employee to a seminar or conference). The recognition must be genuine and must fit the local culture.

The reward may be in the form of bonuses, salary increases, promotion, gain-sharing etc.

## 4.5. ROLE OF MIDDLE AND LOWER MANAGEMENT

Middle managers, supervisors, professional specialists, and the work-force are the people who execute the quality strategy developed by upper management. Role of the middle managers, supervisors and specialists include:

– Nominating quality problems for solutions.

– Serving as leaders of various quality teams.

– Serving as members of quality teams.

– Serving on task forces to assist the quality council.

– Leading the quality activities within their own area by demonstrating the personal commitment and encouraging their employees.

– Identifying customers and suppliers and meeting with them to discover and address their needs.

– The middle managers are required to serve as team leaders as a continuing part of their job, for which they require special managerial skills.

## 4.6. ROLE OF THE WORKFORCE

Workforce means all employees except those in management and the professional specialists. As we have already discussed in earlier chapters that since most quality problems are management/

system controllable, hence the management must: (*i*) direct the steps necessary to identify and remove the causes of quality problems, and (*ii*) provide the system that place workers in a state of self-control. For both of these, co-operation from workforce is essential. The roles of the workforce are :

– Assigning quality problems for solutions.
– Serving as members of various quality teams.
– Identifying elements of their own jobs that do not meet the criteria of self-control.
– Becoming knowledgeable as to the needs of their customers.

The aim is to tap the potential of the workforce by using its experience, training and knowledge. Quality goals cannot be achieved unless we use the heads and the hands of the workforce.

## 4.7. LEADERSHIP

Leadership is the ability to get desirable action, voluntarily and without force, from the followers. Leadership is the process of influencing other members of the organisation or the group to co-operate in achieving the organisational goals. Leadership means to inspire confidence and trust so that there is maximum co-operation from the employees within the control of the manager. Leadership can also be defined as the quality to awaken in others the desire to follow common objectives.

**Types of Leaders**

Leaders can be of following types :

1. Authoritarian leaders.
2. Democratic or participative leaders.
3. Persuasive leaders.
4. Functional leaders.
5. Free-rein leaders.

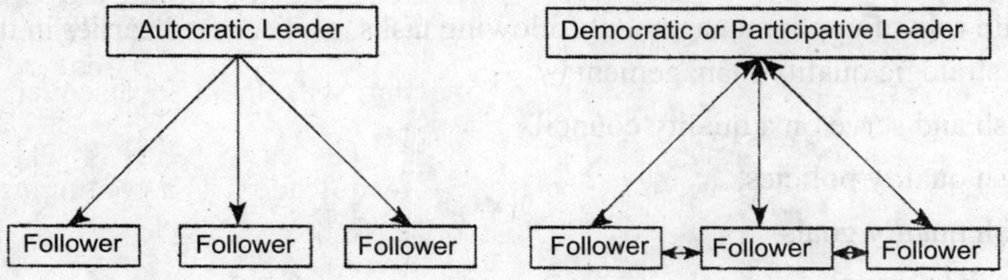


**Fig. 4.3.** Leadership styles

**Leadership Qualities**

Following are some of the qualities, which a good administrative leader must possess:

1. Intelligence and technical knowledge
2. Initiative
3. Decisiveness
4. Persuasiveness
5. Free-rein leaders
6. Ability to inspire
7. Social consciousness
8. Positive attitude
9. Energy
10. Knowledge of human relations
11. Communication skills
12. Teaching ability
13. Maturity
14. Positive attitude
15. Creative and independent thinking
16. Open mindedness
17. Flexibility
18. Self-confidence
19. Foresightedness
20. Faith and respect from followers
21. Vigilant
22. Appropriate risk taking
23. Handling setbacks

### Leadership Role of Upper Management

For leadership role of upper management following tasks, as discussed earlier in this chapter, were identified in strategic quality management:

1. Establish and serve on a quality council.
2. Establish quality policies.
3. Establish quality goals.
4. Provide the resources.
5. Provide problem-oriented training.
6. Serve on quality improvement teams which address cronic problems.
7. Stimulate improvement
8. Provide for reward and recognition.

These activities require nearly 10 percent of the time of upper management. When upper management spends time on above mentioned activities, it provides the evidence of leadership that inspires others. Another form of evidence is upper management quality improvement teams.

There are occasions when opportunities are available for upper management to take dramatic action to demonstrate its commitment to quality.

Leadership styles are also applicable to middle and lower levels of management.

## 4.8. CHARACTERISTICS OF SUCCESSFUL LEADERS

1. Leadership is a process of influencing the group members.
2. Leadership is the function of motivating the people to strive willingly to attain organisational objectives.
3. They empower rather than control, subordinates. Leaders have trust and confidence in the performance of their subordinates.
4. They give more attention to external and internal customers and their needs.
5. They emphasize improvement rather than maintaining status quo.
6. Employees must be satisfied with the type of leadership provided.
7. They enceurage collaboration rather than competition.
8. Instead of direction and supervision, leaders should emphasize on training the subordinates.
9. They establish organisational systems to support the quality efforts.
10. A good leader encourage and recognize team effort.

## 4.9. FUNCTIONS OF A LEADER

Following are the important functions of a leader:

1. Co-ordinate individual efforts.
2. To act as a friend, philosopher and guide.
3. To keep the moral of the group at high level.
4. To encourage teamwork.
5. Channelise the group functioning.
6. To ensure that each member of his group knows his task, if needed, train and develop the members.
7. To achieve his targets, and regularly monitor the progress and evaluate the results.
8. To get best out of each member of the group.

## 4.10. EMPOWERMENT

Empowerment means delegating decision-making authority to lower levels. This necessitates providing additional training to those who are authorised for decision-making.

For this purpose people are encouraged to take the initiative and broaden their scope. In case of empowerment of the workforce, the management must be supportive, if mistakes are made.

Empowerment creates the feeling of ownership and responsibility becomes more meaningful. Empowerment and sharing of confidential business information with employees provide evidence of managements trust. This will clearly be a change in the culture. This concept of empowerment must apply both, to individuals and to workers including self-managed teams.

For the purpose of change in quality culture, more attention is required to be paid on selection and training. Interviews and testing prior to employment assure compatibility of the candidate and the job. Rotational assignments then help in developing a broad base of skills and facilitate in co-operation across departments.

Empowerment can be defined as an environment in which people have the ability, confidence, and commitment to take the responsibility, and ownership to improve the process and initiate the necessary steps to satisfy customer requirements in order to achieve organisational values and goals.

Employee empowerment requires that the individual is held responsible for accomplishing the whole task, thus, the individual is not only responsible but also accountable.

## 4.11. EMPLOYEES INVOLVEMENT (PARTICIPATIVE MANAGEMENT)

Employees participation is a democratic method of the development process which enables people for decision-making and acceptance of changes that affect their lives. It includes:

(*a*) Involvement of people right from planning to execution.

(*b*) Enabling people for decision-making and

(*c*) Combining and utilizing human resources.

Participating management concept is a powerful tool of industrial relation system. It is based on industrial democracy and develops team spirit with the employees, and belongingness in them. This helps in realisation of common objectives.

Participative Management may be defined as a system of communication and consultation either formal or informal to keep employees of the organisation informed about the affairs of the concerns through which they can express their opinions to contribute to management decisions.

### Characteristics of Participation

1. It increases the scope of employees' share of influence in decision-making at different levels of the organisational hierarchy.
2. Participation has to be at different levels of management in regard to policy formulation and execution.
3. It presupposes willing acceptance of responsibilities by workers.
4. Participative forums and practices provide for association of workers' representatives.
5. Its aim is to transfer management functions to the workers.

## Objectives of Workers' Participation

1. Establish a good communication system.
2. To develop a sense of involvement among workers.
3. Promote mutual understanding between management and work-force.
4. To develop a sense of commitment to decisions to which they are a party.
5. To create a sense of belongingness among workers.
6. To create a climate for cordial and harmonious employer-employee relations.
7. To handle resistance to change.

## Forums of Participation

- Quality council.
- Quality improvement teams.
- Quality circles.
- Quality taskforces (appointed by the quality councils.)
- Design review teams.
- Process review teams.
- Plan own work.
- Customer visits.
- Supplier visits.
- Meetings with management.
- Visit other companies to learn about quality activities.
- Conferences.

## Advantages of Participation

**1. Advantages to the employees:**

These include:

- a sense of identity and belongingness
- motivation to perform better. Better performance will mean economic gains in terms of increased wages and incentives and better standard of lining.

**2. Advantages to the organisation.**

These include:

- improved quality of decision-making,
- better implementation of the decisions,
- better quality performances,

- results in better profit,
- easier acceptance of change of technology etc. on the part of employees,
- better materialization of creative ideas and suggestions,
- It reduces labour–management friction and enhances better industrial relations.

## 4.12. QUALITY CIRCLES

Dr. Ishikawa conceived the idea of Quality Control Circles in 1961 in Japan, and in 1967 after visiting Japan, Dr. Juran wrote an article titled "The Quality Control Circle Phenomenon". In 1977, the International Association for Quality Circles was formed in USA, thereafter, the movement started spreading in European countries. In India, this movement was introduced by BHEL in January, 1981.

Conceptually, Quality Circle can be described as a small group of employees of the same work area, doing similar work that meets voluntarily and regularly to identify, analyse and resolve work related problems. This small group with every member of the circle participating to the full, carries of the activities, utilising problem-solving techniques to achieve control or improvement in the work area and also help self and mutual development in the process.

The concept of the Quality Circle is based on "respect for the human individual" as against the traditional assumption, based on suspicion and mistrust between management and its employees. Quality circles built mutual trust and create greater understanding between the management and the workers. Co-operation and non-confrontation is the key element in its operation. Quality Circles aim at building people, developing them, arousing genuine interest and dedication to their work to improve quality, productivity, cost reduction etc.

As mentioned above, Quality Circles were experimented first in 1981, in India at the Hyderabad unit of BHEL. Within about three to four months of their launching, the first Quality Circle could make a presentation of the case studies of the problems identified and resolved by them to the top management. As a result of the success, the workers in other areas started voluntarily coming forward to start new circles. With the BHEL top management, expressing its firm conviction and total support to implementation of Quality Circles, the movement spread rapidly to other units of BHEL. In about two years, since initiation of the concept, all the manufacturing units of BHEL had quality circles operating involving over 4000 employees of grass-root level in activities of over 400 Quality Circles.

As the success story of Quality Circles in BHEL started spreading through articles and news reports, many other organisations started taking interest in this concept. This led to the formation of "Quality Circle Forum of India" (QCFI) which organised a number of Seminars and Workshops on Quality Circles in various parts of the country. QCFI then joined hands with different professional bodies for organising the programmes at different places across different disciplines. This attract overwhelming response testifies to the ever-growing popularity of the participative philosophy in India.

The reason for the success of Quality Circles concept is because it is a **"philosophy of energizing people"** ; **"Improvement through involvement"**, and it is an integrated system, where supervisors and employees work together with trust and co-orperation.

## Objectives

Some of the broad objectives of the Quality Circle are :

(*i*) To improve quality, productivity, safety and cost reduction

(*ii*) To give chance to the employees to use their wisdom and creativity.

(*iii*) To encourage team spirit, cohesive culture and mutual trust among different levels and sections of the employees.

(*iv*) To promote self and mutual development including leadership quality.

(*v*) To fulfill the self-esteem and motivational needs of employees.

(*vi*) To improve the quality of work-life of employees.

(*vii*) Improvement in communication.

(*viii*) Improvement in morale through increased job saticfaction.

(*ix*) Acquiring new skills and knowledge.

(*x*) Improvement in labour-management relations.

(*xi*) Developing quality consciousness.

(*xii*) Waste reduction.

## Implementation of Quality Circles in an Organisation

For the success of Quality Circle programme, following actions are necessary in the Organisation :

(*a*) Few managers representing production, quality control, design, process planning form the Quality Circle (Q.C.) Steering Committee. This acts as a policy-making body and will monitor the Q.C. in the organization.

(*b*) Top management must attend the orientation courses designed for them.

(*c*) A committed top and middle management is necessary.

(*d*) A facilitator must be appointed, who serves as a link between top management, quality circles, steering committee, middle management circle leaders and circle members. Facilitator will co-ordinate regarding training courses, get the support from all concerned including top management, quality circles, steering committee, circle leader and circle members to help the circle leader in conducting the meetings and to provide necessary resources.

## Benefits of Quality Circles (Q.C.)

1. Through the forum of Q.C, the chronic problems of organisations which really create hurdles in work get resolved by the grassroot employees of organisation, whose knowledge and experience otherwise is not fully utilized.
2. With such a capable workforce, any organisation can easily undertake more difficult and challenging assignments for its growth and profit.

3. As the employees gain experience, they take more challenging projects, in due course, they undertake projects on cost reduction, material handling, quality improvement, preventing wastage, improving delivery schedule, improving customer service, improving inspection and test methods, preventing accidents, improving design and process etc.
4. 'Quality circles have good impact on individuals' characteristics as it improves personal capabilities, increase individuals' self-respect and help in improving personality characteristics.
5. Quality circles help in improving individuals' relations with others.
6. Quality circles improve workers attitude towards company, as it instill in the worker a better understanding about the importance of product quality, and compulsions/helplessness in solving their problems by the management. Sometimes collective wisedom helps in solving the problems.
7. Communication is improved between labour, supervisors and management. This also results in improvement of labour-management relations.

## Organisation and Working

Quality circle concept was conceived in Japan, in 1962 as a forum for training its work force for improving the quality of products. Quality circles is a voluntary one and employees are free to join or not to join. 8 to 10 employees including the supervisor from same workshop doing similar work join together as a group and the supervisor can become leader of the group, if the members of Quality Circle so desire.

It is a part time acitivity, members of Quality Circle are allowed to meet for an hour every week. During the various meetings, this group progressively identify, select, analyse and solve the problems. Later they offer proposed solutions to management for consideration, approval and implementation.

Additionally a senior officer from the same workshop is nominated as facilitator, who guide the activities of the group.

A Management Committee at senior level is also formed, which overview the progress of Quality Circle.

Training of members, leaders and facilitator is very important for the success of programme.

## Launching of Quality Circle Programme

The typical steps for launching programme are as under :

(*i*) Orientation Programme for Senior Management Personnel.
(*ii*) Orientation Programme for Managers and Executives.
(*iii*) Orientation Programme for Selected Supervisors.
(*iv*) Orientation Programme for Workers (selected area).
(*v*) Formation of Circles (Minimum 2 and Maximum 4).

(*vi*) Training of Facilitators.
(*vii*) Training of Leaders.
(*viii*) Q.C. meetings for projects

## 4.13. TEAMS AND TEAM WORK

**A team** is defined as a group of people working together to achieve common objectives or goals.

**Teamwork** is the cumulative actions of the team during which each member of the team set aside his individual interests and opinions to fulfill the objectives or goals of the group.

The objective or goal of the team is a need to accomplish something, such as to solve a problem, improve a process, design a product or machine, etc. Most quality and productivity problems can be effectively solved. Since members of the team have their own history of experience, it helps in achieving the objective. Team members are expected to follow discipline, respect others, and listen to the suggestions of others.

Teams are more useful because many heads (members of team) are more knowledgeable than one. Each member of the team has special abilities that can be used to solve problems. The interaction within the team produces results that exceed the contributions of each member.

Quality control circles, as discussed earlier, is considered to be the beginning of the use of teams to improve quality. The quality control circles are groups of people from one work unit who meet together on a regular basis to identify, analyse, and solve quality and other problems within their area.

### Common Barriers to Team Progress

Following are the common barriers to the team. Perusal of these barriers indicate that these are primarily due to the system rather than the team:

1. Insufficient Training.
2. Insufficient compensation and rewards.
3. Resistance by supervisors, as they are reluctant to give up their power.
4. Lack of proper planning.
5. Insignificant project objectives.
6. No clear measure of success.
7. Team is too large.
8. Lack of management support.
9. Access to the information system of the organisation, *e.g.*, business performance, competitive performance, financial data etc.
10. Lack of union support.

## Types of Teams

The current types of teams can be divided into following four main types. These teams may be called by different names depending upon type of work:

1. **Process Improvement Teams.**

   The team members represent each operation of the process. The scope of the work of the team is limited to the work unit. If required, team may include external or internal supplier, and internal or external customer. The team generally has 6 to 10 members and is disbanded when the objective has been achieved. In case, the targeted process includes many work units, a cross – functional team may be more appropriate.

2. **Cross – Functional Teams**

   This team has 6–10 members, representing from different functional areas, such as engineering, marketing, production, quality, human resources, finance etc.

3. **Work Teams**

   This type of team is composed of members from the work unit and a manager is also a part of the team. The management selects the project. The manager should help employees to become comfortable in the team environment.

4. **Self – managed work teams**

   These are an extension of work teams without the supervisor. These not only do the work but also manage it. There is a team co-ordinator to liaison with senior management that may rotate among members.

## Self-managing Teams

Self-managing team is a group of people who work together continuously and who plan, execute, and control their work to achieve a defined output. In this, workers are empowered to make certain decisions previously reserved for supervisor.

**Advantages of these teams are:**

- improvements in productivity
- improvements in quality
- improvements in customer satisfaction
- reduction in cost
- commitment of personnel
- reduction in staff support
- reduction in supervision
- improved decision-making
- improvement in work-methods.

*Problems* experienced due to self-managing teams are :

– costs of salary and training go up.

– resistance by supervisors or lower management

– resistance by staff groups

– conflict between participants and non-participants.

**Self-managing Team v/s Traditional Organisation**

| *Feature* | *Traditional Organisation* | *Self-managing Team* |
|---|---|---|
| 1. Scope of work | Every individual is responsible for a narrow scope. | Team is responsible for a broad scope. |
| 2. Job categories for personnel | Many small categories | A few large categories. |
| 3. Organising, scheduling and assigning work | By supervisor | By team |
| 4. Measuring and taking corrective action | By supervisor | By team |
| 5. Opportunity for job rotation | Minimum | High. |
| 6. Sharing of information | Very limited | Open sharing of information |
| 7. Handling of personnel issues | By supervisor or staff | Many issues handled by team. |
| 8. Training provided | For task assigned to individual | Extensive training for multiple tasks and inter-personal skill |
| 9. Reward system | Related to job and individual performance | Related to team performance and scope of skills acquired by individual. |

**Summary of Types of Teams**

| *Feature* | *Quality Project Team* | *Quality Circle* | *Self Managing Teams* |
|---|---|---|---|
| 1. Purpose | Solve cross-functional quality problems | Solve problems within department. | Plan, execute and control work to achieve defined output |
| 2. Membership | Combination of managers professionals and workforce from multiple departments | Mainly workforce from one department | Mainly workforce from one work-area |
| 3. Basis and size of membership | Mandatory, 4-8 | Voluntary, 6-12 members | Mandatory, all members in work-area (6-18) |

| 4. Continuity | Team disbands after project is completed | Permanent, team remain intact project after project | Permanent |
|---|---|---|---|

## 4.14. MOTIVATION

Today management pays more attention towards motivation of employees. The main task of management is to direct the working force in such a way so that by their collective efforts, objectives of the enterprise are achieved. This is only possible, when the workers take interest in their work and have the desire to do good work. This depends on the fact that the worker is how much motivated. There is basic difference between the "capability to work" and "desire to work."

An employee who is fit to work with all his physical, mental and technical abilities but unless he does not use these qualities for the attainment of objectives, production is not possible. Hence, this is clear that increase in production is the result of motivation explicity. Hence, management should be careful to motivate the workers so that the objectives of the concern are fulfilled to a large extent.

Motivation is a psychological act which attracts the workers to do more work and instigates. If the workers are instigated, they will try to do more than standard work and earn more for themselves which increases their living standard.

Instigation may be positive *i.e.* by encouraging to do more work or negative *i.e.* by punishing for the wrong work. These both schemes tend to increase production and productivity. Motivation has got, in reality no definite source or plan, it is a co-ordinated programme of different schemes organised in such a way that every individual worker is instigated.

### Definition of Motivation

Management is an art of taking work from other persons. Hence, for taking proper work from the persons, to create interest in them for the work and to maintain their interest and instigate them for development is "motivation".

"Instigation" is an element on which organisation's whole performance depends. Work ability and desire to work are separate elements. It is possible that the person may have the work ability but he may not have the desire to accomplish the work and in this way, he cannot accomplish the work so nicely as expected from him. Motivation is a psychological aspect which has relation with mental state and brain.

Motivation is derived from the word "instigation". Some instigation element is necessary to accomplish a job and the object of instigation for the accomplishment of the job is called "motivation".

As put forth by "Brech", Motivation is a general inspiration process which gets the members of the team to do their task effectively, to give their loyalty to the group, to carry out properly the tasks they have accepted and generally to play an effective part in the job that the group has undertaken.

According to "Chael J. Jucius":

"Motivation is the act of stimulating someone or oneself to get a desired course of action, to push the right button to get desired action". As mentioned by "Dalton E. McFarlan":

"The concept of motivation is mainly psychological. It relates to those forces operating within the individual employee or subordinate which impels him to act or not active in certain ways."

## Characteristics of Motivation

(*i*) ***Motivation is a psychological*** concept which should be inherent in every person.

(*ii*) Man as a whole is motivated and not a part.

(*iii*) Motivation is created from aims.

(*iv*) ***Motivation is an unending process.*** Man is a social animal, is needs are unending. Needs instigate to motivation. Because after the completion of a need, commence the second need and hence, act of motivation also is an unending process. Time, place, behaviour and circumstances, uniting together prepare favourable and unfavourable atmosphere.

(*v*) ***Motivation is the strength of work.*** Motivation is that strength which leads to do or not do a work and instigates to do work in the same specific direction.

(*vi*) ***Motivation is different from mental strength.*** There is a difference between motivation and mental strength. Motivation is the strength that instigates a person to do and act, while mental strength is the desire to do a work oneself which is strengthened by motivation.

### Importance of Motivation

**The aim of motivation** is instigation to do work by all the employees working in any organisation so that more good results are attained through less efforts. Effects of motivation comes from all acts of the organisation. Any concern may have best instruments, raw materials in sufficient quantity and sufficient persons and finances but their proper use is not possible till the working persons do not use them properly.

Importance of motivation could be seen under these heads :

(*a*) ***Appropriate use of factors.*** All factors can only be used appropriately through motivation. It satisfies the human needs of individual.

(*b*) ***Kindling of desire to work.*** Capacity to work and desire to work are different things. Any person may be efficient but in the absence of desire to work, he cannot do appropriate work. By motivation, his desire to work is actuated so that he works with full efficiency.

Motivation × Ability = Job Performance

(*c*) ***Lessening in labour turnover, attraction of new persons.*** Labour do not try to go to another place due to motivation schemes, as his gross wages increase. Not only this, the institutions utilising motivation schemes, have the good efficient workers.

(*d*) ***Increase in Production and Productivity.*** It increases the desire to work and hence, it leads to increase in production and there is increase in productivity per worker per machine per hour.

(*e*) ***Basis of co-operation.*** It increases job satisfaction, which increases worker's interest for the organisation. This develops the sense of co-operation, while in the absence of motivation co-operation is not possible.

### Kinds of Motivation

There are two kinds of motivation :

(*a*) Positive Motivation.

(*b*) Negative Motivation.

(*a*) ***Positive Motivation.*** Positive motivation means workers may be instigated to work with some facilities or by giving some prize so that he may do good or more work than was done previously and with less supervision. Prize or facilities may be financial or non-financial. Giving more wages for more work, is the financial motivation, while appraisal of the worker's work, promotion, appreciation etc. are non-financial positive motivation.

(*b*) ***Negative Motivation.*** This is based on punishment or fines, if the labour is not encouraged for work. For less work or for not doing work, he must be punished or fined. This is also of two kinds : financial or non-financial.

In financial punishment, a cut is made in the wages of the labour. Non-financial punishment means giving less facilities, such as to do work for more time, reduction in the facilities of leave, etc. Generally these are for improving him and object is to motivate him for more work.

Positive or negative motivations are the two ends of a rope. Motivation is a psychological aspect and its relation is concerned with the person's brain, to his thoughts and behaviour and hence, they should be motivated accordingly in different ways.

A good manager should use both the ways of motivation at times. At times, good work should be prized but wrong work or no work should be punished. If there is no arrangement for punishment, worker becomes unrestrained, and those who can do good work will do less work as they will think that less work will have no punishment. Under positive motivation, doing more than the prescribed work will fetch them award.

## 4.14.1 Thoughts of Management Philosophy

Douglass McGregore has divided the thoughts of management philosophy in two parts. These are :

(*a*) Traditional or X theory. (*b*) Modern or Y theory.

### (A) 'X' Theory

This theory is based on traditional view, in which management or authority do not trust the labour and use restraining policies so that labour will be unable to act against him. Management considers that work could be extracted from labour through fear, strict discipline and rebukes, their co-operation should not be taken in management. Here, authority or power is thought to be superior. Management acts right or wrong, but labour cannot say anything and thus, mentally he is dependent on management.

**Assumptions of "X" Theory**

This theory is based on the following assumptions :

1. A person is disinclined to work and hence, he always shirks from work.
2. To get work from an employee, he is to be frightened, rebuked necessarily. Through fear, he becomes ready to do the work.
3. Workers try to shirk from responsibility, hence they put off the work till the work is not urgent.
4. Workers are less ambitious. They do not try to do or improve the work through interest but wait for instructions and directions.
5. Workers care mere for security, hence they work slowly.
6. Workers act on the basis of financial greed, if they are paid more wages, they will take more interest in work.
7. Management does not give any importance to labour, they think them to be an instrument of machines. Labour is not given opportunity to show capability or to develop it.
8. This theory has authority for superior. Labour has no right to give his suggestions, and can not do any work without direction, at his own will.

## (*B*) 'Y' Theory

This theory is quite opposite to "X theory". In this, labour is assumed to be partner in the management and what all they are working, it is with the co-operation of labour.

**Assumptions of Y Theory**

1. Every work is not disinteresting. Like a game, playing again and again gives satisfaction.
2. Workers are not instigated to work by fear, out of restraint or strict discipline. They feel responsible for the work for which they are appointed.
3. For the execution of work, it is necessary that it should be recognized. Recognition of work is a great prize.
4. Tendency to escape from the responsibility is not natural, but the reason is lack of ambitions and more stress on security.
5. Generally workers are not instigated to do by financial greed, but non-financial greed also instigates to work.
6. This is based on democratic principles, where everybody has equal chances.
7. Labour can also co-operate to solve the problems of enterprise.
8. This establishes co-ordination between basic personal objectives and the collective objectives of the organisation.
9. Manager works as a leader and gets more good and solid results by the advices of the personnel. Management treats all personnel on equal footing for advices.

### 4.14.2. Herzberg's Motivation-Hygiene Theory

Frederick Herzberg developed a theory of work motivation by indicating the way to better performance through increased job satisfaction. He conducted his study on a group of 200 engineers and accountants from eleven industries from the Pittsburgh area in the U.S.A.

His hypothesis about job satisfaction and job dissatisfaction suggests that:

(*a*) The factors that are present when job satisfaction is produced are separate and distinct from the factors that lead to job dissatisfaction.

(*b*) The opposite of job-satisfaction is 'no job-satisfaction' and not -satisfaction.

(*c*) The opposite of job dissatisfaction is 'no Job-dissatisfaction' and not 'job-satisfaction.'

Herzberg draws a distinction between what he called Motivator and Hygiene factors.

(*i*) **Motivators.** Factors connected with satisfaction or motivation were called as 'Motivators' by Herzberg. Motivators have a positive power to satisfy and produce high performance, and are related to job contents. These factors are :

- Achievement
- Recognition
- Challenging work
- Increase responsibility; and
- Advancement.

(*ii*) **Hygiene Factors.** The factors related to the prevention of dissatisfaction were called as hygiene factors because these factors primarily prevent dissatisfaction, like hygiene prevents sickness. These factors are related to the work environment.

These factors are :

Company policies and administration

Supervision

Inter-personal relations

Salary

Working conditions

Status, and

Security.

These factors prevent losses in the performance of the workers. When these hygiene factors are inadequate in an industry, then these will significantly have negative effect on worker's attitude, but do not have any positive effect, when all the factors are available in the concern.

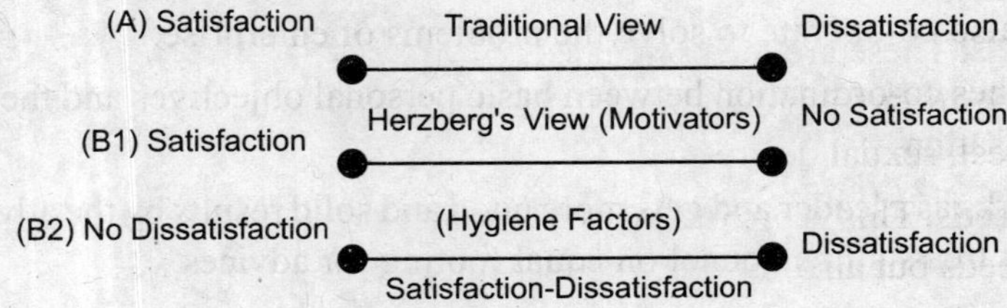

### 4.14.3. Human Needs

The behaviour or nature of every individual is different. There are the three things which require study for his behaviour :

(*i*) To study his behaviour "well".

(*ii*) To understand his behaviour "well".

(*iii*) His behaviour should be changed in a determined direction.

This third point is very important and requires thorough knowledge of the human needs.

When a machine goes out of order, we understand that it needs something, like oil or repairs or replacement of certain parts etc. In the same way, human behaviour should have some reason and if his behaviour is not well, we suppose that some of his wants are not satisfied.

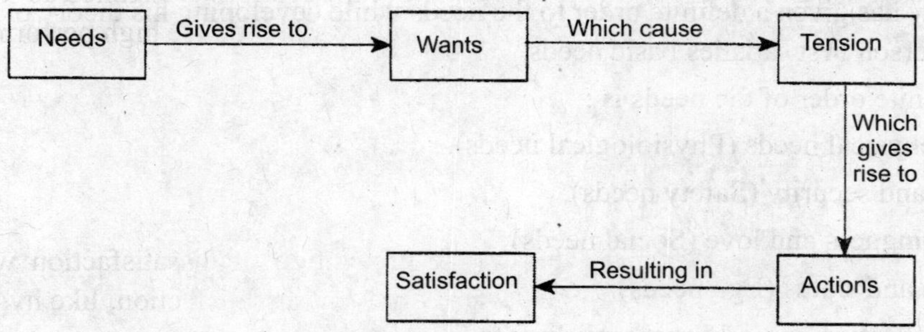


**Fig. 4.4.** Need-want satisfaction chain

Needs create tension in worker. Needs are created by person's culture and for its fulfillment, needs force him to work. For example, a hungry man's primary motive is to satisfy his hunger. Through needs of meals, he feels tension but what meals he will take, depends on his culture e.g., a Bengali will like to eat meat and fish while a Rajasthani will prefer vegetarian meals. To earn his meals, he will do some work which will fetch him wages and by that money he will satisfy his hunger. Series of needs go on. After the fulfillment of one need, another arise.

### Classification of Needs

These can be classified under two heads :

(*i*) Primary needs.

(*ii*) Secondary needs.

1. **Primary Needs.** These are the basic needs of an individual and are found in whole humanity but its intensity differ from man to man. These are essential for everybody, such as meals, air, water, sleep, rest, sexual desire etc.

2. **Secondary Needs.** This is proved by psychological investigations that man works not only for his primary needs but also for other needs which are related to his mind or soul. These needs are learnt by experience and atmosphere.

Secondary needs are of two kinds :

(*a*) Social needs.

(*b*) Egoistic needs.

(*a*) **Social needs.** People want to live with respect in the society. A man wants that he should have relations with different groups of people and they should help during difficulties. These are produced by the social desires existing in men and instigated to lead social life.

(*b*) **Egoistic needs.** These are related to human self-thoughts which are mostly dependent on human nature. These are simulated from the people's personal value and ideals. These instigate a person to self-expression and self-accomplishment.

**Priority of Needs (Maslow's Theory)**

Psychologists are of the opinion that priority of needs has a definite order. Famous scientist A.H. Maslow has given a definite order to the needs while developing his theory of motivation. He said that a person first satisfies basic needs.

The definite order of the needs is :

(*a*) Basic physical needs (Physiological needs).

(*b*) Safety and security (Safety needs).

(*c*) Belongingness and love (Social needs)

(*d*) Esteem and status (Ego needs).

(*e*) Self-realisation and self-accomplishment.

He said that a person satisfies his needs in this order. This conception of Maslow is known as the Maslow's need priority model.

Above mentioned first two needs are called the "low strata" needs, while the rest are called "high strata" needs.

**Low Strata Needs**

A person first satisfies all the necessities of the first kind *i.e.* bodily needs. A hungry person puts his full efforts for earning bread. After coping up the bodily needs , he tries to fulfill his second need of security and safety. This is the reason that he collects grains and some money for future use. He manages for pension and social security.

**High Strata Needs**

Bodily needs are limited, but rest three needs are unlimited. Every man wishes respect and fame. He thinks that he is able and other persons should also think him so and respect him. In more industrially developed countries, the people care more for esteem and status.

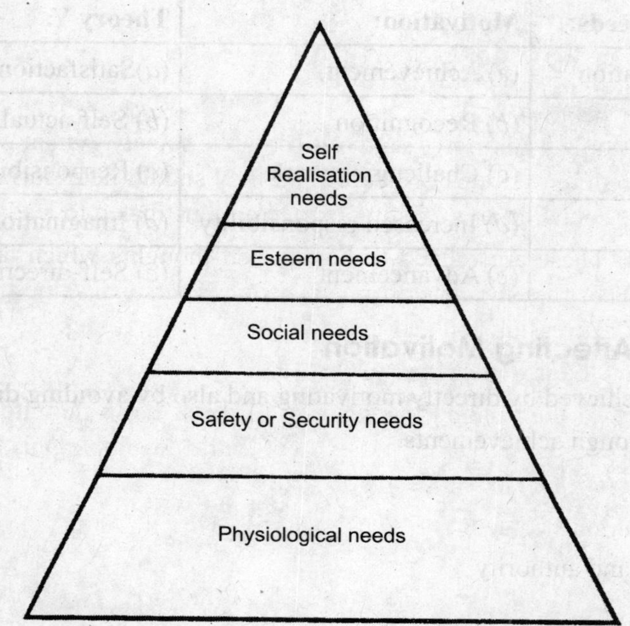


**Fig. 4.5.** Maslow's hierarchy of human needs

The fifth need is self-realisation and self-accomplishment. It means that a person should be what he desires, after the four needs are satisfied for achieving this.

**Comparison of Three Theories**

Hicks and Gullet have compared these theories and had shown the similarity in three theories. This is illustrated in the table.

| ***Maslow*** | ***Herzberg*** | ***Douglass McGragore*** |
|---|---|---|
| **(1) Lower level needs :** | **Hygiene factors:** | **Theory X:** |
| (*a*) Social | (*a*) Company policy and administration | (*a*) Security above all |
| (*b*) Safety | (*b*) Supervision | (*b*) Direction preferable |
| (*c*) Physiological | (*c*) Inter-personal relations | (*c*) Threats or punishment needed. |
| | (*d*) Salary | |
| | (*e*) Working conditions | |
| | (*f*) Status | |
| | (*g*) Security | |

| (2) High level needs: | Motivation: | Theory Y: |
|---|---|---|
| (a) Self-actualisation | (a) Achievement. | (*a*)Satisfaction of esteem. |
| (*b*) Esteem | (*b*) Recognition | (*b*) Self-actualisation needs. |
| | (c) Challenging work | (*c*) Responsibility. |
| | (*d*) Increased responsibility | (*d*) Imagination and creativity |
| | (*c*) Advancement | (*e*) Self-direction and self-control. |

## 4.14.4. Factors Affecting Motivation

Motivation can be achieved by directly motivating and also by avoiding dissatisfaction:

(*i*) Satisfaction through achievements.
(*ii*) Advancement
(*iii*) Growth
(*iv*) Responsibility and authority
(*v*) Recognition
(*vi*) Company policies
(*vii*) Job security
(*viii*) Company administration
(*ix*) Salary including fringe benefits
(*x*) Status
(*xi*) Inter-personal relations
(*xii*) Working conditions
(*xiii*) Personal life

## Motivational Techniques

(*a*) **Positive Motivational Techniques :**

(*i*) Give due credit to workers for their work
(*ii*) Fair wages, incentive and fringe benefits
(*iii*) Promote healthy competition
(*iv*) Improve working conditions
(*v*) Delegate reasonable responsibilities and authorities.
(*vi*) Promote inter-personal relationship
(*vii*) Formulate fair, clear and consistent management policies.

(*viii*) Implement suitable suggestion system.

(*ix*) Provide opportunities for growth and promotions.

**(*b*) Negative Motivational Techniques:**

(*i*) Reprimand

(*ii*) Fines

(*iii*) Demotions

(*iv*) Lay off

(*v*) Discharge

## 4.14.5. Morale

Morale is a mental condition and attitude of employees, either individually or in a group which determines their willingness to co-operate. Morale can also be defined as the extent to which an individual's needs are satisfied and the extent to which he feels satisfaction.

Morale is the degree of enthusiasm and willingness with which the individual member of a group set out to perform the allotted tasks.

High morale is the confident spirit of whole-hearted co-operation.

**Factors Affecting Morale**

Following are some of the factors which affects the morale :

1. **Job Factors :** These may be nature of job, confidence in leadership, confidence in other members of the group, nature of the leader or supervisors, working conditions, condition of working equipment.
2. **Other Factors :** These may be organisational set-up, working system in the organisation, the way in which organisation/management thinks and work, whether organisation goals are clear, justice with the employees in their selections and promotion, importance given to the individual, rewards, incentives, wage structure etc.

**How to Improve Morale**

Following measures have proved to be effective to the process of morale building:

(*i*) Sound wage structure.

(*ii*) Good incentive scheme.

(*iii*) Competent and disciplined worker should be assured security of income and employment.

(*iv*) Sound promotion policy

(*v*) Installation of grievances redressal procedure

(*vi*) Consulting the group of workers on the matters related to their work.

(*vii*) An effective communication system.

(*viii*) Introduction of suitable suggestion scheme.

(*ix*) Adequate welfare schemes.

(*x*) Recreational facilities and social get-together.

**(*A*) High Morale**

High Morale is the spirit of whole-hearted co-operation. High moral means :

(*i*) Loyalty to the organisation and its leadership.

(*ii*) Good discipline

(*iii*) High degree of interest in job

(*iv*) Reasonable initiative from employees.

(*v*) Team spirit.

(*vi*) No frustration

(*vii*) Pride in the organisation.

**(*B*) Low Morale**

Low Morale is the result of:

(*i*) Wrong or improper selection/placement of employees and supervision

(*ii*) Too many supervisors.

(*iii*) Low motivating factors

(*iv*) Improper authority and responsibility

**Results of Low Morale**

(*i*) Higher rate of absenteeism and labour turnover.

(*ii*) Friction, jealousy and frustration.

(*iii*) More complaints and grievances.

(*iv*) Enemity towards the management.

(*v*) Poor inter-personal relations.

## 4.14.6. Motivational Factors and Quality Circles

Motivational factors which have contributed to the development of Quality Circles are :

1. Maslow's self-esteem needs
2. McGregor's Y-theory.
3. Herzberg's motivational theory-providing challenges in work, responsibility and recognition.
4. Argyris' decentralisation of decision-making and developing the maturity level of the people. Argyris theory deals with the development of the maturity level of employees and of providing decision-making powers to the task performers. According to this theory, there are two types of people *i.e.* immature people and mature people, and the people should be developed to mature level.

'*Immature*' people are :

– Passive

– Dependent

– Have short term perspective.

'*Mature* people' have:

– Increased activity.

– Independent.

– Deeper interests.

– Long term perspective.

– Self-control.

*Quality Circles* with autonomy and development, self-discipline and independence evolve long term perspectives and take decisions on work-related problems and recommend solutions to the management.

**Quality Circle Philosophy**

– allows for greater participation

– provides challenges

– increases communication

– develops human and social relation skills

– helps groups to achieve results

– provides recognition

– gives job satisfaction

– integrates people

– increase workers' understanding of the difficulties faced by supervisors

– change some workers' negative attitudes

– helps removal of frustration and thus, eliminates sources of conflicts.

## 4.15. PERFORMANCE APPRAISAL

Performance means doing a job effectively. A good worker is one who performs well in terms of productivity and also minimises problems for organisation by doing work on time, by not remaining absent and by minimising work related problems. *Performance appraisal* is the process through which an individual employees behaviour and accomplishment for a fixed time period are measured and evaluated.

Performance appraisal can be defined as, "the process of assessing the performance and progress of an employee or a group of employees on a given job and his potential for future development".

Performance appraisal can also be defined as "the systematic, periodic and an impartial rating of an employee's excellence in matters pertaining to his present job and his potential for a better job".

Thus, it is the systematic examination of an employee's strengths and weaknesses in terms of the job.

**Objective of Performance Appraisal.**

1. To provide feedback to individual employees so that they know where they stand and can improve their performance.
2. To provide database for the decisions by the management regarding placement, promotion, transfer, punishment etc.
3. To diagnose the strengths and weaknesses of individuals so as to identify training needs.
4. To provide counselling, career planning to subordinates.

**Performance Appraisal Process.**

The process consists of following steps:

1. Establish performance standards.
2. Communicate performance expectations to employees.
3. Measure actual performance.
4. Compare actual performance with standard.
5. Discuss the appraisal with the employee.
6. If necessary, initiate corrective action.

## 4.16. SUGGESTION SYSTEM

Use of suggestion system is most successful bridge between plant improvement efforts and good industrial relations. Suggestion system tap the tremendous store of ideas for performance improvement, which otherwise lying in the minds of the employees. Most employees feel satisfied by volunteering their ideas but they feel reluctant. Therefore, it is necessary to set-up a suitable suggestion system so that employees can give way to their feelings, ideas and valuable suggestions. Most companies give awards for valuable and useful suggestions.

The suggestion system not only enables management to receive ideas for improving the efficiency, but also reduces the complaints and enhances the morale of the employees.

Suggestion systems are designed to provide the individual with the opportunity to be involved by contributing to the organisation. The management commitment is necessary for an effective system. The management must make it easy for employees to give suggestive for improvements. These suggestions are then reviewed promptly and if feasible, implemented.

For encouraging employees to participate in the suggestion schemes, following rules are important:

1. Regularly asking employees for suggestions. Simply putting up a suggestion box is not enough to create desired motivation.
2. Remove fear or hesitation.
3. Simplify the process for participation in suggestion scheme.
4. Take prompt action to suggestions. The evaluation process must be simple and effective
5. Reward the idea and give recognition by giving the publicity.

## QUESTIONS

1. Define organising. How to do organising ?
2. Write short notes on:
   (*a*) Staffing.
   (*b*) Organisational hierarchy and managerial skills.
   (*c*) Role of a quality director.
   (*d*) Role of the workforce on quality.
3. Write an essay on 'evolution of organisation for quality'.
4. Explain the activities of quality organisation.
5. Explain trends emerging in organising for quality.
6. How will you develop an organisation structure for quality?
7. Explain the role of the Quality Director. Mention the Quality Director.
8. Explain in detail the Quality Management System.
9. Describe the main roles of the top management on quality.
10. Write short notes on:
    (*a*) Quality goals
    (*b*) Quality council
    (*c*) Role of middle management on quality
    (*d*) Functions of quality circle leader
11. Explain the term 'Participative management'. Explain 'Characteristics' and 'Objectives' of participation.
12. Explain various forums of participation of workforce on quality.
13. What is a 'Quality circle'? Write an essay on quality circles.
14. Explain the organisation structure for quality circles. Explain about evolution of quality circles in India.
15. Explain how a quality circle can be conducted?

**16.** Write short notes on:

(*a*) Management presentation in respect to Quality Circles

(*b*) Motivation

(*c*) Motivation Theories

(*d*) Human needs and their impact on motivation

(*e*) Motivation techniques.

**17.** Explain the impact of quality circles on motivation.

**18.** What is Self-management? Explain the role of self-management concept.

**19.** Explain in detail about 'Quality in administrative and support operations'.

**20.** (*a*) Define 'Quality-culture'. Explain various quality culture approaches.

(*b*) Write a short note on Identification of training needs.

**21.** Write short notes on:

(*a*) Quality awareness

(*b*) Leadership role on quality

(*c*) Self-development

(*d*) Job enrichment

**22.** Explain in detail about self-development.

**23.** Explain recognition and rewards in relation to quality.

**24.** How much time is expected for changing the culture in an organisation?

# 5 Continuous Process Improvement

## 5.1. INTRODUCTION

Quality improvement is a structured process for reducing the deficiencies that are present in products, processes and services and/or improving performance, whenever there is an opportunity to improve.

Quality management is accomplished by the use of three managerial processes : quality planning, quality control, and quality improvement. These three quality processes provide a methodological approach to addressing quality.

It is general experience that management controllable defects are much more than operator controllable defects. According to J.M. Juran, about 80 percent of the defects are management controllable. Lack of awareness on the part of many industrial managers regarding the fact that majority of defects are management controllable, compels them to believe that most defects are the result of operator carelessness, indifference and sabotage.

Organisations should strive to achieve perfection by continuously improving the businesses and production processes. Although, perfection is impossible, however, we must continuously strive for its attainment.

Improvement is made in following ways:

(*i*) *By viewing entire work as a process*. The work may be associated with the production or business activities.

(*ii*) *By making all processes effective, efficient, and adaptable*.

(*iii*) *By controlling in process performance* using various measures, such as scrap reduction, reduction in cycle time using control charts etc.

(*iv*) *By eliminating waste and re-work*.

(*v*) *By eliminating non - conformities* in all phases at all stages.

(*vi*) *By using benchmarking* to take competitive advantage.

(*vii*) *By adopting lessons learned* into future activities.

(*viii*) *By adopting innovating measures* to achieve breakthroughs.

(*ix*) *By using technical tools and techniques* (explained at appropriate places in the book).

Process as mentioned above, means business and production activities of an organisation. Business processes may be purchasing, financing, accounting, engineering, marketing etc.

Some quality experts have mentioned following five basic ways for improvement:

1. Reduce resources.
2. Reduce errors
3. Meet or exceed expectations of downstream customers. For example, that welding is better which requires less grinding for making the appearance of a finish paint more pleasing.
4. Make the process safer.
5. Make the process more satisfying to the person doing it.

**Dominant Systems**

Before studying 'quality improvement' 'we must know different dominant systems so as to understand the source of defects. Various operational systems (machines, tools, operations etc.) are subject to variation, and the regulation of these variables is the basic problem of process control. Most usual dominant systems (in which one process system dominates the others) are :

1. ***Machine Dominant System :*** The process keeps changing during the manufacturing, requiring periodic check and re-adjustments.
2. ***Operator Dominant System :*** The operation is dependent on the skill and attention of the operator, and this is the major cause of defectives.
3. ***Set-up Dominant System :*** The process has been engineered in such a way that if properly set-up, the entire lot run successfully. In such cases, quality depends on the set-up of the machine.
4. ***Component Dominant System:*** In this system, input materials or components are the main variables affecting the quality of the final product.

The dominant system is not the sole source of defects for the process in question, but it is the main source.

## 5.2. QUALITY PROBLEMS

**Quality Problems** are of the following two types :

1. **Sporadic Quality Problems.** These are detected and acted by the process of quality control (*i.e.* during operation). A sporadic problem is a sudden, adverse change in the status quo, which requires remedy through re-storing the status quo. The variations due to sporadic problems are so significant that they trigger the alarm signals of the control system. The significant variations are a form of sporadic departure from standard which call for quick diagnosis of the cause and removal of the cause to re-store status quo. The sequence of events used to restore the status quo is known as trouble shooting or fire fighting.

These problems are dramatic and must receive immediate attention.

2. **Chronic Quality Problems.** Chronic problem is a long-standing adverse situation, which requires remedy through changing the status quo. For chronic problems, by adopting 'Continuous improvement' concept, better and better levels of performance can be achieved. These problems occur for a long time, and are often difficult to solve, as they are accepted as inevitable.

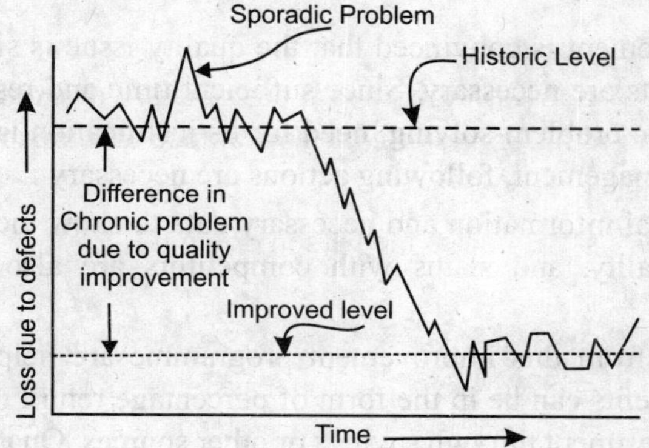


**Fig. 5.1.** Sporadic and chronic quality problems

In chronic problems, the same problem comes up over and over again, suggesting that the cause is not a reported error but a basic deficiency in the design, process, systems etc. Being continuous in nature, these problems are accepted as unavoidable. The solution calls for extensive and complex data collection over long periods, analysis of data by technical and SQC personnel. The solution to these problems, when implemented, provide superior level of performance as compared to that of previous level.

Difference in sporadic and chronic problems is on the following grounds:

1. The approach to solving problems are different. Sporadic problems are attacked by the control process by the local operating supervision using trouble shooting procedures. Chronic problems are solved through the quality improvement process.
2. Sporadic problems are dramatic and must receive immediate attention. Chronic problems occur for a long time. Fire fighting on sporadic problems generally take priority.

## 5.3. STEPS IN PROBLEM–SOLVING (QUALITY IMPROVEMENT)

1. Proving the need.
2. Identifying projects
3. Organising project teams
4. Verifying the project need and mission
5. Diagnosing the causes

6. Providing a remedy, and proving its effectiveness
7. Dealing with resistance to change.
8. Instituting controls to hold the gains.

In the above sequence of steps in quality improvement, first three steps are for setting up the project approach, and last five (4 to 8) steps are for executing the individual projects.

**1. Proving The Need**

In this step management is convinced that the quality issue is significant and companywide improvement efforts are necessary. Since sufficient time and resources for investigation are required for chronic problem-solving, need for its justification is very important. For getting approval of the management, following actions are necessary :

(*a*) Collection of factual information and necessary data to show the gravity of quality problem. Costs of poor quality, and status with competitors are also helpful in convincing the management.

(*b*) Benefits expected from this improvement programme are helpful to justify the requested resources. The benefits can be in the form of percentage return on investment, time required to pay back the investment through savings or other sources. Quantification of quality loss and the potential savings are essential for the justification.

**Languages of Management.** To establish proof of the need, best way to convince higher management is to use the language of money. Some of the statements in money language are given hereunder :

-- 20 percent of sales revenue
-- 24 percent of manufacturing cost
-- Rs. 40.2 lacs per year for scrap and re-work as compared to a profit of Rs. 30 lacs per year
-- 30% of the operating cost of production department.
-- Rs. 80 lacs per year.

**2. Identifying Projects**

This step of project identification consists of nominating, screening and selecting the projects.

***Nominating the projects.*** Nomination for projects (idea for taking up the projects) come from several sources, some of the main sources are:

-- Different levels of management and workforce
-- Analysis of data on cost of poor quality, quality in the marketplace etc.
-- Analysis of field intelligence, like market research, customer feedback, sales personnel.
-- Annual budgeting or management by objectives.
-- Necessity arising out of development in the environment, e.g., government regulation, development in competitive market.

***Pareto Principle:*** Pareto principle states that a few contributors to the cost are responsible for the bulk of the cost. These vital few contributors need to be identified so that the quality improvement resources can be concentrated in these areas.

***Screening of Projects :*** Project nominations as received from various sources are reviewed by middle management and recommendations are then made to higher management for approval. The screening depends on analysis of the project scope and potential benefit. One of the method for screening utilises **'Pareto Priority Index' (P.P.I.)**, which evaluate each of the projects . The index is :

$$\text{P.P.I.} = \frac{\text{Savings} \times \text{Probability of success}}{\text{Cost} \times \text{Time of completion in years}}$$

High value of P.P.I. suggests high priority of project.

***Selection of Project.*** The ideal project should :

(*i*) deal with chronic problem *i.e.* the problem which has been awaiting solution for a long time,

(*ii*) be feasible *i.e.* one which is likely to be a successful and can conclude within about six months,

(*iii*) be significant *i.e.* the end results of which should be useful and of importance, and

(*iv*) be one whose results are measurable in money terms.

**Problem and Mission Statement.** The project selected should have a problem statement as well as a mission statement *e.g.* a problem statement is "During previous year, 6 percent of the total items were replaced under warranty clause". The problem statement should not mention about cause or a solution or blame. A mission statement is based on problem statement and provides direction to the project team e.g. "reduce the rate of items to be replaced under warranty claims to 2 percent or less within next six months".

### 3. Organising Project Teams

A project team consisting of about six to eight persons drawn from different departments is assigned the task of addressing the problem selected as above. The aim of this team is to successfully conclude the project, as defined in the mission statement of the project.

Team members serve in the committee as part time in addition to their regular functional responsibility. The team meets periodically and on completion of the project, the team automatically disbands. The team consists of a leader, a secretary, and other team members. Consulting specialists, if required, can be invited to meetings.

Responsibility of the project manager is to steer the team for carrying out the assigned project. He should have knowledge of the project area, and skill, lead the members from different functional areas, to work as a team. The functions of the secretary of the project team are : to handle documentation, agenda, minutes, reports etc. He is generally a member secretary. Team members, especially for chronic problems, are usually cross-functional and consists of middle management, professional, and workforce personnel. In complex and complicated projects, consulting specialists, preferably from within the company are invited.

***Facilitator Concept :*** Now-a-days, many companies adopt the concept of using a facilitator to help the team in carrying out their first project. Although he is not a member of the team, but plays an important role. His main roles are as follows :

(*i*) Explaining the approach to quality improvement, and how it is different from regular or prior efforts at quality improvement.

(*ii*) Providing assistance in team building.

(*iii*) Assistance in the training of project teams.

(*iv*) Helping the team to avoid a poor choice of project.

(*v*) Revitalizing a stalled project.

***Intra-departmental and Inter-departmental Teams :*** Some of the chronic problems cut across department lines and require cross-functional project teams, while others are centered within one department. Some of these intra-departmental problems can be either solved by concerned individuals, but many of them require departmental teams called 'Quality Circles', which is discussed separately in the book. It is important to mention that both these teams are not alternative to each other, both the types of teams are essential. For the companywide, quality improvement, many such teams are required. Therefore, it is essential for a company to set up a machinery, generally known as 'Quality Council' to select problems and then form, train, monitor the progress of these teams. This Quality Council is a group of higher level managers who develop the quality strategy and guide and support their strategy.

The important differences between project teams and quality circles are indicated hereunder:

| ***Project Teams*** | ***Quality Circles*** |
|---|---|
| 1. Its scope is multi-departmental | 1. Its scope is within a single department |
| 2. It tackles one of the vital few problems | 2. It gives one of the many useful suggestions at a time |
| 3. It draws members from multiple departments | 3. It draws members from a single department |
| 4. The membership is mandatory | 4. Membership is voluntary |
| 5. Members are selected from middle management and specialists | 5. Members are drawn from workforce |
| 6. The team disbands after completion of the project | 6. The circle continues |

Experiences to this approach for quality improvement has shown very good results. Investment required for improvement has been modest and not capital intensive. Mostly the investment is in the time of people doing diagnosis for the projects. Large cost reductions and improved quality of products and services to the customers could be achieved through this approach. According to J.M. Juran, for each dollar invested in improvement activity, the return is between 5 and 10 dollars.

**4. Verifying The Project Need And Mission**

The selected project should be of importance. As discussed under 'Proving the need', the scope of the project and size of the problem should again be reviewed after the team has met once or twice to be sure that whether the mission assigned to the team can be accomplished within about 6 months time. If the project is likely to take more time, it should be divided into number of projects.

**5. Diagnosing The Causes**

Since the diagnosis is the process of studying the symptoms of a problem and determining their cause (*s*), it begins with collection of data on the symptoms and ends with the agreement on the causes. Most managers are of firm belief that most defects are caused during manufacture and are due to worker errors. This belief seldom confirms, but it persists. In view of this, it is useful to conduct studies to separate defects into broad categories of responsibilities. Such studies are for determining the origin of the defects in the design, manufacture etc., and for determining whether defects are management controllable or worker-controllable. "Management-controllable" defects are some times known as "system-controllable" defects. Here, management includes supervisors, design engineers, process engineers etc. According to J.M. Juran and W.E. Deming, authorities on quality, management-controllable defects are of the order of 80 percent, and it is management's responsibility to take care of these more than 80 percent problems traceable to the system.

Some of the terms used here are described as under :

(*a*) *A symptom* is an observable phenomenon arising from and accompanying a defect.

(*b*) *A defect* is any non-fulfillment of intended usage requirement. A defect is also termed as error, discrepency and nonconformance. The examples of defect are : oversize/undersize, or low mean time between failures.

(*c*) *A cause* is a proven reason for the existence of the defect. In case causes are too many, only vital few are tackled first.

(*d*) *A remedy* is a change that can successfully eliminate or neutralize a cause of defects.

***Diagnostic journey*** i.e. from symptom to cause consists of following 3 steps :

(*i*) *Study of symptoms surrounding the defects :*

Records of performance are utilized to quantify the symptom pattern. The frequency and intensity of symptom are of great significance in pointing to directions of analysis.

(*ii*) *Theorizing on the causes of these symptoms :*

Here, a theory means an unproved assertion as to seasons for the existence of defects and symptoms. Several theories are usually advance to explain the presence of the observed phenomena. The theories are formulated in three steps, namely: generation of theories, arrangement of theories, and choosing the theories to be tested.

The theories are generated through brainstorming by involving line managers, technologists, supervisors and workforce. Brainstorming is an activity which promotes group participation and teamwork, and encourages creative thinking and stimulates the generation of as many ideas as possible, in a short period of time. In this, participants are invited on the basis of their particular knowledge and experience, and are expected to contribute to the topic under discussion in an atmosphere where everybody feels free to express themselves. All ideas are recorded. The list of theories, thus, prepared in brainstorming session is then critically reviewed.

(*iii*) *Testing the Theories*

The list so drawn is generally extensive, having 20 or more theories, requires an orderly arrangement. After the theories are arranged in an orderly fashion, priorities must be established for testing the theories. The team then decides whether to test just one theory at a time, one group of inter-related theories at a time, or all theories simultaneously. In the first stage, management controllable theories are tested, while worker controllable theories are tested in the second stage.

**(*a*) Test of Theories of Management–Controllable Problems**

1. Make measurements at intermediate steps in the process so as to discover at which step the defect appears.
2. Process capability analysis is carried out by taking the measurement from the process and analyzing them to determine the amount of variability inherent in the process. This variability is then compared to the specification limits.
3. Various streams used in production like different machines, operators, shifts, suppliers are analyzed on the basis of data recorded separately for each stream.
4. Time-to-time analysis include: (*a*) a sample plot of data on a time scale, (*b*) analysis of the time between abnormalities *i.e.* problems, and (*c*) analysis of rate of change.
5. Piece-part variation analysis which include analysis of different types of variations e.g., piece-to-piece, within piece, and time-to-time .
6. Defect-concentration analysis is used to discover whether defects are located in the same physical area.
7. The data relating symptoms of the problem are analyzed pinpointing process, tools, workers or design.
8. The theories are tested through experiments.

**(*b*) Test of Theories of Worker–Controllable Problems :**

As human errors are of large number of types, they should be tackled by extending the Pareto principle. In this system, errors are first classified into different categories and then vital few are selected for diagnosis. For example, in a department producing a particular type of product produced by 6 workers, 5 types of errors are noticed. The data for these errors are indicated in the following table :

| *Type of Error* | *Worker* | | | | | | *Total* |
|---|---|---|---|---|---|---|---|
| | ***A*** | ***B*** | ***C*** | ***D*** | ***E*** | ***F*** | |
| 1 | 1 | 0 | 1 | 2 | 0 | 4 | 8 |
| 2 | 0 | 0 | 0 | 1 | 1 | 3 | 5 |
| 3 | 0 | 1 | 12 | 0 | 2 | 3 | 18 |
| 4 | 1 | 0 | 1 | 1 | 0 | 4 | 7 |

| 5 | 2 | 3 | 2 | 3 | 2 | 4 | 16 |
|---|---|---|---|---|---|---|---|
| **Total** | **4** | **4** | **16** | **7** | **5** | **18** | **54** |

The table shows that worker *C* produced 16 errors, out of which 12 are only due to type 3 errors. There is nothing wrong with the job specification or the method as other 5 workers had no trouble with type 3 error. Similarly, there is nothing basically wrong with the worker *C*, as he is doing well in other type of errors except type 3 error. It means worker *C* is misinterpreting some instructions.

In type 5 error, all workers made this error more or less uniformly. This is a management controllable problem, and its diagnosis can be done by interviewing the respective workers and supervisors.

Worker *F* made maximum number of errors, and virtually in all error categories. He might have committed so many errors due to inadequate training, lack of capacity to do such work etc. For this purpose, study is required to be conducted on this worker.

Inter-relationship of error pattern and likely cause are indicated hereunder:

| ***Error Pattern*** | ***Likely cause*** |
|---|---|
| 1. No one is error prone and defect pattern is random. | 1. Errors are due to inadvertence. |
| 2. Some workers are consistently error-prone while others are consistently satisfactory. | 2. Errors are due to lack of technique ability, know-how etc. |
| 3. Some workers are consistently error-prone over a wide range of defects. | 3. This may be due to :<br>(*a*) Conscious failure to comply with standards.<br>(*b*) Inherent incapacity to perform this task.<br>(*c*) Lack of training. |
| 4. All workers are error-prone. | 4 Errors are management-controllable. |

**6. Providing A Remedy And Proving Its Effectiveness**

After determining the cause of the problem, the next step is to choose a remedy. Generally, problems have more than one alternative solution. Each of these alternatives are then evaluated to find an optimum solution. Best solution (remedy) is selected by comparing the merits and demerits, gains or losses etc. of each alternative. An essential criterion is that both, company costs and customer costs be optimized. Company costs should include the impact on the cost of poor quality, materials usage, facilities usage, energy consumption, etc. on a companywide basis, similarly customers' costs and their well-being should be evaluated for each alternative remedy.

Before finally adopting a remedy, its effectiveness must be proved. This can be done in two stages, in first stage, reliability is proved through theoretical prediction, run in a pilot plant, or the testing of a prototype. In second stage, final evaluation under real-world conditions is carried out.

After a remedy is proven effective, a proper communication is issued to all concerned parties. The remedy should also be communicated to: (*a*) the ethers who may face similar problems, and (*b*) those who are responsible for planning future products and processes.

**7. Dealing With Resistance To Change**

It is a general tendency that change is resisted by managers/supervisors, workforce, or the union. The change consists of two parts, namely: a technological change, and a social consequence to the technological change. The people generally voice objections on the ground of technological change, but in reality their objection is for the social effect. Therefore, while proposing a change, we must: (*i*) be aware of that we are dealing with a pattern of human habits, beliefs, and traditions, and (*ii*) find out the social effects of the proposed changes.

For introducing a change, following suggestions are kept in view :

(*i*) Provide participation of those who are likely to be affected by the change.

(*ii*) Establish the need for the change.

(*iii*) Enough time to be provided, so as to avoid surprises, and to have proper opportunity for change,

(*iv*) Working with the recognized leadership of the culture.

(*v*) Treating the people with dignity.

Thereafter, while implementing the change, the resistance, if still felt, may be dealt directly through :

(*a*) Persuasion.

(*b*) Offering something for something.

(*c*) Make some changes in the proposals to meet specific objections.

(*d*) Drop the proposal, if not possible to implement it.

The task of dealing with resistance to change is an art and should be done in a methodical way.

**8. Instituting Controls to Hold The Gains**

It is essential to hold the gains so that the benefits continue on and on. For this purpose, following steps are taken :

(*i*) A process capable of holding the gains under operating conditions be provided to the operating forces.

(*ii*) Establish the new operating procedures and train the operating forces.

(*iii*) Systematic means *i.e.* process of control should be provided to hold the gains. The controls should be exercised through feedback mechanism, measuring the actual performance and comparing with the standard.

## 5.4. THE JURAN TRILOGY

Juran expressed his essential message to managers through the **three basic quality related processes:** quality planning, quality control and quality improvement which is known as the Juran trilogy.

### A. Quality Planning

Juran insisted that quality must be planned. Special training must be provided in how to plan for quality. Juran's quality planning road map consists of the following steps:

1. Identify the customers and their needs. By customer, he means end-recipient of the final product as well as internal customer who relies on the output of a particular internal process.
2. Establish quality goals.
3. Optimize the products by developing and optimizing the process which produces this product (i.e. developing and optimizing the product and process of manufacture).
4. Establish process controls and transfer the process to operations.

Every opportunity for improvement, quality-wise and cost-wise should be taken.

### B. Quality Control

As we know that control is the process of detecting and correcting adverse change, as soon as it happens, so that the status quo is maintained.

Conforming to quality specifications and adhering to standards and procedures require prompt corrective action of any sporadic problems, so that the status quo is re-stored.

As per Juran, control involves following **sequence of steps:**

1. Choosing the control subject, i.e. choosing what we intend to regulate.
2. Choosing a unit of measure.
3. Setting a goal for the control subject.
4. Creating a sensor which can measure the control subject in terms of the unit of measure, *i.e.* establish standard of performance.
5. Measuring actual performance.
6. Interpreting the difference between actual performance and the goal.
7. Taking action (if any) on the difference.

Thus, the quality control process addresses sporadic quality problems, while the improvement process addresses chronic quality problems.

Ideal situation is one when quality planning for any task would put the employee into a state of self-control. To be in a state of self-control, people must be provided with: (*a*) knowledge of what they are supposed to do, (*b*) knowledge of their performance, and (*c*) means of regulating performance in the event that they fail to meet the goals.

### C. Quality Improvement

A quality improvement is necessary to reduce substantially the chronic waste and achiene a new improved zone of quality control. Quality improvement is an organized creation of beneficial change. The organized procedures must be found to reduce the incidence of chronic defects and their associated costs. Juran believes that a desire for improvement will get results only when projects are choosen and given priority, and when responsibilities are clear.

The fact remains that the management has the major influence on matters, not the workforce. The workers can only contribute as much as the system allows. The system consists of long-range policies, companywide training, inter-departmental communication and co-ordination, purchased materials etc. When these are taken care of by management, the system improves itself, the workforce can participate and better utilize their education and creativity, and the improvements are a natural consequence.

Juran suggested following **steps for quality improvement:**

1. Prove the need for improvement.
2. Identify specific projects for improvement.
3. Organise project teams.
4. Diagnose the cause.
5. Provide remedies.
6. Prove that the remedies are effective under operating conditions.
7. Deal with the resistance to change.
8. Control to hold the gains.

## 5.5. QUALITY CONTROL V/S QUALITY IMPROVEMENT

In quality control, aim is largely directed at meeting the goals and preventing adverse change, and thus, to hold the status quo, while in 'improvement' focus is on to creating a change *i.e.* bringing improvement in quality, and thus, in contrast to quality control, it changes the status quo. Further, quality control process addresses the sporadic quality problems, whereas the improvement process addresses the chronic problems.

Quality measurement is central to the process of quality control. For quality control, measurement provides feedback and early warnings of problems. For quality planning, measurement quantifies customer needs, and product and process capabilities. For quality improvement, measurement can motivate people, prioritise improvement opportunities, and help in diagnosing the causes.

## 5.6. IMPROVEMENT STRATEGIES

In business, strategy management is now accepted as the discipline of managing resources to achieve long term objectives, and includes long range planning. Fundamental strength of a company depends on the development of strategic success potentials.

A company's potential for strategic success may be defined as those activities which result in above average long term profits. They are generally related to products and markets, and are generally perceived as high quality service standards, public image, low production costs or distribution advantages.

**Strategic Planning.** It includes setting objectives, information analysis about key problems, characteristics of the organisation, internal strengths linked with external opportunities, taking decisions on strategies, and formulating a plan.

**Developing a Strategy.** The basic data are then reinforced through detailed analysis as regards to environment, the market, the competitors, customers and other relevant aspects.

**Implementation of Strategy.** The strategies, for successful implementation, should be correctly defined and specified for each section or department and employee. Capabilities to be developed are identified, company resources are allocated and re-adjusted according to the strategies and monitor the strategies success.

Following are the **four common improvement strategies:**

1. **Repair and Maintenance.** This strategy rectifies the problem, but this does not make the process better than the original design.
2. **Refinement.** It improves the efficiency and effectiveness. It should become an integral part of every employees job. Refinement relies on doing things just but a quicker, better, easier, or with less waste. This is based on *Kaizen* concept (to be discussed later). The change is so gradual that there is little appearance of change.

The repair and refinement improvements are almost immediate with very little cost. These strategies require that all employees have the freedom to solve problems and make incremental improvements in their jobs.

3. **Renovation.** The renovation strategy results in major improvement. Innovation and technological advancements are key factors in this approach. Renovation strategy is costly as compared to the two previous strategies (repair and refinement) and is usually undertaken by teams rather than individuals.
4. **Re-invention or Re-engineering.** Re-invention is the costly improvement strategy. A new product, service, process or activity is developed using teams based on complete understanding of the customers requirement and expectation. This strategy is desirable to maintain organisation vitality or competitive advantage.

Renovation and re-invention are effective in making break–through improvements. These are more costly, take longer to accomplish, and have a greater risk of failure.

**What is Re–engineering**

Re–engineering (or process re–engineering) is focused on break-through improvement to dramatically improve the quality and speed of work and to reduce its cost by fundamentally changing the processes by which the work gets done.

For organisations that want to survive and grow, improvement is not on option but a compulsion. The organisations that seek to thrive, dramatic improvement is often the only key to success.

Small improvements are always necessary, but sometimes quantum leaps are needed, if an organisation is forge ahead.

## 5.7. KAIZEN

Key to Japan's industrial success is the approach of gradual process improvement involving everybody, known as Kaizen. In Japan, Kaizen is everybody's business and many systems have been developed to make managers and workers Kaizen conscious. Kaizen, means step-by-step gradual improvement in the nature of refinements or enhancements.

Japanese business philosophy is based on combination of Kaizen and innovation. Kaizen improvement contrasts sharply with the type of drastic improvement resulting from innovation. Innovation is a short-term dramatic improvement due to the technological breakthrough, based on individual ideas and efforts. It normally requires a large initial investment but little effort to maintain, since it is a one time phenomenon. Kaizen is process-oriented, whereas innovation is result-oriented.

Innovation strategy was favoured by western countries, and were more concerned about quantity than quality, increasing sales than with the reducing costs, western countries ignored the quality-based teachings of the experts, such as W.E. Deming and Joseph Juran.

Kaizen philosophy has following two main features :

1. Never-ending efforts for improvement and gradual change for the better.
2. Build quality into the process.

## 5.8. DEMING CYCLE (P-D-C-A/P-D-S-A CYCLE)

Deming cycle (or as Deming prefers, the Shewart cycle) consists of four main stages, one following another in a specific order which is repeated continuously. The stages are : Plan, Do, Check, Act (P D CA). It is a classic problem-solving self-sustaining quality programme.

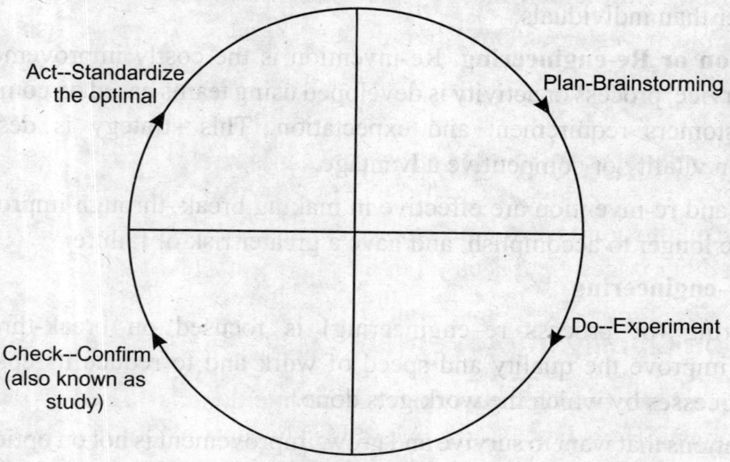


**Fig. 5.2.** Deming Cycle

1. **Plan.** The process of improvement should start in carefully planning the route of action. Planning involve a great deal of understanding, documenting, evaluating and assessing the tools to be used for an effective quality programme. At this stage, decisions should be taken on the objectives to aim for the changes that are needed, the types of measures to be used, and who should be responsible for what. In addition, determination should be made of the availability of resources, the possible implications of the actions and the contingency measures to be taken, when something goes wrong.
2. **Do.** Implementation of the plan should follow by involving everybody. This includes training, survey of customers' needs and expectations, identification of core processes, collecting statistical information, understanding of process control and variation, identification of projects with improvement objectives, formation of project teams, and communication of resulting successes. In this stage, small-scale implementation of any planned change or test will take place and the resulting data is collected.
3. **Check (or Study).** Checking involves measuring and observing the effects of any change or test carried out at the 'do' stage, analysis of results, feedback and review. Using actual data, deviations from the original expectations should be evaluated and investigated. Breaking down the barriers and eliminating fear will prompt people to declare openly what is going wrong and what should be done.
4. **Act.** Changes should be adopted or abandoned based on the results of the previous stage. A study of the current situation, standardizing an improvements and properly documenting any good new processes, and innovative ideas should take place. The review of the checking stage can be used as a leading process, so that knowledge is built into a new plan, which is now broadened with enough information to prevent mistakes from occurring again, and is developed further, utilizing the valuable experiences gained so far.

The results of any change at the action stage can enhance the ability to predict and belief in future. Thus, the Deming cycle is ready to start again i.e.,

**Planning → Doing (Implementing) → Checking → Action→ (New) Plan →**

This cycle should never stop. One should always remember the requirement: *Continuous improvement and innovation*.

## 5.9. QUALITY GYRUS ON QUALITY IMPROVEMENT

Views of renowned quality gurus on quality improvement are being discussed in following sections, where as views on other issues are discussed in the chapter on "Total Quality Management".

### 5.9.1. Crosby on Quality Improvement

Phillip B. Crosby is an American quality expert rose to international standard through his teachings on quality management. He is best known due to his concepts of 'Zero Defects', and 'Do it right first time'.

According to Crosby, the quality improvement process is never-ending. To keep the momentum going, the appropriate culture and attitude about quality have to be embedded throughout the organisation. Crosby has laid own following fourteen steps to help in establishment of quality ethic. The order of these steps is not very important, and they can run in parallel. However, management related 1-6 steps should come first:

1. **Management Commitment.** Senior management has to demonstrate a commitment to quality, and for this a corporate policy on quality should be issued. Quality should be the first item on the agenda of all management meetings.
2. **Quality Improvement Team.** A team should be set up to guide the quality improvement process. For getting definite direction, this team should have clear access to top management. The main task is to change the attitudes and practices of those who run the company; to set up required educational activities, and subsequently to co-ordinate and support the whole effort. In short, this team helps in changing the system to enable quality to flourish.
3. **Measurement.** Every part of any activity, its input, process work and output lends itself to measurement. The type of measurement can be decided by associating concerned people. Once this decision is taken, a reasonable targets can be set and progress can be monitored.
4. **The Cost of Quality.** In order to invite management's attention, it is beneficial to calculate as to how much poor quality is costing the company. This is also necessary for setting the priorities. But Crosby himself is the view that if cost of poor quality is not calculated properly, it can cause more troubles, therefore, he believes that the quality costs need to be identified objectively, pulled together and fed into the regular management process formally, and treated as a positive rather than a threatening item.
5. **Quality Awareness.** He was of the view that through a proper communication system, awareness about quality should spread throughout the organisation and adopted to the company's culture. People should be continuously reminded about the management commitment to quality, the associated policies, the training facilities to offer. Slogans or posters about 'Zero Defects' or 'Do it right first time' to show the importance of quality may be used.
6. **Corrective Action.** The main purpose of it should be to prevent errors or identify and eliminate causes of problems for-ever. Corrective activities need to be based on analysis of past data so that the causes of problems are determined and taken care of permanently.
7. **Zero Defects Planning.** Proper planning is required for properly embedding the 'Zero Defect' (ZD) concept in the organisation culture.
8. **Employees Education.** Crosby is of the view that an investment in quality education can result in quantum leaps in improvement. He summarizes the entire education process in what he calls 'the six Cs':
    1. *Comprehension* (understanding what is necessary, abandonment of old way of thinking and outdated practices).
    2. *Commitment* (management – led dedication to cultural change).
    3. *Competence* (methodical and scientific implementation of the improvement process).

4. *Communication* (complete co-operation throughout the product process, including suppliers and customers).
5. *Correction* (elimination of all causes of problems and prevention of new ones arising).
6. *Continuance* (never-ending effort for improvement).

9. **Zero Defects Day.** Crosby recommends that a Z D Day is planned to reward serious efforts, and is celebrated annually with speakers representing senior management, the customers and unions. This will act as a remainder of the importance of quality and as a demonstration of the commitment towards the Z D principle.
10. **Goal Setting.** In quality, the ultimate goal is 'Zero Defects', and all intermediate goals should move in that direction.
11. **Error Cause Removal.** Permanent removal of the causes of error requires a team effort. Through proper communication system, necessary information is shared about identification of the common sources of error and their permanent elimination, and also in the prevention of the same problems arising in future.
12. **Recognition.** Recognition process needs to be planned carefully and developed gradually. Quality awards should not be taken in monetary terms, but considered as an incentive to others and an example to compete.
13. **Quality Council.** This is a group of all quality professionals, and define the mission, vision, values and policies necessary for managing the improvement process. Their co-ordinated expertise can be more effective in supporting the quality improvement teams in their efforts towards the elimination of hustle and the achievement of Zero Defects.
14. **Do it All Over Again.** The process of learning, participating, experimenting with new methods and improving should never end. Quality improvement has to become the culture of the company through continuous efforts. The momentum should never be allowed to slow down. Continuous re-education and involvement, actively supported by top management are the keys in making quality attainment and enduring way of life.

## 5.9.2. JURAN ON QUALITY IMPROVEMENT

Dr. Joseph M. Juran believes that the majority of quality problems are due to the fault of poor management, rathar than poor workmanship, on the shop-floor. He was of the view that management controllable defects account for over 80% of the total quality problems. He suggested the following 10 steps for quality improvement (known as TQM messages).

1. Create awareness of the need and opportunity for quality improvement.
2. Set goals for continuous improvement.
3. Build an organisation to achieve goals by establishing a quality council, identify problems, select a project, appointing teams and choose facilitators.
4. Give everyone training.

5. Carry out projects to solve problems.
6. Report progress.
7. Show recognition.
8. Communicate results.
9. Keep a record of successes.
10. Incorporate annual improvements into the company's regular systems and processes and thereby maintain momentum.

### 5.9.3. IMAI KAIZEN ON CONTINUOUS IMPROVEMENT

Masaaki Imai has brought together the management philosophies, theories and tools that have been popular in Japan over the years, as a single concept–named as *Kaizen*. In a working environment, Kaizen means continuous process improvement involving everybody. *Kaizen* philosophy advocates ongoing improvement not only in working life, but also in personal life, home life and social life.

*Kaizen* signifies that improvement is constant and gradual, no matter how small, taking place all the time, in every process, involving everyone from all the ranks of management and workforce. When a new standard is achieved, the management should make sure that it is maintained. These improvement require little investment, but a great effort to maintain.

*Imai* has distinguished improvement from innovation. According to him, innvoation results a drastic, dramatic and short term improvement due to a technological break-through, based on individual ideas and efforts. It may generally require a large initial investment but little effort to maintain, since it is usually a one time phenomenon. *Kaizen* and innovation are two complementary aspects and both lead to improvement. K*aizen* is process-oriented, while innovation is result-oriented, western way of thinking chose the innovation path which lead to immediate profit and instant recognition. Whereas, Japanese management always promoted and supported team efforts towards gradual improvement of processes.

Therefore, *Kaizen* is a process-oriented, and people-oriented approach, where efforts for process improvement are properly rewarded which promotes discipline, participation and involvement, skill development, moral and communication. However, efforts for innovation are not excluded. *Kaizen* efforts maintain and improve whenever a new breakthrough is achieved. Efforts for further improvement should never stop.

For achieving and sustaining superior company performance, following are the two pre-requisites:

1. Constant improvement
2. Exceptional care for the customer.

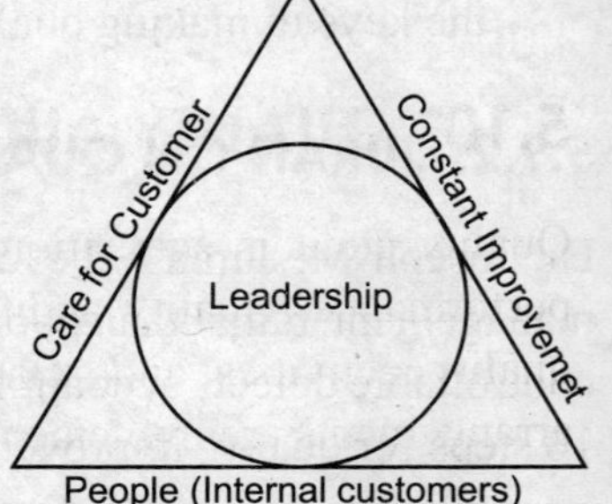


**Fig. 5.2.** Model for superior company performance

### 5.9.4. TAGUCHI ON QUALITY IMPROVEMENT

Professor Genichi Taguchi has devised a quality improvement technique that uses experimental design methods for efficient characterization of a product or process, combined with a statistical analysis of its variability. This approach allows quality considerations to be included at an early stage of new venture : in the design and prototype phase for a product, during routine maintenance or during installation and commissioning of a manufacturing process.

Taguchi has suggested that following steps should always be followed in carrying out experimental studies:

1. ***Define the problem.*** Provide a clear statement of the problem and establish clearly as to what the experiment is aiming to solve.
2. ***Determine the objective.*** Identify the output characteristics to be studied and eventually optimised, and determine the method of measurement.
3. ***Conduct a brainstorming session.*** Managers and operators related to the production process or the product should sit together to determine the controllable and uncontrollable factors and to define the experimental range and the appropriate factor levels.
4. ***Design the experiment.*** Select the appropriate experimental designs assigning the controllable factors. . ,
5. ***Conduct the experiment.*** Experimental trials are performed and data are collected.
6. ***Analyse the data.*** Performance measures are evaluated for each trial run of the inner array and analyse them using the appropriate statistical techniques.
7. ***Interpret the results.*** Identify the variability control factors and target control factors, and select their optimal levels. Predict the 1 process performance under the optimal conditions.
8. ***Run a confirmatory experiment.*** Follow up experimental trials necessary to confirm that whether the new parameter settings have improved the performance measures over their value at the initial settings. If the results are unsatisfactory, additional experiments may be required, and steps mentioned at serial No. 3 to 8 are repeated.

## 5.10. QUALITY AUDITS

Quality audit is evaluation of various aspects of quality performance with a standard for that performance. Quality audit is a systematic and independent examination to determine whether quality activities and related results comply with planned arrangements and whether these arrangements are implemented effectively and are suitable to achieve objectives.

Quality audits are performed to find whether the end-product satisfies the desired quality specifications, proper functioning of all equipment, operators are carrying out their duties as per specified quality plans. Audit should be carried out by unbiased persons and without announcements and cover each and every individual. Audit should be made by check lists and its results recorded and made available to all concerned people.

Audits are of following types :

1. Product audit.
2. System audit.
3. Adequacy audit.

Quality auditing have been discussed in the chapter on "Quality Management System":

## QUESTIONS

1. Define 'quality-improvement'. Explain the different types of quality problems.
2. What is a dominant system ? Explain the different types of dominant systems.
3. Differentiate between 'sporadic' and 'chronic' quality problems. What is the effect of quality improvement process on them ?
4. What steps you will follow during quality improvement process?
5. Write short notes on : (*a*) Proving the need (*b*) Project identification with respect to quality improvement, (*c*) Comparison between 'Project teams' and 'Quality circles'.
6. How will you organise the project teams for the purpose of conducting a quality improvement project?
7. How will you diagnose the cause of quality problem?
8. Explain the different types of errors. What are the possible remedies of these errors?
9. What is resistance to change and how will you deal with it?
10. Explain Crosby's steps on 'quality improvement'.
11. Draw and explain Deming's cycle indicating stages for solving quality problem.
12. Explain the philosophy of 'Imai Kaizen' on quality improvement.
13. Describe the views of 'Taguchi' on Quality improvement.
14. Write short notes on:
    (*a*) Quality audits
    (*b*) Kaizen
    (*c*) Quality control V/S Quality improvement.

# 6

# Customer Satisfaction

## 6.1. INTRODUCTION

Most important asset of any organisation is its satisfied customers. When the customers are satisfied, they will increase in number, buy more, and buy more frequently. From the point of view of customer satisfaction, "quality means meeting or exceeding the customer's expectations". Quality guru Dr. Deming added to this definition that quality also means anticipating the future needs of the customer. Primary goal of the organisation must be the customer satisfaction and not the increase in profit, because the satisfied customer will automatically lead to increased profit.

### CUSTOMER SATISFACTION

As we have seen in chapter second, total quality management is focused on the requirements of the customers, and have a set of expectations and requirements that must be met to win repeat business. Regarding customers, every organisation **must remember that customers are :**

(*i*) most important people,

(*ii*) not dependent on us, rather we are dependent on them,

(*iii*) doing us a favour when they come in. We are not doing them a favour by serving them,

(*iv*) a part of our business, and

(*v*) deserving of the most courteous and attentive treatment, we can give them.

From quality point of view, **requirements of the customers are related to** the following elements :

(*a*) ***Specification :*** to meet the expected requirement from the product.

(*b*) ***Conformance:*** whether the product meets the expectation for which he wants to purchase.

(*c*) ***Reliability :*** whether it can meet the requirement throughout the expected life.

(*d*) ***Value*** **(*cost*)** : whether it fulfills its value.

(*e*) ***Delivery:*** whether it will be available, when desired *i.e.* on delivery date.

In order to achieve the objective of customer satisfaction, following duties should strictly be performed by every individual/department:

1. To monitor performance and customer satisfaction levels.
2. To identify improvements necessary in the customer interface.
3. To assess and agree the customer's requirements.
4. To tailor output to the customer's demand.

## Components of Customer Satisfaction

For achieving the '*customer satisfaction*', two components, namely product features and freedom from deficiencies must be considered.

1. **'Product features'** refer to the quality of design.

   Increasing the quality of design generally results in higher costs. **The product features for manufacturing industries include :**

   (*i*) Performance (*ii*) Reliability
   (*iii*) Durability (*iv*) Ease of use
   (*v*) Serviceability (*vi*) Aesthetics
   (*vii*) Options availability (*viii*) Reputation

   **Product features for 'service industries' may be:**

   (*i*) Accuracy (*ii*) Timeliness
   (*iii*) Completeness (*iv*) Friendliness and courtesy
   (*v*) Anticipating customer needs (*vi*) Aesthetics
   (*vii*) Reputation.

As regards to **'freedom from deficiencies'** the product or services must be free from defects, failures and errors may it be during delivery, use, service, billing or any other business process. This 'freedom from deficiencies' is referred to 'quality of conformance'. Increase in quality of conformance usually results in lower costs, few complaints and hence, increased customer satisfaction.

Increasing global competition has created more demanding customers – as they are seeking best of products and services. Therefore, more and more companies are becoming 'customer conscious' and care for the 'voice of the customer'. Customer satisfaction is not solely dependent on the quality of the product or service, but depends on the whole relationship centered around the product and his perceived expectations. Each member of the customers' chain (end users, dealers, distributors, and contractors) has different expectations, though each one of them have inter-relations with each other.

2. **Freedom from deficiencies** has a major effect on costs through reduction in scrap, re-work, complaints etc,. Deficiencies include errors, defects, failures, off-specification etc. Freedom from deficiency means quality of conformance and this increases customers satisfaction.

Freedom from deficiencies shall reduce the waste, warranty cost, claims, cycle time etc., which will lead to reduction in cost and enhance profit for the company.

**Types of Customers**

Customers are of following two types:

1. External customers.
2. Internal customers.

An **external customer** is one who uses the product or service, the one who purchases the product or service, or the one who influences the sale of the product or service. External customers exist outside the organisation. Valuable customer satisfaction information can be provided to the organisation by the current,prospective, and lost customers.

**Care of external customers :** It is most important to give topmost priority to long-term total satisfaction of the customer. This satisfaction can only come with a quality product that fully conforms to the customer's expectations, and with a proper after-sales service. Customer's complaints must be viewed as an opportunity for improvement.

**Care of internal customers :** As explained earlier, the persons within the company who receives the work of another individual/department and then adds his contribution to the product or service before passing it onto someone else, is known as internal customer. If the internal customers' requirements are agreed and met, a chain of quality is made that reaches to the external customer. This concept of internal customer is a start of a total quality process.

## 6.2. CUSTOMER COMPLAINTS

The customer complaints are the reactive feed back. As a dis-satisfied customer can easily become a lost customer, it is always advisable to take proactive action on informations received on feedback gathered from surveys conducted by the organisation.

Each complaint poses different problems requiring programmes of action, such as:

1. **Satisfy the customer.** This involves prompt action for restoration of service and re-storation of goodwill.
2. **Preventing a recurrence of complaint.**
3. **Identify the 'vital few' servius complaints,** which demand in-depth studies to discover basic causes and their remedy.

Field complaints are not a foolproof measure of product performance, because some users may complain despite the fact that the product is fit for use while others do not complain despite the fact that a product is not fit for use. Thus, a low complaint rate is not proof of consumer satisfaction. However, high complaint rate is proof of dissatisfaction, and therefore, it should be measured and watched closely.

It is always better to take positive approach, on complaints, as an opportunity to obtain information which will help in providing better service to the customer. For handling complaints, following actions can be taken by the organisations:

1. Investigate the complaints and take suitable actions promptly.
2. Empower front – line personnel for resolving complaints
3. Identify process and / or material variations and then eliminate the root cause
4. Establish customer satisfaction measures and constantly monitor them.
5. Utilize complaint analysis for identifying the customers expectations.
6. Monthly complaint report should be provided to the quality council for their information and further action, as required.
7. Communicate complaint information, as well as the results of investigations and solutions, to all the sections / departments in the organisation.

## 6.3. AVOID CUSTOMER DEFECTIONS (CUSTOMER RETENTION)

Customer defection occurs when a customer switches to another brand. When customers defect, the profit–making potential goes with them for many years. The longer a company keeps a customer, the larger the profit will be. Research conducted in service industries indicates that reducing the defection rate can have a dramatic impact on boosting the profits.

Customer retention is more effective than customer satisfaction, because customer retention represents the activities that produce the necessary customer satisfaction which results into customer loyalty. Surveys, interviews and observations of customers help in determining as to what they think about the product or service.

It is, therefore necessary, that organisations must continually:

(*i*) Improve the methods of obtaining correct information concerning the customer's needs and expectations, and

(*ii*) Fine – tune their operation to achieve incremental improvements.

## 6.4. CUSTOMER PERCEPTION OF QUALITY

Customers form perception of quality during three phases – before purchase, at the point of purchase, and after purchase. Customers perception of quality depends on many aspects, such as performance, service, warranty, price and reputation. These aspects are being discussed in this section.

### 6.4.1. Factors Influencing Customers Perception of Quality

It is important to examine the factors that influence customer perception of quality. Some of the main factors influencing customer perception of quality are :

**1. *Before Purchase*:**

- Brand name and image of company
- Previous experience

- Opinion of friends
- Published test results
- Advertised price for performance.

**2. At the Time of Purchase:**

- Specifications
- Performance
- Comments of salespeople
- Warranty provisions
- Service and repair policies
- Quoted price for performance.
- On-time delivery

**3. After Purchase**

- Ease of installation and use
- Handling of claims, repairs and warranty
- Availability of spare parts
- Effectiveness of service
- Reliability
- Comparative performance.

**Important aspects of customers perception are discussed hereunder in detail:**

**1. Performance.**

Field performance can be adjudged in two phases ; namely, preuse phase and use phase. **Preuse phase** includes packing, shipping, receiving and storage. This includes the activities like package design and the purchasing and testing of packaging materials. Handling and transportation of the product must take care of the temperature changes, humidity, vibration, shock, carelessness. All our efforts must be made for systematic storage of materials including finished products to avoid deterioration and degradation. In such cases, "first come —first go" principle should strictly be followed.

**Use phase** includes installation, operation and maintenance. The installation is done either at site *i. e.* at user's premises by the specialists of the manufacturing firm or by the users themselves. Installation and operation thereafter by the specialists also include the checking out of the product, its demonstration for proper operation and maintenance and necessary instructions, and training to the operation and maintenance staff of the user. For the help of users, manufacturers prepare and provide operating manuals for proper use and maintenance.

Performance involves the phrase "fitness for use" (discussed in the chapter on "introduction to quality concept") which means that the product or service is ready for use of the customer at the time of purchase.

Other considerations in performance are:

(*a*) *availability*, which is the probability that a product will operate, when required,

(*b*) *Reliability*, which is the freedom from failure over time, and

(*c*) *maintainability*, which is the ease of keeping the product operatable.

The above three terms have been discussed in the chapter on "Reliability",

**2. Service**

Service include several small things, which changes the customers perception and contribute to customer satisfaction.

In service industry, a contact is made by the customer at the service counter. This illustrates the quality of the transactions involved, both the technical adequacy of the result and the social skills of the frontline person who conducts the transaction.

In such cases, three factors emerge as important: selection of the frontline employee, training of that employee, and the empowerment of that employee to act to meet customer needs. In "person-to-person" type of transactions, these frontline employees provide an immediate, direct, and lasting impact on customer perception.

**3. Safety and Product Liability**

The manufacturer is responsible for providing safe products. Product liability refers to the legal obligation of a manufacturer to compensate for injury or damage caused, if any, by a product.

**4. Warranty**

A warranty is a form of assurance that a product is fit for use or, failing this, the user will receive some kind of compensation. Consumer product warranties are either "full" or "limited". In limited warranties, the warranties as to quality were limited to replacement or repair of the product during the warranty period. This may exclude labour costs, require the purchaser to pay transportation charges and may be limited to the original purchaser of the product.

In full warranties, it refers to the customer's full rights about quality, and means that:

(*i*) Manufacturer will replace any defective product free of charge.

(*ii*) No limit about time

(*iii*) If the manufacturer is unable to make adequate repairs, the consumer may choose a refund or replacement.

(*iv*) The warranty does not exclude or limit payment for consequential damages.

(*v*) Not only the original purchaser but also any subsequent owners of the product during the warranty period are entitled to make claims.

**5. Price**

Normally selling price depends upon the benefit which the customers expect to drive by using the product. This benefit is translated by the customer in terms of money which he can pay or in other words, this is the value which the customer places on the article or service for its purchase. This amount is entirely based on the wishes of the customer and has nothing to do with the money spent on producing the article.

Thus, the price at which the product sells or can sell in the market is a measure of its value to the customer. Customer pays the assigned price for the product because he considers the satisfaction derived from its use worth that price. He is generally unconcerned about what it costs the manufacturer to produce the product.

**6. Reputation**

Most people rate organisations by their overall experience with them. Total customer satisfaction is based on the entire experience with the organisation, not just the product. Customers are willing to pay a premium for a known and trusted brand name.

## 6.5. SERVICE QUALITY

Like a product quality, the service quality is also based on 'fitness for use.' The service must be according to the needs of customer, in price, in delivery schedule and suitability to meet the purpose. The fitness for use is determined by those features of the service that customer recognises as beneficial to him.

Service Quality can be controlled through service characteristics. The requirements of a service is defined in terms of characteristics that are observable and subject to customer evaluation against defined standards of acceptability. Examples of some of the service characteristics are:

1. Waiting time.
2. Delivery time.
3. Accuracy of service.
4. Accuracy of billing.
5. Completeness of service.
6. Responsiveness.
7. Credibility.
8. Security.
9. Reliability.
10. Courtesy.
11. Hygiene.
12. Safety.
13. Aesthetic.

## 6.6. CUSTOMER NEEDS

Identifying customers, analyzing their needs and understanding the quality status of the company relative to competition, help in establishing new product quality goals that will lead to a competitive advantage. In order to understand the needs of customers, it is necessary to first identify internal as well as external customers and suppliers. It should also be recognized that some customers are more important than others, it has been noticed that in most cases, about 80 percent of the total sales volume goes to about 20 percent customers. Thus, these are the 'vital few' customers who command priority.

While understanding customer needs, we must be able to differentiate between stated needs and real needs. Sometimes, a product designed for some specific purpose is used by the customers for other purpose. Although from designer's point of view, this is a misuse, but it necessitates to consider alternative design concepts. Sometimes, needs may be perceptional, or cultural. Some time back computer was treated as a source which will create very serious unemployment problem. Sometime, customer needs or expectations increases in steps *i.e.* when level 1 needs are fulfilled, level 2 needs started and so on. The aim should be to create customers and their needs be discovered and served.

There should be an information system which include alarm signals arising from decline in sales, field failure reports, customer complaints, claims etc. The problem become serious when the product is inexpensive, complaint rates are a poor indicator of customer satisfaction. If customer is not satisfied, in such cases, he simply switch over to other brands without complaining. Sometimes, a product may be failure free, even than it is not salable, because the competitor's design is superior and has a lower price. The solution to these problems is well-planned marketing research studies.

For this purpose, customers may be asked to select attributes, the relative importance is then measured as the percent of customers selected each attribute. For example, relative importance of attributes of a typical product is given below :

– Quality of product
– Meeting delivery schedule
– In-field reliability
– After sales service
– Technical assistance
– Price
– Product aesthetics
– Capability of field service.

## 6.7. CUSTOMER REQUIREMENTS

As we know, quality means 'customer satisfaction' i.e. 'conformance to customer requirements'. Therefore, quality is explained as those product features which meets the needs of customers and thereby provides product satisfaction. Marketing function of the company works as an interface between the customer and the production system to establish the quality requirements of the products, which can meet the customer satisfaction. Marketing helps in setting the quality objectives, and for this purpose, marketing department should perform the following functions :

1. Conduct market survey and determine the customer needs for a product or service.
2. Define the market demand, market segment and sector
3. Determine the quality grade, price and time estimates for the product or service.

4. Prepare a product brief, which should include : performance ; characteristics ; sensory characteristics like colour, smell, taste, installation standards, statutory regulations, packaging requirements.
5. Determine informations about competitive products.

From the above, we see that in quality 'focus is on customer'. Therefore, a clear 'commitment to quality of product or service' and a 'considerate mechanism for dealing with customer complaints' should be there. From the point of view of customer satisfaction, following elements are considered:

1. *Specification. i.e.* expectation of the customer from product.
2. *Conformance to the specification i.e.* whether it meets the expectations to the product.
3. *Reliability i.e.* whether it continues to meet expectation.
4. *Value* (*cost*) *i.e.* whether customer is willing to pay the price of product or service.
5. *Timely delivery.* Delivery should be at the time, when it is desired by the customer.

Form the above criteria, we can say, 'quality is fully satisfying agreed customer requirements at the lowest internal cost.'

'Customers' requirements can be met by listening to him and responding to what he wants and to what is agreed. Customers are of two types : external to the company *i.e.* the people outside who are end users of products or services, and internal customer who is the person within the company who receives the work of another and then adds his contribution to the product or service before passing it onto someone else. In a manufacturing concern, the internal customer is the next person down the line who builds the product. If the internal customer's requirements are met, a chain of quality is made that reaches out to the external customer. Although it is most important to give top most priority to long term total satisfaction of the customer, but you will never achieve quality externally until you have quality internally. The customer satisfaction can only come with a quality product that fully conforms to the customer's expectations, and with a proper after-sales service. Customers' complaints must be viewed as an opportunity for improvement.

## 6.8. CUSTOMER FEEDBACK

The marketing function should establish an information monitoring and feedback system. All informations pertinent to quality of product or service should be analysed, investigated, compiled, interpreted and communicated for appropriate action.

It is essential to minimize customers dissatisfaction by collecting, analyzing and responding to customer complaints. Customer surveys generally cover product, service, sales, and administration support. A questionnaire should be prepared for collecting field information on all the aspects related to the product. (including equipment/appliance), service, sales and administration support. The result of the survey are used to take immediate action on customer problems.

Feedback should be obtained through mail surveys and /or from company personnel and is a continuous process. Feedback requires a variety of actions to make the process as convenient and effective as possible for improving the quality and promptness.

If the activities on product complaints are not sufficient to increase customer satisfaction, the dissatisfied customer may defect. A customer defection occurs, when a customer switches to another brand. When customers defect, the profit-making potential goes with them.

Customer feedback must be a continuous process and regularly monitored. Since Customers continuously change and they also change their mind, therefore, feedback is an ongoing and active probing of the customers' mind. Customer needs and the level of their satisfaction / dissatisfaction can be more effectively addressed, when field data are available.

The results of surveys are used to take immediate action on customers problems. Similar information is obtained from users of competitors products, which enable providing competitive benchmarking data.

Customer feedback is required for following purposes:

(*i*) Discover customer dissatisfaction.

(*ii*) Discover relative priorities of quality.

(*iii*) Identify customer needs.

(*iv*) Discover opportunities for improvement.

## 6.9. PRODUCT LIABILITY

It is the responsibility of the manufacturer to provide safe products. Manufacturer of the product has a liability to compensate for injury or damage caused by the product. Now-a-days due to consumer movement, number of law suits and size of awards to victims are increasing. The basic defence against liability is prevention—by eliminating the causes of the injuries or damange.

In such cases, following precautions should be taken:

1. Promptly notify the insurance company
2. Qualified experts should be assigned to make the investigation.

Consumer Protection Act of 1986 safeguards consumer's interests and is intended to provide justice which is less formal, and involves less paperwork, delay and expenses. This Act has received wide recognition as poor man's legislation.

Local, state, and central laws regulate many products, such as buildings, fireworks, toys etc. so as to enhance safety in order to protect their citizens.

Product liability law, also known as "product lability" governs the liability of manufactures, wholesalers, distributors and vendors for injury to a person or property caused by dangerous goods or defective products.

### Prevention of liability

Products are, in many cases, insured by the manufactures. In such cases, insurance companies make the initial payments from products liability losses, however, the organisation ultimately has to pay the price. The manufacturer of the consumer product protect himself against the risk of products liability litigation or atleast reduce the risk. So as to achieve this goal, a **products liability prevention programme** is prepared by the organisation.

For having an effective products liability prevention programme, a formal product – safety committee should be formed with either a safety engineer or an outside safety consultant as a member of the committee.

**Other liability prevention measures are:**

- All employees should be made aware of the importantce of product safety.
- Continuing education and training programme should be a part of action plan.
- New product should be reviewed by a team constituted for the purpose. This team must look for all possible hazards.
- Production review must also be carried out to evaluate the manufacturing plan.
- To carry out periodically the production audit to verify the effectiveness of the quality control system. This is a requirement of ISO: 9000.
- Continually review the warranty, advertising literature, catalogue, and technical publications regarding language of terms and conditions, analysis by legal counsel, warranty provisions, language of agreements etc.
- Provide adequate warning lables and operating instructions be given at appropriate places
- Customers generally co-operate, if the redressal system is effective. Organisations can improve customer loyalty through an effective redress policy.

## QUESTIONS

1. 'Quality of any product or service is regarded as the degree to which it fulfills the requirement of customers'. Discuss this statement.
2. 'Quality management system is required to meet the inter-related needs of company as well as of customer'. Discuss.
3. Write an essay on 'Customer Satisfaction'.
4. 'For any quality system, quality and customer satisfaction are the most important objectives'. Explain this statement.
5. How will you plan for assessing customer requirements? What element will you consider from the point of views of customer-satisfaction ?
6. Explain the procedure for planning the 'marketing as a customer service'.
7. What is meant by 'understanding customer needs' ? How it can be done?
8. Write short notes on:
   (*a*) Marketing goals (*b*) Customer feedback
   (*c*) Customer perception of quality
9. What do you understand by "Customer satisfaction ? Explain it in detail.
10. "Customer satisfaction can be achieved through two components, viz. product features, and freedom from deficiencies". Elaborate the statement.

# 7 Supplier Partnership

## 7.1. INTRODUCTION

A survey, conducted by the Directorate of Industrial Statistics showed that the average material cost is 64 percent of the sales value, and wages, overheads, profit etc. account for only 36 percent. Poor quality of supplier items are the source of more than half of the quality problems. Poor quality of supplier items results in extra costs for the purchaser.

These facts themselves show the importance of right source of supply. A good supplier is he, who maintain the quality, quantity and time schedules at competitive price. Proper selection of supplier helps in the development of better products and materials services to a manufacturing industry.

Inventory carrying costs alone come out to be about 20 percent of the material cost. Inventory carrying cost comprises interest charges on the cost of inventory, storage and material handling, insurance, physical deterioration and obsolescence. Under the "Just–in–time" philosophy, goods are received from suppliers only in the quantity and at the time that they are needed for production. In this just–in–time (JIT) concept, the buyer stocks no inventories.

Since materials are supplied just – in – time for use of factory floor, it is important to have close relationships with suppliers on long – term basis who are geographically close for frequent deliveries of small and exact quantities. For the success of JIT, co-operation from the company's vendors is essential. In this concept, vendors are virtually an extension of the company. JIT vendors have to deliver goods to production line at the required time, which must be quite frequent – say every 3 or 4 hours.

Till 1980s, procurement decisions were based on price, thereby awarding supply contract to lowest bidder. As a result, quality and timely delivery of supply were sacrificed. This concept of supply have now been stopped by the manufactures, as price has no basis without quality. Now–a – days, concept of single supplier for each item is gaining popularity, as it helps in developing long – term relationship of loyalty and trust, and shall ultimately lead to improved products and services.

The practice of continuous improvement has also caused development of partnership between suppliers and manufacturer's organisation. In recent years, many original equipment manufacturers

(OEMs) are developing strategic partnerships with their suppliers. In the development of new products, many suppliers are becoming involved in product design.

## 7.2. PARTNERING (CUSTOMER-SUPPLIER RELATIONSHIP)

Partnering (partnership) is a long term commitment between two or more organisations for achieving: (*i*) specific business goal, and (*ii*) objectives by maximising the effectiveness of resources of each participants.

This partnership is based on following:

– trust,

– dedication to common goals and objectives,

– understanding the expectations and values of each participants.

**Benefits of partnership are:**

(*i*) Improving quality.

(*ii*) Increased efficiency.

(*iii*) Lower cost.

(*iv*) Use of latest technology possible.

(*v*) Continuous improvement of products and services

Partnership involves business issues alongwith quality. Teamwork between manufacturing and supplier organisations vary greatly with regards to:

– training a supplier's staff in quality technique,

– design review meeting to gain ideas on how supplier parts can be used,

– sharing sales projections with suppliers to assist in suppler production scheduling.

Co-operation between buyers and suppliers can best be achieved by setting up multiple channels of communication e.g., designers with designers, quality specialists with quality specialists etc.

**Key elements to a partnering relationship are:**

1. *Long-term commitment*.
2. *Trust* enables the resources and knowledge of each partner to be combined to eliminate an adverse relationship. The parties should have access to each other's business plans and technical informations.
3. *Shared vision*. Each of the partnering organisations must understand the need to satisfy the final customer/end user.

Thus, the partnership can be achieved through:

(*a*) Joint economic planning.

(*b*) Joint technological planning.

(c) Co-operation during contract execution.

### Customer-Supplier Relationship

A revolution in the relationship between customers (buyers) and suppliers has emerged in the form of "supplier partnership". Supplier partnerships require joint economic planning, joint technological planning, and cooperation during contract execution.

Supplier relations are measured on the basis of input from customer and its evaluation.

### Principles of Customer-Supplier Relations

According to Dr. Kaoru Ishikawa following principles ensure quality products and services and eliminate unsatisfactory conditions between the customer and the supplier:

1. Customer and the supplier both are responsible for the control of quality.
2. Both of them should respect each other's independence.
3. The customer is responsible for providing the supplier with clear and sufficient requirements so that supplier can understand precisely what to produce.
4. Customer and the supplier both should enter a clear contract with respect to quality, quantity, price, delivery method, and terms of payments.
5. The supplier is responsible for providing the quality that will satisfy the customer.
6. The customer and supplier both should decide the method to evaluate the quality of the product or service to the satisfaction of both the parties.
7. Both of them should establish in the contract the method for an amicable settlement of dispute, if any.
8. Both of them should continually exchange informations, sometimes using multi-functional teams, in order to improve the product or service quality, if any.
9. Both of them should perform activities, like procurement, production, inventory planning, record keeping etc. so that an emicable and satisfactory relationship is maintained.

As discussed earlier, a true partnering relationship exists with long term commitment, trust and shared vision.

## 7.3. SOURCING

A firm has two categories of suppliers: (1) the firm itself, and (2) outside suppliers. Here in this chapter we shall concentrate on outside suppliers. A good supplier make a direct contribution to the firms success. Such suppliers can assist in product development, value analysis, and timely delivery of the desired level of quality. Selection and management of the right supplier is the key to obtaining the desired level of quality, on time, and at the right price, the necessary level of technical support, and the desired level of service.

Experiences have shown that when suppliers are involved early in the buyer's design process, they can apply their expertise in the fields of: material specification, tolerances, standardisation, order sizes, packaging, transportation etc.

Issue of deciding number of suppliers is most important. **Single source is justified when:**

(*i*) better pricing due to higher volume,

(*ii*) quality considerations dictate,

(*iii*) lower costs are incurred in finding source, process, expediting, inspection, coordination etc.

(*iv*) lower freight costs due to higher volume,

(*v*) reduced inventory,

(*vi*) an improved commitment.

**Dual or multiple sourcing is justified when:**

(*i*) to protect during times of shortages, strikes etc.,

(*ii*) to maintain competition and provide a back-up source,

(*iii*) to meet customer's volume requirements.

Purchasing methodology decide, whether to purchase from local source, national or international source; or from manufacturer or distributor.

### Types of Sourcing

Following are the three types of soaring:

1. **Sole Source.** In sole source of supply, organisation is forced to use only one source of supply, because this situation is due to factors, such as patents, technical specifications, raw material location, only one organisation producing the item or the item being produced by the same organisation in another plant or division.
2. **Multiple Sourcing.** Multiple sourcing is the use of two or more suppliers for an item. In this system, suppliers are chosen considering their performance in terms of price, quality and delivery. The principle behind this method is that the competition will result in better quality, lower costs, and better service.
3. **Single Sourcing.** Single sourcing is a planned decision to select one supplier for an item when several sources are available. It results in large, long–term contracts and a partnering relationship. With a guaranteed future volume, the supplier can direct its resources to inprove the processes for reducing the production cost, better end product with less variability and supplier loyalty.

## 7.4. SUPPLIER SELECTION

Selection of suppliers starts with the decision as to whether to 'make' (manufacture) or 'buy' (outsource) a particular item. This decision is a strategic decision and is taken at the design stage, and requires consideration on following three questions:

1. How critical is the item to the design of product?
2. Whether the organisation have the technical knowledge to manufacture the item technically?

3. Are there suppliers available who specialise in the production of that item?

These factors are considered with regards to cost, delivery, quality, safety and the availability of technical knowledge.

Once a decision is taken to 'buy' a particular item, the procedure for selection of supplier is started. The selection decision depends on following:

- Skills and facilities needed
- Plant capacity
- Ability to meet delivery schedules
- Assessing the capability of supplier
- Qualifying the supplier's manufacturing process.
- Supplier Quality survey. This aspect not only covers the final quality results, but also covers the entire quality system.

## Stages in Source Selection

**I. Stage–Searching.**

Once the list of items to be purchased and their specifications are received, purchase officer starts looking for suitable suppliers who are reliable. This process is known as searching of sources. This procedure involves in preparation of an exhaustive list of suppliers, which will then be sorted out in second phase. Normally comprehensive information can be obtained from the following sources:

(i) *Interviews with the salesmen.* This will enable the purchase officer to get all the relevant information about the supplier.

(ii) *Technical and descriptive catalogues.* Normally large vendors brought out technical and descriptive catalogues of their products. This serves as a valuable guide for the selection of supplier.

(iii) *Trade directories.* These contain necessary informations about an item produced or marketed by different sources.

(iv) *Trade Journals.* National or International Journals are published for various trades which include informations and advertisements of various products by their suppliers.

(v) *Trade fairs and conventions.* The fairs, exhibitions and conventions also provide informations about their products. These are organised by the manufacturers or their area representatives.

(vi) Advertisements in newspapers.

(vii) Telephone directories, yellow pages.

(viii) Routine sale calls of the supplier or their representatives, face to face talks, telephonic conversations, offer letters etc.

**II. Stage—Selection.**

The list of all possible sources prepared in first phase is sorted out in this second phase, to bring down their number to a reasonable limit with whom purchase department should deal. In this phase, emphasis is on getting more specific informations on the suppliers' financial strength, quality of product supplied, reliability price facilities offered and efficiency with which orders are handled. On the basis of all such and other informations, list of suppliers prepared under first phase is sorted out. The idea behind this is that the suppliers with whom the purchase officer will deal should meet the purchase parameters, discussed in the chapter on 'Purchasing'.

In short, source selected should be managerially, technically, and financially sound. A supplier should be selected after considering the following factors :

1. **Technical ability.** This is the most important factor which should be considered by purchase officer while selecting a source of supply. The supplier must have all the necessary manufacturing facilities for producing the product of desired quality.
2. **Production capacity.** The purchase officer must satisfy himself that supplier has sufficient production capacity and he can meet his requirement of quantity within the required time. If the supplier fails to deliver the material in required quantity at required time, it may affect the production of the organisation.
3. **Location and transport facilities.** Purchase officer should always try to locate the supplier nearer to his plant or factory, as it saves time, and freight charges. It also helps in chasing or contacting him, whenever necessary.
4. **Financial position.** Supplier's firm should be financially sound. If the supplier's firm is not sound enough, it may not be possible for them to supply the ordered quantity in time.
5. **Performance reports as received from other organisation.** While selecting a new source, it is necessary to be convinced about the satisfactory performance of the supplier regarding quality, meeting the schedules, after-sales service. The quality aspects can be ascertained by discussing and examining the sample. The other aspects can be enquired from the other organisations to whom this seller has supplied the same items.
6. **Labour relations.** Labour relations of the supplier's firm should be good, otherwise if the relations are not good there may be strikes or lockouts etc. which may affect timely delivery.
7. **Stockists and dealers.** When the requirement is not very high, big manufacturers are not interested in accepting these small value orders. In such cases stockists, dealers or distributors are selected as probable source of supply.
8. **Open Tenders.** When for a particular item, the firm do not have permanent list of suppliers, method of open tender system is employed. Tenderers may be asked to furnish certain informations which may help to evaluate their performance and reliability.

While purchasing capital equipment or other important items, **two bid system** is followed. First bid contains information which may help in ascertaining the quality of product and firm's credibility. Second bid of the bidder is opened only when purchase officer is satisfied about the product and the firm.

Large technically oriented firms for major supply or works/services use a modified system of competitive bidding, called "two-step bidding" or "two bid" system. This method of source selection and pricing is used in situations, where specifications are inadequate or use of high technology is required. In the first step, bids are requested only for technical proposals without any prices. Bidders are required to submit their proposals about technical details describing how they would produce the required materials, products or services and also their capabilities in dealing with such works. After the technical bids are evaluated and it is decided that which are the proposals, those are technically satisfactory, the second step is followed.

In the second step, requests for price bids are sent only to those sellers who submitted acceptable technical proposals in the first step. These sellers (bidders) at this stage compete for the business on a price basis. Sometimes to reduce time, both the bids are invited in separate covers simultaneously, but the second bid (price bid) is opened only for those bidders who qualify after first bidding.

9. **Plant Visits.** By visiting a supplier's plant or distribution facility, the sourcing team can obtain first-hand information concerning the adequacy of the firm's technological capabilities, manufacturing or distribution capabilities, and its management's technical know-how and orientation. Factors to be seen during the visit are :

1. Attitude and stability of the top and middle management teams.
2. R & D capability.
3. Appropriateness of equipment.
4. Effectiveness of the production control, quality assurance, and cost control systems.
5. Competence of the technical and managerial staffs.
6. Morale of personnel at all levels,
7. Industrial relations.
8. Quality of back orders.
9. Past performance.
10. Selection from existing suppliers.

The procedure and criteria for selecting the suppliers from existing regular suppliers is different than that of selecting a new supplier. As in this case selection is done on the basis of past performance and records of the firms. This selection is based on vendor analysis.

**III. Stage---Negotiations and Trial Orders**

After preliminary screening and selection, process of negotiation is started. In this, the suppliers are called for negotiations, which may be done either individually or jointly. Negotiations should be carried out smoothly and in a cordial atmosphere. The negotiations are carried out for terms of delivery, price, quality or payment terms etc.

The negotiation process is adopted to lead to a complete understanding of all issues of the procurement and greatly reduces subsequent quality and schedule problems. Negotiations have already been discussed in detail in the chapter on "Purchase Procedure".

After successful negotiations, trial orders are placed, when the item to be procured is crucial, otherwise purchase order can be placed directly. Since in case of crucial items, purchase officer can not take a risk, he places trial order. If the quality and delivery schedule of supplies of trial order are found satisfactory, the firm can be finally selected as supplier of the product.

## 7.5. SOURCE–DEVELOPMENT

Source development, also known as supplier development means to develop long-range collaboration with a supplier and therefore, reduce uncertainties of material inflow. Source development is based on the philosophy that the buyer's enterprise helps the supplier to help ownself. The policy of source development is framed by the top management, if they consider it useful for itself. The source development is necessary, when selected sources do not satisfy with what is available from them. Examples of such cases are : the item is new and has not been manufactured previously, time constraints, and/or technical constraints for their manufacture, existing source of supply is not efficient, and/or located at quite a distance etc.

To develop small scale industries, government organisations and public sector undertakings allow price preference of 10 to 15% on the products manufactured by them. Sources are mostly developed by the large manufacturing concerns in order to purchase semi-finished products or components to be used in assembling a major product.

By adopting a source development policy, a company has following advantages:

(*i*) Conserve working capital.

(*ii*) Low cost in buying as compared to manufacturing.

(*iii*) Easier to buy in certain cases.

(*iv*) More number of vendors permit uninterrupted supply even when anyone of them is in problem.

## 7.6. SUPPLIER (VENDOR) ANALYSIS

Supplier/Vendor analysis is done by calculating overall performance of the vendor. Overall performance is the sum of the quality performance, quantity performance, and delivery performance, (each of these performances are multiplied by a weightage factor before final summation). The example of vendor anlaysis is given hereunder :

**Vendor Analysis**

Vendor's Name and Address Date....

**1. Quality Performance**

(*a*) Quantity Received

(*b*) Quantity Accepted

Weightage, 50%

Quality Rating $\frac{b}{a} \times 50$......

**2. Delivery Performance**

Purchase order No. and date ........

Scheduled delivery date ........

Actual delivery date

(*a*) Days allowed

(*b*) Days taken

Weightage 40%

Delivery Rating $\frac{b}{a} \times 40$......

**3. Quantity Performance**

(*a*) Quantity promised

(*b*) Quantity supplied ......

Weightage 10%

Quantity Rating $\frac{b}{a} \times 10$......

Overall Performance = 1 + 2 + 3

## 7.7. SUPPLIER (VENDOR) EVALUATION

Supplier/Vendor evaluation is earned out by the buyers in following two situations :

(*a*) Evaluating the performance before placing the order.

(*b*) Evaluating the performance after the deliveries have been made by the vendor.

In case, buyer does not have full direct evidence on the results, achieved by the vendor, he must get information in other ways. This includes :

(*i*) General reputation of vendor.

(*ii*) Data from other buyers.

(*iii*) Vendor surveys.

For having good vendors, purchase department must make a list of vendors who have good reputation in the market and also, if they are already supplying materials, their performance is monitored and the list is updated.

**Informations collected about the vendor's organisation are :**

1. Organisation structure, commitment to quality, quality policies, attention towards reliability.
2. Manufacturing process, process capabilities, production capabilities.
3. Purchasing of materials and their specifications.
4. Quality control system and laboratories.

**A good vendor (supplier) is one:**

– who is at all times honest and fair in his dealing with the customers and his own employees;

– who has adequate plant facilities and know-how so as to meet the buyer's specifications, timings and the quantities required:

– whose financial position is sound;

– whose prices are reasonable both to the buyer and himself; and

– whose management policies are progressive.

## Methods of Evaluating the Suppliers

**1. Subjective Evaluation**

In this method managers of the concerned departments, such as production, engineering, quality, purchasing, warehousing etc. prepares a list of factors important from their point of view. They meet and evaluate the suppliers against each of these factors. These factors are usually evaluated in terms of 'Good', 'Satisfactory' or 'Poor'. On the basis of these ratings, each of the supplier is given overall subjective rating, such as 'Good', 'Satisfactory', 'Poor'.

**2. Weighted Point Evaluation**

In this case buyer decides important factors for the evaluation of vendors, and then each factor is given its weightage. Weightages of all the factors when added should be 100. As per one of the such plans :

Timely delivery is given 40 points weightage, quality of goods supplied is given 30 points weightage and the relative price of offer is given 30 points weightage.

## 7.8. SUPPLIER RATING

Periodic and systematic performance evaluation is called as Supplier/Vendor Rating.

Objectives of periodic monitoring and evaluation for vendors performance are :

1. To help in future source selection.
2. To provide information which is helpful in subsequent negotiations with the suppliers.
3. To provide information which the buyer can act upon for any corrective measures.

Vendors can be rated on the basis of following characteristics :

1. **Timely Delivery.** The capacity to deliver the supply on time as per orders.

$$\text{Index of delivery service} = \frac{\text{Number of timely deliveries}}{\text{Total number of orders placed}}$$

2. **Adherence to Quality.** The capacity to deliver as per quality specifications.

$$\text{Index of quality} = \frac{\text{Percent of good quality items supplied}}{100}$$

$$= \frac{100 - \text{percent rejects}}{100}$$

3. **Prices Offered.** The capability to offer goods at competitive prices.

$$\text{Index of price} = \frac{\text{Average price}}{\text{Price at which supplied}}.$$

The purpose of vendor rating scheme is to establish a procedure by which corporate objectives of obtaining quality with minimum cost can be achieved. An efficient vendor rating system helps in selecting the best vendor for the organisation, so as to save time and money. Vendor rating method should be able to rate the entire performance of the vendor systematically and scientifically, and should also give the purchaser information about the capabilities of the vendor regarding know-how, testing, transport, contractual willingness etc.

Vendor rating is done with the help of records maintained or procured from some other sources. Generally a combination of price, quality, quantity, delivery time, service etc. giving relevant weightages to these factors is used for vendor rating. In addition, a checklist can also be used to facilitate rating. Some of the points of checklist are :

1. What is his financial ability ?
2. What is his technical ability ?
3. What is his management ability ?
4. Is the supplier reputable and stable ?
5. Is the supplier's integrity above doubt ?
6. Is his competitive strength with regard to price, quality etc. proved by past experience ?
7. Is he going alongwith product improvement ?
8. What service does he offer ?
9. How well can he control quality?
10. Can he offer other related products ?
11. Is he capable to help in solving difficult problems ?
12. Does he assume delivery in time ?
13. Are his stocks locally available, and or at short notice ?
14. Can supplier plan his supply to minimise buyer's inventory?
15. Whether he has eminent after-sales service ?

16. Can the supplier help building mutual markets ?

**Example 7.1.** Vendor firm *Z* has made 18 deliveries on time out of 20 orders placed on them, has given an average of 5 percent rejects and has delivered at the performance index of ₹ 110, when the average price performance index is ₹ 100.

Determine the overall evaluation of rating for this firm.

**Solution.**

Performance rating of the supplier can be evaluated, on the basis of each factor, as shown in the Table below:

| *Factor* | *Weight* | *Performance* | *Performance Evaluation* |
|---|---|---|---|
| 1. Delivery | 40 | 18 out of 20 deliveries in time | $(40) \times \frac{18}{20} = 36.0$ |
| 2. Quality | 30 | 5 percent rejects | $(30) \times \left(\frac{100-5}{100}\right) = 28.5$ |
| 3. Price | 30 | index of Rs. 110 against an average price performance index of Rs. 100 | $(30) \times \frac{100}{110} = 27.3$ |
| **Total** | **100** | -- | **91.8** |

Thus, overall evaluation of this *Z* firm is **91.8. Ans.**

**Example 7.2.** List price of a cloth is Rs. 40.00 per metre, if purchased in quantities of 1000 metres or more. If less than 1000 metres are purchased on the list price of ₹ 42.00 per metre. A trade discount of 20-10-5 is available. If a small firm buys 1300 metres of this cloth and gets the complete trade discount. The supplier also offers a cash discount of 2 percent, if payment is made within 10 days. If the firm makes the payment within a week of the receipt of the bill, how much was the payment ?

**Solution.**

Rate applicable for the purchase = 40.00 Rs. per metre,

(being more than 1000 metres)

Considering the discount, price per metre can be calculated as

List price = Rs. 40.00

Less 20 percent of 40.00 = $\frac{8.00}{32.00}$

Less 10 percent of 32.00 = 3.20

Less 5 percent of 28.80 = $\frac{28.80}{1.44}$

∴ Net invoice price per metre = 27.36

∴ Total Net invoice price for 1300 metres 4 1300 × 27.36 = Rs. 35568

Since payment has been made within 10 days, the firm is entitled to get a cash discount of 2%.

$$\therefore \text{Payment made} = 35568 \times \frac{100-2}{100}$$

$$= ₹\ \mathbf{34857\ Ans.}$$

## 7.9. SUPPLIER – BUYER RELATIONSHIP

To cultivate and maintain good relations with suppliers is one of the basic objectives of materials management department. Since corporate plans are based on the assumptions that materials and supplies will be forthcoming at right time, in right quantity and quality, it is most essential that good relations between buyers and sellers are maintained. After sales department, materials management is the only department which has more outside contacts with many firms and individuals. Therefore, buyer has the chance to enhance the reputation and goodwill of the company by cultivating and maintaining good buyer-seller relations.

Smooth running of the business of a company is based on healthy buyer-seller relations. Materials management and especially purchase department has a crucial responsibility for establishing and maintaining cordial working relations with the suppliers.

It has been noted that the most successful supplier-buyer relation results are obtained, when the buyer and the supplier view their relationship as a "partnership". *Partnerships* are based on mutual inter-dependency, co-operation and respect. Supplier partnership begin with careful source selection during the product design and development process. At this point, the buying firm needs a dependable supplier to provide the required design and technological input.

In turn, the supplier needs a responsible customer for its products and services. Whenever unexpected problems arise, "we shall overcome" attitude is required to be demonstrated by the partners. During production also, the buyers and suppliers must mesh their schedules. Long-term partnering agreement encourage suppliers to invest on research and development in order to propose technological developments, cost-effective and high-quality solutions to the needs of buying firms. Long-term agreements also encourage suppliers to invest in the equipment, training and appropriate management systems. The buyer must also agree to protect the supplier partner from sudden changes which might leave the supplier with unusable raw materials and finished goods.

### Essentials for Good Buyer-Seller Relationship :

1. Completeness and clarity of communication of essential and helpful information.
2. Mutual confidence and interests of both the parties must be taken care of by avoiding unreasonable demands.
3. Co-operation in prompt shipment, payment of invoices and sharing relevant information.
4. Objective should be for sustained and ethical relations, both for short as well as long-term.
5. Regularly evaluate relations and plug any loop-holes in time.

6. Both parties must feel and appreciate that the other understands his problems and is willing, able, and eager to help in solving the problems.
7. Developing methods for identifying the qualified vendors, and for eliminating those who are unable to meet the quality requirements.
8. Performance of the vendor should be reviewed regularly through vendor rating.

## Principles of Buyer / Supplier Relationship

1. Both, the buyer and the supplier are fully responsible for the control of quality.
2. Both of them should respect each others
3. Buyer should provide clear and sufficient requirement to the supplier so that he can know precisely as to what is to be produced.
4. Both of them enter into a contract agreement with regard to quality, price, delivery method and schedule, and terms of payment.
5. The supplier is responsible for providing the quality that will satisfy the buyer.
6. Both of them should jointly decide the method to evaluate the quality of product or service.
7. Both of them should establish in the contract the method of settlement of dispute that may arise.
8. Both of them should continually exchange information so as to improve the quality of product or service.
9. Both of them should perform business activities, such as procurement, production and inventory planning etc. so that good relationship is maintained.
10. While dealing with business transactions, both of them should always have the best interest of the end user in mind.

The idea behind these principles is to have family–type relationship, where each party preserves their identity and independence.

## Relationship Development

The points so far discussed in the chapter contribute to the establishment of the relationship.

Further, inspection, training, teamwork, and recognition and reward contribute towards the maintainability and growth of the relationship. These aspects have been discussed in detail in the book at appropriate places. Here, we are discussing them in brief, as to how they help in maintaining good relationship.

1. **Inspection.** The goal of inspection is to eliminate or substantially reduce the inspection activity. This can be achieved in 4 phases:
   (*a*) 100 percent inspection,
   (*b*) Sampling inspection, with statistical process control,

(*c*) Random sampling with auditing the performance.

(*d*) Identity checks by adopting statistical control of process and continuous improvement of the process.

Both the parties starts from phase 1 and move to second phase after they gains confidence in first phase. Similarly, they move from phase two to phase three after gaining confidence in phase two, and them from phase three to phase four. Experience have shown that it takes about four to five years to achieve final level of quality.

2. **Training.** The buyer or a consultant starts the training process in which the supplier is invited to attend the training courses or present the course at the suppliers premises. Such a training and type of courses may be as per requirement. The training should be treated as an investment and not an expense.
3. **Team Approach.** Joint teams of buyer (customer) and supplier are formed in various areas, like product design, process design and quality assurance system. It is advisable to held team meetings at both parties plants so as to develop greater understanding.
4. **Recognition and Reward.** It is a good strategy for quality improvement to create incentive for suppliers so that they remain committed to quality. Incentive may be in the form of many ways, such as recognition in the publication in house journal, news letter regarding outstanding contribution, a letter of commendation or declaring the supplier as preferred supplier.

## QUESTIONS

1. How the right source of supply is important task of purchase officer? Explain.
2. Explain the term "sourcing" with regards to supply of materials.
3. Explain the different stages followed in selecting the right source of supply.
4. Write an essay on 'Buyer-seller relationship'.
5. Explain the term 'vendor rating'. How it is done?
6. Explain the following:
   (*a*) Vendor evaluation
   (*b*) Vendor / supplier rating.
7. Explain the term 'vendor analysis'. How a supplier is selected from the existing regular suppliers?
8. Explain the term "Source development".
9. "A good supplier is an invaluable resource to the organisation requiring its product or service". Explain.
10. What are the characteristics of a "Supplier partnership"? What are the dangers associated with partnership?
11. What are the reasons for conducting a tour of the suppliers facilities ? What areas typically receive more attention? When should a plant visit be made and who should make the visit?

# Performance Measures

## 8.1. INTRODUCTION

Performance measures are very essential for managing an organisation. These play a vital role in the success or failure of an organisation. In order to quantify, it is necessary to create a system of measurement consisting of:

(*i*) a unit of measure, which quantifies the feature which permits evaluation of that feature.

(*ii*) a method or instrument, which can carry out the evaluation and state the finding in terms of the unit of measure (this is known as sensor).

Units of measures for product and process performance are generally expressed in technological terms ; for example:

(*i*) fuel efficiency is measured in terms of distance travelled per volume of fuel,

(*ii*) timeliness of service is expressed in minutes, hours, days etc. required to provide the service.

Units of measure for product deficiency is expressed as a fraction. In this, numerator may be defects per failure, number of field failures or cost of warranty claims. The denominator may be number of units produced, number of units serviced, volume of sales, length or of time in service.

As there may be large number of control subjects, only few vital controls are carried out by supervisors and managers, while some others are carried out by the workforce. Remaining majority of control subjects are handled by non-human beings *e.g.*, automated processes, servo-mechanisms, stable processes etc. Therefore, instruments for measuring performance must be economical and easy to use, besides providing accurate and precise data which may be helpful in taking critical decisions.

It is useful to establish a limited number of control stations for measurement. Each control station should also be responsible for giving feedback of desired control subjects. Control stations are usually located at principal junctures, *e.g.*

(*a*) at changes of jurisdiction,

(*b*) after creation of critical quality,

(*c*) at dominant (vital few) process variables, and

(*d*) before embarking on an irreversible path.

For each control station, it is necessary to define :

(*i*) work to be done,

(*ii*) which control subjects are to be measured,

(*iii*) goals and standards to be met,

(*iv*) procedures to be used,

(*v*) instruments to be used,

(*vi*) data to be recorded, and

(*vii*) the decisions to be made including the responsibility for making each decision.

## 8.2. ACTUAL PERFORMANCE VERSUS GOALS.

Quality goals are required to be set with the aim of controlling the quality targets. The goals are set for a variety of control subjects ranging from those for products, processes, service in departments to that of an entire organisation. The goals should be:

- Legitimate.
- Measurable.
- Attainable.
- Comparable.

For setting the quality goals, various bases are available *e.g.*, engineering studies or norms, competitive market place, and history of previous performance.

A goal can be defined as an achievement of an end–point and is stated in quantitative terms. Goal represent the desired future results / conditions, which organisation strives to achieve. The goals are the relatively long term targets.

### Interpreting the difference between Actual Performance and the Goal

In quality control process, measurements are compared with the goals, and decision is taken whether the difference is significant enough to justify action. The process variations are due to two types of causes : (*a*) random or chance causes, and (*b*) assignable causes (also known as specific or special causes). A process can have random causes, and the process operating without assignable causes of variation is said to be "in a state of statistical control". Random and assignable causes are represented on control charts (discussed in statistical control section of this book). When the actual variation exceeds the control limits, it is a signal that assignable causes have entered the process and the process should be investigated. Variation within the control limits means that only random causes are present. The control charts provide an early warning of problems. Sometimes, the non-conformance are so numerous that it becomes necessary to establish priorities for action, based on economic significance and related parameters.

### Taking Action on the Difference

In the final step of control of process, action is taken to re-store the process to a state of meeting the goal. Action may be taken for : elimination of chronic sources of deficiency, elimination of sporadic sources of deficiency, and continuous process regulation to minimise variation. Sporadic trouble arises due to some adverse changes, and it can be eliminated in two stages. First stage is diagnostic stage, in which adverse change is discovered. In second stage, known as remedial stage, adverse change is removed and status quo is re-stored. This trouble shooting process is carried out in following steps :

(*i*) State the deviation
(*ii*) Specify the deviation
(*iii*) Identify the unique characteristics of deviation
(*iv*) Search for changes
(*v*) Develop possible causes
(*vi*) Test the possible causes against the specification
(*vii*) Verify the cause.

## 8.3. QUALITY MEASURES

Performance rating is the process during which the performance is compared with that of normal (standard) performance.

In mathematical term,

$$\text{Performance Rating} = \frac{\text{Qbserved performance}}{\text{Normal performance}}.$$

Performance measures (rating) in some of the common fields of production and service industries are given hereunder:

### 8.3.1. Quality Measurement in Marketing

Management should have provision for measurement of quality-related activities in marketing, field performance, customer service and other fields. Some examples of quality measurement in various fields are given below :

| ***Subject*** | ***Unit of measurement*** |
|---|---|
| 1. Marketing | (*a*) Percentage of orders cancelled |
| | (*b*) Percentage of successful bidding |
| | (*c*) Number of misprocessed orders |

| | |
|---|---|
| 2. Complaints | (*a*) Total number of complaints |
| | (*b*) Number of complaints per 1000 units of products |
| | (*c*) Number of complaints per crore Rs. of sales |
| | (*d*) Value of material returned |
| | (*e*) Cost of claims paid. |
| 3. Failures | (*a*) Mean Time Between Failures (MTBF). |
| | (*b*) Mean usage between failures. |
| | (*c*) Mean time between repair calls. |
| | (*d*) Failure per 1000 units under warranty. |
| 4. Maintainability | (*a*) Mean Time To Repair (MTTR). |
| | (*b*) Mean downtime. |
| | (*e*) Number of repeated service calls for same complaint. |
| | (*d*) Ratio of maintenance hours to operating hours. |
| | (*e*) Repair cost per unit under warranty |
| 5. Design aspects | (*a*) Cost of poor quality. |
| | (*b*) Number of design changes. |
| | (*c*) Number of waivers to specifications. |
| 6. Reliability | (*a*) Ratio of predicted reliability to actual reliability. |
| | (*b*) Ratio of actual reliability to reliability requirement. |

### 8.3.2. Quality Measurement in Supplier Relations

Following are some of the quality measurement to assess supplier relations:

| ***Subject*** | ***Units of measurement*** |
|---|---|
| 1. Quality of lots | (*a*) Percentage of lots rejected |
| | (*b*) Cost of poor quality |
| | (*c*) Percentage of lots accepts as waiver |
| 2. Business relationship | (*a*) Average number of suppliers per item |
| | (*b*) Percentage of purchase as single source |

| | |
|---|---|
| | (*c*) Percentage of purchases to lowest bidders |
| | (*d*) Average time to secure bids. |
| 3. Supplier relations | (a) Percentage of product samples approved on first programme. submission |
| | (*b*) Percentage of production shipments approved on first submission |
| | (*c*) Average time to resolve problems |
| 4. Adequacy of inventory service | Percentage of stockouts |

## 8.3.3. Performance of Vendors

Performance of vendor (supplier) is evaluated and rated periodically with the objective of monitoring and continuous improvement. This aspect has been discussed in detail in the previous chapter. Here, we are mentioning important vendor rating criteria based on the following characteristics:

1. Timely Delivery.

$$\text{Delivery service index} = \frac{\text{Number of timely deliveries}}{\text{Total number of orders placed}}$$

2. Adherence to Quality

$$\text{Index of quality} = \frac{\text{Percent of good quality items sup plied}}{100}$$

$$= \frac{100 - \text{Percent rejects}}{100}$$

## 8.3.4. Quality Measures in Maintenance

(*i*) $\text{Frequency of break – down} = \frac{\text{Number break–downs}}{\text{Available machine hours}}$

(*ii*) $\text{Maintenance–Cost ratio} = \frac{\text{Total maintenance cost}}{\text{Total annual sales}}$

(*iii*) $\text{Equipment availability ratio} = \frac{\text{Equipment running time}}{\text{Total available time}}$

$$= \frac{\text{MTBF}}{\text{MTBF} + \text{MTTR}}$$

where,

(*a*) MTBF = mean time between failures

$$= \frac{\text{Equipment operating time}}{\text{Number of observed failures}}$$

(*b*) MTTR = mean time to restore (repair)

(*vi*) Achieved Availability $= \frac{MTBF}{MTBF + M}$

where,

M = Mean active maintenance downtime due to both, preventive and corrective maintenance

(*v*) Operational availability $= \frac{\text{MTBF}}{\text{MTBF + MDT}}$

where,

MDT = Managerial down time (This is the downtime due to maintenance, administrative reasons and due to supply)

### 8.3.5. Measures of Productivity

(*i*) General measure of productivity.

$$\text{Productivity} = \frac{\text{Output}}{\text{Input}}$$

(*ii*) Labour productivity

$$= \frac{\text{Production in standard hours}}{\text{Actual man - hours}}$$

(*iii*) Material productivity $= \frac{\text{Material cost}}{\text{Number of units produced}}$

(*iv*) Machine productivity $= \frac{\text{Output in standard hours}}{\text{Actual machine – hours}}$

(*v*) Overall productivity

$$\text{Return of capital employed} = \frac{\text{Profit}}{\text{Capital employed}}$$

### 8.3.6 Financial Ratios

(*i*) Return on operating assets

$$= \frac{\text{Operating profit before interest and taxes}}{\text{Average operating assets}} \times 100$$

(*ii*) Return to ordinary shareholders

$$= \frac{\text{Profit after tax and preference dividends}}{\text{Average equity of ordinary shareholders}} \times 100$$

(*iii*) Net profit margin $= \frac{\text{Operating profit}}{\text{Sales}} \times 100$

(*iv*) Asset turnover = $\frac{\text{Sales}}{\text{Average operating assets}}$

(*v*) Debt / equity ratio = $\frac{\text{Long term debt}}{\text{Long term debt plus equity}} \times 100$

(*vi*) Current ratio = $\frac{\text{Current assets}}{\text{Current liability}}$

(*vii*) Liquid assets ratio = $\frac{\text{Current asset – Stock/inventories}}{\text{Current liability}}$

(*viii*) Stock turnover = $\frac{\text{Costs of goods sold}}{\text{Average stock}}$

### 8.3.7 Other Typical Measurements

| *S.No.* | *Fields* | *Measures* |
|---|---|---|
| 1. | Human Resource | Absenteism, turnover, employee satisfaction index, training hours per employee, number of active teams, number of grievances received and redressed, number of suggestions received and implemented, time lost due to accidents. |
| 2. | Production | Amount of scrap/re-work, defect per million units, machine downtime, number of products returned, cost per unit, inventory turns. |
| 3. | Customers | Number of complaints, number of on–time deliveries, number of parts replaced, customer satisfaction index, time to resolve complaints, mean time to repair. |

## 8.4. OBJECTIVES OF PERFORMANCE MEASURES

Performance measures are helpful in achieving following objectives:

1. To establish baseline measures and indicate trends.
2. To determine as to which processes are required to be improved.
3. To know process gains and losses.
4. To compare goals with actual performance.
5. To provide information for making right decisions.
6. To determine the overall performance of the organisation.

## 8.5. COST OF QUALITY

"Cost of quality" is an important approach to measure and track financial impact of various quality activities. The cost of quality have been discussed in detail in the first chapter under heading "Introduction to Quality Concept" in the section "Quality Cost (Economics of Quality)".

The cost of quality is not merely the resources allocated to the quality function and are not only limited to factory operations, but also extended to support functions. A large amount of cost is on account of poor quality (as discussed in the chapter on "Quality Planning" under the heading "Assessment of Quality").

The trend analysis over a long period of time helps in monitoring the progress of improvement actions. It has generally been observed that in initial stages, share of failure costs in the total cost of quality is significant. Total cost of quality reduces with the passage of time.

## 8.6. PERFORMANCE STRATEGY

Before studying the performance strategy, we must know the meaning of "strategy'. Strategy is a unified, comprehensive and integrated plan that relates to strategic advantages of the firm to the challenges of the environment and that is designed to ensure the basic objectives of the enterprise are achieved through proper execution by the organisation.

Strategic management allows firms to anticipate changing conditions, and provide clear objectives and direction for employees. Strategic quality management has already been discussed in detail in the chapter on "Quality Planning " (Chapter 3).

Strategic quality management is the process of establishing long range quality goals and defining the approach for meeting these goals.

Since the 'Quality Council' has the overall responsibility for the performance measures, it ensures that all the measures are integrated into a total system of measures. In order to develop the system, the quality council obtain necessary informations from all the stake–holders and utilize the core values, goals, mission, and vision statement as well as the objectives as given above. With the help of all these input information, the strategic measurement system is created.

After the strategic measurement system is developed, the functional areas develop their systems by involving their departments and workgroups. Then the responsibilities are assigned and the procedure for continuous improvement is developed.

Quality council meetings should be held every month for monitoring current activities and planning for future. The **monitoring report** is prepared which should include the following:

(*i*) performance measures,

(*ii*) narration on competition, opportunities, and concerning important events, and

(*iii*) system audits.

## 8.7. PERFORMANCE MEASURES OF SERVICE QUALITY

As already explained in the chapter on "Customer Satisfaction", service quality like product quality, is also based on 'fitness for use'. The fitness for use is determined by those features of the service that customer recognises as beneficial to him. Service quality can be controlled through service characteristics. These characteristics are observable and subject to customer evaluation against defined standards of acceptability.

The quality characteristics can be grouped into four categories, namely:

(*i*) Human factors and behavioural characteristics.

(*ii*) Timeliness characteristics.

(*iii*) Service non – conformity characteristics.

(*iv*) Facility related characteristics.

Quality of a service can be broken down into two categories: (*a*) effectiveness, and (*b*) efficiency.

**Effectiveness** deals with meeting the desirable service attributes that are expected by the customer. **Efficiency,** on the other hand, concerns the time required for the service to be rendered.

Service quality characteristics and their measures are mentioned hereunder:

**1. Human Factors and Behavioural Characteristics**

Service quality is influenced by the attitude and behaviour of the service provider and customer. Human factors include intensity and eagerness to help, thoughtfullness, courtesy etc. Some of the traits are inherent, while others can be developed through training. A primary source of customer complaints is discourteous behaviour. On the other hand, the attitude of the customer is largely beyound the control of the service provider.

In view of the above, measurement of attitudes and behavioural characteristics is not simple and well-defined. However, number of customer complaints/ compliment related to behavioural and human traits of persons involved in service can be the measure of service quality.

**2. Timeliness Characteristics**

The timeliness with which a service is performed is critical to customer satisfaction. These can be measured as:

(*i*) Waiting time prior to start of service.

(*ii*) Time required in providing service including post – service time

**3. Service Non–conformity Characteristics**

The goal of the service organisation is to achieve the target level i.e. meeting the customer expectations, and then to exceed it through quality improvement measures.

Non–conformity characteristics deal with deviation from target performance levels. The examples for measuring such characteristics are :

(*i*) Number of errors by bank employees in processing 100 vouchers.

(*ii*) Number of billing errors per 1000 customer.

(*iii*) Number of complaints per hundred service customers.

The target performance level for these examples is zero non–conformities.

**4. Facility Related Characteristics.**

Facilities related characteristics associated with a service and its delivery have an impact on customer satisfaction. These characteristics are not as clearly defined and measurable as service non–conformity characteristics. However, these are more quantifiable than behavioural characteristics.

Some of the examples of measuring these characteristics are as under:

(*i*) Number of complaints regarding;

Waiting area in a hospital, availability of amenities in a hotel etc.

(*ii*) Number of complaints due to uncomfortable bed in a hotel room.

(*iii*) Shabby appearance of reception room and the staff in a hotel.

After going through different types of service characteristics, we can say that in terms of ease of quantification and measurement, these categories can be ranked in the following order:

1. Service non – conformity,
2. Timeliness,
3. Facility related,
4. Human behavioural factors.

Since the success of many service functions is determined by the interaction between the service provider and the customer, measurement and evaluation of service quality is difficult because it is subjective. Another difficulty in measuring the service quality is that significant differences exist between individuals.

## 8.8. PERFORMANCE AFTER USING QUALITY MEASURES

After using quality measures an organisation is expected to be benefitted as under:

1. Improve in quality, productivity, reliability, market share, revenue, profits and growth.
2. It helps in developing a well-documented quality system.
3. Improvement in percent of scrap, rework, and non-conformities.
4. Improvement in production reliability. This can be measured by the number of breakdown per month, percentage of time dedicated to emergencies and percent of downtime per shift.
5. Improvement in product acceptance by customers without inspection, and reduction in claims of non-conforming product or returned product.
6. Timely delivery of products in market.

7. Improvement in gross margin.
8. Maintaining a good public/community relations/image.
9. Improving defence posture in litigation.
10. Reducing incidents that result in liability.
11. Conserving input materials and energy.
12. Improving industry/government relations.
13. Effective decision making.
14. Improved team-work.
15. Improving the internal (workplace) and external environment.
16. Enhanced internal communications.
17. Prevention of pollution due to reduced air, water pollution, and solid waste.

## 8.9. RECOGNITION AND REWARDS

**"Recognition"** is a public acknowlegement of superior performance of specific activities. Recognition can be provided at several levels: — individuals, teams, and business units.

**"Rewards"** are benefits which are conferred for superior performance against goals. These play an important role in inspiring people on quality.

### 8.9.1. Malcolm Baldrige National Quality Award

The Malcolm Baldrige National Quality Award (MBNQA) is an annual award to recognize organisations from U.S. in the field of performance excellence. The award criteria supports a systems approach in maintaining organisation – wide goal alignment and goal – based diagnosis.

The award promotes awareness of the requirements for performance excellence and competitive improvement, sharing of information on performance strategies, and the benefits derived from using these strategies. Out of following **6 categories**, 18 awards may be given each year:

1. Manufacturing.
2. Service.
3. Small business.
4. Health care.
5. Education.
6. Non – profit public, private, and government organisations.

The **award criteria** are built on the following core values:

1. Visionary leadership,
2. Customer,–driven excellence,
3. Organisational and personal learning.

4. Valuing employees and partners,
5. Focus on the future,
6. Managing for innovation,
7. Management by fact,
8. Social responsibility,
9. Focus on results and creating value, and
10. Systems perspective.

Seven categories determine the framework for evaluation. Following table shows the award criteria categories, subcategories, and point values of the "Criteria for Performance Excellence."

**Table: Criteria for Performance Excellence**

| | ***Categories and Items*** | ***Point*** | ***Values*** |
|---|---|---|---|
| 1. | Leadership | | 120 |
| | 1.1. Senior Leadership | 70 | |
| | 1.2. Governance and Societal Responsibilities | 50 | |
| 2. | Strategic Planning | | 85 |
| | 2.1. Strategic Development | 40 | |
| | 2.2. Strategic Deployment | 45 | |
| 3. | Customer and Market Focus | | 85 |
| | 3.1. Voice of Customer | 40 | |
| | 3.2. Customer Engagement | 45 | |
| 4. | Measurement Analysis and Knowledge Management | | 90 |
| | 4.1. Measurement, Analysis and Improvement of Organisational performance | 45 | |
| | 4.2. Management of Information, Knowledge and Information Technology | 45 | |
| **5.** | Workforce Focus | | 85 |
| | 5.1. Workforce Environment | 45 | |
| | 5.2. Workforce Engagement | 40 | |
| **6.** | Process Measurement | | 85 |
| | 6.1. Work Processes | 45 | |
| | 6.2. Operational Effectiveness | 40 | |

| 7. | Results | | 450 |
|---|---|---|---|
| | 7.1. Product and Process Results | 120 | |
| | 7.2. Customer Focussed Results | 85 | |
| | 7.3. Workforce Focussed Results | 85 | |
| | 7.4. Leadership and Governance Results | 80 | |
| | 7.5. Financial and Market Results | 80 | |
| | **Total points** | | **1000** |

## 8.9.2. Rajiv Gandhi National Quality Award (RGNQA)

RGNQA was instituted by the Bureau of Indian Standards ((BIS) in 1991, with a view to encourage Indian manufacturing and service organisations to strive for excellence and giving special recognition to those who are considered to be the leaders of quality movement in India.

This award is intended to drive the products and services to higher levels of quality and equip industry to meet the challenges of the domestic and international markets. This helps Indian Industry to improve the quality.

The award has been designed in line with similar awards like Malcolm Baldrige National Quality Award in U.S., and Deming Prize in Japan.

For this award, the assessment of the applicant, organisation is carried out based on following criteria:

(*i*) Leadership.

(*ii*) Policies, objectives and strategies.

(*iii*) Human Resource management.

(*iv*) Resources.

(*v*) Processes.

(*vi*) Customer focussed results.

(*vii*) Employee's satisfaction.

(*viii*) Impact on environment and safety.

(*ix*) Business results.

## 8.9.3. Ramkrishna Bajaj National Quality Award (RBNQA)

RBNQA is the Indian equivalent of MBNQ and was introduced in 1996. It was named after Ramkrishna Bajaj, whose motto was "Trust in Quality and Business Ethics". This award is based on the 14 business philosophies of Deming Prizes (an award for Japanese companies). Most of these philosophies relate to the psychology and understanding of human behaviour.

The evaluation for this award is done on same criteria as that of MB NQA with the total score of 1000.

In addition to the above 3 awards, following are the other important awards:

4. **Deming Prize.** This is one of the highest award in TQM. Deming prize for any organisation is given to those who have achieved the distinctive performance improvement through application of TQM in a designated year.
5. **CII – EXIM Bank Award.** As the name suggest, this award was jointly installed by CII and EXIM Bank in 1994 to promote business excellence amongst Indian Industries. The award is based on the internationally recognised 'European Foundation for Quality Management' (EFQM) Excellence Model.

## QUESTIONS

1. Write an essay on "Economics of Quality".
2. Explain the term "Quality Cost". Illustrate the different types of Quality Costs.
3. What is 'Quality Loss'? Explain in detail.
4. Write a short note on each of the following:
   (*a*) Prevention cost.
   (*b*) Appraisal detection cost.
5. Explain the term 'cost of poor quality' in detail.
6. How will you measure quality in marketing?
7. How will you measure the quality in supplier relations?
8. Explain the term 'strategic quality management'.
9. Classify different quality characteristics.
10. How will you measure performance?
11. How will you differentiate between actual performance and goal?
12. What performance measures would you recommend for the following organisations:
    (*a*) A large bank.
    (*b*) Health – care facility
    (*c*) A large departmental store.
13. Write short notes on:
    (*a*) Creating a system of performance measurement.
    (*b*) Units of measure for product deficiency.
    (*c*) Actual performance versus goals.
14. How will you measure performance of vendors ? Explain.
15. Explain the following:

(a) Quality measures in maintenance.

(b) Measures of productivity

(c) Financial ratios.

**16.** What are the measures of performance in respect of human resource; production, and customers?

**17.** Mention various objectives of performance measures.

**18.** Explain in details with regard to cost of quality.

**19.** Write an essay on performance strategy

**20.** Explain in detail about the performance measures of service quality.

**21.** Explain in brief on performance measures of service quality with respect to the following:

(a) Human factors and behavioural characteristics

(b) Timeliness characteristics.

(c) Service non–conformity characteristics.

(d) Facility related characteristics.

**22.** Explain in detail about recognition and rewards. Discuss any two important national level quality awards in India.

**23.** Explain in detail about the "Malcoln Baldrige National Quality Award" in detail.

**24.** List benefits in organisational performance after implementing quality measures.

# Quality Gurus (Pioneers) of Total Quality Philosophy

## 9.1. INTRODUCTION

By adopting the learnings from the quality gurus, the Japan which was a largely illiterate, semi-industrialized country in fifties, manufacturing cheap and unreliable copies of western products, has now became a nation with world's highest per capita income and a producer of best quality goods.

Views of quality gurus on quality improvement have already been discussed in the concerned chapter. Now other views of some of the renowned quality gurus are given here :

## 9.2. W. EDWARDS DEMING'S PHILOSOPHY

As discussed in first chapter on "Introduction to Quality concept", Dr. Deming was the first American quality expert to reach Japan in 1947 to teach Japanese managers methodically about quality. His 14 points provide a theory for management to improve quality, productivity, and competitive position. He has authored a number of books as well as 161 scholarly studies".

Deming said that over 85% problems can be solved only by management, as they involve changing the system of operation and are not influenced by the workers. He believed to plan for the long – run and provide a course of action for the short–run.

Deming also believed in the adoption of a total quality programme and emphasized the never ending nature of quality control in the quality improvement process. Such a programme achieves the desired quality goals of improved quality, customer satisfaction, higher productivity, and lower total costs in the long– run.

His approach demands for a total cultural transformation and TQM must become a way of life. Total commitment of the management is necessary, and there is need for management and workers to speak a common language of statistical process control.

Dr. Deming expands the traditional organisational boundaries to include suppliers, customers, investors, employees, the community and the environment. He termed this expanded boundary as the **'extended process'**. According to him, an organisation consists of people, materials, machines, methods, and money. Primary goal of the organisation is to satisfy the consumer. Achieving this primary goal automatically causes realisation of secondary goals i.e reasonable rate of return.

Deming's cycle (PDCA cycle) has already been discussed in chapter 5.

### 9.2.1. Deming's 14 points for Management

As discussed above, as per Deming's view, without management commitment, the adoption and implementation of a total quality system will not succeed, because a major proportion of problems can be solved by management. As per him, it is managers that create the **corporate culture** that enables workers to feel comfortable enough to recommend changes.

**Deming's Fourteen Points for Management**

Deming's points on promoting product or service quality are :

1. ***Be consistant and purposeful*** For continual improving products and services. Aim is to be competitive, to stay in business, to meet long-term needs.
2. ***Adopt new philosophy.*** Commonly accepted delays, mistakes, defective workmanship can no longer be tolerated.
3. ***Stop depending on mass inspection,*** Demand statistical evidence of quality being build into manufacturing and purchasing functions.
4. ***Work to minimise total cost not just initial cost.*** Move towards a single supplier for any one item on a long-term relationship of loyalty and trust.
5. ***Improve the system continually.*** Make better every process for planning, production and service to improve quality, increase productivity and decrease costs.
6. ***Institute modern methods of on-the-job training.*** New skills are required to keep up with changes in material, methods, product design, machinery, techniques and service.
7. ***Set-up new ways of supervising production workers.*** Improvement of quality will automatically improve productivity. Management should initiate action in response to reports of inherited defects, maintenance needs, bad tools, confused operational definitions and other things that lead to poor quality.
8. ***Drive out fear,* so that everyone may work effectively for the company.**
9. People in research, design, sales and production should work as a team to deal effectively with problems of products and service.
10. Eliminate numerical goals, slogans, exhortations (like zero defects).
11. Use statistical methods for continuous improvement of quality and productivity.
12. Abolish performance appraisal and management by objectives.
13. Institute a vigorous programme of education and retraining. Competitive advantage is always rooted knowledge.

14. Push every day to progress the thirteen preceding points and take action to make the total transformation happen.

According to Deming, following are the major obstacles in implementing his philosophy :

1. Preoccupation with short-term profits.
2. Lack of consistency.
3. Reliance on only visible figures.
4. Performance appraisal.
5. Managerial job mobility.

### Reduce Variation

Deming's philosophy can be summarized in just two words: "Reduce variation". These two words are fundamental to the principle of: (*i*) continuous improvement, and (*ii*) to the achievement of consistency, reliability and uniformity. In other words, this " reduce variation" means trust worthiness, competitive position and success.

In implementing Deming's 14 points for management, certain practices of management, which Deming labels as 'deadly diseases or sins', must be eliminated.

He is of the view that a major cause of organisational instability is the short tenure of management. Due to short tenure, continuity is difficult *i.e.*, frequent changes, sabotage, consistency of purpose. To reduce mobility, top management can promote from within, institute job enrichment programmes, and practice job rotation.

## 9.3. JOSEPH M. JURAN'S PHILOSOPHY

Joseph M. Juran founded the Juran Institute which offers consulting and management training in quality. Jurans views on 'quality improvement' and his 'quality trilogy' has already been discussed in chapter 5 on "Continuous Process Improvement".

Dr. Juran has authored many books on the subject of quality planning, control, management and improvement. Like Deming, Juran also visited Japan in the early 1950s to conduct training courses in quality management.

He believed that management should adopt a unified approach to quality. He defined the quality as 'Fitness for Use' (as explained in the chapter 1) which means the focus should be on the needs of the customer.

Juran developed his TQM message around the following ten steps:

1. Create awareness of the need and opportunity for quality improvement.
2. Set goals for continuous improvement.
3. Build an organisation to achieve goals for establishing a quality council, identifying problems, selecting a project, appointing teams and choosing facilitators.

4. Give training to everyone
5. Carry out projects to solve problems
6. Report progress
7. Show recognition
8. Communicate results
9. Keep a record of successes
10. Incorporate annual improvements into the company's regular systems and processes and thereby maintain momentum.

## 9.4. DEMING V/S JURAN

It has been noted that teachings of Deming and Juran, are most of the time complementary, though sometimes are different; but many of their fundamental principles are basically the same. The background of both of them is similar, as they both studied under Schewart, they were both invited to teach the Japanese in the early 1950s, they both are world authorities in the field of quality. Deming in his approach is concerned with education and training, whereas Juran is more concerned with actual implementation. In general, Deming provides the philosophy, whereas Juran provides the specific structure which can help in the materialization of these principles.

**The similarities in the fundamental principles are:**

(*a*) ***The role of top management.*** The main responsibility for guidance towards quality lies with the senior management, as they are mainly responsible for most of the company problems (Juran put these problems as 80%, while Deming's latest revised estimate for management controllable errors to 94%).

(*b*) The importance of the customers.

(*c*) ***The necessity of quality.*** Juran refers to the habit of quality, while Deming to an obsession with quality, in order to satisfy the customer and survive in the competitive world market.

(*d*) The importance of 'continuous improvement'.

(*e*) The need for scientific knowledge.

(*f*) ***Distinction of the causes of problems.*** Deming's special and common causes while Juran's sporadic and chronic causes.

(*g*) Training as an investment for future.

## 9.5. PHILLIP B. CROSBY'S PHILOSOPHY

Phillip B. Crossby founded Philip Crosby Associates in 1979. He listed 4 essentials, also known as absolute of quality management, in chapter 1. His views on quality improvement has been discussed in chapter 5 on "Continuous Process Improvement:.

## 9.6. COMPARISON OF DEMING, JURAN AND CROSBY PHILOSOPHIES

All the three philosophies advocate integration of total quality system with a continual drive for improvement. There are many similarities in these three approaches, some differences also exist. These are compared on main issues as under:

**1. Definition of Quality**

(*a*) **Deming's Definition.** It emphasises use of statistical process control charts.

(*b*) **Juran's Definition.** It emphasises on fitness of a product for its intended use.

(*c*) **Crosby Definition.** It emphasises on conformance to requirements based on customer needs.

Thus, Deming concerns about the quality of process, while Juran and Crossby focuses on customer.

**2. Management Commitment.**

(*a*) **Deming Philosophy**. His 14 points are aimed at management, implying that management's attention is necessary for total quality system.

(*b*) **Juran's Philosophy.** His quality planning, control, and improvement process seeks management support at all levels. He believes in quality improvement by getting managers involved and assigning responsibilities to each.

(*c*) **Crosby Philosophy.** He stresses the importance of management communicating its understanding and commitment. He also focussed on the creation of 'quality culture', which can be attained through management commitment.

Thus, all three philosophies stress the importance of top management commitment.

**3. Strategic Approach.**

(*a*) **Deming Strategy.** It involves top management and creates a structure to promote continuous quality improvement.

(*b*) **Juran Strategy.** A quality council should be constituted, which guides the quality improvement process. It suggests creation of: (*i*) diagnostic arms, for analysing problems and tracking their causes, and (*ii*) steering arms, for directing problem – solving efforts.

**(*c*) Crosby Strategy.** It suggests: (*i*) sequencing the quality improvement approach, and (*ii*) creation of quality improvement teams.

**4. Quality Measurement.**

All the three philosophies view quality as a measurable entity. Often, top management has to be convinced of the effects of good quality in financial Terms. The aim of the quality strategy is to reduce and eliminate scrap and re-work which will reduce the cost of quality. The total cost of quality may be divided into prevention, appraisal, internal failure and external failure costs.

**5. Never – ending Process of Improvement**

All these philosophies believe in the never – ending (continuous) process improvement.

**6. Education and Training.**

(*a*) **Deming Philosophy.** He referred to training of all employees, and need for retraining to keep pace with changing needs of the customer. He also focussed on education in statistical techniques.

(*b*) **Juran Philosophy.** He was of the view that people must be knowledgeable to diagnose defect and determine remedies. However, he did not clearly mentioned for education and training.

(*c*) **Crosby Philosophy.** He stressed on quality education and emphasizes developing a quality culture within the organisation.

**7. Causes of Problems.**

(*a*) **Deming's Approach.** He mentioned two types of causes of problems: (*i*) *special causes* arise due to something unusual *viz*. poor quality of material, improper tool. (*ii*) *common causes* that are inherent to the system *e.g.*, inherent machine variability or worker capability and are controllable only by management.

Deming suggested the use of statistical techniques to identify special causes and common causes through statistical process control and control charts. Variations outside the control limits are attributed to special causes and these are worker controllable. Variations within the control limits are considered as the result of common causes and requires management action.

(*b*) **Juran's Approach.** This is similar to Deming's approach and according to him, special causes create sporadic problems and common causes create chronic problems. He categorizes operator error as being inadvertent, willful, or due to inadequate training or improper technique.

(*c*) **Crosby's Approach.** He promotes the zero defects programme. He also suggested a course of action for error cause removal, whereby employee identify reasons for non–conformity.

**8. Goal Setting**

(*a*) **Deming's Views.** He asserted that arbitrary established numerical goals, and short–term goals without regard to quality are unacceptable.

(*b*) **Juran's Views.** Juran recommends an annual quality improvement programme with specific goals for even short–term periods. He believes that such goals help in measuring the success of the quality projects undertaken in a given year. The goals should be set considering the customers requirements.

(*c*) **Crosby's View.** He believes that employees be asked to set measurable goals even for short – period.

## 9.7. OTHER QUALITY GURU'S PHILOSOPHY

Other famous quality gurus are:

1. Massaki Imai.
2. Genich Taguchi.

The philosophy of these two quality pioneers have already been discussed in chapter 1 on "Introduction to Quality Concept", and chapter 5 on "Continuous Process Improvement".

3. Kaoru Ishikawa.
4. William E. Conway.

Works of these two pioneers have been discussed in chapter 1 on "Introduction to Quality Concept".

5. Walter A. Shewhart.

   Dr. Shewhart developed control chart theory with control limits, assignable and chance causes of variation. In 1931, he had written a book, "Economic Control of Quality of Manufactured Product," which is regarded as a complete and thorough work of the basic principles of quality control. The PDSA cycle was first developed by Shewhart which was then modified by deming and known as PDCA or Deming cycle.

## 9.8. TQM FRAMEWORK

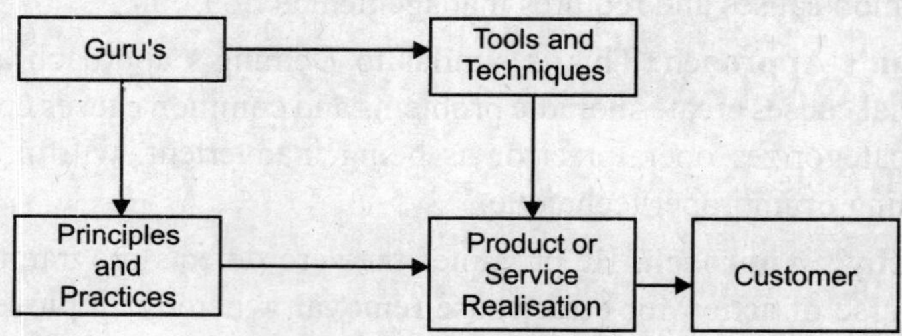


**Fig. 9.1.** TQM Framework

Fig. 9.1. shows the framework for the TQM system. The framework begins with the knowledge provided by quality gurus (pioneers). The main quality gurus are Deming, Juran, Crosby, Massaki Imai, Taguchi, Ishikawa, Conway and Shewhart.

As shown in the figure, these gurus contributed to the development principles and practices and/or the tools and techniques.

**Principles and practices** developed by these gurus are mainly:

1. **People and Relationships:**
   - Leadership,
   - Customer satisfaction,

- Employees involvement, and
- Suppler partnership.

2. **Approach:**
   - Continuous process improvement.
3. **Measure:**
   - Performance measures:

**Important Tools and Techniques** developed/recommended by the quality gurus are:

- Information Technology
- Quality Management Systems.
- Management Tools.
- Quality Function Deployment
- Failure Mode and Effect Analysis.
- Product and Service Liability.
- Process Capability
- Benchmarking.
- Environmental Management Systems.
- Statistical Process Control.
- Total Productive Maintenance.
- Quality by Design.
- Experimental Design

Till now we have discussed about main quality gurus and principles and practices developed by these gurus in the book. Now in the later part of the book, we shall discuss tools and techniques, as suggested by these gurus for the use in product and or service realisation activity.

Feedback from customers ( internal as well as external) or interested parties provide information to continually improve the organisation's systems, product and/or service.

## 9.9. ROLE OF TQM LEADERS

Important roles of TQM leaders are:

1. Senior management must practice the philosophy of "Management by Wandering Around (MBWA)". In this philosophy management must get out of their offices and visit customers, suppliers, departments within the organisation and plants. In this way they learn what is happening with a particular customer, supplier, department, or project. This system of MBWA substantially reduce paper work, and encourage subordinates to write only important message that need to be part of the permanent record.
2. Senior management's role is to make sure that the team's decision is aligned with the quality statements of the organisation. Problem solving and decision making job should be shifted to the lowest appropriate level by delegating authority and responsibility.
3. Senior managers must remain well informed on the topics of quality improvement by reading books and articles, attending seminars, and talking to other TQM leaders.
4. The needed resources must be provided to train employees in the field of TQM tools and techniques, technical requirement of the job, and safety.

5. The senior managers must ensure to celebrate the success of their organisation's quality efforts by personally participating in award and recognition ceremonies. A simple handshake along with a sincere "well done" is a powerful form of recognition.
6. The senior mangers must be engaged in the quality efforts by serving on teams, coaching teams, and teaching seminars. They should lead by demonstration, communicating and reinforcing the quality statements.
7. The senior managers after listening to customers and suppliers through visits, focus groups, and surveys, translate the information into core values and process improvement projects.
8. The senior managers' another important role is communication, through which awareness is created about the importance of TQM.
9. Senior managers should be able to breakdown barriers, remove system roadblocks, minimise resistance to change, and change the culture.

From the above we can visualize that, TQM can be a success only with the involvement of senior managers.

## QUESTIONS

1. Explain Crosby's steps on 'Quality Improvement'.
2. Draw and explain Deming's cycle indicating stages for solving quality problem.
3. Explain the philosophy of 'Imai Kaizen' on Quality Improvement.
4. Describe the views of 'Taguchi' on Quality Improvement.
5. Name any three most important pioneers of total quality movement and explain their views.
6. Explain Deming's quality model and compare it with that of Juran.
7. Mention Deming's 14 points for improved quality, productivity and competitive positions.
8. Discuss Juran's philosophy on quality improvement.
9. Explain the Juran Trilogy.
10. Mention Deming's 14 points for management of quality.
11. Explain the works done by Deming and Juran of TQM and compare their views.
12. Explain the works done by following pioneers on quality:
    (*a*) Ishikawa (*b*) Massaki Imai
    (c) Genichi Taguchi (*d*) Crosby
13. Explain the philosophy of Crosby on quality.
14. Compare the views of Deming, Juran, and Crossby on TQM.
15. Discuss the role of TQM leaders.

# TQM Tools And Techniques – 1

## 10.1. INTRODUCTION

We have already discussed under "TQM Framework" that the knowledge provided by quality gurus (pioneers) have contributed to the development of principles and practices and / or the tools and techniques. A large number of tools and techniques are used for quality improvement. These tools and techniques are being discussed in this chapter and next chapter. So far in the book, we have already discussed certain management Techniques; such as total employee involvement, Deming (PDCA) cycle, and quality control circles. Other Techniques are being discussed hereunder.

These tools and Techniques analyse the quality process and then used for quality improvement:

## 10.2. SEVEN NEW QUALITY MANAGEMENT TOOLS

These are the tools developed for the purpose of 'creative output', and are in fact "art" of scientific thinking and can also be termed as seven management tools. Ishikawa strongly recommended these seven elemental techniques and are widely used for quality improvements.

### 10.2.1 Affinity Diagram

This is an organising tool and is used, when a large amount of information, ideas, opinions have been collected in situations when a process needs defining, or customer requirements need identifying, or when a problem needs solving. The technique organises the collected pieces of information into groupings based on the natural relationships that exist among them. The number of groupings is limited to a maximum of 10 in which ideas are generated by brainstorming. A heading is created for each group, capturing its meaning. The diagram may present the relationship between function and their objective in grading or pairs of two or three functions with goals, pictorially for particular topic.

The technique is useful in reducing an otherwise unmanageable amount of information into a smaller number of homogeneous groups which are much easier to handle independently, prioritise in order of significance (Pareto principle), or allocate to specific project for further study or investigation.

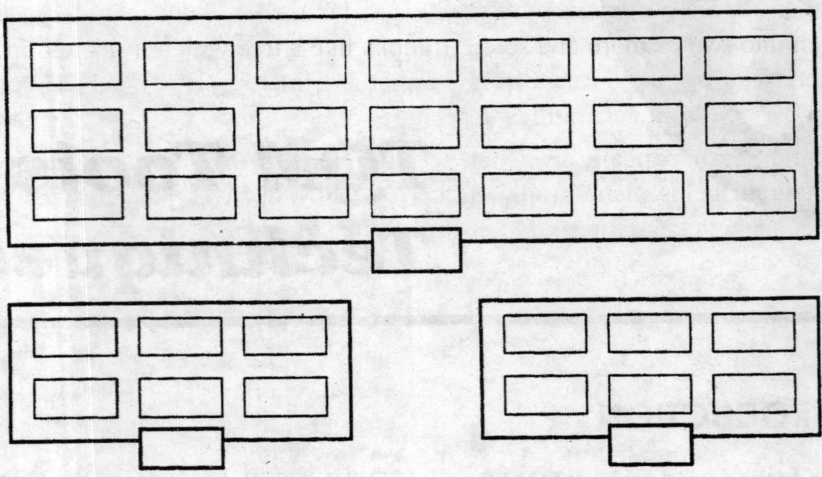

**Fig. 10.1.** Affinity diagram

### 10.2.2 Inter-relationship Diagram (Cause Identification)

These are used to relate complex cause and effect relationships. This diagram explores and displays inter-related factors involved in complex problems. This diagram shows relationships between inter-related factors. (Refer Fig. 10.2).

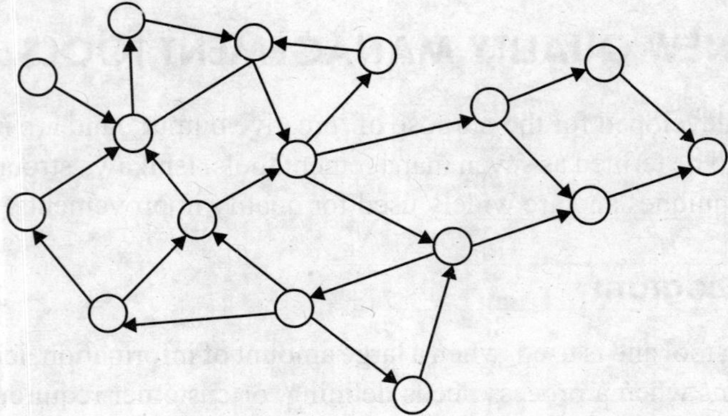

**Fig. 10.2.** Inter-relationship diagram

A relationship diagram allows a team to identify root causes from subjective data, systematically explores cause – and – effect relationships, encourages members to think multi-directionally, and develops team harmony and effectivness.

## 10.2.3. Tree Diagram (Systematic Diagram)

Tree diagram or tree analysis starts with one item that branches into two or more, each one of which further branch into two or more and so on. It looks like a tree with a trunk and multiple branches. It is used to break-down broad categories into finer and finer levels of detail. It helps in moving the thinking step-by-step from generalities to specifics.

This diagram systematically maps out the full range of tasks/methods needed to achieve the goal. This diagram helps planning effectively so that objectives are achieved. This is done by showing the sequencing and inter-relationships so that the resulting actions are error free.

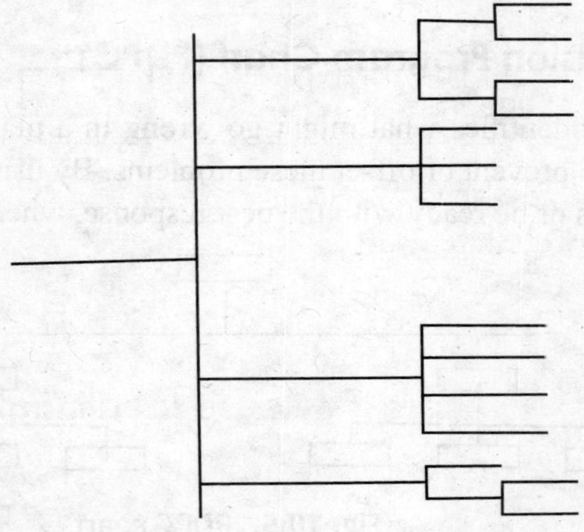

**Fig. 10.3.** Tree diagram

## 10.2.4 Matrix Diagram

These diagrams display the relationship between necessary tasks and people or other tasks often to show responsibility for tasks. These may have L, T, Y, X or C shaped configurations. This helps to clarify. The problems through multi-dimensional thinking.

| | | | | | *A* | | | | *B* | | |
|---|---|---|---|---|---|---|---|---|---|---|---|
| | | 1 | 2 | 3 | 4 | 5 | 6 | 7 | 8 | 9 | 10 |
| | 1.1 | 1.11 | | | | | | | | | |
| 1 | | 1.12 | | | | | | | | | |
| | 1.2 | 1.21 | | | | | | | | | |
| | | 1.22 | | | | | | | | | |
| 2 | 2.1 | 2.11 | | | | | | | | | |
| | | 2.12 | | | | | | | | | |
| | 2.2 | 2.21 | | | | | | | | | |
| | | 2.22 | | | | | | | | | |

**Fig. 10.4.** Matrix diagram

### 10.2.5. Matrix Data Analysis (Prioritization Matrices)

This matrix, also known as the criteria matrix, is used to compare choices relative to criteria like price, ease of use, service and any other desired factor. This tool when used effectively, is of great help for project teams for decision – making. These tools prioritize the issues, tasks, characteristics etc. based on weighted criteria using a combination of tree and matrix diagram.

This requires complex mathematical skills and relies on systematic organisation and presentation of data so that relations can be examined. It shows the strength of the relationship between variables which have been statistically determined.

### 10.2.6. Process Decision Program Chart (PDPC)

This chart systematically identifies what might go wrong in a plan under development. Counter measures are developed to prevent or offset these problems. By using PDPC, one can either revise the plan to avoid problems or be ready with the best response, when a problem occurs.

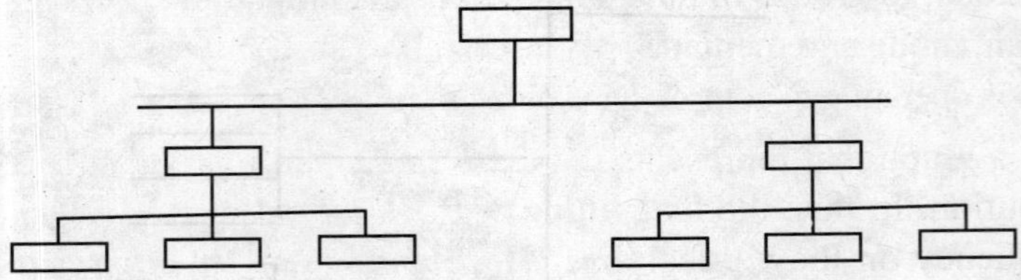

**Fig. 10.5.** PDPC chart

This is a detailed planning purpose tool and helps to select best process to use to obtain the desired results. It not only evaluates existing process, but also looks at alternatives through newly gained knowledge. It is a dynamic approach and PDPC maps out every conceivable event that may occur, when moving from a problem statement to the possible solution.

### 10.2.7. Arrow Diagram (Activity Network Diagram)

This diagram is also a detailed planning purpose tool and is used to plan the most appropriate schedule for any task and to control it effectively during the progress. This is a combination of Gantt chart and PERT/CPM charts.

It allows the project team to schedule a project efficiently. This diagram shows completion times, simultaneous tasks, and critical activity path.

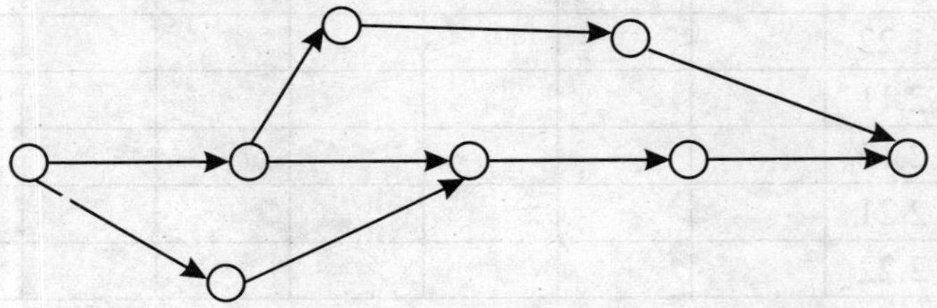

**Fig. 10.6.** Arrow diagram

## 10.3. SEVEN BASIC (TRADITIONAL) TOOLS OF QUALITY

These seven basic technical tools not only controls the process, but also has the capability to improve it. These tools are:

1. Histogram.
2. Pareto Analysis.
3. Scatter diagram.
4. Control charts.
5. Cause and Effect (Fish bone) diagram.
6. Check sheets (data collection)
7. Flow diagram.

### 10.3.1. Histogram

Histograms are graphical representations of the spread or distribution of data. They are also called "frequency distribution". These are used to monitor a process to see, if it consistently meets customer requirements. The information presented in historgrams is represented by a series of rectangles which are proportional to groups of data. Histograms also illustrate the various measures of central tendency, the mean, mode and median. This information can be helpful in understanding the extent to which a process is operating in control. Deviations from normal can help teams to locate root cause (*s*).

Histogram is a graph that represents the class frequencies by vertical adjacent rectangles in a frequency distribution. In this, the magnitude of the class interval is plotted along the horizontal axis and the frequency on the vertical axis. Since each class has lower and upper values, hence two equal vertical lines represent the frequency. Upper of these two lines, representing the class interval, are joined together. Height of rectangle thus obtained are proportional to their frequencies. Histograms are some times called as 'Block diagram'.

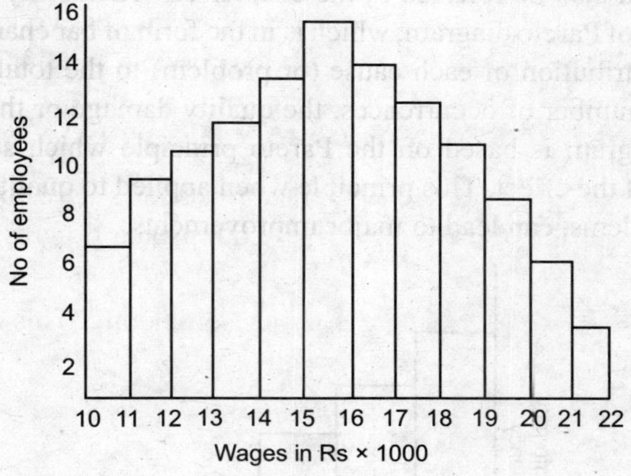


**Fig. 10.7** (a) Histogram

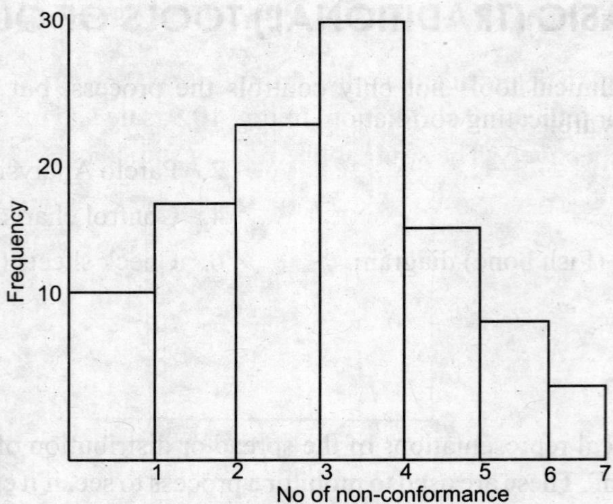


**Fig. 10.7.** (b) Histogram

## 10.3.2. Pareto Analysis/Diagram

### 6. Pareto Analysis

Pareto analysis is a technique for arranging the causes or problems from the most to the least significant. Thus, the most significant problems are identified (Juran has called them as "the vital few") and efforts can be concentrated on those, so as to get maximum benefits with least efforts in minimum time.

Pareto analysis can also be referred in the chapter on "Reliability Improvement". The Pareto analysis takes the help of Pareto diagram, which is in the form of bar chart and displays in decreasing order, the relative contribution of each cause (or problem) to the total. This relative contribution may be based on the number of occurrences, the quality damage or the cost associated with each cause. The Pareto diagram is based on the Pareto principle which states that a few causes are responsible for most of the effect. This principle when applied to quality improvement *i.e.*, solving a few key quality problems, can lead to major improvements.

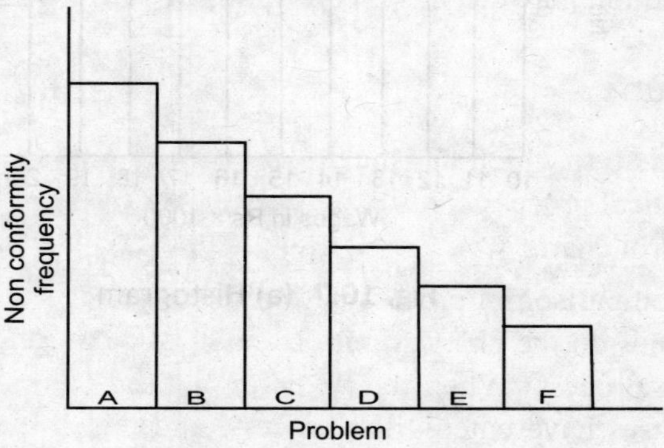


**Fig. 10.8.**

## 10.3.3. Scatter Diagram

A scatter diagram is used to determine if a relationship, exists between two variables. This is a most valuable graphic tool for indicating correlation. In Fig. 10.9, sale and income are plotted on vertical and horizontal scale respectively. The straight line relationship between sales and income is at once apparent.

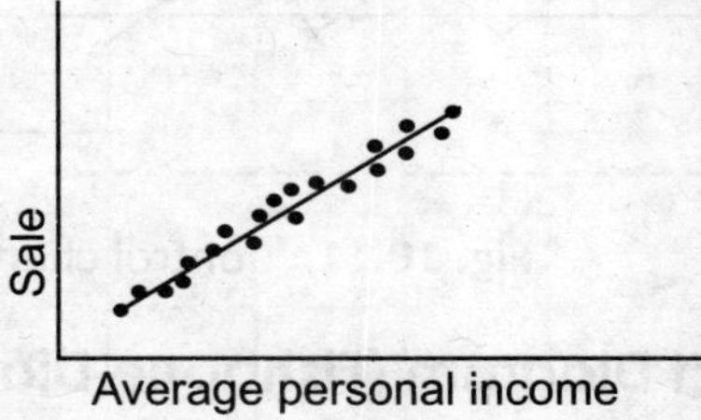


**Fig. 10.9.** Scatter diagram

Based on the relationship indicated in scatter diagram shown in Fig. 10.9, company would forecast average sales based on the average income forecast.

In an another example of speed and averge fuel consumption (mileage), a cause–and–effect relationship can be determined between these two variables by plotting a scatter diagram. Fig. 10.10 shows their relationship.

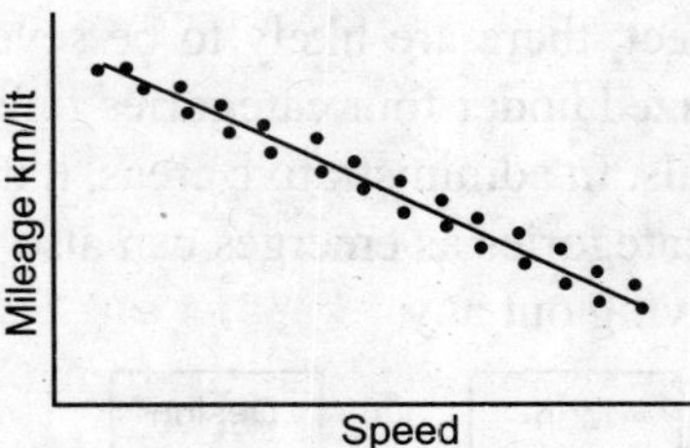


**Fig. 10.10** Scatter diagram

The automotive speed (cause) is controlled and the mileage (effect) is measured. The values of $x$ and $y$ are plotted to know the relationship or correlation between the two variables. In this case, there is a negative correlation between the two variables, because as $x$ increases, $y$ decreases.

## 10.3.4. Control Charts

A control chart is a line chart to which statistically determined limits have been added. Control chart is the main tool of statistical process control, and has been discussed in the chapter on "statistical process control and control charts."

These are graphic comparison of process performance data to be computed 'statistical control limits, drawn as limit lines on the chart. Main objective of a control chart is to detect assignable causes of variation in a process. When the variation exceeds the statistical control limits, it is a signal that special causes have entered the process, and the process should be investigated to identify the causes of excessive variation.

Thus, control chart detects whether there is any change in the characteristics of item, since the start of the product run. It immediately tells about the undesired variations.

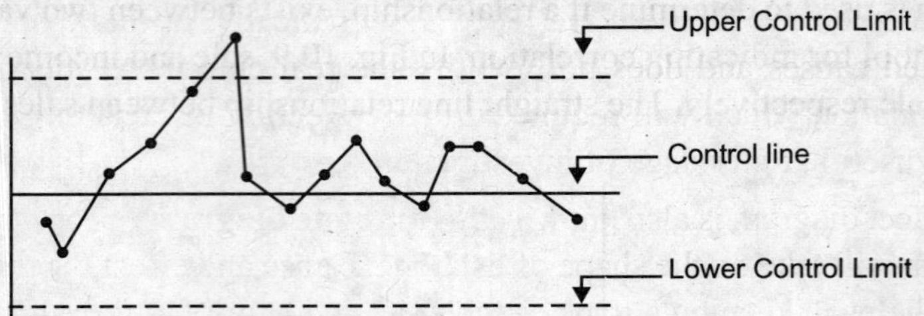


**Fig. 10.11.** Control chart

## 10.3.5. Cause and Effect Diagram (Fishbone Diagram)

This diagram is a useful tool for formulating possible causes of quality problems. This is an effective technique to obtain the leads to improve the understanding of problems experienced in work-area. Any defect or a problem or an effect on quality/performance of a component, a product or service could be due to one or more causes. The "Cause and Effect diagram" was developed by Koran Ishikawa of Japan (hence, also known as Ishikawa Diagram) and represents the relationship between some "effect" (problem) and all the possible "causes" influencing it.

The effect or problem is stated on the right side of the diagram and the major causes are listed on the left. For every effect, there are likely to be several major categories of causes. The major causes might be summarized under four categories referred to as the 4 M's, i.e. Manpower, Machines, Methods and Materials. In administrative areas, it may be 4 P's i.e. Policies, Procedures, People and plant. Other major categories as emerges can also be listed *e.g.*, Design, Customer etc. so that there is no change of leaving out any.

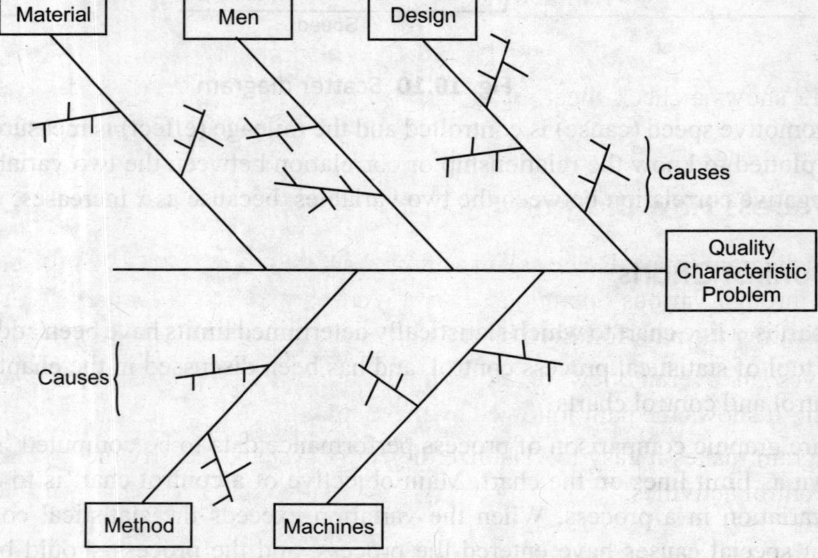


**Fig. 10.12.** Causes and effect diagram

Preparation of the diagram will need a brainstorming session among representatives of different functional groups so that the problem is looked at in its totality. All possible factors suspected to have some influence on the problem are listed systematically. In this emphasis is given only to listing of suspected causes and does not identify the real culprit. As identification shall require a process of elimination which will require further collection of facts or experimentation. Pareto technique will be useful at this stage of investigation.

Cause and Effect diagram is also known as **"Fishbone diagram"** because a well-detailed cause and effect diagram will take on the shape of fishbone. Cause and effect diagram is not an answer to a problem, but it helps in keeping a track of the issue and helps in quickening the process.

## 10.3.6. Check Sheet

A check sheet is a list of check-off items that permit data to be collected, quickly and easily in a simple standardised form for analysing. Cheek sheets should be carefully designed so that data collected are useful and have a clear purpose. In this happenings are recorded, as they occur against a list of possible events. Thus, it is a simplified data collection, and ensures that no items are omitted.

| *Type of defects* | *Tally* | *Sub Total* |
|---|---|---|
| 1. Surface finish | 1111 1111 11 | 12 |
| 2. Cracks | 111 | 3 |
| 3. Dimension | 1111 1111 111 | 13 |
| 4. Welding defect | 1111 1111 | 9 |
| 5. Other miscellaneous defects | 1111 111 | 8 |
| **Grand Total** | | **45** |

**Fig. 10.12.** Check sheet

Fig 10.12 shows a check sheet for monitoring the different types of defects in manufacturing of a product.

## 10.3.7. Process Flow Diagram

Process flow diagram (may also be called as flow diagram) show the flow of the product or service, as it moves through various operations. It is a plan view of a work to a certain scale and a line diagram indicating the path followed by the object under study.

This gives an overall view of an existing or proposed process and is used for making improvement. It shows the path followed by the material, man or equipment.

The diagram makes it easy to visualize the entire system, identify the potential trouble spots, and locate control activities.

## 10.4. OTHER TOOLS AND TECHNIQUES

Other tools and techniques used for TQM in a concern may be:

1. **Block Diagram**

   In block diagram, every activity which is part of process is represented by a block (box) and all blocks are connected by lines representing the interfaces between activities, a macrolevel view of the process is obtained. The diagram traces the paths that any information, necessary actions or materials can take between the original input and the final output of the process.

2. **Bar Charts**

   A bar chart is a graphical representation of discrete groups or categories of data, shown in such a way that clear comparisons can easily be made. The bar chart is normally used to emphasize the variation and uneveness in data. Using this information, further investigation can be made to determine the reasons for occuring the variations. When the data are spread across a continuous range of values, a bar chart is equivalent to a histogram.

3. **Line Graphs**

   A line graph is a simple way of graphical representation data. Direct relationships between the two qualities can be shown easily without looking at the actual data. These can be used to summarize the complex information, to point out trends, fluctuations and relationships, and generally to effectively organize the data and communicate important results. These are drawn to display the relationship between two variables, and are useful in monitoring trends of a variable interest.

4. **Brainstorming**

   Brainstorming is an activity which promotes group participation and teamwork, encourages creative thinking and stimulates the generation of as many ideas as possible within a short period of time. The participants in a brainstorming meeting are invited on the basis of their particular knowledge and experience, and are expected to contributed the topic under discussion.

5. **Break-even Analysis**

   Break-even analysis helps in "cost-volume-profit analysis" or simply known as cost-benefit analysis. For studying the relationship between sales volume, cost (fixed and variable), prices and profits, cost-volume-profit analysis is carried out. Thus, it helps the management to seek the most profitable combinations of costs and volume.

   The break-even analysis not only highlights the areas of economic strength and weaknesses in the firm, but also helps in finding out the ways which can enhance its profitability. With the help of this, analysis management of a production firm can take decisions related to the following:

   (*a*) Volume needed to attain target profit.

   (*b*) Change in price and its effect.

   (*c*) Whether to expand production capacity or not?

(*d*) How much cost can be incurred for improving the quality?

(*e*) Whether to add a new product or drop production of any product?

(*f*) Whether to make or buy?

(*g*) Selection of production machinery so as to get maximum profit for a particular volume of the product.

(*h*) Improving profit performance, by:

  (*i*) increasing the volume of sales, and or

  (*ii*) improving the quality, and or

  (*iii*) increasing the selling prices,

(*i*) When to discard a machine?

(*j*) How much sale should increase, to offset a wage increase or increase in expenses on quality improvement?

As mentioned above, break-even analysis technique helps in cost–benefit analysis which is used for assessing the viability of an action in monetary terms. In this analysis, the cost of taking a particular action are compared to the benefits achievable from the future outcome. It can also be used to compare, in many terms, a number of problem solutions or plans of action.

**6. Quality Circles**

Quality circles have been discussed in detail in the chapter on "Organising (Leadership) for Quality".

**7. Statistical Tools**

Various statistical tools have been described in detail in the chapter on "Statistical Concept" and also on "Statistical Control Charts".

**8. O.C. Curve**

Operating characteristic curve (O.C. Curve) qualifies manufacturer's (producer's) risk and consumer's (purchaser's) risk. This is a graph of the percentage defective in a lot versus the probability that the sampling plan will accept a lot.

O.C. curve have been discussed in the chapter on "Acceptance Sampling and O.C. Curves".

**9. Risk Analysis**

The purpose of risk analysis is to identify and qualify all risks which could hamper the quality improvement effort. Appropriate risk management can control and possibly eliminate each risk. Risk analysis alongwith risk management,can reduce costs and effort, can assess potentially damaging circumstances and control any slippage in the project plan. Main element of risk analysis are as follows :

1. Identify and list potential areas of risk.
2. Quantify the risks.
3. Develop contigency plans
4. Monitor and review the risks

**10. Kaizen**

*Kaizen* means gradual unending improvement, doing little things, better settings and achieving higher standards. Following this strategy Japanese, during the past three decades, improved productivity, quality and flexibility and emerged as a leader of world market. Now-a-days Kaizen philosophy is being extended to such fields as labour managements, relations, marketing practices and supplier relations. Middle managers, supervisors and workers are also actively involved.

*Kaizen* is the process oriented rather than individual task-oriented, where most emphasis is placed on individual performances and rewards.

**Salient features** of Kaizen philosophy :

(*i*) It has a long term and long lasting but undramatic effect.,

(*ii*) Small steps of improvements.

(*iii*) Continuous process resulting in gradual change.

(*iv*) It involves everybody.

(*v*) Its approach is collective and system-oriented.

(*vi*) It requires little investment but great efforts to maintain it.

This Kaizen concept is based on Deming's P-D-C-A cycle.

**11. Poka Yoke (Fool-Proofing)**

*Poka-Yoke* is a Japanese word which means "to avoid unintentional errors". The basic philosophy behind Poka Yoke is that human beings are liable to commit error unknowingly during any operation, they perform. If there is a system which prevents them from committing the error, the mistake can be eliminated. Poka Yoke aims at the total elimination of the possibility of human error. Thus, Poka Yoke is an effective method of achieving zero defect objective.

Thus *Poka Yoke* is designing the work process to eliminate human mistakes. Fool-proofing create devices that can discover defectives/disorders. The process of fool proofing is standardised to ensure that stable quality can be assured. Fool-proofing can be achieved by following ways:

(*i*) by designing of the machines and tools so as to make human error impossible,

(*ii*) by providing redundancy,

(*iii*) by magnifying normal human muscle strength and senses through programmed indexing of fixtures, optical magnification, viewing through closed-circuit television, simultaneous signals to multiple senses etc.

**Some of the commonly used methods for fool-proofing are :**

1. If any step is missed during production process, the device does not allow goods to be mounted to jigs or the machine does not start processing.
2. If a disorder is found in goods, the device does not allow the machine to start processing.
3. The disorder that has occurred in preceding process, is examined at the next process, the device will stop defectives.

Thus, in the Pokayoke, emphasis is placed on preventing defects, during the production process instead of correcting defects after the item is produced.

Objective of the fool-proofing can be accomplished by following principles:

(*i*) Eliminate the possibility of error.
(*ii*) Substituting a more reliable process.
(*iii*) Making the work easier to perform.
(*iv*) Detecting the error before further processing.
(*v*) Minimizing the effect of the error.

**12. Kanban System**

The word *Kanban* means a signboard of a store or shop, but here, it means any small sign displayed in front of a worker. *Kanban* has two functions:

(*i*) To contain information that serves as a work order which gives information that about what, how much, when, by what means to produce and how to transport it; and
(*ii*) To move with actual material.

Since material and Kanban moves together no overproduction will occur, control of material and production becomes easier. For implementing Kanban following rules are followed :

(*i*) Do not send defective products to subsequent process.
(*ii*) Subsequent process comes to withdraw only what is needed. The is known as the "path system of demand".
(*iii*) Produce only the exact quantity withdrawn by the subsequent process.
(*iv*) Equalise production.
(*v*) Stabilise and rationalise the process.

In this system chain of withdrawal and production is continuous from the end product to the beginning of the process.

**13. "5-S" (The Principles of House-keeping)**

The upkeep of workplace is of most important, as it helps in quality and productivity improvement. It has been proved that the first step towards quality improvement is workplace utilisation. The Japanese have developed five simple words as a directive for achieving workplace utilisation. The five words starting from letter "S" are :

1. **SEIRI (Sort)-Proper Arrangement:**

   "Seiri" means sort out unnecessary items. Unwanted things at workplace occupy precious space and create confusion and obstacle to working.

2. **SEITON (Set)-Orderliness:** The word "Seiton" means a place for everything in its place. Everything should be kept in a pre-determined place and maintained so that it need not to be searched, whenever it is required by any body.

3. **SEIKETSU (Sound)-Cleanliness :** In the Japanese world "Seiketsu" means prevent problems by keeping things clean. It is important to keep the work-area very clean with no oil spots, burns, dirt or dust. This will provide a pleasant working environment and result in quality products.
4. **SEISO (Shine)-Clean up:** "Seiso" means after work cleaning up and maintenance. To have consistent quality output, it is important to clean the machine and workplace and to maintain the machine by carrying out routine checks like lubrication, check-ups etc.
5. **SHITSUKE (Self Discipline).** The word "skitsuke" means maintaining good habits like following work instructions/standards, safety precautions, punctuality etc., to achieve consistent desired quality of products and good work culture.

**14. Just-in-time (JIT) Philosophy**

Just-in-time is not just an inventory reduction programme or **kanban**, or material requirement planning, or a production control technique. It is a corportate strategic philosophy and aims at elimination of waste. It is based on the following factors :

1. Unnecessary complexity in the design of products should be removed for producing it at least cost.
2. Plant layout should be changed to eliminate or shorten material movement and reduce time-loss.
3. Provide incentives to workers to tap their knowledge to develop methods of eliminating waste of all forms.
4. People should be accountable for accuracy and institute programmes to measure it.
5. Reduce paperwork. Use of on-line, real-time data update and retrieval and interaction decision-making is important.
6. Scrap should be completely avoided, as scrap is more costly than mere material.
7. Reduce inventories by eliminating large queues and many kinds of safety stocks. When ordering purchase of parts from vendors, negotiate prices based on long term commitments and then schedule frequent releases to support the flow of production with minimal inventory.
8. In order to strive for continuous improvement, set goals and when they are achieved, set them higher.

JIT means a structural approach in a manufacturing organisation focussed on improving timeliness, quality, productivity and flexibility utilising various methods of work simplification and waste elimination. The company following the JIT philosophy want to do work systematically, remove excess work, eliminate waste, un-evenness and unreasonableness and thereby raise their productivity.

JIT concept when applied, results in smaller set-up costs which justifies smaller lot sizes and provide greater flexibility for changeovers from one product to another. Companies adopting JIT concept found improvement in productivity, reducing set-up lime, reducing inventory, improving quality, saving space and reducing lead times. Reduction in economical batch sizes lead to reduction in-process inventory. This leads to productivity improvement in the following way :

- Smaller lot size inventories
- Smaller buffer inventories
- Less indirect cost of inventories
- Less space for inventories
- Less equipment to handle inventories
- Less inventing accounting
- Less physical inventory control effort
- Less scrap
- Less direct labour wasted on re-work.
- Reduction in delays and scrap also improve market response.
- Because of speedy changeover, reduces production lead times, better delivery dates can be promised, as the product mix and quantities can be changed quickly as demand and forecasts of demand change.

For reduction in in-process inventories use of Kanban is very helpful.

**JIT Purchasing**

JIT purchasing emphasises on supplying materials just in time for use on factory floor, equally important are the close relationships with suppliers on long-term basis, who are geographically close for frequent deliveries of small and exact quantities. For the success of JIT, co-operation from the company's vendors is essential. In this concept, vendors are virtually an extension of the company. JIT vendors have to deliver goods to production line at the required time ; which may be quite frequent – say every 3 or 4 hours. In view of this, JIT purchase agreements need to be simple, specifying price, specifications, and an overall quantity to be delivered in accordance with long-term production schedules. The specifications are focused on product performance rather than being highly detailed.

The objective of this system alongwith Kanban is to have right number of parts or components at the right place at the right time.

**JIT Production System**

In this concept, factory produces the required goods only at the times, when they are needed in the quantity that is needed, and in this situation, the inventory of the finished goods and work in progress would be almost zero. If we make raw material, suppliers also agree to deliver their goods only at a time in quantities we need them, then we are almost eliminating raw materials as well. In such a situation, we shall have near zero inventories.

In this system, workers go to the preceding process to withdraw the required parts or components for their operations using the Kanban system. If there are fluctuations in the rates of which these materials are withdrawn, then the preceding process must hold buffer in-process inventories to give off-the self-service. This require minimising production fluctuations on the final assembly line by scheduling small lots of individual models.

In JIT production processes are so designed that it need less specialisation of workers, and the physical layout is so arranged that a worker can operate two or three different machines for providing flexibility in processes. The organisation of multi-functional workers have following benefits :

(*i*) A decrease in the number of workers required, resulting in increase in productivity.

(*ii*) Increased worker satisfaction because of more broadly defined gobs.

**JIT Implementation Methods**

(*i*) **Autonomation.** This means "autonomous defects control" or worker controlled quality control. Although JIT systems control production quantities, the production flow would be interrupted, if the items delivered were defective. The **autonomation system** is designed to ensure that theoretically 100 percent good units flow to subsequent operations.

2. **Self-Discipline.** For the success of JIT systems, positive human relations is most essential. Here, each worker is his own boss, as he produces and checks his own work and ensures zero defectives in his output that is sent to the next process in line.
3. **Waste and its Elimination.** Anything other than the minimum amount of plant, material, parts, energy, space, and people's time which are absolutely essential to add value to the product or service, is waste. Cost reduction can be achieved through elimination of wasteful operations. There are many types of wastes which needs elimination are : storage, material handling, set-up time, inspection, expediting, machine breakdowns, paperwork, over-production, queuing (or waiting), unnecessary stock, idle time, idle cash, motion without work, talent misuse etc. All these add cost, without adding value.
4. **Good House-keeping.** Workplace should be organised with a purpose and to attain unidirectional flow of process. "5-S" principles, as discussed earlier should be followed.
5. **PokaYoke (Fool proofing):** As discussed earlier PokaYoke is designing the work process to eliminate human mistakes.

## 10.5 SIX – SIGMA (6 σ)

Six-sigma concept have already been discussed in chapter 2 under heading "TQM Concept' in section 'Right First Time or Zero Defect'.

The term sigma (σ) is a Greek alphabet letter and also known as standard deviation in statistics and has been used to define a curve known as 'normal distribution curve'. Most of the quality characteristics vary and happen to follow a normal distribution so long the manufacturing process remains stable. All the quality parameters, in the six-sigma quality system have been named as characteristics.

Quality levels with respect to 1 σ , 2 σ, 3 σ, 4 σ, 5 σ, and 6 σ, as represented by the area under normal distribution curve indicate defectives, as shown below for a population of 1 million:

| Sigma quality level | Parts per million (ppm) without shift | | Parts per million with shift of 1.5σ | |
|---|---|---|---|---|
| | Percent conformance | Defective ppm | Percent conformance | Defective ppm |
| ± 1. Sigma | 88.27 | 317300 | 30.23 | 697700 |
| ± 2. Sigma | 95.45 | 45500 | 69.13 | 308700 |
| ± 3 Sigma | 99.73 | 2700 | 93.32 | 66810 |
| ± 4. Sigma | 99.9937 | 63 | 99.3790 | 6210 |
| ± 5. Sigma | 99.999943 | 0.57 | 99.97670 | 233 |
| ± 6. Sigma | 99.9999998 | 0.002 | 99.999660 | 3.4 |

**Note.** This shows that when there is no shift *i.e.* with a centered normal distribution between ± 6 Sigma limits, only two parts per billion fail to meet the specification target. With 1.5 σ shift 3.4. ppm fail to meet specifications.

Six – Sigma concept is usually applicable, where objective of the firm is 'Right First Time or 'Zero Defect'.

## Methodology

Six – Sigma concept is applied in following phases:

1. **Define Phase.** In the define phase, customer needs are translated to specific attributes which are essential for meeting such needs. They may be essential (critical) from quality, delivery, or cost considerations. Identification of these attributes will create a framework for six – sigma study.
2. **Measure Phase.** This phase consists of identifying matrices for process performance. This includes the establishment of baseline levels. Key process input and output variables are also identified. In this phase, it must be ensured that the measurement system itself is stable. Such a system should have gauge system, and benchmark measures of process capability *e.g.*, defects per unit of product, non-performing parts per million, proportion of final product that has no defects.
3. **Analyze Phase.** In this phase, the objective is to determine which of the multitude of factors affects the output variable (*s*) significantly, through analysis of collected data. Tools used for this purpose may be graphical tools, pareto chart to identify vital few from the trivial many, a cause – and – effect diagram etc.
4. **Improve Phase.** This phase consists of identifying the significant factors to optimise the performance measure chosen.
5. **Control Phase.** This phase deals with the methods to sustain the gains identified in the preceding improve phase. Statistical process control using control charts are commonly used methods (tools). Process capability measures are also helpful in this control phase.

## QUESTIONS

1. Write short notes on:
   (*a*) Zero Defect (*b*) Ten Mantras for TQM
   (*c*) Pareto Analysis (*d*) Kaizen
2. Explain the different types of tools and techniques for TQM.
3. Explain the Cause and Effect Diagram in detail.
4. Explain seven new quality improvement tools.
5. Write short notes on:
   (*a*) PokaYoke (Fool-proofing) (*b*) Kanban system
   (*c*) "5-S"-the principles of housekeeping.
6. What is Just-in-time philosophy? Explain it in detail. Discuss JIT purchasing, production system, and its implementation methods.
7. Construct a flow diagram for the manufacture of product or providing a service.
8. Design a checksheet for the maintenance of your bicycle.
9. Write short notes on:
   (*a*) '5 – S' Compain (*b*) Fishbone diagram
10. Name seven new management tools and explain any 4 in detail.
11. Explain the following in brief:
    (*a*) Tree diagram (*b*) Arrow (network) diagram
    (*c*) Affinity diagram
12. Name seven traditional tools of quality. Explain any three of them in detail.
13. Write short notes on:
    (*a*) Pareto analysis (*b*) Scatter diagram
    (*c*) Cause and effect diagram (*d*) Control charts
14. Explain the following in brief:
    (*a*) O.C. Curve (*b*) Brainstorming
    (*c*) Bar charts (*d*) Kaizen
15. Write short notes on:
    (*a*) Poka Yoke (b) Kanban
    (c) Break – even analysis
16. Explain Six – Sigma Concept. Discuss its methodology for a product.

# TQM Tools And Techniques – 2

## 11.1. BENCHMARKING

Benchmarking can be defined as a systematic method by which an organization can measure itself against the best industry practices. In this, the organization strive to be better than the best competitor. In other words, benchmarking is the practice of identifying best practices in industry and thereby setting goals to compete them. Since companies can not afford to stagnate, this guarantees a loss of market to the competition. Specific steps for benchmarking vary from company to company, but the fundamental approach is the same.

The essence of benchmarking is the process of borrowing ideas and adapting them to gain competitive ideas. Thus, it is a tool for continuous improvement. This tool is used extensively by both, manufacturing and service organizations. The benchmarking stipulates that quality goals/targets and objectives be based on competitive products.

Benchmarking is, therefore, defined as the systematic search for best practices, innovative ideas, and highly effective operating procedures. Benchmarking, the experience of others and adapt it.

Benchmarking has two main elements. First element is measuring the performance. The performance of best – in class are the target benchmark. In second part, managers are required to understand why their performance is less than the best. These managers are then required to develop a thorough and in depth knowledge of both the processes (own process as well as best – in class process). This will enable them to make efforts to improve their performance and meet the goal.

### 11.1.1 Reasons for Benchmarking

For critical business activities, organisations must continue to innovate as well as follow best – in – class practices of competitors. For this purpose, organisations must constantly scan the external environment and use the important informations obtained for improving the process. In addition, benchmarking organisation should locate the technological breakthroughs and adopt at an earliest.

As discussed earlier, benchmarking is a powerful tool to achieve business and competitive objectives, when used for the right reasons and aligned with firm's stralegy . It should be remembered that it is simply one tool which help organisation to develop its strengths and reduce weaknesses.

Traditionally, next year's goals/targets are set by extrapolating from last years performance, while benchmarking allows targets to be set objectively on external information obtained.

Since benchmarking involves initiation and adaptation, it is time and cost effective, because it provide, a working model of an improved process, which reduces some of the planning, testing and prototype efforts.

### 11.1.2. Benchmarking Process

Organisations for benchmarking, adapt the process which is best fit for their own needs and culture. Following steps are required for benchmarking process, however, they may vary from organisation to organisation:

1. Decide what is to be benchmarked.
2. Understand current performance.
3. Study others process.
4. Develop the benchmarking plan.
5. Analyse and learn from the data.
6. Use and integrate the findings.
7. Take action and continue improvement.

In should be remembered that organisations must ensure that business ethics are maintained in obtaining the data and avoid copying the process blindly. Benchmarking is a source of ideas from outside the organisation and can be adapted to any business or production process.

## 11.2. QUALITY FUNCTION DEPLOYMENT (Q.F.D.)

Quality function deployment (QFD) is a planning tool that focuses on product design, engineering, and production and provides in-depth evaluation of a product. By correctly implementing QFD organisation can improve engineering knowledge, productivity and quality. It reduces cost, product development time and engineering changes. QFD is a team-based management tool in which customer expectations are used to drive the product development process. Conflicting characteristics or requirements are identified early and resolved before production.

Quality function deployment is defined as a system for translating consumer requirements into appropriate company requirements at every stage, from research, through product design and development, to manufacture, distribution, installation and marketing, sales and services.

Thus, Quality Function Deployment (QFD) is a process which brings together the essential elements and crucial characteristics of the various phases in the lifecycle of a product, from its conception through design, development, manufacture, distribution and use. It encourages teamwork between marketing people, design engineers and manufacturing staff.

By recognising the inter-relationship between the engineering properties of the product and the customer's requirements, appropriate actions can be taken at every stage of the product's development, so that the customer needs are anticipated, prioritized and effectively incorporated into the product.

The products that only satisfy the basic needs of performance and specification, but miss out on additional desirable or 'excitement' features available elsewhere, will probably cause the intending purchaser to select the competitor's product.

Therefore, the management of QFD ensures that vital customers satisfaction and excitement attributes are recognized and developed, so that the company can achieve a competitive edge. QFD is used as a planning tool to fulfill the customer requirement/expectations to achieve product design, engineering, production and a methodology for in depth evaluation of a product.

QFD when implemented can improve knowledge, productivity and quality, in addition, this also reduces cost and product development time.

QFD is employed to translate customer expectations, in terms of engineering and technical characteristics that can be deployed through:

(*i*) Product planning.

(*ii*) Part development.

(*iii*) Process panning.

(*iv*) Production planning,

(*v*) Service.

### 11.2.1. QFD Team

Quality function deployment is a team–based management tool in which customer expectations are used to drive the product development. Conflicting characteristics or requirements are identified early in the QFD process and need to be resolved before production.

QFD teams are of two types: (*i*) designing a new product, (*ii*) improving on existing product. Teams are composed of members from marketing, design, quality finance and production. This team modifies the QFD process by utilizing their full potential and inter–team communication. Time spent by the team is an essential resource in getting the QFD project done on schedule. By using inter–communication to its fullest extent, unforeseen problems are removed so that the project runs smoothly.

Team meetings are held under the directions of the team leader, who ensure that the meetings are conducted in most efficient manner and that the members are kept informed about the QFD process. Team leader is also required to keep the team focussed on quality improvement goals/ target.

### 11.2.2. Benefits of QFD

Benefits of QFD can be summarized as under:

1. Reduced product development time.
2. Improved customer satisfaction.
3. Improved quality.
4. Improved company performance.
5. Reduced cost in design and manufacture.
6. Reduced design changes/problems.
7. Improved product reliability.
8. Reduced planning time.
9. Improved productivity.
10. Improved communication.
11. Reduced warranty claims.
12. Improved documentation.
13. Improved marketing opportunities.
14. Improved profitability.

### 11.2.3. QFD Process

Under QFD, customer information is obtained and presented as a series of charts cascading from concept of manufacturing detail. Because of its shape, the drawing is known as the "**house of quality**". In this, every person downstream is regarded as a customer, the last operation is performed in a manner that satisfies the end – user. Everything upstream is done so that the next downstream activity can be undertaken correctly. The QFD procedure is undertaken by a multi – disciplinary team, therefore, it is necessary to break the protective vertical communication lines and consensus can be achieved.

Following procedure is carried out in QFD:

1. As a first step, survey both the expressed and latent quality demands of customer, i.e, customer requirements.
2. Place these customer requirements in quality deployment chart as **WHAT'S.**
3. Find out the quality characteristics which will affect these customer requirements.
4. Place these quality characteristics as **HOW's** in quality deployment chart.
5. Fill up relationship matrix that correlates **WHAT's** and **HOW's** with appropriate symbols given in relationship matrix.
6. Fill up customer importance rating.
7. If possible, try to evaluate customer competitive assessment and fill up the house with the same information.

8. To have better information, fill up the roof with appropriate symbols given in correlation matrix to correlate HOW's among themselves.
9. Fill up present values of preliminary target. For this, some experimentation may be required.
10. Decide final target values that are to be achieved after QFD. Place these final values in the house.
11. If required, next phase is started, in which:
    (*a*) Transfer vital HOW's of I-phase as new WHATS .
    (*b*) Write down new HOW's.
    (*c*) Repeat the procedure as in I-phase.
12. Concentrate on vital HOW's of both the phases.
13. Work out for improved design methods for these vital HOW's to obtain "customer requirements integrated into product design to obtain quality product".

## 11.2.4. House of Quality

As discussed above, primary tool used in QFD is the 'house of quality'.

The house of quality translates the voice of the customer into design requirements that meet specific target values and matches those against how an organization will meet those requirements. Many managers and engineers consider the house of quality to be the primary chart in quality planning.

The structure of QFD can be thought of as a framework of a house, as shown in Fig. 11.1

The parts of the house of quality are described as follows :

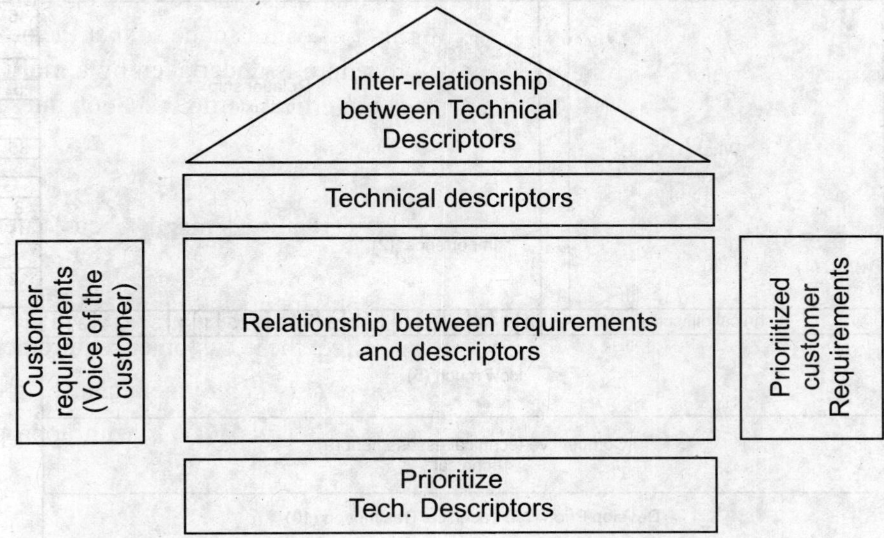


**Fig. 11.1.** House of quality

The exterior walls on the left side is a listing of the voice of customer, or what the customer expects in the product on the right side are the prioritized customer requirements, or planning matrix listed are items, such as customer benchmarking customer importance rating, target value, scale up factor and sales point.

The ceiling or second floor of the house contains the technical descriptors. Consistently of the product is provided through engineering characteristics, design constraints and parameters.

The interior walls of the house are the relationship between customer requirement and technical descriptors. Customer expectations (customer requirement) are translated into engineering characteristics (technical descriptors).

The roof of the house is the inter-relationship between technical descriptors items, such as the technical benchmarking degree of technical difficulty and target value are listed.

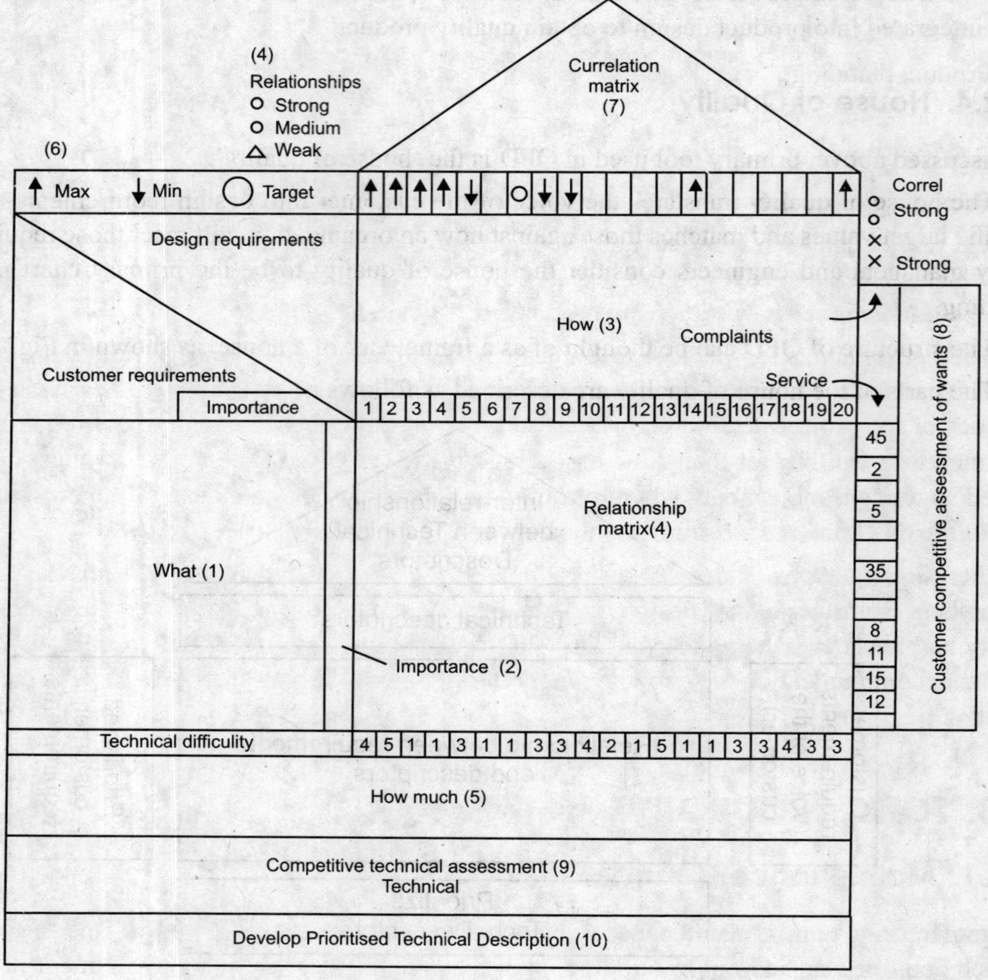


**Fig. 11.2.** Elements of house of quality

House of quality, as shown in Fig. 11.2., has the following elements:

1. What customer wants (Requirements)?
2. Rank (relative importance) of customer wants?
3. How these wants can be met out?
4. Relationship between what and how?
5. How much these wants can be met out?
6. Target values of customer wants.
7. Inter-relationship (technical)
8. Competition from other existing product (Rating).
9. Compare with benchmark
10. Develop privatised technical description.

Further, the QFD process can be split in four major phases *i.e.*:

(*i*) Product planning
(*ii*) Part development
(*iii*) process planning
(*v*) Production planning

On further analysis, product is developed on, the basis of customer and design requirements which are orthogonally and inter-related. So, design is inter-related to quality, then to process operations: process operations to production requirements.

When an organization decides to implement QFD, the projects manager and team members need to be able to commit a significant amount of time to it, especially in the early stages. The priorities of the project need to be defined and told to all departments within the organization so team members can budget their time accordingly. Also, the scope of the project must be clearly defined so that questions about why the team was formed do not arise. One of the most important tools in the QFD process is communication.

There are two types of teams: New product or improving an existing one. Teams are composed of members from marketing, design, quality, finance and production. The existing product team usually has fewer members, because the QFD process will only need to be modified. Time and inter-team communication are two very important things that each team must utilize to their fullest potential.

## 11.3. TOTAL PRODUCTIVE MAINTENANCE (TPM).

### 11.3.1. Maintenance Concept

In manufacturing plants, maintenance (which is also used for reliability improvement) consists of all such activities carried out to building, services, machineries, tools and equipment in order to ensure that these are kept serviceable at all times with acceptable levels of operational efficiency.

This avoids production hold-ups, interruptions or loss of their individual standard efficiency of operations. Increased availability of well-maintained plants should be matter of considerable importance, as it directly affects plant capacity, productivity and profitability.

Maintenance is carried out to retain an item in, or re-store it to an acceptable standard of performance. The function of maintenance department is to keep the facilities of the organisation in an optimum operating conditions so that the intended functions are performed satisfactorily. The aim of maintenance is to reduce the frequency and severity of failures so as to ensure the availability and efficiency of the existing plant, equipment and buildings at an optimum level.

In order to make the maintenance function more effective than other departments, such as design, engineering, purchasing, finance, R&D, and production be also involved. This concept of involving other departments for maintenance is given name as 'terotechnology'. It is concerned with the specifications and design for reliability and maintainability of plant, equipment, building with their installation and commissioning, modification and replacement, alongwith the feedback of informations on all these aspects.

Both the Maintenance system and Operation system are the subsystems of Production system, and work with the production equipment. When an equipment is used, its different components are subjected to stresses, which causes wear and deterioration. This affects the condition and functioning of the component and after some time, it leads to an unacceptable functioning, and the component requires the repair or replacement so as to re-store it to the acceptable condition.

Therefore, the term "maintenance" can be defined as :

"All activities necessary to keep an equipment in or re-store it to a specified condition."

## Preventive Maintenance

Preventive maintenance is sometimes termed as "planned maintenance" or "scheduled maintenance" or "systematic plant maintenance" etc. It is an extremely important function for the reduction of maintenance cost and to keep the good operational condition of equipment and hence, increases the reliability. Preventive maintenance aims to locate the sources of trouble and to remove them before the breakdown occurs. Thus, it is based on the ideas "prevention is better than cure". Scheduled maintenance is always economical than unscheduled maintenance, as we all know that "a stitch in time saves nine."

Preventive Maintenance is defined as a maintenance activity conducted on a machine as per laid down schedule or frequency by making necessary or need-based re-placement and/or re-conditioning of component (*s*) within the pre-fixed time period of the said work in order to reduce and avert breakdown (*s*).

Best safeguard against costly breakdown is to inspect, lubricate and check up the equipment as frequently as possible. To take full use of equipment and to maintain it in reliable condition, necessary measures should be taken to prevent overloading, dampness, negligence and misuse of machines. Frequency of inspection should be decided on the basis of the importance of the machine; wear and tear of the machine and its delicacy. This periodic inspection or checking helps to find out the reasons leading to breakdown and to rectify them, when they are in minor stages. Thus, the repair can be done when one wants to do it, i.e., when it has least effect on the production schedule. Further this repair-requires lesser time as compared to that of breakdown repair and thus, down time is reduced by doing preventive maintenance.

## Predictive or Condition Based Maintenance

This is also used alongwith preventive maintenance. In this, health of the equipment is regularly monitored and recorded in the form of mechanical vibrations, noise, acoustic, thermal emissions, changes in chemical compositions, smell, pressure, relative displacement etc. This helps in diagnosis and detection of faults, if any. Vibrations and noise are most valuable signals. **Condition monitoring** can be applied in the following three ways :

(*i*) Qualitative checks based on look, sound and feel, through simple inspection.

(*ii*) Condition checking by measuring some parameters regularly.

(*iii*) Trend monitoring by making measurements and plotting them in order to detect gradual departure from a norm.

## Objects of Preventive Maintenance

Preventive maintenance has the following main objects ;

- To obtain maximum availability of the equipment by avoiding breakdowns and by reducing the shutdown periods to a minimum.
- To keep the machine in proper condition so as to maintain the quality of the product.
- By minimising the wear and tear, preserve the value of the equipment.
- To ensure for the safety of the workers.
- To keep the plant at the maximum production efficiency.
- To achieve all the objectives with most economical combination.

## Functions or Elements of Preventive Maintenance

Following are some of the important functions of the preventive maintenance programme:

- Inspection or check-ups.
- Servicing including cleaning, cooling and lubrication.
- Planning and scheduling.
- Records and analysis.
- Training to maintenance staff.
- Storage of spare parts.

### 11.3.2. TPM Philosophy

Total productive maintenance involves both, operation and maintenance personnel to meet the goals of zero breakdown and zero defects by adopting preventive maintenance coupled with predictive maintenance and condition monitoring. Where this concept of TPM have been implemented, results have shown sizeable improvement in reduced equipment breakdown maintenance costs, inventory costs, substandard products, production loss, maintenance cost per unit and increased labour productivity.

This concept of TPM came to light in late 1980s due to increasingly urgent need to reduce costs and ensure reliable capacity of the equipment. Total productive maintenance (TPM) keeps the plant and equipment at its highest productive level through co-operation of all areas of operation. Individuals working together without regard to organisational structure, using their skills and expertise, have a common objective i.e. total productivity or peak performance.

This TPM function should be directed towards the elimination of unplanned equipment and plant maintenance. Surprise equipment breakdowns should not occur.

**The overall goals of TPM are:**

(*i*) Maintaining and improving equipment capacity.

(*ii*) Maintaining equipment for life.

(*iii*) Using support from all areas of the operation.

(*iv*) Encouraging input from all employees

(*v*) Using teams for continuous improvement.

From the above, we can conclude that TPM is an extension of TQM philosophy to the maintenance function. For implementing and promoting the TPM philosophy, senior management must spent significant time and they must sell the idea and let the employees know that they are totally committed to its success.

Managers at all levels should be taught or trained about the TPM philosophy. Senior management must spend time learning about and understanding for applying this philosophy in their organization. First line supervisors need to learn their role in implementing the new philosophy. The maximum benefit of TPM is the cross-pollination of ideas between maintenance technicians and production operators.

### T.P.M. covers the following :

(*a*) TPM is aimed for re-storing and maintaining equipment at optimal levels.

(*b*) Understanding failure modes and controlling the source of their cause.

(*c*) Planning maintenance based on actual equipment condition.

(*d*) Improving reliability, maintainability and operability.

(*e*) Applying predictive and condition based monitoring.

## Main functions of T.P.M. are :

- Eliminate unnecessary and unplanned downtime.
- Eliminate equipment related quality problems and improve machine operability and maintainability.
- Rigorous preventive maintenance programme, coupled with predictive and condition monitoring, be adopted to control deterioration with the co-operation of operations and maintenance personnel.
- To impart training to upgrade operations and maintenance skills.
- Quality maintenance team to identify and control the equipment conditions to assure key product quality characteristics.
- Information system be developed for operation, adjustment and maintenance with higher reliability.

## Losses to be prevented by TPM are :

(*a*) Losses of production and in repair due to breakdown.

(*b*) Set-ups and adjustment loss after shutdown is over.

(*c*) Idling and other minor stoppages loss after shut down.

(*d*) Loss due to lesser speed of equipment because of its poor condition.

(*e*) Quality defects due to poor condition of equipment.

# 11.4. FAILURE MODE AND EFFECT ANALYSIS (FMEA)

FMEA is a tool used for reviewing the design of any new product before it is sent for production. It is also used as an effective tool to eliminate future problems on a running product. It helps to review the design of the product to meet the customer requirements or specified product performance.

FMEA is basically used for analysing the effect of failure of individual components on the system as a whole. FMEA is a "before – the – event" action requiring a team effort to easily and inexpensively reduce changes in design and production.

Failure Mode and Effect Analysis (FMEA) some times also known as Failure Mode and Effects Criticality Analysis (FMECA) is a systematic procedure for systematic evaluation of the impact of potential failures and thereby determine a priority of possible actions that will reduce the occurrence of such failures.

It can be applied at the: (*i*) system level (*ii*) at the design levels for a product or service, (*iii*) at the process level for manufacturing or services, or (*iv*) at the functional level of a component or sysystem level.

FMEA is an analytical technique that combines the technology and experience of people in identifying foreseeable failure modes of a product or process and planning for its elimination. Thus, FMEA is a group of activities, intended to:

(*i*) Recognize and evaluate the potential failure of a product or process and its effects.

(*ii*) Identify actions that could eliminate or reduce the chance of potential failures.

(*iii*) Document the process.

In products involving safety issues, FMEA assists in a thorough analysis of what the various failure modes could be, their impact and effect on the customer, the severity of the failure, the possible causes that may lead to such a failure, the chance of occurrence of such failures, and the chance of detection of such failures.

Based on the information specified above, a **risk priority number** (RPN) is calculated, which indicates a relative priority scheme to address the various failures. The risk priority number is the product of severity, occurrence, and detection ratings. The larger the RPN, the higher the priority for actions for each failure mode. Based on this action, the ratings are revised.

The objectives of the recommended actions are to reduce severity and/or occurrence of the failure modes and to increase their detection through appropriate controls, such as evaluation techniques or detection equipment. Whereas, severity can be reduced only through a design change, occurrence may be reduced through design or process improvements.

For most products, it is not economical to conduct the analysis of failure mode and failure effect for each component. Instead, engineering judgement is used to single out items which are critical to operation of the product.

The analysis include following matters:

1. Safety of the user.
2. Downtime of the system until repairs are made.
3. Access to remove and repair the failed component.
4. Repair planning to decide special repair tools needed and anticipated repair time.
5. Recommendations about changes in design or specifications, instructions to be included in manuals of operation, or maintenance.

## Reliability

Reliability is one of the most important characteristics of any product. Customer always wants that the products which he purchases, must be reliable. Reliable means that these products should meet requirements without failure for a considerable time. For this purpose, manufacturers continually re-design their products to rectify defects and discrepancies.

The generally accepted definition of reliability is as under:

"Reliability is the probability of a device (product) performing its purpose adequately for the period (time) intended under the given operating conditions encountered".

One important consideration, when performing reliability studies is the safety of the product or the process. The criticality of a product or process changes drastically, when human safety considerations are involved.

### 11.4.1. Failure Rates and Product Life-cycle

One cannot expect a product or device or a system to work for ever and that too in the same condition. The product or device wears out with time and hence, the capability of the device is to perform its task adequately depends upon its age. Experience has shown that failure characteristics of most of the products (or devices or systems), follow a definite pattern, known as 'bath tub curve' and is indicated in the figure 11.3. To understand clearly, we can divide the product life in following three periods :

(*a*) **Burn-in-period (Infant Mortality Period).** When system is given a trail run during initial period, there may be rapid failures known as initial failures.

These failures are concerned with malfunctioning due to poor design, poor workmanship and poor quality. The sub-standard components are located and then replaced. This will improve the reliability.

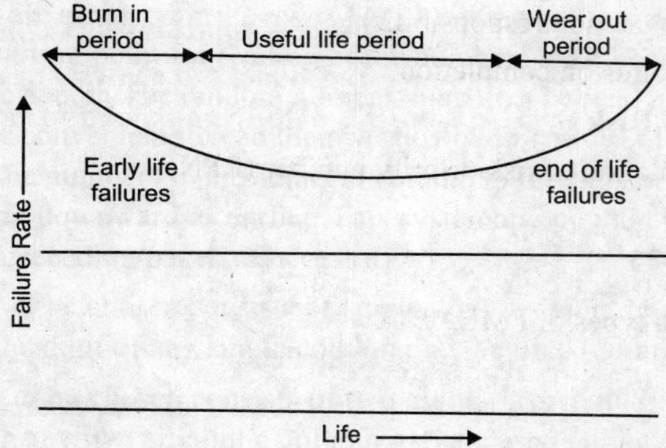


**Fig. 11.3** Curve to indicate failure rate and product life-cycle

(*b*) **Useful Life Period.** After the burn-in period actual useful life of normal use starts. During this period, failure rate is low but occurs unexpectedly and at random intervals, such failures are known as 'Normal failures' or 'Chance failures.

(*c*) **Wear-out Period.** Beyond its useful life period, failure rate increases very much. This is due to excessive wear after the expected useful design life of the device or system has been exceeded. The failures during this period are known as 'Ageing failure' or 'Wearout failures'.

The curve shown in Fig. 11.3 is sometimes referred as the 'Bath Tub' characteristics.

### 11.4.2. Stages of FMEA

FMEA is performed in the following 4 stages:

1. **Specifying the Possibilities**

   (*a*) Functions of the item.

   (*b*) Potential failure mode.

(*c*) Root causes.

(*d*) Potential effect (s) of failure.

(*e*) Detection / prevention.

**2. Quantifying the Risk**

(*a*) Potential causes of failure.

(*b*) Severity of effect.

(*c*) Effectiveness of control to detect and prevent cause.

(*d*) Risk priority number (RPN).

**3. Correcting High-Risk Causes**

(*a*) Prioritising work.

(*b*) Detailing action.

(*c*) Assigning action responsibility.

(*d*) Check points on completion.

**4. Re-evaluation of Risk**

- Re-calculation of risk priority number (RPN)

### 11.4.3. FMEA Types

Following are the main types of FMEA:

- System FMEA
- Design FMEA
- Process FMEA
- Equipment FMEA
- Maintenance FMEA
- Service FMEA
- Environmental FMEA

For all intents and purposes, all the types of FMEA can be broally categorised under either: (*i*) design FMEA, or (*ii*) process FMEA. System FMEA is a combination of design and process FMEA.

**1. Design FMEA**

Design FMEA helps in the designing by identifying known and foreseeable failure modes and then ranking failures according to relative impact on the product.

Implementing design, FMEA helps in establishing priorities based on expected failures and severity of those failures and helps in uncovering oversights, misjudgement, and errors that may have been made.

It reduces development time and and cost of manufacturing processes by eliminating many potential failure modes prior to operation of the process and by specifying the appropriate tests to prove reliability of designed product.

**2. Process FMEA**

Process FMEA is used to identify potential process failure modes by ranking failures and helping to establish priorities according to relative impact on customer.

Implementing process, FMEA helps in identifying potential manufacturing or assembly failure causes in order to establish controls for occurrence, reduction and detection.

## 11.5. TAGUCHI METHOD

As discussed in chapter on "Continuous Process Improvement", Professor Genichi Taguchi has devised a quality improvement technique that uses experimental design methods for efficient characterisation of a product or process, combined with a statistical analysis of a variability. This approach allows quality considerations to be included at an early stage of new venture in the design and prototype phase for a product, during routine maintenance, or during installation and commissioning of a manufacturing process.

In this section we shall discuss the philosophy and experimental design principle devised by Taguchi. Taguchi supported the neverending cycle of quality improvement. The subject of designing quality of product and corresponding process is known as **'Quality Engineering'**. It directs quality improvement efforts upstream from the manufacturing process to the design phase and is, therefore, referred to as an **off-line quality control** method. The techniques of statistical process control, are known as **on-line quality control** methods.

The Taguchi's off-line methods are effective in improving quality and cutting down the costs. It also improves product manufacturability and reduce product development and lifetime costs.

In this Taguchi's method quality is measured by the deviation of a characteristics from its target value. A loss function (discussed in the chapter on "Quality Concept") is developed for this deviation. Uncontrollable factors, known as **noise**, cause such deviation and thereby lead to loss. Since the elimination of noise factor is impracticable and often impossible, the **Taguchi method** seeks to minimise the effects of noise and to determine the optimal level of the important controllable factors based on the concept of robustness.

### Taguchi Philosophy (Loss Function)

As discussed in the chapter on "Quality Concept", the principle idea in the Taguchi philosophy is that statistical testing of a product should be carried out at the design stage in order to make the product and the process robust to variations in the manufacturing and use environment.

According to Taguchi, "Quality is the loss imparted to society from the time a product is shipped." Taguchi attaches a monetary value to quality because he feels that this will make quality improvement understood by all stake holders.

Total loss include following types of losses:

(*a*) The cost of customer dis-satisfaction which may lead to a loss of reputation and goodwill for the company.

(*b*) Direct loss to the company arising from warranty and service costs.

(*c*) Indirect loss due to reduction in market share.

(*d*) Increased marketing efforts needed to overcome lack of competitiveness.

(*e*) Loss to society due to depletion of raw materials and labour when making the product or rendering the service.

(*f*) The cost of environmental pollution falls into this category.

(*g*) The loss due to those products which break or need to be repaired or replaced.

(*h*) During production, costs such as inspection, scrap, and rework contribute to loss.

Profit increasing measures such as productivity improvement and waste reduction are linked by such factors as labour and material costs and technology. Real growth in market share is influenced by customer satisfaction. Any cost incurred by the customer or any loss resulting from poor quality have a significant negative impact. On the other side, a satisfied customer who realize savings from using the product or service will help to greatly improve market share.

## 11.6. ROLE OF I.T. IN TQM

Information Technology (I.T.) is a tool which has major impact on all business processes and quality function. Data collection and analysis has been extremely efficient and fast. Like other tools, it helps the TQM organisation achieve its goals. Since last few decades, computers and quality management practices have evolved together and have supported each other.

We can define Information Technology as computer technology (either hardware or software) for processing and storing information as well as communications technology for transmitting information. Organisation should be proficient in converting information into knowledge.

Computers play an important role in the quality function. They perform very simple operations at fast speeds with an exceptionally high degree of accuracy.

Computers can be programmed to perform complex calculations, to control a process or test, to analyze data, to write reprots, and to recall information on command.

A quality information system (QIS) is an organised method of collecting, storing, analysing, and reporting information on quality to assist decision makers at all levels. Inputs needed for a quality information system include:

1. Market research information on quality.
2. Product design test data.
3. Information on design evaluation.
4. Information on purchased parts and materials.
5. Process data.

6. Final inspection data.
7. Field performance data.
8. Results of quality measurement.

The planning of a computer-based QIS starts with an analysis of customer needs, creation of design specification for the system, and preparation of a proposal indicating costs and time required. On approval of the proposal by the management, the system is developed, tested, and implemented. In the end, provisions are made for review of system performance. System must be tailored to meet the needs of both internal and external customers of an organisation.

The role of the computer in quality information systems seems to be without limit. We are moving towards the "paperless organisation". Application software packages are available in the market for a wide variety of needs. In creating new software, the primary issue is the lack of sufficient communication between the user and the software developer.

The quality function needs to be served by the computer are:

(*i*) data collection,
(*ii*) data analysis and reporting,
(*iii*) statistical analysis,
(*iv*) process control,
(*v*) test and inspection, and
(*vi*) system design.

In addition to the above, the computer serves as the platform for Internet and internet utilisation.

## Internet and Other Electronic Communication

The internet is a worldwide network of computer networks. The internet contains an incredible amount of information and knowledge on subjects. The autonomous agents or search engines are used to determine all those locations that contain a particular requested subject.

Within organisation, local-area networks (LANs) efficiently share data among users by keeping large amounts of transaction data on large central computers, while connecting personal computers (PCs) to them. LANs facilitate data sharing such as e-mail messages, transactions, decisions and searches, scheduling, and access to the internet. The most recent data are stored on the central computer, and authorised individuals have access to it.

Internet is also helpful in "video conferencing", which is a technique where people at remote locations participate in a conference. In addition, internet also allows, e-learning, e-government, e-commerce, website design etc.

## QUESTIONS

1. What are the advantages of using 'quality function deployment? What are some key ingredients that are necessary for its success?

2. Discuss 'house of quality' in detail.
3. Describe the steps of benchmarking relating to a company that develops food processors. What is the role of top magement in this process?
4. What is 'total productive maintenance? Explain in detail.
5. Write an essay on "importance of the maintenance".
6. Explain how preventive maintenance is better that breakdown maintenance.
7. Efficiency has been defined as "doing things better" and effectiveness as "doing better things". Describe how benchmarking can be used to improve both, efficiency and effectiveness.
8. Explain how an organisation might benefit from benchmarking?
9. What are the advantages by using benchmarking as an improvement tool? What are the disadvantages?
10. What is benchmarking? Explain in detail.
11. Explain the reasons for benchmarking.
12. Discuss benchmarking procedure.
13. What is quality function deployment? Explain in detail.
14. What are the benefits by using QFD as a management tool?
15. Write short notes on:
    (*a*) QFD team. (b) QFD process
16. What is 'house of quality'? Explain in detail. How it is constructed?
17. Explain the application of 'house of quality".
18. What is 'total productive maintenance'? Explain its philosophy.
19. Write short notes on:
    (*a*) Goals of TPM (*b*) Risk priority number
    (*c*) Reliability
20. What is 'Failure Mode and Effect Analysis? Explain in detail.
21. Explain failure rate and product life-cycle in detail.
22. List out the stages of FMEA.
23. What are the different types of FMEA? Explain design FMEA and Process FMEA.
24. Discuss Taguchi's philosophy for quality improvement. Also discuss his loss function and its contributions.
25. Describe Taguchi's method for quality improvement in detail.
26. Discuss the role of I.T. in TQM in detail.
27. Using the internet or other sources, discuss role of computers in quality functions.

# Fundamentals of Statistics

## 12.1. STATISTICS

Statistics can be defined as :

1. "Statistics are numerical statement of facts in any department of enquiry placed in relation to each other".

   According to this definition, only numerical values can be termed as statics and non-numerical facts cannot be processed statistically.

2. "By statistics we mean quantitative data affected to a marked extent by multiplicity of cause". This definition refers to numerical data affected by a mupltiplicity of causes. For example, price of an item depends upon supply, demand, competition, circulation of money etc.

3. "By statistics we mean aggregate of facts affected to a marked extent by multiplicity of causes, numerically expressed, enumerated or estimated according to reasonable standard of accuracy, collected in a systematic manner for a pre-determined purpose and placed in relation to each other."

   This definition possess the following characteristics :

   (*i*) Statistics are aggregate of facts.

   (*ii*) Statistics are affected to a marked extent by multiplicity of causes.

   (*iii*) Statistics are numerically expressed.

   (*iv*) Statistics should be enumerated or estimated.

   (*v*) Statistics should be collected with reasonable standard of accuracy.

   (*vi*) Statistics should be collected in a systematic manner for a pre-determined purpose.

   (*vii*) Statistics should be placed in relation to each other.

4. "Statistics may be defined as the collection, presentation, analysis and interpretation of numerical data".

First 3 definitions are based on the consideration of "statistics as data", while 4th definition considers "statistics as methods". The real purpose statistical methods is make sense out of facts and figures, to prove the unknown, and to cast light upon the situation. Thus, statistics is a body of methods for making decisions in the face of uncertainty.

**Statistics is a tool to translate complex facts into simple and understandable statement of fats, and can be used in decision-making in various fields.**

## 12.2. SAMPLING

All the items *i.e.* complete group of persons or objects for which the results are to apply, which fall within the purview of the statistical study are known as universe or population. The statistical population can be either: (*a*) finite population, which can be counted and definite, or (*b*) infinite population, which cannot be counted and is infinite.

Statistical informations can be collected in two ways-census method and sample method. The object of a census or complete enumeration is to collect information for each and every unit of the population. In the sample study, only a part of the population is studied. It is based on the principle that to arrive at valid conclusions, it is not necessary to enumerate all or nearly all of the population. We may study a sample drawn from the large population and, if that sample is adequately representative of the population, we should be able to arrive at valid conclusions. The results obtained from the sample study can be applied to whole universe or population. The characteristics of the population can be studied from the sampling, which will give a correct idea of the universe.

Sampling aspects have already been discussed in detail in the chapter on "Acceptance Sampling".

**Essentials of Sampling**

1. It must be representative, *i.e.* sample should have similar characteristics as that of universe.
2. Homogeneity, *i.e.* samples should have similar nature as that of universe.
3. Adequate samples. It is necessary to make the result more reliable.
4. Optimisation *i.e.* to optimize results in terms of cost and efficiency, proper size of sample should be maintained.

**Methods of Sampling :**

1. Random Sampling
2. Non-Random Sampling

**Law of Statistical Regularity**

The Law of Statistical Regularity formulated in the mathematical theory of probability lays down that a moderately large number of items chosen at random from a very large group are almost sure on the average to have the characteristics of large group.

**Statistical Errors**

1. Errors arising on account of inappropriate definitions of statistical units, defective questionnaire etc.
2. Errors of inadequacy *i.e.* incomplete data, inadequate number of items in the sample etc.
3. Errors of interpretation.
4. Errors of manipulation *i.e.* clerical errors, arithmetical slips.

**Sampling errors can be classified as:**

1. **Biased Errors.** These may arise due to a bias or prejudice on the part of the informant or enumerator or investigators. These also arise due to defect in the methods of collection of data, defect in method of organising data, and defect in the method of analysis of data.
2. **Unbiased Errors.** These may arise accidentally without any bias or prejudice. These errors occur due to faulty planning of statistical investigation.

**Reducing Sampling Errors**

Element of error reduces with the increase in sample size.

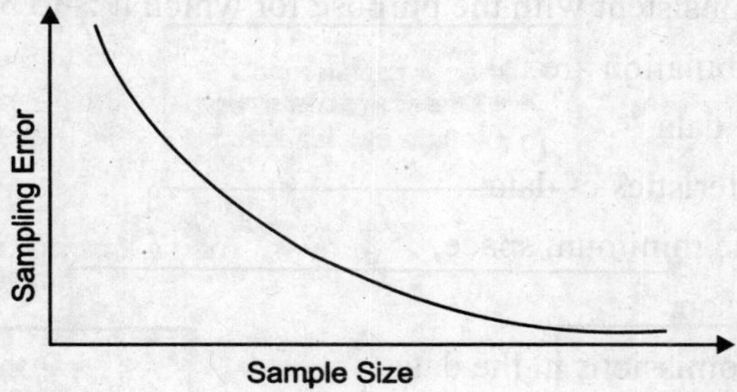


**Fig. 12.1.** Sample size and sampling error

Fig. 12.1 shows that when the sample size is very small, sampling error is very large. Thus, the sample, with an increase in its size, becomes more representative of the population.

## 12.3. CLASSIFICATION AND TABULATION

"The collected data in a statistical study are known as 'raw data', and they cannot be easily understood as such. For the purpose of further analysis and interpretation, they are required to be classified and arranged. Therefore, after having collected and edited the data, they are organised in a systematic manner.

**Classification** is the process of arranging the available facts into homogeneous groups or classes according to resemblances and similarities. The objects of classification are :

(*i*) to condense the mass data

(*ii*) to present the facts in a simple form

(*iii*) to bring out clearly the points of similarity and dissimilarity.

(*iv*) to facilitate comparison,

(*v*) to bring out the relationship.

(*vi*) to prepare data for tabulation.

(*vii*) to facilitate the statistical treatment of the data.

Following are the four important types of classification :

1. Geographical *i.e.* areawise.
2. Chronological or historical *i.e.* on the basis of time.
3. Qualitative by character or by attributes.
4. Quantitative or by magnitudes.

**Tabulation**

By tabulation we mean, a systematic presentation of numerical data in columns and rows in accordance with some salient features or characteristics. It facilitates comparison and analysis. Tabulation helps in understanding complex numerical data and makes them in a simple and clear way. The purpose of a table is to summarise a mass of numerical information and to present it in the simplest possible form, consistent with the purpose for which it is to be used.

Main objectives of tabulation are :

(*i*) to simplify complex data,

(*ii*) to clarify the characteristics of data,

(*iii*) to present facts in the minimum space,

(*iv*) to facilitate comparison,

(*v*) to detect errors and omissions in the data,

(*vi*) to depict trend and tendencies of the problem under consideration,

(*vii*) to facilitate statistical processing.

From the above, we have seen that the data are first classified and then they are presented in tables. Thus, classification is the basis for tabulation. In other words, classification is a process of statistical analysis, while tabulation is a process of presenting data in suitable structure.

**Statistical Series**

These are prepared to present the collected and classified data in a properly arranged way. It may be defined as things or attributes of things, arranged according to some logical order. According to L.R. Corner, "if two variable quantities can be arranged side-by-side so that the measurable differences in the one correspond to the measurable differences in the other, the result is said to form a statistical series."

Raw data arranged in descending or ascending order of magnitude is called an array. This helps in noticing highest and lowest values, dividing data in sections, values appearing more than once, distance between succeeding values in the data.

The purpose of the characteristics of the data is to enable us to see quickly some of the characteristics of the data, we have collected. We look for things, such as the range, apparent patterns, what values the data may tend to group around, what values appear most often and so on. The more information of this kind we can know from sample, the better we can understand the population from which it came. This also helps in making better decisions.

## 12.4. FREQUENCY DISTRIBUTION

Frequency distribution can be defined as "a classification according to the number possessing the same values of the variables". In this, data are grouped into classes and the number of cases which fall in each is recorded in the form of a table. It shows the frequency of occurrence of different values of a single variable.

The frequency distribution are of following types :

1. **Individual Observations**

   This is a simple listing of items singly after each observation.

2. **Discrete Frequency Distribution**

   In a discrete series, the data are presented in such a way that exact measurements of units are clearly indicated. In discrete frequency distribution, we count the number of times, each value of the variable occurs in the given data. This is facilitated by Tally bars.

For drawing discrete frequency distribution, all possible values of the variables are placed in the first column. Tally bars are placed in the second column against the value of the variable. For showing tally bars upto four times, they are shown vertically like 1111, but fifth is put as cross tally mark on four tally bars like 1111 to give a block at 5. This facilitates the counting of number of occurrences at the value of the end. In the third column, the number of frequency is written, after counting the tally bars. This type of representation of the data, known as discrete frequency distribution, is shown in the example given below :

To illustrate, an example of frequency distribution is dealt hereunder:

**Example, 12.1** A machine produces the following component:

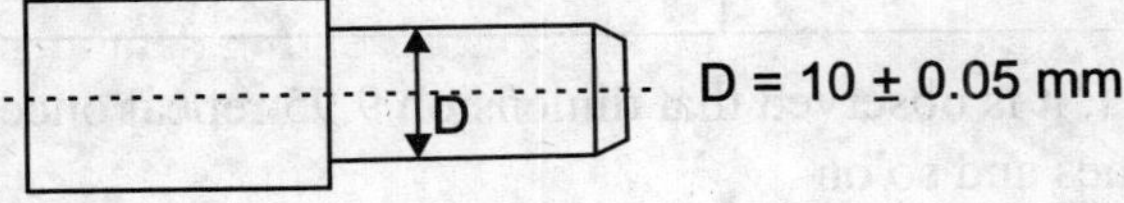


**Fig. 12.2**

*Out of 1000 pairs manufactured, 100 are measured to the nearest of hundredth a mm. The measurement, recorded are shown in the table. Explain what do these measurements tell about the machine or process?*

| 10.03 | 10.02 | 10.04 | 10.00 | 10.03 | 9.98 | 9.97 | 10.01 | 10.02 | 10.04 |
|---|---|---|---|---|---|---|---|---|---|
| 9.99 | 9.99 | 10.03 | 10.04 | 10.00 | 9.98 | 10.00 | 10.03 | 10.02 | 10.01 |
| 9.97 | 9.90 | 10.01 | 10.02 | 10.02 | 10.03 | 10.00 | 10.04 | 10.00 | 9.99 |
| 10.02 | 10.00 | 10.01 | 10.00 | 10.00 | 10.02 | 10.01 | 9.99 | 9.99 | 9.98 |

| | | | | | | | | | |
|---|---|---|---|---|---|---|---|---|---|
| 10.04 | 10.01 | 9.98 | 9.99 | 9.99 | 10.01 | 10.02 | 10.00 | 10.00 | 9.97 |
| 9.98 | 10.01 | 9.97 | 9.96 | 9.99 | 9.98 | 10.01 | 10.04 | 10.01 | 9.99 |
| 10.01 | 10.03 | 10.03 | 9.97 | 10.02 | 9.95 | 9.96 | 9.99 | 9.98 | 10.00 |
| 10.00 | 10.00 | 9.96 | 10.03 | 10.02 | 10.00 | 9.98 | 9.97 | 9.97 | 9.98 |
| 10.10 | 10.02 | 9.97 | 10.05 | 10.02 | 10.00 | 9.99 | 9.96 | 9.96 | 10.01 |
| 10.00 | 9.99 | 10.01 | 9.98 | 9.97 | 9.99 | 9.99 | 9.98 | 9.98 | 10.02 |

**Solution.** For the above data, discrete frequency distribution sheet is plotted as follows :

| ***Dimension*** | ***Tally*** | ***Frequency*** |
|---|---|---|
| 9.95 | I | 1 |
| 9.96 | 卌 I | 6 |
| 9.97 | 卌 IIII | 9 |
| 9.98 | 卌 卌 II | 12 |
| 9.99 | 卌 卌 IIII | 14 |
| 10.00 | 卌 卌 卌 I | 16 |
| 10.01 | 卌 卌 IIII | 14 |
| 10.02 | 卌 卌 II | 12 |
| 10.03 | 卌 IIII | 9 |
| 10.04 | 卌 I | 6 |
| 10.05 | I | 1 |

From this tally sheet, it is observed that dimension 9.95 repeat once, dimension 9.96 six times, dimension 9.97 nine times and so on.

**3. Continuous Frequency Distribution**

A collection of items, which cannot be exactly measured, but placed within certain limits, is called continuous series. In this type of distribution, there are two methods of forming class-intervals:

(*a*) ***Exclusive Method*** **(*Overlapping*).** In this method, the upper limit of one class-interval is the lower limit of the next class, for example:

| *Income (Rs)* | *Number of persons* |
|---|---|
| 1000–1500 | 10 |
| 1500–2000 | 20 |
| 2000–2500 | 15 |
| 2500–3000 | 20 |
| 3000–3500 | 10 |
| **Total** | **75** |

This method ensures continuity of data. A person having income between Rs. 1000 and 1499 would be included in the 1000-1500 class. A person having income of Rs. 1500 would be included in the class 1500-2000. To avoid confusion in class 1000-1500, we must clarify as : 1000 and more but under 1500. Similarly, in class 1500-2000, we may mention as : 1500 and more but under (or less than) 2000.

(*b*) ***Inclusive Method* (*Non-overlapping*):** In this method, the upper limit of one class is included in that class itself. For example:

| *Income (Rs)* | *No. of persons* |
|---|---|
| 1000-1499 | 10 |
| 1500-1999 | 20 |
| 2000-2499 | 15 |
| 2500-2999 | 20 |
| 3000-3499 | 10 |
| **Total** | **75** |

**4. Cumulative Frequency Distribution**

As we have seen that a frequency distribution shows how the frequency of a particular variable or class is occurring. Now, we are discussing cumulative frequencies, which are derived by the cumulation of the frequencies of successive values. Cumulative frequency of a given variable or class represents the total frequency of all previous variables including the variable or the class. This is shown below considering the previous example of income distribution:

| *Income (Rs)* | *Frequency* | *Cumulative frequency* |
|---|---|---|
| 1000–1500 | 10 | 10 |
| 1500–2000 | 20 | 10 + 20 = 30 |
| 2000–2500 | 15 | 30 + 15 = 45 |
| 2500–3000 | 20 | 45 + 20 = 65 |
| 3000–3500 | 10 | 65 + 10= 75 |
| | **Total** | **75** |

It is easy and quick to find out the number of persons who have income less than a particular mark. For example, number of persons who have income less than Rs. 3000 are 65, and therefore, number of persons who have income more than Rs. 3000 are (75 - 65) *i.e.* 10.

## 12.5. MEASURES OF CENTRAL TENDENCY (AVERAGES)

Measures of central tendency describes the characteristics of the entire mass of data, and reduces the complexity of data and makes them easy to compare. According to Prof. R.A. Fisher, "The inherent inability of the human mind to grasp in its entirety, a large body of numerical data compels us to see relatively few constants that will adequately describe the data." A simple figure is used to describe the series which must be a representative number. This figure is generally called "measure of central tendency or average".

This can also be defined as follows :

"Average is a value which is typical or representative of a set of data."

"Average is an attempt to find out single figure to describe whole figures". The 'average' is used :

(*i*) to facilitate quick understanding of complex data,
(*ii*) to facilitate comparison,
(*iii*) to know about the universe from a sample,
(*iv*) to help in decision-making,
(*v*) to establish mathematical relationship.

**Kinds of Averages**

Out of the above types, following are common and are being described in succeeding paragraphs:

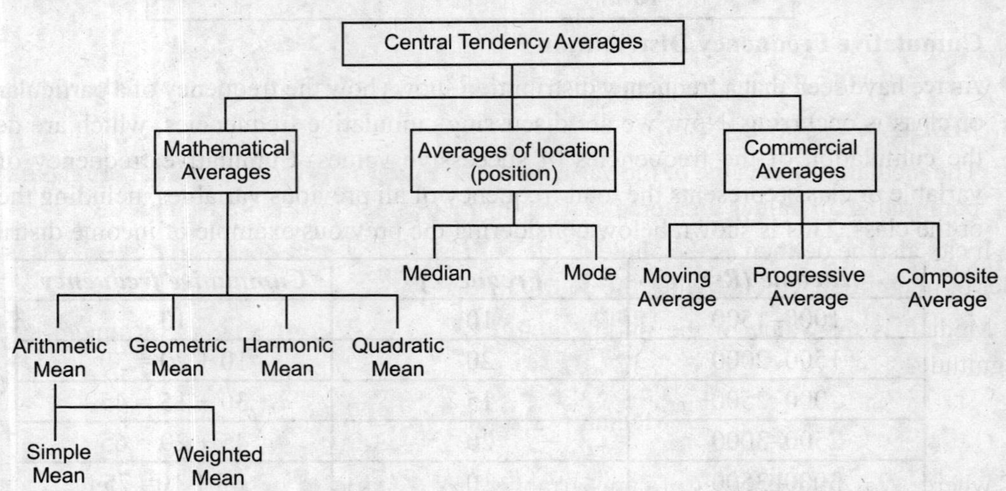


1. Simple arithmetic mean
2. Weighted arithmetic mean

3. Median
4. Mode.

## 1. MEAN

### 1. Simple Arithmetic Mean

Simple arithmetic mean of a series is equal to the sum of variables divided by their number.

$$\overline{X} = \frac{X_1 + X_2 + X_3 + .....X_n}{N}$$

$$= \frac{\sum X}{N}$$

where, $\overline{X}$ = mean

$\Sigma X$ = The sum of variables

$N$ = Number of observations.

### 2. Weighted Arithmetic Mean

Simple arithmetic mean gives equal importance to all the items of distribution, but in practice, in certain cases, relative importance of the items in the distribution is not the same. Where, the importance of the items is different, it is necessary to allocate weightage to the items according to the relative importance of the items.

Therefore, weighted average can be defined as an average whose component items are multiplied by certain values (weights) and the aggregate of the products are divided by the total weights. In weighted arithmetic mean,

$$\overline{X} = \Sigma\left(\frac{W_1X_1 + W_2X_2 + W_3X_3 + ...W_nX_n}{W_1 + W_2 + W_3 + ...W_n}\right)$$

$$= \frac{\Sigma WX}{\Sigma W}$$

where, $W_1$, $W_2$, $W_3$...are the respective weights and $X_1$, $X_2$, $X_3$ .... represents the variables.

## 3. MEDIAN

The median is that value of the variable which divides the group into two equal parts, one part comprising all values greater, and the other, all values less than median.

It can also be defined as the value of the item, actual or estimated, when a series is arranged in order of magnitude which divides the distribution into two parts.

Median is the value of the middle item in a series, when items are arranged according to magnitude.

$$\text{Median} = \text{size of} \left(\frac{N+1}{2}\right)^{th} \text{item}$$

where, $N$ = Total number of items arranged in ascending or descending order.

### Location of Median in Discrete Series

In this, median is calculated after arranging the data in ascending or descending order and then determining the cumulative frequencies. This will be clear from the following example.

**Example 12.2.** Locate median from the following data :

| *Size of shoes* | 5 | 5.5 | 6 | 6.5 | 7 | 7.5 | 8 |
|---|---|---|---|---|---|---|---|
| *Frequency* | 10 | 16 | 28 | 15 | 30 | 40 | 24 |

**Solution.** For calculating the median, the cumulative frequencies are calculated as follows :

| *Size of shoes* | *Frequency (f)* | *Cumulative frequency ($C_f$)* |
|---|---|---|
| 5 | 10 | 10 |
| 5.5 | 16 | 26 |
| 6 | 28 | 54 |
| 6.5 | 15 | 69 |
| 7 | 30 | 99 |
| 7.5 | 40 | 139 |
| 8 | 24 | 163 |

$$\text{Median} = \text{size of } \left(\frac{N+1}{2}\right)\text{th item}$$

$$= \text{size of } \left(\frac{163+1}{2}\right) \text{ th item}$$

$$= \text{size of 82 nd item} = \mathbf{7 \text{ Ans.}}$$

### Median in Continuous Series

For calculating median in a continuous series, following formula is used:

$$\text{Median} = L + \frac{\frac{N}{2} - C_f}{f} \times i$$

where, $L$ = Lower limit of the median class

$f$ = Frequency of the median class

$C_f$ = Cumulative frequency of the class preceeding median class *i.e.* total frequency of all lower classes.

$i$ = Class interval of median class.

**Example 12.3.** Calculate the median from the data given in the following table:

| *Marks* | *Frequency* |
|---|---|
| 10–25 | 6 |
| 25–40 | 20 |
| 40–55 | 40 |
| 55–70 | 26 |
| 70–85 | 5 |
| 85–100 | 3 |

**Solution.** From the data given in the table, cumulative frequencies are calculated as under :

| **Marks** | **Frequency (*f*)** | **Cumulative Frequency ($C_f$)** |
|---|---|---|
| 10–25 | 6 | 66 |
| 40–40 | 20 | 26 |
| 40–55 | 40 | 66 |
| 55–70 | 26 | 92 |
| 70–85 | 5 | 97 |
| 85–100 | 3 | 100 |

$$\text{Median (approx.)} = \frac{N}{2} = \frac{100}{2} = 50$$

Thus, median lies between 40-55 marks group. Therefore, using the formula,

$$\text{Median} = L + \frac{\frac{N}{2} - C_f}{f} \times i$$

where, $L = 40,\ \frac{N}{2} = 50,\ C_f = 26,\ i = 15, f = 40$

$$\therefore \quad \text{Median} = 40 + \frac{50-26}{40} \times 15$$

$$= 40 + 9 = \mathbf{49\ marks.\ Ans.}$$

## 4. MODE

The mode is that value of the variable which occurs or repeats itself maximum number of mes. Modes can be defined as :

(*i*) the value occurring most frequently in series of items and around which the other items are distributed most densely.

(*ii*) the value at the point where the items tend to be most heavily concentrated.

(*iii*) the value which has the greatest frequency density in its immediate neighbourhood.

**Example 12.4.** Find out the mode in following cases :

(*a*) 1100,950,1050, 1000, 850, 900, 1000, 975, 1000

(*b*) 40, 44, 53, 47, 51, 58

(*c*) 45, 48, 50, 43, 45, 47, 53, 50

**Solution.**

(*a*) Since 1000 repeats 3 times (maximum number of times), the mode is **1000**.

(*b*) Since no value is repeated, there is **no mode**.

(*c*) Since 45 and 50 both are repeated two times, it has two modes *i.e.* **45** and **50**.

## 12. 6. DISPERSION

Measures of central tendency *i.e.* Mean, Median , Mode etc. indicated the central position of the series, but this do not reveal the degree of the spread out or the extent of the variability in individual items of the distribution. This can be known by 'Measures of Dispersion' or 'Measures of Variation'.

Dispersion can, therefore, be defined as:

(*i*) Dispersion is the measure of the variation of the items.

(*ii*) Dispersion is a measure of extent to which the individual items vary.

(*iii*) The measurement of the scatteredness of the mass of figures in a series about an average is called measure of variation or dispersion.

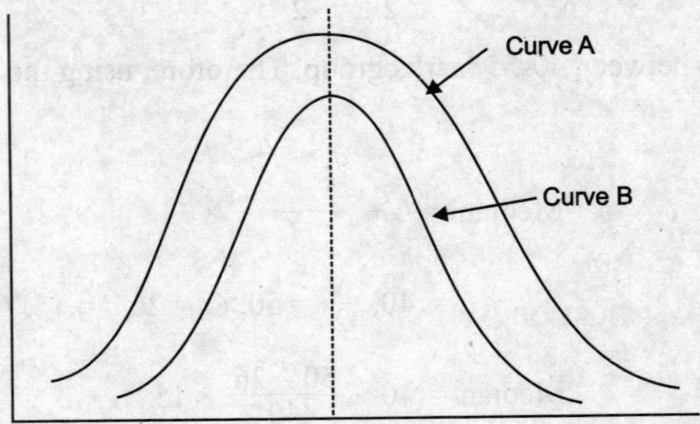


**Fig. 12.3.** Comparison of dispersion: Curve a has A wider-spread or dispersion than curve B

(*iv*) The degree to which numerical data tend to spread about an average value is called the variation or dispersion of the data.

An average is meaningful, when viewed with the help of dispersion (scatteredness). The average discovers the representative value of a series and the dispersion finds how individual values are scattered away from the central tendency.

**The purposes of measuring dispersion are :**

1. To test the reliability of an average
2. To serve as a basis for control or variability
3. To compare two or more series with regard to their variability.
4. To facilitate as a basis for further statistical analysis i.e. for correlation, regression, analysis of fluctuations, cost control etc.

**Measure of Dispersion**

1. Range.
2. Mean Deviation or Average Deviation.
3. Standard Deviation.

### 12.6.1. Range

Range is a rough measure of dispersion, and depends upon the extreme items and not on all the items. It does not tell anything about the distribution of values in the series relative to a typical or representative value.

Range = Largest value – Smallest value

*i.e.* $$R = L - S$$

$$\text{Co-efficient of Range} = \frac{L - S}{L + S}$$

**Example 12.5.** Find the range and co-efficient of range of heights of 7 students. 50, 53, 55, 56, 58, 59, 61 inches.

**Solution.**

Range = $L - S = 61 - 50 =$ **11 Ans.**

$$\text{Co-efficient of range} = \frac{L - S}{L + S} = \frac{61 - 50}{61 + 50}$$

$$= \frac{11}{111} = \textbf{0.10 approx. Ans.}$$

### 12.6.2. Mean Deviation or Average Deviation

Mean deviation is the arithmetic mean of the deviations of a series computed from any measure of central tendency, i.e. the mean, median or mode. In this case +ve and -ve signs are ignored. It can be defined as follows:

Average deviation is the average amount of scatter of the items in a distribution from either the mean or the median, ignoring the signs of the deviations.

Mean deviation can be denoted by M.D. or 5 (delta). It is generally computed from mean,

$$\text{Mean Deviation} = \text{M.D.} = \frac{\Sigma|D|}{N}$$

where, $\Sigma|D|$ = sum of the deviations,

and $N$ = Number of items.

*Co-efficient of Mean Deviation.*

$$\text{Co-efficient of M.D.} = \frac{\text{Mean deviation}}{\text{Mean or Median or Mode.}}$$

**Example 12.6.** Calculate the mean deviation from mean and median for the following data:
100, 150, 200, 300, 325, 350, 400, 500, 600
Also, calculate the co-efficient of mean deviation.

**Solution.** In this case,

$$\text{Mean, } \overline{X} = \frac{\Sigma X}{N}$$

$$= \frac{100 + 150 + 200 + 300 + 325 + 350 + 400 + 500\ 600}{9}$$

$$= \frac{2925}{9} = \textbf{325 Ans.}$$

$$\text{Median} = \text{value of} \left(\frac{N+1}{2}\right) \text{th item}$$

$$= \text{Value of} \left(\frac{9+1}{2}\right) \text{th item}$$

$$= \text{Value of 5th item} = \textbf{325 Ans.}$$

(In this example, value of mean and medium are same, but this may not be same in other cases.)

For calculating the value of deviation $|D|$, we draw the following table:

| $X$ | $\|D\| = X - \overline{X}$ *i.e.* $X - 325$ | $\|D\| = x -$ *median i.e.* $x - 325$ |
|---|---|---|
| 100 | 225 | 225 |
| 150 | 175 | 175 |
| 200 | 125 | 125 |
| 300 | 25 | 25 |
| 325 | 0 | 0 |
| 350 | 25 | 25 |
| 400 | 75 | 75 |
| 500 | 175 | 175 |
| 600 | 275 | 275 |
| $\Sigma X = 2925$ | $\Sigma\|D\| = 1100$ | $\Sigma\|D\| = 1100$ |

**Mean Deviation**

**1.** As Mean Deviation from mean

$$= \frac{\Sigma|D|}{N}$$

$\therefore$ *MD* from mean = $\frac{1100}{9} = 122.22$

and Co-efficient of

$$MD = \frac{MD}{X} = \frac{122.22}{325} = 0.376 = \mathbf{37.6\%}\ \textbf{Ans.}$$

**2.** Similarly, Mean Deviation from median

$$= \frac{\Sigma|D|}{N}$$

$\therefore$ MD from median $= \frac{1100}{9}$

$= 122.22$

and Co-efficient of MD $= \frac{\text{M.D}}{\text{Median}}$

$= \frac{122.22}{325} = 0.376$

$=$ **37.6% Ans.**

## 12.6.3. Standard Deviation

It is a widely used concept in many statistical formulae. Standard deviation is also called as Root-Mean Square Deviation. It is the square-root of the mean of the squared deviation from the arithmetic mean.

Standard deviation is defined as positive square-root of the arithmetic mean of the squares of the deviations of the given observation from the arithmetic mean. It is denoted by the Greek letter 0 (sigma).

Methods of calculating standard deviations can be understood from the following examples:

**Example 12.7.** Calculate the standard deviation from the data given below :

*9, 14, 22, 15, 20, 17,11, 12*

**Solution.**

From the given data,

$$\overline{X} = \frac{\Sigma X}{N} = \frac{120}{8} = 15$$

| *Variables X* | $X-\overline{X}$ | $(X-\overline{X})^2$ |
|---|---|---|
| | $(X-15)$ | |
| 9 | −6 | 36 |
| 14 | −1 | 1 |
| 22 | 7 | 49 |
| 15 | 0 | 0 |
| 20 | 5 | 25 |
| 17 | 2 | 4 |
| 11 | −4 | 16 |
| 12 | −3 | 9 |
| $\Sigma X = 120$ | | $\Sigma(X-\overline{X})^2 = 140$ |

As Standard Deviation,

$$\sigma = \sqrt{\frac{\Sigma(X-\overline{X})^2}{N}} = \sqrt{\frac{140}{8}} = \textbf{4.18 Ans.}$$

**Alternatively**

This example can also be solved by using variables directly *i.e.* without calculating deviations. The formula used in this case is,

Standard deviation,

$$\sigma = \sqrt{\frac{\Sigma X^2}{N} - \left(\frac{\Sigma X}{N}\right)^2}$$

Calculating the values $\Sigma X$ and $\Sigma X^2$ :

| *Variables (X)* | $X^2$ |
|---|---|
| 9 | 81 |
| 14 | 196 |
| 22 | 484 |
| 15 | 225 |
| 20 | 400 |
| 17 | 289 |
| 11 | 121 |
| 12 | 144 |
| $\Sigma X = 120$ | $\Sigma X^2 = 1940$ |

$$\therefore \quad \sigma = \sqrt{\frac{\Sigma X^2}{N} - \left(\frac{\Sigma X}{N}\right)^2} = \sqrt{\frac{1940}{8} - \left(\frac{120}{8}\right)^2}$$

$$= \sqrt{242.5 - 225} = \sqrt{17.5} = \mathbf{4.18\ Ans.}$$

**Deviation taken from assumed mean**

Earlier we have discussed the method in which deviation is taken from actual mean. In certain cases, when calculating deviation from above method becomes difficult and time consuming, this short cut method is used, which save time and labour. The formula used in this case is :

$$\sigma = \sqrt{\frac{\Sigma d^2}{N} - \left(\frac{\Sigma d}{N}\right)^2}$$

where, $d$ = deviation from the assumed mean.

**Example 12.8.** 10 students of a class have obtained the following marks in a subject out of 100 marks. Calculate the standard deviation.

| Serial No. | 1 | 2 | 3 | 4 | 5 | 6 | 7 | 8 | 9 | 10 |
|---|---|---|---|---|---|---|---|---|---|---|
| Marks | 5 | 10 | 20 | 25 | 40 | 42 | 45 | 48 | 70 | 80 |

**Solution.** Determination of $\Sigma d$ and $\Sigma d^2$ using the following table : (Assumed mean is say 40).

| *S. No.* | *Marks* | *d = (X–40)* | $d^2$ |
|---|---|---|---|
| 1 | 5 | –35 | 1225 |
| 2 | 10 | –30 | 900 |
| 3 | 20 | –20 | 400 |
| 4 | 25 | –15 | 225 |
| 5 | 40 | 0 | 0 |
| 6 | 42 | 2 | 4 |
| 7 | 45 | 5 | 25 |
| 8 | 48 | 8 | 64 |
| 9 | 70 | 30 | 900 |
| 10 | 80 | 40 | 1600 |
| N = 10 | | $\Sigma d = -15$ | $\Sigma d^2 = 5343$ |

Using the formula,

$$\sigma = \sqrt{\Sigma\frac{d^2}{N} - \left(\frac{\Sigma d}{N}\right)^2} = \sqrt{\frac{5343}{10} - \left(\frac{15}{10}\right)^2}$$

$$= \sqrt{534.3 - 2.25} = \sqrt{532.05} = \mathbf{23.07\ Ans.}$$

**Standard Deviation for Discrete Series**

For discrete series,

$$\sigma = \sqrt{\frac{\Sigma fd^2}{\Sigma f}}$$

where,

$d = X - \overline{X}$ = deviation fro the mean

$f$ = frequencies

**Example 12.9.** Calculate the standard deviation from the following:

| *Marks* | *No. of students* |
|---|---|
| 10 | 8 |
| 20 | 12 |
| 30 | 20 |
| 40 | 10 |
| 50 | 7 |
| 60 | 3 |

**Solution.** Computation of standard deviation from actual mean can be done in the tabular form as shown below:

| *Marks* ($x$) | $f$ | $f.x$ | $d = X - \overline{X}$ $= X - 30.8$ | $d^2$ | $f.d^2$ |
|---|---|---|---|---|---|
| 10 | 8 | 80 | -20.8 | 432.64 | 3461.12 |
| 20 | 12 | 240 | -10.8 | 116.64 | 1399.68 |
| 30 | 20 | 600 | -0.8 | 0.64 | 12.80 |
| 40 | 10 | 400 | 9.2 | 84.64 | 846.40 |
| 50 | 7 | 350 | 19.2 | 368.64 | 2580.48 |
| 60 | 3 | 180 | 29.2 | 852.64 | 2557.92 |
| $\Sigma = 210$ | $N = 60$ | $\Sigma fx = 1850$ | | | $\Sigma fd^2$ $= 10858.40$ |

Here, Mean, $$\overline{X} = \frac{\Sigma fx}{\Sigma f} = \frac{\Sigma fx}{N} = \frac{1850}{60} = 30.8$$

Standard deviation, $$\sigma = \sqrt{\frac{\Sigma f.d^2}{N}}$$

$$\sigma = \frac{\sqrt{10858.40}}{60} = \mathbf{13.45\ Ans.}$$

## 12.7. NORMAL DISTRIBUTION

The normal distribution was first discovered by the English mathematician De-Moivre in 1673 to solve the problem in game of chances. Later on, it was applied in natural and social sciences by the French mathematician La Place.

The normal distribution have already been discussed in the previous chapter. This distribution is widely used in the Statistical Quality Control. This type of distribution is applicable, when there is a concentration of observations about the average and it is equally likely that observations will occur above and below the average. Variation in observations is usually the result of many small causes.

**Characteristics of the Normal Curve**

Important properties of normal distribution are :

1. The curve is symmetrical and bell-shaped. The distribution of the frequencies on either side of the maximum ordinate of the curve is exactly the same. The number of cases above the mean value and below the mean value are equal. The height of the curve is maximum at the mean value, and this ordinate divides the curve into two equal parts.
2. Since the Mean = Median = Mode, these will coincide because the distribution is symmetrical and single peaked.
3. It has only one mode occurring at μ. The maximum ordinate is at,

$$x = \mu$$

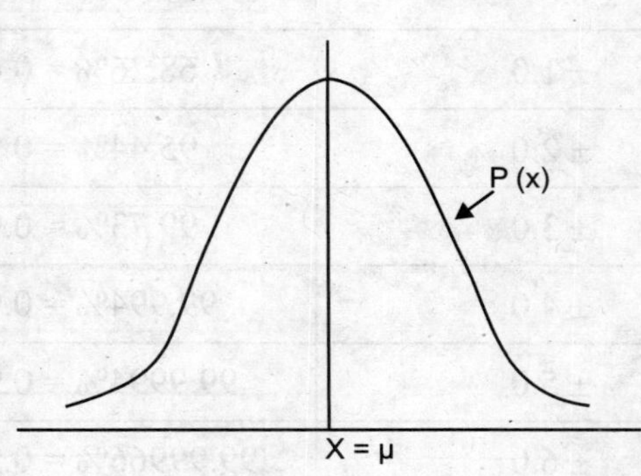


**Fig. 12.4**

4. The range is unlimited, infinite, in both directions, but as the distance from μ increases, the curve approaches the horizontal axis more and more closely. Theoretically, it never reaches the horizontal axis.

The value of maximum ordinate is $\frac{1}{\sigma\sqrt{2\pi}}$, When the standard deviation increaees, the maximum ordinate decreases and vice versa.

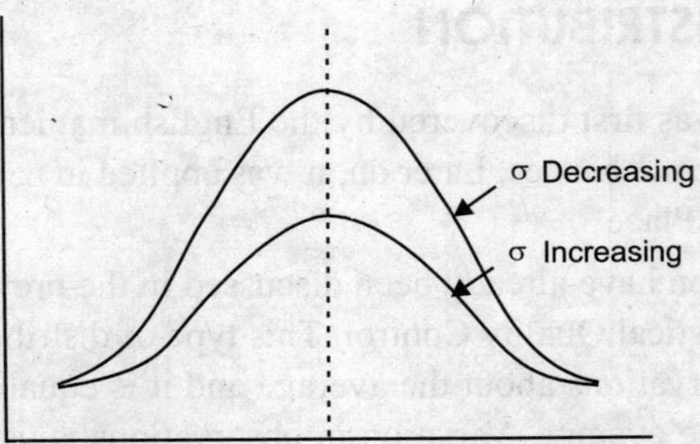


**Fig. 12.5**

6. Change in the value of mean and standard deviation or in both, will alter the position or shape, but the curve will always be symmetrical about the maximum ordinate.
7. At various standard deviation, the distances are in a fixed proportion to the ordinate at the mean. There is a fixed relationship between the total area of the curve and the areas between the mean ordinate and the ordinate at the various standard deviation distances. The area under the normal curve for some important values are as follows:

| *Distance from the mean ordinate in terms of* $\pm \sigma$ | *Area under the curve* |
|---|---|
| ± 0.6745 | 50% = 0.50 |
| ± 1.0 | 68.26% = 0.6826 |
| ± 2.0 | 95.44% = 0.9544 |
| ± 3.0 | 99.73% = 0.9973 |
| ± 4.0 | 99.994% = 0.99994 |
| ± 5.0 | 99.9994% = 0.999994 |
| ± 6.0 | 99.99966% = 0.9999966 |

**Importance of Normal Distribution**

1. It is applicable in many situations in which it is necessary to make inferences by taking samples.
2. It comes close to fitting actual observed frequency distributions of many phenomena.

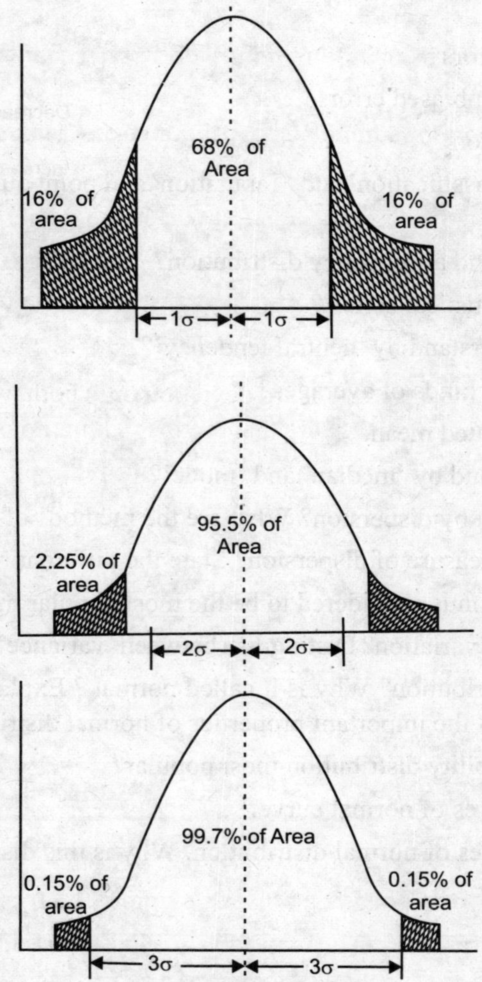


**Fig. 12.6** Relationship between the area under the curve and the distance from the mean measured in standard deviations.

## QUESTIONS

1. (*a*) What is Statistics?

   (*b*) Discuss the meaning and scope of Statistics.
2. Distinguish between the census and sampling methods on collecting data.
3. Explain the importance and significance of sample.
4. What is random sampling? How can a random sample be selected?
5. Define the law of statistical regularity.

6. Write short notes on:
    (*a*) Statistical errors
    (*b*) Biased and unbiased errors
    (*c*) Sampling errors.
7. Explain the terms 'Classification' and 'Tabulation' and point out their importance in statistical investigation.
8. (*a*) What is an array and a frequency distribution?
    (*b*) What is a statistical series ?
9. (*a*) What do you understand by 'central tendency'?
    (*b*) What are the kinds of averages?
    (*c*) Define weighted mean.
10. What do you understand by 'median' and 'mode'?
11. Explain what is meant by dispersion? What are the methods of computing dispersion ?
12. What is meant by a measure of dispersion? State the different methods of measuring it.
13. Why standard deviation is considered to be the most popular measure of dispersion ?
14. What is co-efficient of variation? Distinguish between 'variance' and 'co-efficient of variation'.
15. What is a normal distribution? Why is it called normal ? Explain its importance in statistical theory. Also, point out the important properties of normal distribution.
16. Why is normal probability distribution most popular?
17. State the salient features of normal curve.
18. List the chief properties of normal distribution. Why is this distribution given a central place in statistics?

# Acceptance Sampling and O.C. Curves

## 13.1. SAMPLING CONCEPT

Sampling is a technique used to discover facts about a particular population by considering a small part of that population. Here, the population means the total number of items in the whole field under investigation. While taking a sample, some checking is necessary to ensure that it is representative of the population. Sampling is based on statistical techniques and well-known laws of probability. The samples are drawn from a population to obtain information about the population itself. In order to get a reliable information, it is necessary that the samples chosen are representative.

### Types of Sampling

Following are the important ways of drawing a representative sample :

**1.** Judgement sampling. **2.** Random sampling.

**1. *Judgement* (*Non random*) *Sampling***

In this, a person estimate the characteristics of a population merely by sight. Because of the inaccuracy, this system is not commonly used. This sampling can, however, be used as a trial or pilot sampling to decide as to how to take a random sample.

**2. Random Sampling (*a*) *Simple Random* (*Probability*) *Sampling***

In this sampling we draw a sample of a certain size from a population in such a way so as to ensure that each member of the population has an equal chance of being included in the sample. The best way of drawing such a sample is to give a serial number to each number of the population and then make withdrawals according to a Random Number Table.

**(*b*) Systematic Sampling**

Systematic sampling of population is made by drawing an item at regular intervals that is measured in time, order or space *e.g.*, every fifth or tenth item, or an item produced every fifth or tenth minute.

**(c) Stratified Random Sampling**

In this sampling, the population is split into groups according to some characteristics and a simple random sample is drawn from each group, and a weightage is given to the results according to the group's proportion of total population.

**(d) Cluster Sampling**

In this, population is divided into groups or clusters, and then a random sample of these clusters is selected. It is assumed that these individual clusters are representative of the population as a whole. For example, dividing the city into blocks (clusters) as per territary maps.

We have seen that in both stratified and cluster samplings, the population is divided into well-defined groups. Stratified sampling is used, when each group has small variation within itself, but there is a wide variation between the groups. The cluster sampling is used, when there is considerable variation with in each group, but the groups are essentially similar to each other.

## 13.2. SAMPLING INSPECTION

To understand 'sampling inspection' properly, we must first discuss the two words 'sampling' and 'inspection'.

### Sampling

A sample may be defined as the number of items or component parts drawn from a lot, batch or population. Sampling is an act of drawing samples from a batch on random basis. Since sampling depends upon statistical probability, samples must be drawn from all sides and different depths of the box containing the batch of component parts, for inspection, so that every part has an equal chance of being selected. The samples should be collected at regular intervals from entire production run, so as to obtain a sample truly representative of the lot.

### Inspection

Every manufactured item or component is expected to perform certain functions. The act of checking whether the item or component will be able to perform that function, is known as inspection. The act of inspection separates defective items from non-defective ones to ensure the adequate quality of the product. It also locates defects in raw materials and flaws in the processes which otherwise cause problems at final stage.

## 13.3. ATTRIBUTES AND VARIABLES

In *attributes*, the number of articles conforming and number of articles failing to conform to any specified requirement are indicated, whereas in *variables*, an actual measured quality characteristics, such as dimension in cms, pressure in Kg/cm$^2$, temperature in degree centigrade, hardness in Rockwell units, weight in Kgms, life in hrs etc., are expressed.

### Inspection by Attributes or Variables

Quality of a characteristic can be inspected as :

(*i*) Inspection by attributes. (*ii*) Inspection by variables.

**(*i*) Inspection by Attributes**

In this system, it is seen whether an item satisfies a particular characteristic or not. Example of this type of inspection is, inspection by 'Go' and 'Not-Go' gauges. Attribute inspection, also known as Yes or No inspection, is used to differentiate between a defective and a non-defective part and the part is rejected or accepted without using quantitative measures. In this, inspection of sample is conducted on the basis of determining whether or not the product in the sample conforms to the specified tolerances.

Most requirements are necessarily stated in terms of attributes rather than variables. For example, the glass cover of a pressure gauge is either cracked or not cracked, a paper either has certain desired colour or not, in a spot welding in sheet metal either has not caused crack in the sheets or it has. These are used, where it is very difficult and costly to measure the quality characteristic of a product, *e.g.* measuring a quality of a paint on a transistor cabinet, or where it is not necessary to measure the exact dimension.

**(*ii*) Inspection by Variables**

In this system of inspection, a characteristic is measured on a continuous scale. Inspection using variables is mostly done on the shop floor and is important for the control of operations. Inspection using variables is more detailed, and contains more information, but involves-higher costs per unit as compared to inspection by attributes. Based on the requirement of the product, manufacturer decide as to which type of inspection is needed at a particular stage.

## 13.4. APPLICATION OF SAMPLING INSPECTION

The following are the important places, where sampling inspection is widely used:

(*i*) At all the places where destructive testing of product is not avoidable. In such cases 100% inspection is not possible.

(*ii*) Where 100% inspection causes lot of 'Fatigue'.

(*iii*) Where inspection cost is too high.

(*iv*) To determine the acceptability and quality of incoming raw materials, components and finished products.

(*v*) To determine the acceptability and quality of outgoing products, *i.e.*, the products which are complete and ready for shipment.

(*vi*) To determine the acceptability of work-in-process for further processing with-in the plant.

(*vii*) To improve and control the quality of product.

**Advantages**

Advantages of sampling inspection as compared to 100% inspection are :

(*i*) Less amount of inspection for achieving a pre-decided degree of certainty about the quality.

(*ii*) It is less expensive and less time consuming.

(*iii*) Since less fatigue and boredom is experienced by inspectors, their operating efficiency is high.

(*iv*) Since fewer parts are inspected, no damage to remaining pieces, where destructive test is necessary for inspection.

(*v*) Fear for rejection of entire lot, pressurizes for improvement in quality.

(*vi*) This is widely suitable in mass production.

(*vii*) The inspector can easily and efficiently be 'trained' on this 'technique'.

**Disadvantages**

It does not give definite assurance for the conformation of the specification.

## 13.5 DEFECTS (ERRORS)

Before discussing defects, their causes and remedies, we must first understand following terms:

1. **Defect.** A defect is any non-fulfillment of intended usage requirements. A defect can also be named as error discrepency or non-conformance.
2. **Symptom.** A symptom is an observable phenomenon arising from and accompanying a defect. Many times, a defect have multiple symptoms.
3. **Cause.** A cause is a proven reason for the existance of the defect. Often, there are multiple causes, in which case Pareto principle (*i.e.* the vital few causes dominate the rest) is followed for remedial action.
4. **Remedy.** A remedy is a change that can successfully eliminate or neutralize a cause of defects.

For the quality improvement, two journeys are followed:

**(*a*) Diagnostic journey: Symptom → Cause**

**(*b*) Remedial journey: Cause → Remedy.**

### Diagnosis

Diagnosis is the process of studying the symptoms of a problem and determining their cause(s). Diagnostic journey consists of:

1. A study to determine the origin of the defect in the design, manufacture etc.
2. A study to determine whether defects are primarily management-controllable (here "management" includes not only people in supervisory position, but also others who influence quality, such as design engineers, process engineers etc. or worker-controllable. In general, defects are more than 80 percent management controllable (some people term it as system-controllable) and less than 20 percent worker-controllable.

Diagnosis of management-controllable defects requires a study of current management practices and current technology. A successful diagnosis can take place by conducting the following:

(*i*) An analysis of symptoms.

(*ii*) A systematic formulation of theories for the causes of the symptoms, through brainstorming involving as many supervisors/managers as possible.

(*iii*) Thorough testing of the theories by: (*a*) analysing prior in-house data, (*b*) studying current operations and processes, and (*c*) conducting off-line experiments.

**Remedial Action**

Once a problem has been diagnosed, there may be many alternative remedies to choose from. The choice depends upon optimisation of company costs and customer costs. Activities that add no further value as far as customer is concerned, should be avoided. Most important remedial actions are those associated with the management-controllable problems, the majority of all company problems.

## Types of Errors

Majority of worker-oriented errors fall into one of the following three categories:

1. **Inadvertant Errors.** These are those errors which workers are unable to avoid because of human inability to maintain attention. These are unintentional, unpredictable errors occuring randomly, which the operator (worker) is unaware of making.

   Remedies for such errors involve two approaches:

   (*a*) Reducing the extent of dependence on human attention. This can be achieved through automation, alarm signals, or fail-safe designs etc.

   (*b*) Making it easier for human beings to remain attentive. This can be achieved by making the job more interesting or making it easier for the operator to retain attention. Other examples of remedies in this category are: re-organization of work to reduce fatigue and monotony, job rotation, and use of templates, masks, gauges etc.,

2. **Technique Errors.** Technique errors arise from lack of knowledge of an essential new technique. These errors are unintentional, specific and unique to certain defect types and are unavoidable (as the operators do not know fully about the technique) and consistent (the operator who does not possess the technique, make more defects than workers who possess the technique).

   The sequence of identifying, analysing and remedial measures are given hereunder:

   (*i*) For the defect types under study, collect the data which can disclose any significant differences between worker-to-worker.

   (*ii*) Analyse the data so collected to discover whether consistency is present.

   (*iii*) Identify the consistently best and consistently worst performers.

   (*iv*) Study the work methods used by the best and worst performers to identify their differences in technique.

(*v*) Study these differences further so as to discover the superior habits and bring everyone upto the level of the best through appropriate remedial action, such as training and job instruction programme.

3. **Conscious (wilful) Errors.** These are the errors that the operator makes intentionally and persistently. Examples of conscious errors include short-cut methods adopted by workers to meet arbitrary targets imposed by the management. Frustated or demotivated workforce also result into these errors. Fear induced by management may cause the operator not reveal the true levels of scrap and current defect rates so as to avoid being planned and therefore, opportunities for prevention of further mistakes are lost.

The remedial measures regarding conscious errors emphasize changes in behaviour through motivational factors.

**Some of the remedial measures for conscious errors are:**

1. **Motivate the workers:**
   (*a*) by allowing participation and involvement in the company's future,
   (*b*) by proper training and providing proper tools and techniques,
   (*c*) by making the jobs inherently interesting, and
   (*d*) by allowing the workers to take pride in their job. This shall encourage the state of self-control.
2. Improve communication and explain the impact of errors on internal or external customers.
3. Create positive competition with non-financial incentives.
4. Establishing individual accountability arid tracebility.
5. Providing balance between productivity and quality.
6. Remind workers about specific defects.
7. Re-assigning or rotating the work.
8. Conduct periodic quality audits.

**Defects Classification**

In sampling, the defects in a product can be classified in to three categories. These defects are also known as quality characteristics of any product and are:

(*a*) **Critical.** It is that defect which renders the use hazardous.

(*b*) **Major.** It is the defect which could result in the failure of the product or materially affect its usability, operation and performance.

(*c*) **Minor.** It is that defect which do not materially affect the quality, operation or performance of the product.

## 13.6. ACTION ON REJECTED LOT

If a lot consisting of work-in-process or complete product is rejected, it can be subjected to 100% inspection to take out all the defectives which can be sent directly to repair or sold as seconds or be scrapped entirely which ever procedure involves the least loss.

Secondly, as soon as any lot is rejected, the shop foreman must be informed immediately so that he can check the trouble and correct the faulty worker, process or equipment that may be responsible for the defective lot. Thus sampling inspection provides most important service to the shops by immediately stoping the flow of defective products and permits remedy before materials and time are needlessly wasted.

### 13.6.1. Random Sampling

Appendix A contains a portion of random number table. For convenience of readers, the digits are grouped into sets of 3 and are arranged in 12 rows. For obtaining random number, a pencil may be dropped blindly and the starting point for reading of the numbers shall be the random digit nearest to the spot indicated by the pencil. The random number, may then be read up or down, right or left, but it may perhaps be more convenient to read them vertically downward till the bottom of the page is reached and thereafter, the numbers in the adjacent column to the right are read starting from the top of the page and moving downward as earlier. This systematic method of reading the numbers may be carried on to the succeeding pages, if necessary.

If the random number to be chosen consists of single digit (as would be the case when lot size does not exceed 10, then the digit of any single column may be used, taking 0 to represent 10.

If the random number to be chosen consists of two digits ( as would be the case when lot size does not exceed 100) when any two adjoining column may be used taking 0 to represent 100.

If the random numbers to be chosen consist of three or more digits, then a similar method, as explained above may be followed.

**Example 13.1.** Suppose it is required to obtain a sample of 10 components from a lot of 200. If the components in the lot are assigned serial numbers upto 200, the problem then becomes to obtain 10 random numbers in the 1 to 200. Taking the 3 digited random numbers from Appendix A and starting from any number, say 190, occurring in the eleventh row, third coloumn proceeding downwards, the numbers so obtained are 190, 91, 45,10, 90, 29, 93, 83, 65 and 28. While in upward direction, these are 190, 48, 17, 22, 44, 40, 93, 33, 72 and 62. The components in the lot corresponding to these numbers shall then be selected to constitute the required random sample of size 10.

**APPENDIX A**

**Table 13.1 3 Digits Random Number Table**

ROWS

| | | | | | | | | | | | |
|---|---|---|---|---|---|---|---|---|---|---|---|
| 110 | 450 | 961 | 514 | 031 | 264 | 177 | 264 | 492 | 084 | 119 | 481 |
| 439 | 112 | 626 | 718 | 311 | 581 | 076 | 362 | 024 | 540 | 809 | 115 |

| 397 | 266 | 725 | 966 | 552 | 259 | 256 | 965 | 070 | 280 | 309 | 292 |
|---|---|---|---|---|---|---|---|---|---|---|---|
| 062 | 101 | 336 | 207 | 318 | 266 | 501 | 990 | 915 | 518 | 317 | 542 |
| 919 | 719 | 933 | 233 | 214 | 316 | 392 | 849 | 807 | 246 | 216 | 400 |
| 689 | 321 | 404 | 509 | 529 | 744 | 132 | 958 | 965 | 107 | 905 | 590 |
| 726 | 072 | 444 | 217 | 002 | 249 | 831 | 216 | 639 | 301 | 867 | 291 |
| 344 | 277 | 229 | 261 | 945 | 017 | 356 | 671 | 289 | 394 | 216 | 479 |
| 085 | 727 | 175 | 495 | 650 | 239 | 907 | 320 | 939 | 417 | 270 | 577 |
| 424 | 760 | 481 | 511 | 168 | 319 | 153 | 563 | 345 | 278 | 762 | 070 |
| 961 | 752 | 190 | 197 | 457 | 057 | 367 | 150 | 954 | 275 | 909 | 927 |
| 194 | 057 | 913 | 507 | 499 | 226 | 206 | 161 | 161 | 602 | 462 | 356 |
| 096 | 978 | 450 | 975 | 249 | 710 | 244 | 138 | 271 | 547 | 015 | 176 |
| 757 | 035 | 101 | 957 | 733 | 232 | 459 | 995 | 032 | 760 | 484 | 893 |
| 112 | 306 | 902 | 365 | 325 | 709 | 562 | 548 | 646 | 024 | 859 | 290 |
| 945 | 029 | 290 | 077 | 930 | 232 | 306 | 459 | 046 | 378 | 455 | 012 |
| 534 | 349 | 932 | 321 | 929 | 202 | 106 | 155 | 011 | 282 | 512 | 733 |
| 411 | 145 | 838 | 667 | 282 | 018 | 523 | 176 | 731 | 115 | 013 | 649 |
| 118 | 253 | 657 | 974 | 169 | 954 | 403 | 587 | 191 | 825 | 821 | 541 |
| 134 | 491 | 289 | 102 | 253 | 218 | 456 | 436 | 252 | 518 | 276 | 721 |
| 155 | 031 | 603 | 886 | 984 | 320 | 552 | 520 | 202 | 726 | 408 | 851 |
| 473 | 057 | 403 | 394 | 971 | 239 | 852 | 651 | 761 | 319 | 556 | 003 |
| 097 | 874 | 927 | 047 | 003 | 202 | 902 | 998 | 841 | 033 | 007 | 312 |
| 340 | 180 | 385 | 798 | 800 | 136 | 407 | 469 | 780 | 297 | 304 | 261 |
| 409 | 540 | 286 | 029 | 999 | 190 | 774 | 119 | 533 | 187 | 373 | 165 |
| 704 | 238 | 043 | 643 | 104 | 366 | 665 | 242 | 061 | 874 | 494 | 374 |
| 797 | 066 | 903 | 330 | 713 | 202 | 876 | 699 | 959 | 702 | 567 | 394 |
| 434 | 432 | 405 | 805 | 265 | 584 | 454 | 361 | 039 | 642 | 915 | 782 |
| 809 | 088 | 378 | 472 | 512 | 259 | 302 | 739 | 076 | 225 | 406 | 058 |

## 13.7. PROBABILITY CONCEPT

The basic idea in the theory of probability is the law of large numbers. Probability concept states that certain mass phenomenon have a tendency towards regularity in behaviour *i.e.* if sample is drawn from the mass of universe (population) without any bias that sample is quite likely to display those characteristics that are found in the whole mass. Therefore, inferences drawn from the study of such a sample can be relied upon as being representative of the 'whole mass'.

**Universe.** 'Universe' means a group of items from which a sample is drawn.

Sampling enables us to draw conclusions about a mass of items based upon the careful study of a small number of items. This number of items is known as 'sample'. The chief application of the theory of probability is in Statistical Quality Control. Inspection of each individual item of production to determine whether it meet specifications or not may be too expensive and monotonous. Therefore, samples are regularly taken at random from a lot and information from the study of samples tell us the extent to which specifications are being met.

Probability concept have been discussed as a separate chapter in this book.

## Application of Probability Concept in Quality Control

1. **Probability of finding defectives in a Sample.** Let us take 100 units, out of which 10 are known to be defective. Now, if a sample of $n$ units is taken and if it is used to study the true character of the lot, we are expected to receive 0.9 $n$ good units and 0.1 $n$ defectives. Therefore, the probability that a unit taken from the lot at random would be a good one is 0.90 and that it would be defective is 0.10. Similarly, the chances that the two units taken in succession would be all right are $0.90 \times 0.90$ or the chances that three good units in a lot would be $0.90 \times 0.90 \times 0.90$, *i.e.* $(0.90)^3$. So, in this way we can conclude that the probability in a sample of $n$ units will have no defective is given by – $q^n$.

Here, $q$ = actual proportion of good units in the lot.

$n$ = sample size.

2. **Frequency Distribution.** Frequency Distribution can be applied in following fields of Quality Control:
   1. To determine performance of incoming materials.
   2. To determine the amount of variation from that expected.
   3. To determine the performance of new product to facilitate its design.
   4. To determine the operating accuracies of machine tools and other processing equipment.
   5. To examine the difference between the dimensional characteristics of parts produced by two machine tools or two moulds.
   6. To examine the accuracy of fits between mating parts.
   7. To determine the effect of tool wear on a machine tool.

Frequency distribution patterns reveral the relative amount of variation in a lot. It also help us to determine whether or not the product is within the tolerance limits.

# 13.8. ACCEPTANCE SAMPLING

Sampling is the tool or technique of statistical quality control. Webster defined a sample as a product to represent the quality of the whole lot. Frequently, we in our daily life come in contact with sampling. For example, if we purchase a bag of potatoes, only a few potatoes can be observed from the whole bag, however, we draw an inference about the whole bag by only inspecting a few. If these look alright, it is assumed that all the potatoes in that bag will be alright.

As already discussed, the basic concept of sampling lies in testing the samples for acceptance or rejection. Some products, such as electric bulbs, radio valves, razor blades, bolts etc. require to be subjected to destructive tests so as to ascertain their life. A cent-percent inspection and destructive testing of such type of products cannot be possible and also sometimes the cost of cent-percent inspection is extremely high. Therefore, for such problems, acceptance sampling can be widely used.

In this method samples are collected at regular intervals and subjected for inspection.

For the purpose of acceptance, inspection is carried out at many stages in the process of manufacturing. These stages maybe: inspection of incoming materials and parts, process inspection at various points in the manufacturing operations, final inspection by a manufacturer of his own product and finally inspection of the finished product by the purchaser.

Inspection for acceptance is generally carried out on a sampling basis. The use of sampling inspection to decide whether or not to accept the lot is known as Acceptance Sampling. A sample from the inspection lot is inspected, and if the number of defective items is more than the stated number (the number is decided using statistics after a decision is taken about confidence level depending upon the place of application of the product and its criticality) known as Acceptance Number, the whole lot is rejected.

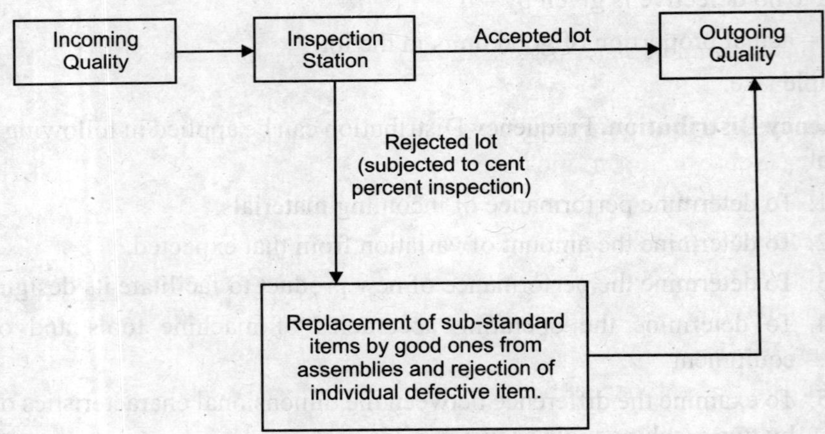


**Fig. 13.1.** Dealing with lot rejected in sampling inspection

The purpose of Acceptance Sampling is, therefore, to decide whether to accept or reject the lot. It does not control the quality during the process of manufacturing.

**Role of Acceptance Sampling**

Acceptance Sampling is very widely used in practice due to the following merits :

1. Acceptance Sampling is much less expensive than 100 percent inspection.
2. It is general experience that 100 percent inspection removes only 82 to 95 percent of defective material. Very good 100 percent inspection may removes at the most 99 percent of the defectives, but still cannot reach the level of 100 percent. Due to the effect of fatigue involved in 100 percent inspection, a good sampling plan may actually give better results than that achieved by 100 percent inspection.

3. Because of its economy, it is possible to carry out sample inspection at various stages. Acceptance number is evaluated using sampling plan and confidence level.
4. The 100 percent inspection is not possible, where quality can be tested only by destroying the items . In such cases, sampling inspection is the only solution.
5. Since handling of items is itself a source of damage, and as it handles lesser number of items, there are less chances of damage to the items.
6. Inspection takes lesser time.
7. Acceptance sampling is helpful in designing the prevention programmes.

Main disadvantage of the acceptance sampling is sampling risks: risks to the customer or to the manufacturer (as discussed under "OC curve" in the later part of this chapter). With the growing emphasis on statistical process control, the acceptance sampling is no longer a valid concept.

## 13.9. ECONOMICS OF INSPECTION

Lots are evaluated by adopting one of the following alternatives :

1. **No Inspection.** If same lot has been inspected earlier by qualified laboratories *e.g.* in other divisions of the same or sister organisation or by an organisation of repute, there is no need for inspection.
2. **Small Samples.** Sample of small size can be considered as adequate in cases where: (*a*) the process is inherently uniform, and (*b*) the product is homogeneous due to its fluidity (*i.e.* gases or liquids).
3. **Large Samples.** Large samples are drawn, when there is no prior knowledge about the product. Information about the lot quality is derived in such cases, by taking large samples drawn through random sampling.
4. **100 percent Inspection.** When results of sampling show that the level of defects present in lot is too high, 100 percent inspection becomes necessary.

Economic evaluation of these alternatives is explained hereunder:

Let, $N$ = Number of items in a lot

$n$ = Number of items in sample

$p$ = Proportion defective in the lot

$A$ = Damage cost, if a defective slips through inspection

$I$ = Inspection cost per item.

$P_a$ = Probability that lot will be accepted by sampling plan.

Total cost of each of the alternatives available for inspection are :

1. No inspection = $Np\,A$.
2. Sampling inspection = $nI + (N - n)\,p\,A\,P_a + (N - n)\,(1 - P_a)\,I$.

3. 100 percent inspection = $NI$

If we assume,

* No inspection error occurs
* Cost to replace a defective found in inspection is borne by the producer
* Cost to replace the defective found in inspection is small compared to the damage or inconvenience caused by a defective.

The sampling or 100 percent inspection is decided on the basis of break-even-point $p_b$,

$$P^b = \frac{I}{A}.$$

If lot quality $p$ is less than $p_b$, total cost will be lower with sampling inspection. If $p$ is greater than $p^b$, 100 percent inspection is economical.

## 13.10. SAMPLING PLANS

A decision required to be taken by quality men, for determining the acceptability of a lot of manufactured products. For this purpose, the lot is required to be evaluated by carrying out sampling inspection according to certain plans. The sampling plans are of following two types :

1. **Attributes Sampling Plans.** In this plan, a random sample is taken from the lot and each unit is inspected and classified as acceptable or defective. The total number of defective (non-conforming) items in the sample is then compared with the acceptance number in the plan, and a decision is made to accept or reject the lot. Attributes sampling plans are based on AQL, RQL, and AOQL. (Discussed under "Quality Indices" later in this chapter).
2. **Variables Sampling Plans.** In this plan, a sample is taken and a measurement of a specified quality characteristics is taken and recorded for each item in the sample. These measurements are then summarised and sample average is taken and the observed value is compared with an allowable value defined in the plan. A decision is then made to accept or reject the lot.

It may be mentioned that if the lot quality is uniform and the lot comprises of homogeneous items, then a small sample can be taken to represent the lot. However, each of the important quality characteristics needs to be evaluated against a separate variables acceptance criterion.

## 13.11. PROCEDURE OF SAMPLING INSPECTION

For setting up acceptance sampling inspection, following steps are taken:

1. Setting of inspection lots.
2. Arranging for rational lots.
3. Establishing an allowable percent defective.
4. Selecting sampling plan.

## 1. Setting of Inspection Lots.

Under sampling inspection, the lot size varies from about 300 products upto any number. Theoretically, there is no upper limit for the lot size, but in practice lots should be kept small enough so that they are easy to move and do not require special handling. For lots smaller than 300, either process inspection or screening is economical and, therefore, preferable.

Another factor influencing lot size is, how frequently you wish to inspect the work from one machine or process.

## 2. Arranging for Rational Lots.

A 'rational lot' is one whose units have been produced from the same source. As far as possible, a lot should consist of products manufactured from one batch of raw materials, one production line, one pattern or die and one and the same shift. Often it is not possible in practice to separate product as strictly as that but it should adhere to the rule of arranging rational lots as closely as possible. If we mix up products from different sources and find a bad lot, we cannot put our finger immediately on the source of trouble which can be pointed out, if there are rational lots.

## 3. Establishing an Allowable Percent Defective.

In mass production, it is often not possible to continually produce hundred percent satisfactory products. It can be assumed that certain percentage of defectives will always be present in certain processes; however, if the percentage do not exceed a certain limit, it is more economical to allow the defectives to go through rather than to sort out each lot. This limit is called the 'Allowable Percent Defective'.

But how to establish the Allowable Percent Defective? To do this, watch the product for some time while it is under regular operation. Collect sufficient data over a period of one to two weeks to determine the percentage of defective normally occurring in the products from certain equipment or process.

## 4. Selecting Sampling Plan

Now-a-days three important plans are in use :

(*a*) Single Sampling Plan.

(*b*) Double Sampling Plan.

(*c*) Sequential or Multiple Sampling Plan.

## (a) Single Sampling Plan

In inspection, defective product is one that fails to conform to specifications. The most common system in this plan is to take a single sample from the lot at random. Single sample does not mean one unit, it may have number of units. The acceptance and rejection of the lot depends on the number of defectives in the sample. For designing a sampling plan, the following symbols may be used :

$N$ = Number of products in a given lot.

$n$ = Number of samples drawn from the lot ($N$) at random.

$A$ = Acceptance number. It means the maximum allowable number of defectives in a sample size, $n$.

$R$ = Rejection number.

**Selection of *N* and *n*.** Selection of the values of $N$ and $n$ can be done in two ways :

1. Sample inspected may have some fix percentage of lot, i.e.

$$\frac{n}{N} \times 100 = \text{constant.}$$

In such methods, percentage varies from 10 to 20%.

This method is used, when lot size is comparatively small.

2. In this method, the value of $n$, *i.e.* sample size is obtained from Master Table for Single Sampling plan.

The procedure of single sampling plan is explained as under :

(*i*) Inspect a sample of n pieces.

(*ii*) If the number of defects found in the sampling does not exceed ($A$) accept the lot.

(*iii*) If the number of defects found in the sample exceeds ($A$) inspect all the pieces in the remainder of the lot.

(*iv*) Correct or replace all the defective pieces found.

For example, let us take that the allowable percent defective for a certain item is 1 per cent. Lot size is 400. From the master Table, the sample size requirement is 75, then acceptance number is 1 and rejection number 2.

Now from the lot size of 400 units, take 75 units at random. Accept the lot, if not more than one defective piece is found, since the acceptance number is 1. If two or more defectives are found, reject the lot, since rejection number is 2.

## (b) Double Sampling Plan

In the single sampling plan, if the sample for inspection is found defective, then the entire lot is rejected. To overcome this, double sampling plan is a sort of modification on single sampling plan. In this method, the lot is not rejected but again a second sample is taken to judge the quality. The procedure is explained as flow diagram shown in Fig 3.2.

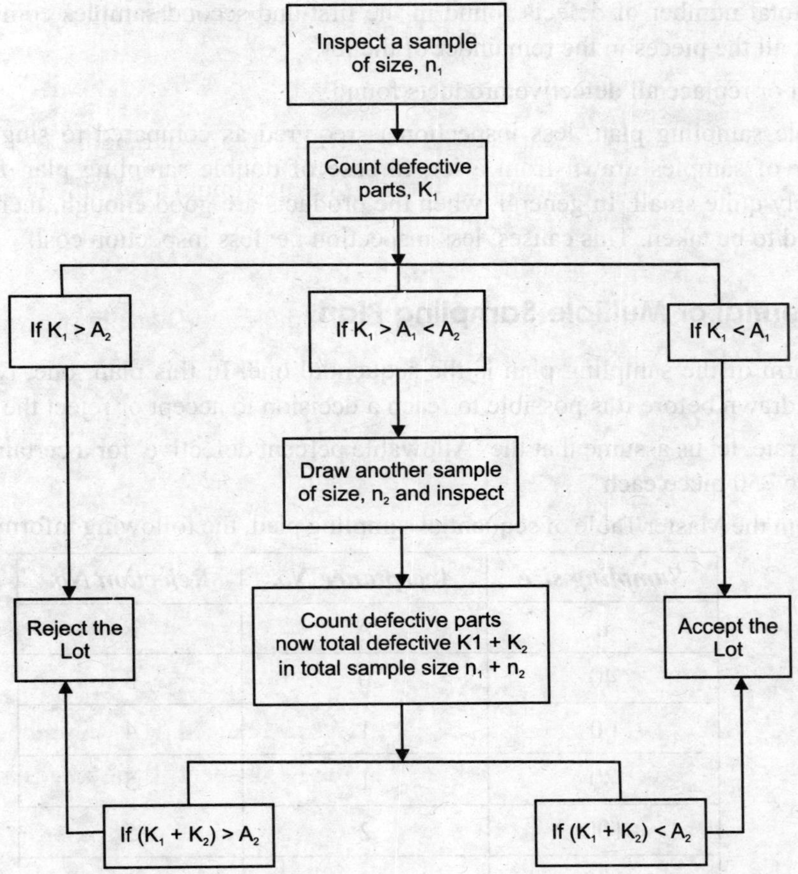


**Fig. 13.2.** Double sampling plan

Let, $n_1$ = Number of products in the first sample.

$A_1$ = Acceptance number for first sample.

$n_2$ = Number of products in the second sample.

$A_2$ = Acceptance number for both the samples.

(*i*) Inspect first sample of $n_1$ pieces.

(*ii*) If the number of defects found in the sample does not exceed $A_1$, accept the lot.

(*iii*) If the number of defects found in the first sample exceeds $A_2$, inspect all the products in the remainder of the lot.

(*iv*) If the number of defects in first sample exceed $A_1$, but does not exceed $A_2$, inspect a second sample of $n_2$ pieces.

(*v*) If the total number of defects in the first and the second sample combined does not exceed $A_2$, accept the lot.

(*vi*) If the total number of defects found in the first and second samples combined exceeds $A_2$, inspect all the pieces in the remainder of the lot.

(*vii*) Correct or replace all defective products found.

In double sampling plan, less inspection is required as compared to single sampling plan. The number of samples drawn from a lot, in case of double sampling plan for first sample is comparatively quite small. In general, when the products are good enough, then very few second samples need to be taken. This causes, less inspection i.e. less inspection cost.

## (c) Sequential or Multiple Sampling Plan

The third form of the sampling plan is the sequential one. In this plan, one, two, three or more samples are drawn before it is possible to reach a decision to accept or reject the lot.

To illustrate, let us assume that the 'Allowable percent defective' for a certain product is 2 percent. Lot size 750 piece each.

Now from the Master Table of sequential sampling plan, the following information is collected:

| ***Sampling size*** | ***Acceptance No.*** | ***Rejection No.*** |
|---|---|---|
| n | A | R |
| 40 | 0 | 3 |
| 60 | 1 | 4 |
| 80 | 1 | 5 |
| 100 | 2 | 5 |
| 120 | 4 | 5 |

Now begin by selecting 40 sample pieces at random from the lot. If there are no defectives accept the lot, since acceptance number is 0. If there are three or more defectives, reject the lot a the rejection number is 3. But when the defectives found are between the acceptance and rejectio numbers, *i.e.* 1 to 2 in this case, the lot can neither be accepted nor rejected. Now, collect additiona information by taking another sample of 20 from the lot. This brings the total sample size to 60 = (40+20).

Again compare the total number of defectives found to determine whether to accept or rejec the lot or to continue sampling. This process may go on until the highest sample size 120 is reache at which the gap between the acceptance and rejection number disappears and the problem o acceptability solved.

The following table shows the comparative size of samples with their acceptance and rejectio numbers developed for single, double and sequential sampling plans.

| | | | | Combined sample | |
|---|---|---|---|---|---|
| ***Type of Sampling*** | ***Sample*** | ***Sample size*** | ***Size*** | ***Acceptance number*** | ***Rejection number*** |
| Single | First | 225 | 225 | 14 | 15 |
| Double | First | 150 | 150 | 9 | 24 |
| | Second | 300 | 450 | 23 | 24 |
| Sequential | First | 50 | 50 | 1 | 6 |
| | Second | 50 | 100 | 3 | 9 |
| | Third | 50 | 150 | 7 | 13 |
| | Fourth | 50 | 200 | 10 | 16 |
| | Fifth | 50 | 250 | 13 | 19 |
| | Sixth | 50 | 300 | 16 | 22 |
| | Seventh | 50 | 350 | 19 | 25 |
| | Eighth | 50 | 400 | 24 | 25 |

From the table, it is found that sequential sampling requires comparatively much less inspection than single and double sampling, hence widely adopted. Still there are some plans where single sampling is preferred. The reason being their material handling problems. For example, if the product is heavy and difficult to transport, such as heavy coils, large castings, heavy large machine parts etc., it will be less costly to move a large number of sample articles to a place of inspection once instead to transport much smaller number of articles several times.

## 13.12. QUALITY INDICES

Quality indices for acceptance sampling plans are :

1. ***Acceptance Quality Level (AQL).***

   It is a fraction defective that can be tolerated without serious effect on further processing operation or customer reaction. In other words, AQL is the maximum percent defective that for the purpose of sampling inspection, can be considered satisfactory as a process average. AQL can also be termed as maximum number or percentage of defective pieces in a 'good' lot.

**Table 13.2 Master Table of Single Sampling Plan**

| Lot size | Sample Size | *Allowable Percent Defective* | | | | | | | | | | | | | | | | | | | | | |
|---|---|---|---|---|---|---|---|---|---|---|---|---|---|---|---|---|---|---|---|---|---|---|---|
| | | 0.025 | | 0.50 | | 0.75 | | 1 | | 2 | | 3 | | 4 | | 5 | | 6-7 | | 8 | | 9-12 | |
| | | A | R | A | R | A | R | A | R | A | R | A | R | A | R | A | R | A | R | A | R | A | R |
| 499 to less | 75 | | | | | | | 1 | 2 | 2 | 3 | 3 | 4 | 4 | 5 | 5 | 6 | 6 | 7 | 8 | 9 | 10 | 11 |
| 500 to 799 | 115 | | | | | ↓ | | 2 | 3 | 3 | 4 | 4 | 5 | 6 | 7 | 8 | 9 | 9 | 10 | 11 | 12 | 14 | 15 |
| 800 to 1299 | 150 | | | ↓ | | 1 | 2 | 3 | 4 | 4 | 5 | 5 | 6 | 8 | 9 | 10 | 11 | 12 | 13 | 15 | 16 | 20 | 21 |
| 1300 to 3199 | 225 | | | 1 | 2 | 2 | 3 | 4 | 5 | 5 | 6 | 8 | 9 | 11 | 12 | 14 | 15 | 17 | 18 | 21 | 22 | 29 | 30 |
| 3200 to 7999 | 300 | ↓ | | 2 | 3 | 3 | 4 | 5 | 6 | 7 | 8 | 10 | 11 | 14 | 15 | 18 | 19 | 22 | 23 | 26 | 27 | ↑ | |
| 8000 to 21,999 | 450 | 1 | 2 | 3 | 4 | 4 | 5 | 6 | 7 | 9 | 10 | 14 | 15 | 20 | 21 | 26 | 27 | ↑ | | ↑ | | | |
| 22,000 to 99,999 | 750 | 2 | 3 | 4 | 5 | 5 | 6 | 8 | 9 | 13 | 14 | 23 | 24 | ↑ | | ↑ | | | | | | | |
| 100,0000 to up | 1500 | 3 | 4 | 6 | 7 | 8 | 9 | 13 | 14 | 23 | 24 | ↑ | | | | | | | | | | | |

*A* = Acceptance Number, *R* = Rejection Number

Arrows → : When there is an arrow, below given, *i.e.* Allowable Percent Defective, use first sampling data below arrow in upper left-hand corner (Forming large lot, if possible) or first sampling data above arrows in lower right hand, as the case may be.

## Table 13.3 Master Sampling Table of Sequential Plan

| Lot Size | Sample Size | Allowable | | | | | | Percent | | | | | | | | | | Defective | | | | | | | | | | | | | |
|---|---|---|---|---|---|---|---|---|---|---|---|---|---|---|---|---|---|---|---|---|---|---|---|---|---|---|---|---|---|---|---|
| | | 0.25 | | 0.50 | | 0.75 | | 1 | | 1.5 | | 2 | | 3 | | 4 | | 5 | | 6 | | 7 | | 8 | | 9 | | 10 | | 12 | |
| | | A | R | A | R | A | R | A | R | A | R | A | R | A | R | A | R | A | R | A | R | A | R | A | R | A | R | A | R | A | R |
| (1) | (2) | (3) | | (4) | | (5) | | (6) | | (7) | | (8) | | (9) | | (10) | | (11) | | (12) | | (13) | | (14) | | (15) | | (16) | | (17) | |
| | 40 | | | | | | | 0 | 1 | 0 | 2 | 0 | 3 | 1 | 4 | 1 | 4 | 2 | 6 | 2 | 6 | 7 | | 3 | 7 | 3 | 8 | 4 | 9 | 4 | 9 |
| | 50 | | | | | | | 0 | 2 | 0 | 3 | 1 | 3 | 1 | 4 | 2 | 5 | 2 | 6 | 3 | 7 | 2 | 8 | 4 | 9 | 4 | 9 | 5 | 10 | 5 | 11 |
| 499 to | 60 | | | | | | | 0 | 3 | 1 | 3 | 1 | 3 | 2 | 5 | 2 | 6 | 3 | 7 | 4 | 8 | 4 | 9 | 5 | 10 | 5 | 11 | 7 | 12 | 8 | 11 |
| less | 70 | | | | | | | 1 | 3 | 1 | 4 | 1 | 4 | 2 | 5 | 3 | 6 | 4 | 8 | 5 | 9 | 5 | 9 | 6 | 10 | 7 | 11 | 8 | 13 | 7 | 13 |
| | 80 | | | | | ↓ | | 2 | 4 | 3 | 4 | 3 | 4 | 4 | 5 | 5 | 6 | 7 | 8 | 8 | 9 | 8 | 9 | 9 | 10 | 10 | 11 | 12 | 13 | 8 | 13 |
| | 40 | | | | | | +1 | | +2 | 0 | 3 | 0 | 3 | 0 | 4 | 1 | 5 | 1 | 5 | 1 | 6 | 1 | 7 | 2 | 8 | 2 | 8 | 2 | 9 | 4 | 10 |
| | 60 | | | | | | +1 | 0 | 2 | 0 | 3 | 1 | 4 | 1 | 5 | 2 | 6 | 2 | 7 | 3 | 8 | 3 | 9 | 4 | 10 | 5 | 11 | 5 | 11 | 6 | 12 |
| 500 to | 80 | | | | | 0 | 2 | 1 | 3 | 1 | 4 | 1 | 5 | 1 | 6 | 3 | 7 | 3 | 8 | 5 | 10 | 5 | 11 | 6 | 12 | 7 | 13 | 8 | 14 | 9 | 15 |
| 799 | 100 | | | | | 0 | 2 | 1 | 3 | 2 | 4 | 2 | 5 | 2 | 6 | 4 | 8 | 5 | 9 | 6 | 11 | 7 | 13 | 8 | 14 | 9 | 16 | 10 | 17 | 12 | 18 |
| | 120 | | | ↓ | | 1 | 2 | 2 | 3 | 2 | 3 | 4 | 5 | 5 | 6 | 7 | 5 | 8 | 9 | 10 | 11 | 12 | 13 | 13 | 14 | 15 | 16 | 16 | 17 | 18 | 19 |
| | 40 | | | | +1 | | +1 | | +2 | | +3 | 0 | 3 | 0 | 4 | 0 | 5 | 0 | 6 | 1 | 6 | 1 | 7 | 1 | 8 | 2 | 8 | 2 | 9 | 2 | 10 |
| | 60 | | | | +2 | 0 | 2 | 0 | 2 | 0 | 3 | 0 | 4 | 1 | 5 | 1 | 6 | 2 | 7 | 2 | 8 | 3 | 9 | 3 | 10 | 4 | 11 | 4 | 11 | 5 | 12 |
| 800 to | 80 | | | 0 | 2 | 0 | 2 | 0 | 3 | 1 | 4 | 1 | 5 | 2 | 6 | 2 | 7 | 3 | 8 | 4 | 10 | 5 | 11 | 5 | 12 | 6 | 13 | 8 | 15 | 8 | 15 |
| 1299 | 100 | | | 0 | 2 | 0 | 2 | 0 | 3 | 1 | 4 | 1 | 5 | 2 | 6 | 3 | 8 | 5 | 10 | 5 | 11 | 7 | 13 | 7 | 14 | 9 | 15 | 10 | 17 | 10 | 18 |
| | 120 | | | 0 | 2 | 1 | 3 | 1 | 3 | 2 | 5 | 2 | 6 | 3 | 7 | 5 | 9 | 6 | 11 | 7 | 13 | 8 | 14 | 9 | 16 | 11 | 18 | 12 | 19 | 13 | 21 |
| | 160 | ↓ | | 1 | 2 | 2 | 3 | 3 | 4 | 4 | 5 | 5 | 6 | 7 | 8 | 9 | 10 | 11 | 11 | 13 | 14 | 15 | 16 | 16 | 17 | 18 | 19 | 19 | 20 | 22 | 23 |
| | 50 | | +1 | | +1 | | +2 | | +3 | | +3 | 0 | 4 | 0 | 4 | 0 | 5 | 0 | 6 | 1 | 7 | 1 | 8 | 2 | 9 | 2 | 10 | 3 | 10 | 3 | 11 |
| | 75 | | +1 | | +1 | 0 | 2 | 0 | 3 | 0 | 4 | 0 | 5 | 1 | 5 | 2 | 7 | 2 | 8 | 3 | 9 | 4 | 10 | 4 | 12 | 5 | 12 | 6 | 14 | 6 | 15 |
| 1300 to | 100 | | +1 | 0 | 2 | 0 | 2 | 1 | 4 | 1 | 4 | 1 | 5 | 2 | 6 | 3 | 8 | 4 | 9 | 5 | 11 | 6 | 12 | 6 | 14 | 8 | 15 | 9 | 17 | 10 | 18 |
| 3199 | 125 | 0 | 2 | 0 | 2 | 1 | 3 | 1 | 4 | 2 | 5 | 2 | 6 | 3 | 7 | 4 | 9 | 5 | 11 | 7 | 13 | 8 | 15 | 9 | 16 | 11 | 18 | 12 | 20 | 13 | 21 |
| | 150 | 0 | 2 | 0 | 2 | 1 | 3 | 2 | 5 | 2 | 5 | 3 | 7 | 4 | 8 | 9 | 10 | 7 | 13 | 9 | 15 | 10 | 17 | 11 | 19 | 14 | 21 | 15 | 23 | 15 | 25 |
| | 200 | 1 | 2 | 1 | 2 | 2 | 3 | 4 | 5 | 5 | 6 | 6 | 7 | 8 | 9 | 10 | 11 | 13 | 14 | 17 | 18 | 17 | 18 | 20 | 21 | 22 | 29 | 25 | 26 | 27 | 28 |
| | 50 | | +1 | | +2 | | +2 | | +3 | | +3 | | +4 | + | 5 | 0 | 6 | 0 | 7 | 0 | 8 | 1 | 9 | 1 | 10 | 1 | 11 | 2 | 11 | 2 | 12 |
| | 100 | | +1 | | +2 | 0 | 3 | 0 | 4 | 1 | 4 | 1 | 5 | 1 | 7 | 2 | 8 | 3 | 10 | 4 | 12 | 5 | 13 | 5 | 15 | 6 | 16 | 8 | 17 | 9 | 19 |
| 3200 to | 150 | 0 | 2 | 0 | 3 | 1 | 4 | 1 | 5 | 2 | 5 | 2 | 8 | 5 | 11 | 5 | 15 | 8 | 14 | 9 | 17 | 10 | 17 | 10 | 19 | 11 | 21 | 13 | 23 | 15 | 25 |
| 7999 | 200 | 0 | 2 | 1 | 3 | 2 | 4 | 2 | 5 | 3 | 6 | 3 | 8 | 5 | 10 | 7 | 13 | 8 | 16 | 12 | 19 | 13 | 21 | 15 | 24 | 16 | 26 | 19 | 29 | 21 | 31 |
| | 250 | 0 | 2 | 1 | 4 | 2 | 3 | 2 | 6 | 4 | 8 | 5 | 9 | 6 | 11 | 9 | 15 | 11 | 18 | 15 | 22 | 17 | 25 | 19 | 28 | 22 | 32 | 25 | 35 | 28 | 38 |
| | 300 | 1 | 2 | 3 | 4 | 4 | 5 | 5 | 6 | 7 | 8 | 8 | 9 | 10 | 11 | 15 | 18 | 18 | 18 | 22 | 23 | 25 | 26 | 29 | 30 | 32 | 33 | 36 | 37 | 39 | 43 |

| | | | | | | | | | | | | | | | | | | | | | | | | | | | | | | | |
|---|---|---|---|---|---|---|---|---|---|---|---|---|---|---|---|---|---|---|---|---|---|---|---|---|---|---|---|---|---|---|---|
| 8000 to 9999 | 100 | | +2 | | +3 | | +3 | | +4 | 0 | 5 | 0 | 5 | 0 | 7 | 1 | 9 | 1 | 11 | 3 | 12 | 3 | 14 | 4 | 16 | 5 | 17 | ↑ | | ↑ | |
| | 150 | | +2 | | +3 | 0 | 4 | 0 | 5 | 1 | 6 | 2 | 7 | 2 | 9 | 3 | 11 | 4 | 14 | 6 | 16 | 7 | 17 | 9 | 20 | 10 | 22 | | | | |
| | 200 | 0 | 2 | 0 | 3 | 0 | 5 | 1 | 6 | 2 | 7 | 3 | 8 | 3 | 10 | 6 | 13 | 7 | 17 | 10 | 19 | 11 | 12 | 13 | 14 | 16 | 27 | | | | |
| | 250 | 0 | 2 | 0 | 4 | 1 | 5 | 2 | 6 | 2 | 8 | 4 | 9 | 5 | 12 | 8 | 16 | 10 | 19 | 13 | 22 | 15 | 25 | 18 | 29 | 19 | 32 | | | | |
| | 300 | 0 | 3 | 1 | 4 | 2 | 6 | 2 | 7 | 3 | 8 | 5 | 11 | 6 | 19 | 10 | 18 | 12 | 22 | 16 | 26 | 19 | 29 | 23 | 33 | 24 | 37 | | | | |
| | 400 | 1 | 3 | 1 | 4 | 3 | 7 | 4 | 8 | 5 | 10 | 5 | 14 | 10 | 16 | 14 | 22 | 18 | 27 | 23 | 33 | 27 | 37 | 31 | 42 | 34 | 47 | | | | |
| | 500 | 2 | 3 | 3 | 4 | 6 | 7 | 7 | 8 | 9 | 10 | 13 | 14 | 16 | 17 | 22 | 23 | 28 | 29 | 34 | 35 | 40 | 41 | 45 | 46 | 50 | 51 | | | | |
| 22,000 to 99,999 | 100 | | +2 | | +3 | | +4 | | +5 | | +6 | | +8 | 0 | 8 | 0 | 11 | 2 | 19 | 2 | 16 | ↑ | | ↑ | | ↑ | | | | | |
| | 200 | | +3 | | +4 | 0 | 6 | 1 | 7 | 1 | 7 | 1 | 10 | 3 | 11 | 3 | 15 | 6 | 18 | 8 | 20 | | | | | | | | | | |
| | 300 | 0 | 3 | 0 | 4 | 1 | 6 | 1 | 8 | 2 | 9 | 3 | 12 | 5 | 14 | 7 | 19 | 11 | 23 | 14 | 26 | | | | | | | | | | |
| | 400 | 0 | 3 | 1 | 5 | 2 | 7 | 3 | 9 | 4 | 11 | 5 | 14 | 8 | 17 | 11 | 23 | 16 | 28 | 21 | 23 | | | | | | | | | | |
| | 600 | 1 | 4 | 2 | 6 | 3 | 9 | 5 | 11 | 7 | 14 | 10 | 18 | 14 | 23 | 19 | 31 | 27 | 28 | 34 | 46 | | | | | | | | | | |
| | 800 | 1 | 4 | 3 | 7 | 5 | 11 | 8 | 14 | 11 | 17 | 14 | 28 | 20 | 28 | 27 | 28 | 37 | 49 | 46 | 58 | | | | | | | | | | |
| | 1000 | 3 | 4 | 6 | 7 | 10 | 11 | 13 | 14 | 17 | 18 | 22 | 23 | 30 | 31 | 40 | 41 | 53 | 54 | 65 | 66 | | | | | | | | | | |
| 100,000 and up | 200 | | +3 | | +5 | | +7 | | +8 | 0 | 9 | 0 | 13 | 2 | 13 | 2 | 18 | ↑ | | ↑ | | | | | | | | | | | |
| | 400 | | +4 | 0 | 6 | 0 | 8 | 0 | 10 | 3 | 12 | 3 | 17 | 7 | 18 | 9 | 25 | | | | | | | | | | | | | | |
| | 600 | 0 | 4 | 1 | 7 | 2 | 10 | 2 | 12 | 5 | 15 | 7 | 20 | 12 | 22 | 17 | 23 | | | | | | | | | | | | | | |
| | 80 | 1 | 5 | 1 | 8 | 4 | 11 | 5 | 14 | 8 | 18 | 11 | 14 | 28 | 29 | 24 | 40 | | | | | | | | | | | | | | |
| | 1000 | 1 | 5 | 3 | 9 | 5 | 13 | 7 | 17 | 11 | 21 | 15 | 28 | 23 | 25 | 32 | 47 | | | | | | | | | | | | | | |
| | 1200 | 2 | 5 | 3 | 9 | 7 | 15 | 9 | 19 | 14 | 24 | 19 | 32 | 28 | 40 | 39 | 55 | | | | | | | | | | | | | | |
| | 1600 | 4 | 5 | 8 | 9 | 14 | 15 | 19 | 20 | 24 | 25 | 33 | 24 | 45 | 46 | 61 | 62 | | | | | | | | | | | | | | |

2. ***Rejectable Quality Level (RQL).***

   This is also known as 'lot tolerance percentage defective (LTPD). It represents the percentage defectives in a lot that can be tolerated in only a specified proportion of lots. By adopting a sampling plan that will reject most of the lots offered that would cause too much unfavourable reaction of the customer. This RQL helps in real protection against unsatisfactory material, reaching the customer. RQL or LTPD can also be expressed by the minimum number or percentage of defective pieces in a "bad" lot. This can also be termed as 'Limiting Quality Level' (LQL)

3. ***Average Outgoing Quality Limit (AOQL).*** This is the limit of quality, worst than which a consumer will not get any lot. AOQL represents the maximum average percent defective in the outgoing products.

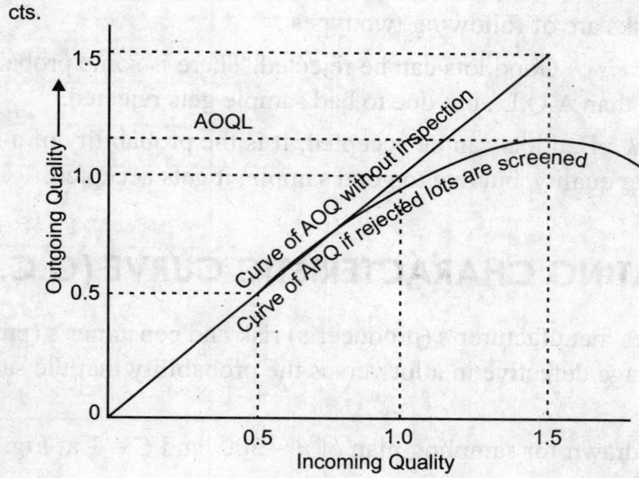


**Fig. 1.3.3.** A.O.Q.L.

4. ***Acceptance Sampling Number (ASN).*** It is the maximum allowable number of defective pieces for acceptance of the lot.

## DODGE-ROMING SAMPLING TABLES

Dodge and Roming have developed an extensive and valuable set of readymade sampling tables, the plans of which are very simple and useful. These have been developed to minimise the total inspection. These provide four sets of attributes plans emphasizing either lot-by-lot quality *i.e.* lot tolerance percentage defective (LTPD) or long-run quality *i.e.* average outgoing quality limit (AOQL):

1. Single-sampling for lot tolerance tables (LTPD).
2. Double-sampling for lot tolerance tables (LTPD).
3. Single-sampling AOQL tables.
4. Double-sampling AOQL tables.

In these plans, all rejected lots are 100 percent inspected and the defective items are replaced with acceptable items. Because of this feature, these plans are called **rectifying inspection plans.**

The readymade plans like, Dodge-Roming tables, ABC standard tables, ABC-STD-105 tables; and IS : 2500 (part II)-1965 plans are also known as **"published sampling plans".**

## 13.13. SAMPLING RISKS

Neither sampling nor 100 percent inspection can guarantee that no defective item in a lot will be found. A risk is involved in the sampling that the sample will not adequately reflect the conditions in the lot. Even 100 percent inspection has the risk that monotony and other factors may allow some of the defectives to escape.

The sampling risks are of following two types :

1. *Manufacturer's risk :* Good lots can be rejected. There is some probability that a batch being good *i.e.* better than A.Q.L., but due to bad sample gets rejected.
2. *Consumer's risk :* Bad lots can be accepted. It is the probability of a lot being bad *i.e.* worse than the limiting quality, but due to good sample, it gets accepted.

## 13.14. OPERATING CHARACTERISTIC CURVE (O.C. CURVE)

O.C. Curve quantifies manufacturer's (producer's) risk and consumer's (purchaser's) risk. This is a graph of the percentage defective in a lot versus the probability that the sampling plan will accept a lot.

An O.C. Curve drawn for sampling plan of $n = 300$ and $C = 1$ at Fig. 3.4 below indicates the following :

$AQL = 0.02$ or 2%

Manufacturer's, risk = 0.05

Consumer's risk = 0.10

LTPD (Bad quality) = .05 or more defectives.

All practical sampling plans have an operating characteristics curve, briefly called O.C. curve. Following points need emphasis regarding O.C.curves:

(*i*) There is some chance that good lots will be rejected.

(*ii*) There is some chance that bad lots will be accepted.

(*iii*) These risks can be calculated by the theory of probability and depends on the number of samples inspected, the acceptance number, and the percent defectives in the lot offered for sample inspection.

Given,

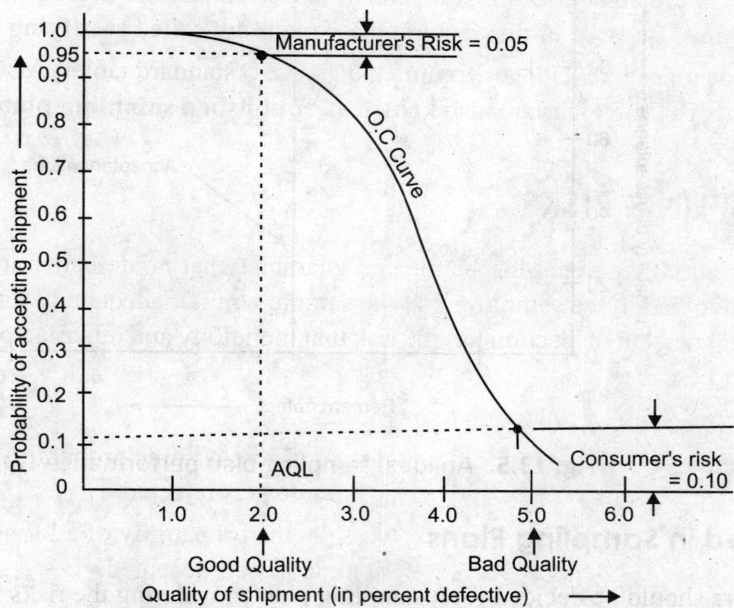


**Fig. 13.4.** O.C. Curve indicating sampling risks.

the amount of risks which can be tolerated, a sampling plan can be devised to meet these requirements.

(*iv*) The larger the sample used for inspection, the nearer the O.C. curve approaches the ideal. However, beyond a certain point, the added cost in inspecting a large number of parts far exceeds the benefit derived.

In any acceptance sampling plan, three parameters are specified. The first parameter is number of articles *N* in the lot from which sample is to be drawn. The second parameter is the number of articles *n* in the random sample drawn from the lot, and the third is the acceptance number *C*. This acceptance number *C* is the maximum allowable number of defective articles in the sample. If more than *C* defectives are found in a sample, the lot is liable to be rejected. Since the lot size has little affect on the probability of acceptance, therefore, lot size is generally ignored in deriving a sampling plan.

O.C. Curve of an acceptance sampling plan (i.e. for a particular combination of n and C) shows how well the sampling plan discriminates between good and bad lots. In order to examine the suitability of an acceptance sampling plan, it is necessary to compare their performance over a range of possible quality levels of the product. The graph of this performance is known as operating characteristic curve (O.C. curve). Fig. 3.5 below shows an ideal O.C. Curve, where it is desired to accept all lots having 3% or less defectives, and to reject all lots having more than 3% defectives. In this curve, all lots with less than 3% defectives have a probability of acceptance of 100%, while all lots with more than 3% defectives have a probability of acceptance as 0%. However, such a plan does not exist in reality.

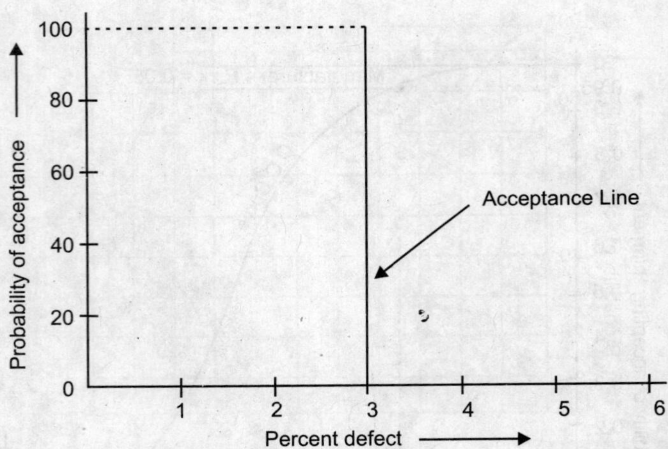


**Fig. 13.5.** An ideal sampling plan performance

## Risks Involved in Sampling Plans

Following factors should be decided for a sampling plan considering the risks involved:

(*i*) ***Acceptance Quality Level* (*AQL*)** $P_1$. To measure the producer's risk, a minimum percent of defective items in a lot is decided below which the lot should be accepted. This is known as A.Q.L.

(*ii*) ***Rejectable Quality Level* (*R.Q.L.*)**, $P_2$. To measure the customer's risk, we must decide maximum percent of defective items in a lot which he can accept. This is called R.Q.L, or Lot Tolerance Percent Defective (L.T.P.D.)

(*iii*) ***Producer's Risk.*** This is probability of rejecting a good lot.

(*iv*) ***Consumer's Risk.*** This is probability of accepting a poor lot.

## 13.14.1. O.C. Curves for Single Sampling Plan

Graph 13.6 is an OC curve for a sampling plan with *n*-50 and C = 1.

Graph 13.6 shows the probability of acceptance of lot for various values of percent defectives in the lot. Suppose, if the actual bad quality were 1 percent, samples on $n = 50$ would accept the lot as satisfactory about 94 percent of the time and reject it about 6 percent of the time.

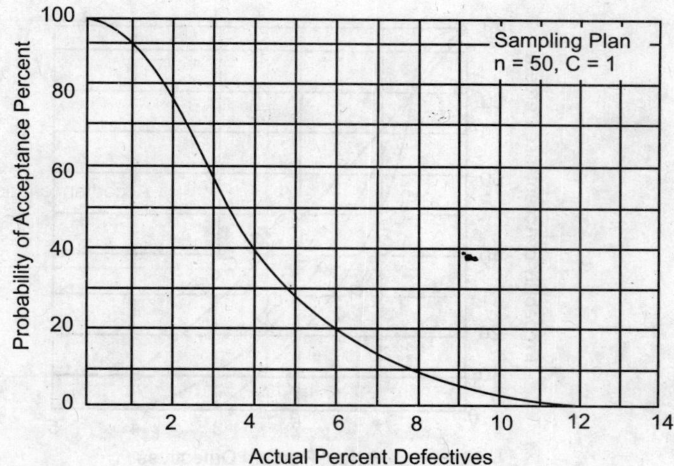


**Graph. 13.6.** OC curve for a sampling plan with n = 50 and C = 1

Note, however, that if the actual quality of the lot were somewhat worse than 1% defective, say 5% the probability of accepting these lots drastically to about 29%. This is the situation, we would like in a sampling plan. If the actual quality is good, then there should be a high probability of acceptance, but if the actual quality is poor, then the probability of acceptance should be low. Thus, in this way the OC curve shows how well a given sampling plan discriminates.

## Affect of Sample Size on the Sampling Plan

The discriminating power of any sampling plan depends largely on the size of the sample. Graph 13.7 shows the OC curves for sample sizes of 100, 200 and 300 with the acceptance number remaining in the proportion to the sample size. Graph 13.7 shows that the OC curve becomes steeper as the sample size goes up. If the discrimination power of all the three plans shown in the graph is compared, it is found that these would accept lots of about 0.7% defectives about 80% of the time (the approximate cross over points of the three curves). However, if actual quality falls to 3 percent defectives, the plan with n = 100 accepts lots about 28% of the time, n = 200 about 10% of the time, and n 300 less than 1% of the time. Therefore, it shows that the plans with larger sample sizes are definitely more effective.

What happens to the OC curve, if any of the acceptance number changes ? Graph) 13.8 shows OC curves for sample of n = 50 and acceptance number of C = 0, 1, 2 and 3. Graph indicates that the effect is mainly to change the level of the OC curve so that lower acceptance number make the plan "tighter".

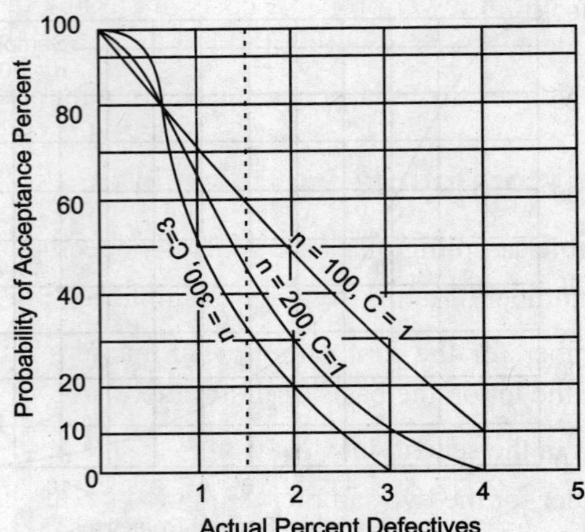


**Graph. 13.7.** OC curves for different sample sizes with acceptance numbers in proportion to sample size

A sampling plan that discriminated perfectly between good and bad lots would have an OC curve that was vertical; that is, it would follow the dashed lines of Graph 13.5. For all lots having percent defectives to the left of the dashed line, the probability of acceptance is 100. For all lots having percent defectives to the right of the line, the probability of acceptance is zero but the only plan which could achieve this discrimination is one requiring cent-percent inspection. Therefore, the proper justification for the selection of a sampling plan is the balance between inspection costs and the probable cost of rejected parts. By making sampling plans more discriminating

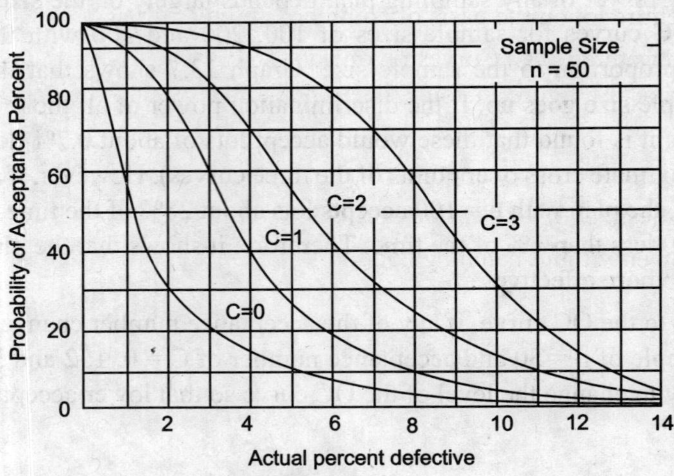


**Graph. 13.8.** OC curves with different acceptance numbers for a sample size $n = 50$.

(increasing sample size) or tighter decreasing acceptance numbers, we can approach any desired level of outgoing quality that we please but at increasing inspection cost. This increased inspection effort would result in lower probable costs of passing defectives and at some point, the combination of the incremental costs is a minimum.

This minimum point defines the most economical sampling plan for a given situation.

## 13.14.2. O.C. Curves for Double Sampling Plan

As discussed earlier, double sampling plans are generally specified by following :

$n_1$ = number of items in the first sample,

$c_1$ = acceptance number for the first sample (*i.e.* maximum number of defectives that will permit the acceptance of the lot on the basis of first sample)

$n_2$ = number of items in the second lot

$c_2$ = acceptance number for the two samples combined *i.e.* maximum number of defectives that will permit the acceptance of the lot on the basis of two samples.

For example, interpretation of following sampling plan is given hereunder:

$n_1 = 30$ $c_1 = 0$ $n_2 = 60$ $c_2 = 3$

1. Inspect a first sample of thirty items from a lot.
2. Accept the lot on the basis of first sample, if the sample contains *o* defectives.
3. Reject the lot on the basis of first sample, if the sample contains more than 3 defectives.
4. Inspect a second sample of 60 items, if the first sample contains 3 defectives.
5. Accept the lot on the basis of both the samples combined together (30 +60 = 90 items), if the defectives are 3 or less.
6. Reject the entire lot on the basis of combined sample, if the defectives are more than 3 items.

Fig. 13.9 shows three O.C. Curves involved in the analysis of this double sampling plan. These three curves divide the figure in four zones indicating following possibilities for acceptance or rejection :

1. I zone (lowest zone) - Acceptance after first sample.
2. II zone (highest zone) - Rejection after the first sample.
3. III zone (lower without hatching zone) - Acceptance after second sample.

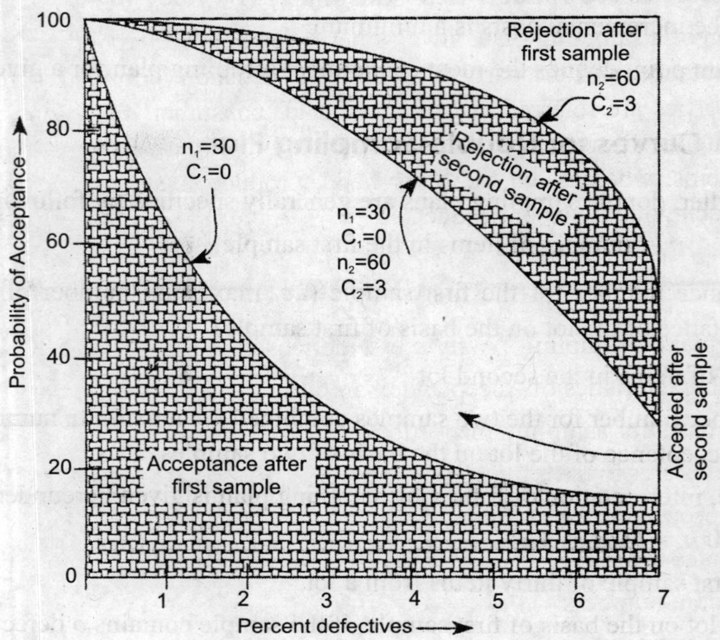


**Fig. 13.9.** Characteristics of a double sampling plan

4. IV zone (higher with hatching zone) - Rejection after second sample.

Characteristics of the lowest curve is $n = 30$ and $C = 0$

Characteristics of the highest curve is $n = 30$ and $C = 3$

Characteristics of the middle curve is the actual O.C. curve of the double sampling plan.

### 13.14.3. Zones of O.C. Curve

O.C. curve can be divided into following 3 zones :

(a) ***Acceptance Zone.*** In this zone, all the batches are accepted, therefore, the O.C. curve should be so selected that its acceptance zone accepts what is considered to be satisfactory lot.

(b) ***Rejection Zone.*** In this zone, all the batches are rejected. Hence, the O.C. curve selected should be such that it rejects what is considered to be an unsatisfactory lot.

(c) ***Zone of Indecision.*** This is the zone where there is no surety that whether any particular batch or lot will be accepted or rejected. This problem can be solved either by adopting 100% inspection or by taking larger sample, but these will increase the inspection costs. A batch or lot in this zone is worse than acceptable lot, and better than those what is considered unacceptable. Thus, its quality is borderline and practically does not matter much whether a lot is finally accepted or rejected from this zone.

**Conflicting Interests of Producer and Consumer**

In the selection of a sampling plan, always there are two affected parties; the party submitting the items for acceptance, and the party for whom the decision is made regarding acceptance or rejection. These parties are referred as 'producer' and 'consumer' respectively. Both these have completely opposite viewpoints, as consumer wants to be protected against the acceptance of too many defective items, whereas, on the other hand, producer wants to be protected against the rejection of too much good items or products.

## QUESTIONS

1. What is Acceptance Sampling ? Why it is widely used in practice?
2. Explain the characteristics of Acceptance Sampling.
3. What are the basis for sampling inspection ? Explain each of them.
4. Where do you prefer to use sampling inspection for quality control?
5. Describe the procedure for sampling inspection.
6. Write short notes on :
   (*a*) Random numbers.
   (*b*) Sampling plan.
   (*c*) Advantages and disadvantages of sampling inspection.
   (*d*) Producer's risk and consumer's risk in acceptance sampling.
7. What is the use of operating characteristic curves in inspection?
8. Plot the O.C. curves for different values of *n* and *C* and make the inferences from the plot drawn.
9. Write a short note on the objectives of O.C. curves.
10. Define O.C. curves and explain its significance.
11. What is sampling ? Explain the different types of samplings.
12. Explain the following:
    (*a*) Inspection
    (*b*) Sampling inspection
    (*c*) Attributes and variable.
    (*d*) Economics of inspection.
13. Explain as to how will you inspect the quality of characteristic: (*a*) by attributes (*b*) by variables?
14. Write short notes on :
    (*a*) Limitation of sampling.
    (*b*) Application of sampling inspection.

(*c*) Disposition of defective products.

(*d*) Sampling risks.

**15.** What is the role of acceptance sampling ?

**16.** (*a*) Explain 'double sampling plan'.

(*b*) Explain 'sequential sampling plan'.

**17.** Explain following terms :

(*a*) Acceptance Quality Level (AQL)

(*b*) Rejectable Quality Level (RQL)

(*c*) Average Outgoing Quality Level (AOQL)

**18.** Explain O.C. Curve for double sampling plan. Indicate various zones on it.

**19.** Write short notes on :

(*a*) Different types of sampling plans.

(*b*) Dodge-roming sampling tables.

(*c*) ABC standard with reference to O.C. Curve.

**20.** Define the terms : defects; because of defect, symptoms and remedy.

**21.** Explain 'Diagnostic Journey' and 'Remedial Journey' for the quality improvement.

**22.** Explain the different types of errors.

# 14 Statistical Process Control and Control Charts

## 14.1. STATISTICAL QUALITY CONTROL (S.Q.C.)

These days, the Statistical Quality Control is used more or less in every kind of industry. It is now becoming an integral part of Management Control. Statistical Quality Control involves the statistical analysis of the inspection data obtained from the samples. Statistical Quality Control technique was introduced during II World War by Dr. Walter A. Shewartan American scientist. The quality in statistical quality control is usually related to measurements made, of the items manufactured. A good quality item is an item which conforms to specified standards, and is not mean having highest standards of manufacture. Most desirable situation is which represents consistency in quality standards rather than the absolute standards.

### Definition

Before understanding S.Q.C., we must first know the meaning of each word in the term statistical quality control.

**Statistics.** It means data, sufficient enough to obtain reliable results.

**Quality.** It is a relative term and can be defined as fitness for the purpose.

**Control.** Control is a system for measuring and checking. It suggests when to inspect, how often to inspect and how much to inspect. This also incorporates a feedback mechanism to explore the causes of poor quality and takes corrective steps.

Thus, statistical quality control is a quality control system employing the statistical techniques to control quality by performing inspection, testing and analysis to conclude whether the quality of the product is as per laid quality standards. Relying on the probability theory, S.Q.C. evaluates batch quality and controls the quality of processes and products.

The purpose of statistical quality control is to ensure, in a cost efficient manner that the product shipped to customers meets their specifications. Inspecting every product is costly and inefficient, but the consequences of shipping non-performing products can be significant in terms of customer dissatisfaction. Statistical quality control is the process of inspecting enough products from given lots to probalistically ensure a specified quality level.

**Techniques** of SQC can be divided into two categories :

1. **Acceptance Sampling**—already discussed in the book.
2. **Control charts**—being discussed in this chapter.

## Advantages of SQC

Statistical Quality Control is one of the tools for scientific management, and has following main advantages over 100 percent inspection:

(*i*) **Reduction in cost.** Since only a fractional output is inspected, hence, cost of inspection is greatly reduced.

(*ii*) **Greater Efficiency.** It requires lesser time and boredom as compared to the 100 percent inspection and hence, the efficiency increases.

(*iii*) **Easy to Apply.** Once the statistical quality control plan is established, it is easy to apply even by man who does not have extensive specialised training.

(*iv*) **Accurate Prediction.** Specifications can easily be predicted for the future, which is not possible even with 100 percent inspection.

(*v*) **Can be used where inspection needs destruction of items.** In cases, where destruction of product is necessary for inspecting it, 100 percent inspection is not possible (which will spoil all the products), sampling inspection is resorted to.

(*vi*) **Early detection of Faults.** The moment a sample quality point falls outside the control limits, it is taken as a danger signal and necessary corrective measures are taken. Whereas, in 100 percent inspection, unwanted variations in quality may be detected after large number of defective items have already been produced. Thus, by using the control charts, we can know from graphic picture that how the production is proceeding and where corrective action is required and where it is not required.

This also helps in early and easily identification of trends over times, so as to enable in taking advance corrective action.

(*vii*) **Helps management in decision-making.** If the process remain within statistical control in long term, the management can take a decision for reducing process variability and vice-versa.

(*viii*) Knowing that a process is in statistical control worker feels confidence and he shall not make any unnecessary adjustments etc. in the machine, tools, fixtures etc.

## 14.2. STATISTICAL PROCESS CONTROL (S.P.C.)

Traditional methods of quality control in a manufacturing process have been: (*a*) 100% inspection and (*b*) sampling inspection. Both these methods concentrate on the final output of the process.

When the products were of critical nature or when the production used to be in small quantities, 100% inspection of the final output was adopted for quality control. For the large production, full 100% inspection was prohibitive in terms of cost and time, sampling inspection was preferred as a method for quality control. In the sampling inspection method for quality control sampling plans are drawn so that samples are taken until there is a sufficient amount of confidence to accept or reject the batch. This aspect has been discussed in detail in the chapter on "acceptance sampling and O.C. curves". In this method, the producer has to accept a certain amount of risk that some defective products will slip through the quality control net. As acceptance sampling does not help to catch in-process problems. This contradicts the principle of total quality. This necessitated the use of alternative methods of quality control which will give their products a high degree of precision and reliability.

A valuable alternative is provided by the technique of statistical process control (SPC). Sampling plans and SPC have a common characteristic. As in the case of sampling plans, SPC attempts to utilize the connection between the properties of a sample and the properties of the parent population. The main difference is that SPC provides the operator with a opportunity of correcting or appropriate tuning the production process in time to avoid whole batches being rejected later. It encourages continual process improvement.

In the statistical process control, we built a model based on as to how the process will perform and calculate the control limits for the expected measurements of the output of the process. Then, we collect data from the process and compare the data to the control limits. The majority of measurements should fall within the control limits. Measurements that fall outside the control limits are examined.

In this chapter, control charts are being discussed in detail, as other techniques have already been covered in the chapter on "total quality management".

Statistical Process Control (SPC) technique is aimed to prevent defective work being produced by focusing on the production process rather than on the final product. This technique is definitely superior to sampling inspection plans which is aimed to trap the defects after they have been produced. This feature makes the sampling inspection simply an appraisal procedure rather than making effort for improvement.

Statistical Process Control (SPC) is an approach to controlling non-uniformity, and it detects and eliminate non-random (sporadic) variations as they arise while the process is operating. The process is said to be *in control* when all variations, are random and is *out of control,* when some variation are sporadic. The process is monitored periodically by examining sample units of output. *Control Charts* are the primary tool for SPC.

When the output of some process is found to be unreliable, not always conforming to requirements, we need to carefully examine the process and see how it can be controlled. There are two kinds of variations that are observed in the output from most processes :

(*a*) Random variation (sometimes called *common*, *inherent*, or *chance cause* variation)

(*b*) Systematic variation (sometimes called *assignable* or *special cause* variation.)

These two kinds of variations call for different managerial responses. If the process is *out-of-control*, because there is still some special cause variation present, identify and correct the cause of that variation. Thereafter, when the process has been brought *in-control*, quality can be improved by re-designing the process to reduce its inherent variability.

Catch phrase of many quality management problems is "*Variation is the enemy of quality*".

Statistical process control involves studying variation to emphasize control — once the process is measured, we can eliminate or control non-random sources of variation and improve the process to reduce random variation.

Statistical process control can be defined as the application of statistical methods to the measurement and analysis of variation in any process. A process is a unique combination of machines, tools, methods, materials, and people that attains an output in goods, software, or services. We have already discussed methods of collecting, summarizing and analyzing data; probability concepts; statistical concepts; measurements; process capabilities, now we shall discuss use of control charts in analyzing and minimizing variations and other techniques for process improvement.

## 14.3. VARIABLES AND ATTRIBUTES

Measurements used in process control are of two types, namely by variables and by attributes. In certain situations, we must measure a product characteristic on a continuous scale, such as its length, weight, hardness strength, pressure, temperature or volume, each of which is a variable characteristic. An attribute characteristic can be measured by a simple rating of good or bad, success or failure, etc.

Measuring of attribute is quicker and easier, as they offer more economical data gathering and storage. While variable measurements contain more potential information. Variables measurements provide the capability data, and they also provide more useful information for controlling the process.

## 14.4. STATISTICAL CONTROL CHARTS

These are graphic comparison of process performance data to computed "statistical control limits", drawn as limit lines on the chart. The process performance data usually consists of groups of measurements that come from regular sequence of production while preserving the order of data. Main objective of a control chart is to detect assignable causes of variation in a process.

As we have already discussed that process variations are due to two kinds of causes :

**1.** Common, random or chance causes, which are inherent in the process, and

**2.** Special or assignable causes, which cause excessive variation.

Ideally only common or chance causes should be present in a process because they represent a stable and predictable process which leads to minimum variation. A process which is having only common causes and no special or assignable causes of variation is said to be "in a state of statistical control". The objective of a control chart is to reduce variation.

When the variation exceeds the statistical control limits, it is a signal that special causes have entered the process, and the process should be investigated to identify the causes of excessive variation. Here, it is pointed out that the control chart only detects the presence of a special cause but does not find the cause.

∴ Control chart detects whether there is any change in the characteristics of item since the start of the production run. It immediately tells about the undesired variations and helps in exploring the cause and eliminating manufacturing troubles.

All processes whether semi-automatic or automatic are susceptible to variations which result in changes in dimension or other characteristics of the product. These variations occur due to following reasons:

(*i*) due to use of different machine tools,
(*ii*) due to use of different cutting tools,
(*iii*) due to use of materials with different properties,
(*iv*) due to change in working conditions, *e.g.*, light, humidity, temperature,
(*v*) due to workers of different skills,
(*vi*) due to change in jigs, fixtures etc.

## Advantages of Control Charts

Control charts are advantageous from following reasons :

(*a*) It indicates whether the process is *in-control* or *out-of-control* at particular point of time.
(*b*) It ensures level of quality, and hence, built up the reputation of the organisation due to customers satisfaction.
(*c*) It detects unusual variations taking place in a process.
(*d*) It helps in reducing the rejection, as it warns in time, so that process can be rectified in time.
(*e*) It helps in setting of tolerance limits.

### 14.4.1 Types of Control Charts

1. Shewhart control chart for measurable quality characteristics – charts for variables–X $\overline{X}$ and $R$ (average and range) charts.
2. Shewhart control chart for fraction defective – charts for attributes – $p$ charts.
3. Shewhart control chart for number of defects per unit – $C$-chart.

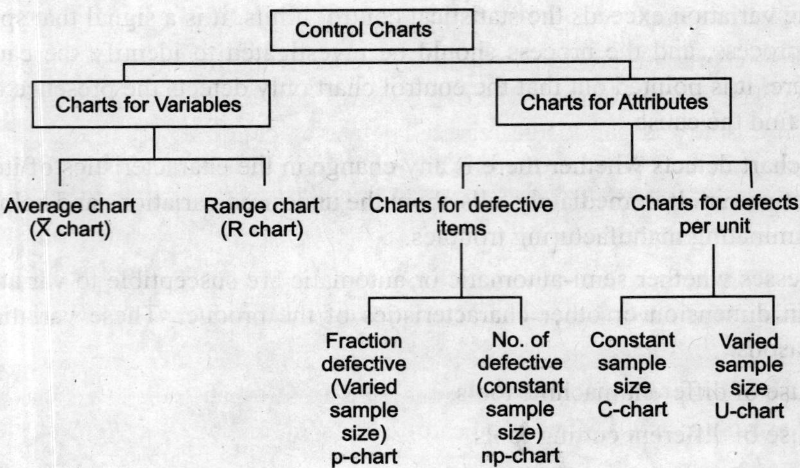


## 14.4.2. Setting Up a Control Chart

Following steps are generally followed for setting up a control chart:

1. Selecting the characteristics to be charted:
   (*a*) Use Pareto analysis for giving high priority to characteristics which are currently running with high defective rate.
   (*b*) Identify the process variables and conditions contributing to the end-product characteristics
   (*c*) Selecting measurement methods which will provide the kinds of data needed for diagnosis of problems.
   (*d*) Selecting the points in production process at which testing is to be done.
2. Selecting the type of control chart.
3. Deciding the centerline, which may be the average of past data, or it may be desired average. Limits are then set, usually at ± 3 standard deviation.
4. Selecting the "rational subgroup (or sample)" to represent as a point on the control chart.
5. Deciding a system for collecting the data.
6. Deciding control limits and providing instructions regarding the interpretation of the results and the actions which are to be taken by different production personnel
7. Take steps for :
   (*a*) ensuring cooperation,
   (*b*) training of involved personnel,
   (*c*) keep up interest,
   (*d*) assess effectiveness at regular intervals, and
   (*e*) review the chart.

### Data Collection Plan

The control charts are prepared to obtain a reliable and unbiased picture of how the process is performing. The success of this objective depends on the way the data are collected. Therefore, before any SPC study is conducted, careful plans for data collection, adequate training of the operating personnel, and well-maintained/calibrated measuring devices are available. For accurate reflection of process performance, collection of correct data are necessary. For this purpose following factors are considered:

1. **Quality Characteristics** should be easily measurable and representative of key operation which has a significant impact on : factory and business performance.
2. **The data to be collected** should either be expressed: (*a*) quantitatively and measured on a scale for variable data, (*b*) in a yes/no format (*i.e.*, go/no), pass/fail, conforming/non-conforming etc. for attribute data. Different types of control charts are used depending upon the type of data.
3. **Sample size and frequency** of sample collection depend upon the type of data, practical experience and past knowledge of process. The number for sample size should be higher at the beginning of the SPC effort, and when further process data become available and confidence is built up, these numbers can decrease.
4. **Cost effectiveness** should be considered for every improvement effort.

## 14.5. CONTROL CHARTS FOR VARIABLES

Control charts for variables are based on the properties of the normal distribution, for which over 99% of the values fall within a band of 6 standard deviations *i.e.* $\pm 3\sigma$ from the central line. Normal distribution can be applied to the subgroup (or sample) averages also. This follows the principle of the 'central limit theorem', which states that, "irrespective of the distribution of the individual readings, the sample means are normally distributed with the same mean but narrower standard deviation than that of the individual readings." It further states that some nice properties of the normal distribution hold for the population of the sample means.

99.73% of the sample means fall within $\pm 3\sigma$ measured outwards from the central value. The $\pm 3\sigma$ lines define the control limits in the control chart. The probability of a point falling outside the control limits is equal to 0.0027 (1 – .9973) *i.e.* roughly 3 in 1000, and is so slight that, if it does occur, it can be assumed that it has occurred not by chance, but because a special cause of variation is present. Since the presence of a sample mean outside the control limits is an unlikely event, providing a sufficient evidence that special cause of variation is present.

Many experts prefer to introduce warning limits in the system. These are the lines drawn at $\pm 2\sigma$ from the mean. These lines are drawn in addition to the control limits drawn at $\pm 3\sigma$ from the mean. Action should be taken, when atleast two consecutive points fall outside the warning lines.

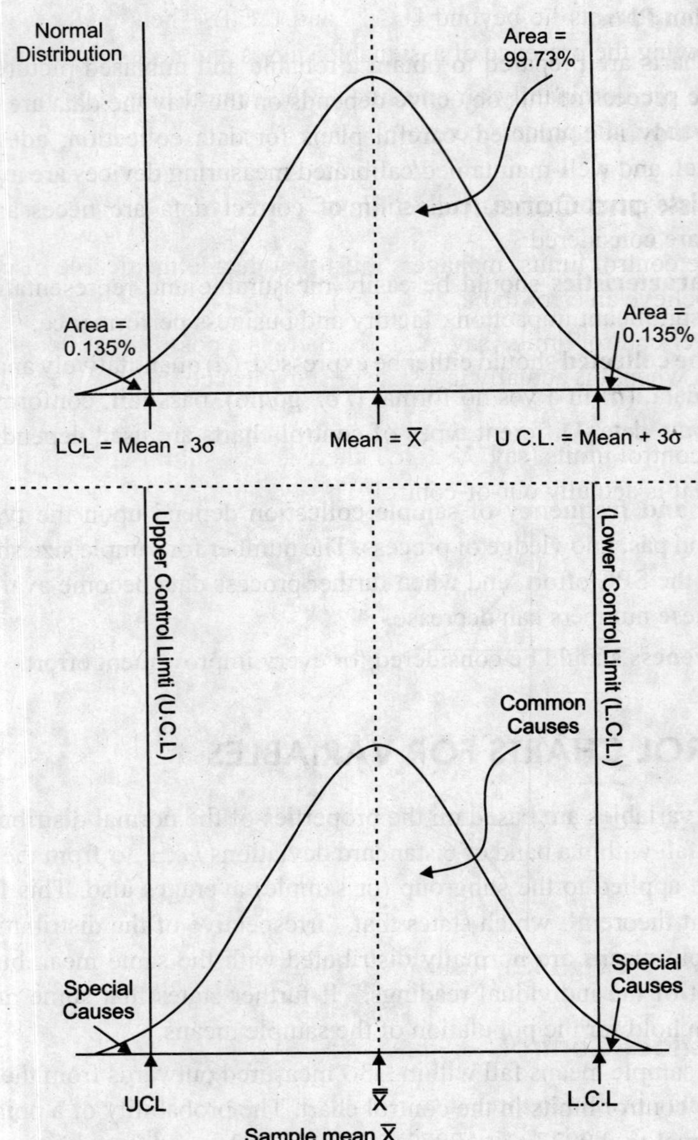


**Fig. 14.1** Principles of control chart.

## Interpretations of Control Chart

Following interpretations can be made by the study of control chart:

1. If all the points lie within U.C.L. and L.C.L., then the process is said to be in-control, indicating the presence of chance causes only.

2. If one or more points lie beyond U.C.L. and L.C.L. Then, the process is said to be out-of-control showing the presence of assignable causes and necessity of some remedial measures.
3. If points lie pre-dominantly on one side of the central line, then it is not safe to derive any conclusion about the process control.

## Producer's Risk and Consumer's Risk

While setting the control limits, managers must first decide the degree of certainty based on how important they believe an error to be.

With narrower control limits (say $\overline{X} \pm 1\sigma$, there is a possibility of concluding that the process is out-of-control, when it is actually in a state of statistical control. This is called the producer's risk or type *I* error.

With wider control limits (say $\overline{X} \pm 3\sigma$), there is a possibility of concluding that the process is in-control, when it is actually out-of-control. This is called as consumer's risk or type II error.

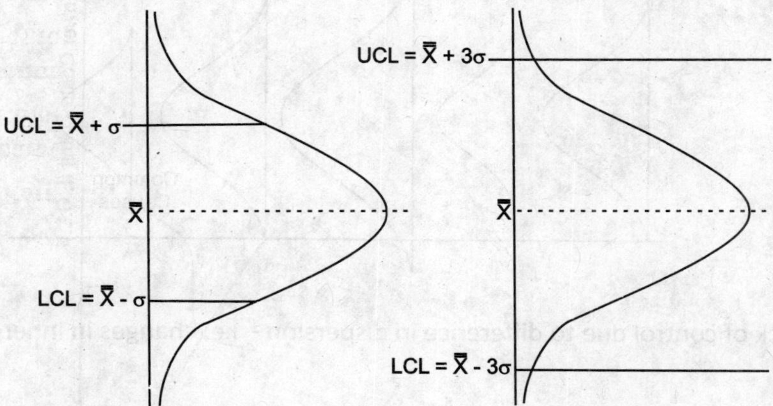


**Fig 14.2.** Risks involved in using 1 σ (*a*), and 3 σ (*b*).

## Lack of Statistical Control

Lack of control may be due to three different situations :

1. They may differ in average only. This influence the control chart for $\overline{X}$ and *R*.
2. They may differ in dispersion only. This also influence the $\overline{X}$ and *R* both.
3. They may differ in both, average and dispersion.

Fig. 14.3 slows the different situations about lack of statistical control.

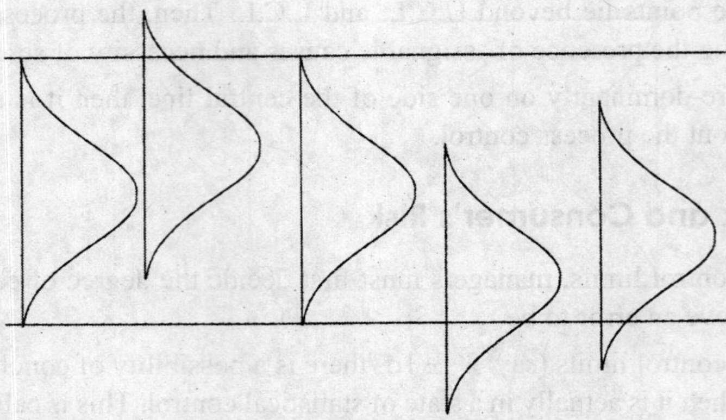

(a) Lack of control due to difference in averages – i.e. shifting quality level.

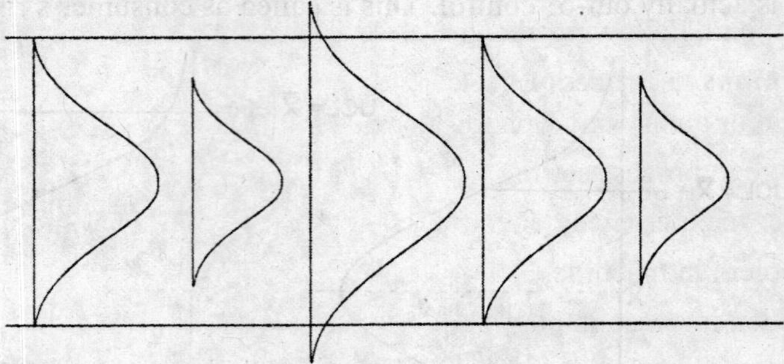

(b) Lack of control due to difference in dispersion – i.e. changes in inherent variability.

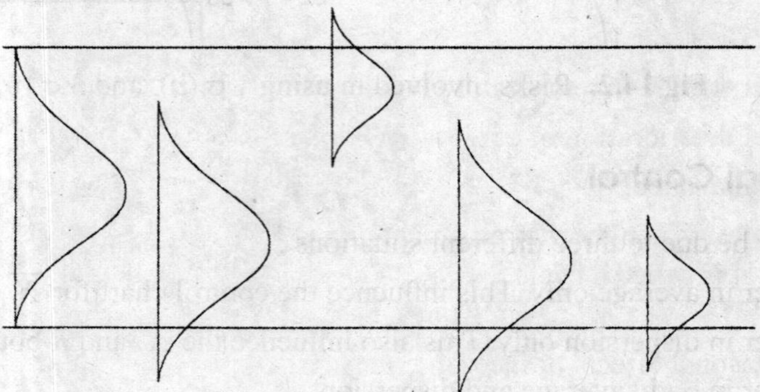

(*c*) Lack of control due to changes in both, average and dispersion – *i.e.* both, quality level and inherent variability

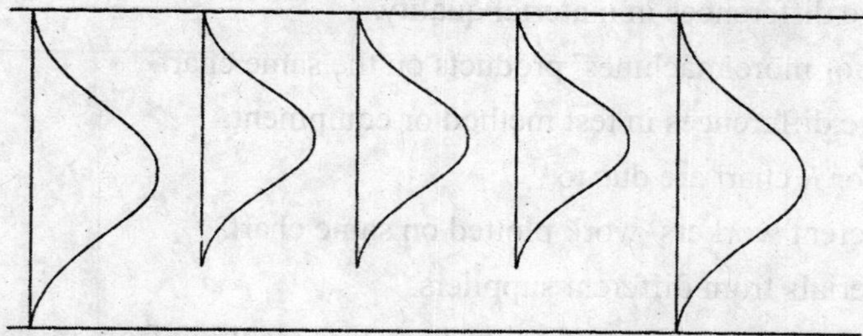

(d) A statistically controlled process

**Fig. 14.3.** Lack of statistical control-chances cause system may change in different ways.

**Interpreting Patterns of Variation on $\overline{X}$ and *R* Charts :**

The control chart tells us *when* to look for trouble but it cannot, by itself, tell where to look or what cause will be found. Following changes are seen in the charts due to various causes of trouble:

1. **Changes or Jumps in Process Level.** This type is concerned with a sudden change in process level (average) for an $\overline{X}$ and *R* chart. This is due to :
   (*i*) Change in process setting,
   (*ii*) new or inexperienced operator,
   (*iii*) a problem in machine,
   (*iv*) a sudden increase in play, and
   (*v*) greater variation in incoming material.
2. **Trend or Steady Change in Level:** Some reasons for steady progressive changes on $\overline{X}$ chart are :
   (*i*) tool or die wear,
   (*ii*) gradual change in temperature or humidity,
   (*iii*) gradual deterioration of equipment,
   (*iv*) no maintenance.
3. **Recurring Cycles.** When the plotted points on an $\overline{X}$ or *R* chart show a wave or periodic high and low points, it is called a cycle. For an $\overline{X}$ chart, some of the causes of recurring cycles are due to :
   (*i*) The seasonal effects of incoming material.
   (*ii*) The recurring effects of temperature and humidity.
   (*iii*) Daily or weekly chemical, mechanical or psychological event.
   (*iv*) Periodic rotation of operators or machines.
4. **Two Universes.** When there are large number of points near or outside, both the control limits (upper and lower), a two-universe situation may be present. For an $\overline{X}$ chart, this situation can be due to :

(*i*) Large differences in material quality.

(*ii*) Two or more machines' products on the same chart.

(*iii*) Large differences in test method or equipment.

Some causes for *R* chart are due to :

(*i*) Different workers' work plotted on same chart.

(*ii*) Materials from different suppliers.

5. **Mistakes.** Some causes of out-of-control patterns resulting from mistakes are:

(*i*) Measuring equipment out of calibration.

(*ii*) Errors in calculations.

(*iii*) Errors in using test equipment.

(*iv*) Taking samples from different universes.

(*v*) Inspection error.

**Process Variability**

No process can turn out an identical product. Even with the best equipment, and most skilled operators, no two pieces will be alike. This fact reflects the variability of the process. The variability cannot be eliminated, but efforts can be made to keep it to minimum or within specification limits.

To compute the process variability, it is generally sufficient to take ten samples of equal number of items produced under similar conditions. The first step is then to compute simple range (*R*)--the difference between highest and lowest readings of the sample. Similarly, the value of *R* is computed for all the samples. Then, the process variability will be:

$$\therefore \qquad \overline{R} = \frac{R_1 + R_2 + .... + R_9 + R_{10}}{10}$$

## 14.5.1. $\overline{X}$ AND R CHARTS (CONTROL CHARTS FOR VARIABLES)

These charts are used for quality characteristics which are specified as variables *i.e.* on the basis of actual readings taken. The purposes or objectives of these charts are :

(*a*) To establish whether the process is in statistical control or not.

(*b*) To determine whether the process capability is compatible with the specifications.

(*c*) To detect trends in the process so as to assist in planning, adjustment and re-setting of the process.

(*d*) To show when the process is likely to be out of control.

A number of samples of components coming out of the process are taken over a period of time. Each sample must be taken at random and the size of sample is generally kept as 5, but 10 to 15 units can be taken for sensitive control charts. For each sample, the average value $\overline{X}$ of all the measurements and the range *R* are calculated. The grand average $\overline{\overline{X}}$ (equal to the average value of all the sample averages $\overline{X}$) and $\overline{R}$ ($\overline{R}$ is equal to the average of all the sample ranges $R$) are found and from these, we can calculate the control limits for the $\overline{X}$ and $R$ charts. Therefore,

For $\overline{X}$ charts :

Upper Control Limit,

$$UCL\overline{x} = \overline{X} + A_2\overline{R}$$

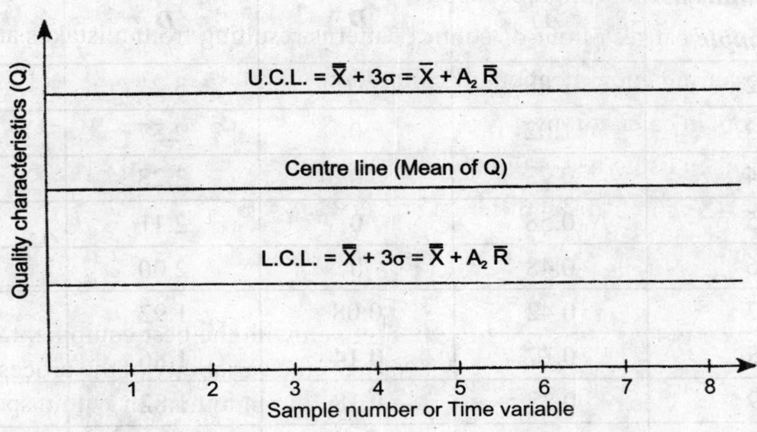


**Fig, 14.4.** Control Limits,

Lower Control Limit,

$$LCLx = \overline{X} - A_2\overline{R}$$

$\overline{X}$ and $\overline{R}$ are also called right line values.

For R chart:

$$UCL_R = D_4\overline{R}$$

$$LCL_R = D_3\overline{R}$$

Here, the factors $A_2$, $D_4$ and $D_3$ depend on the number of units per sample. Larger the number, the close the limits. The value of the factors $A_2$, $D_4$ and $D_3$ can be obtained from Statistical Quality Control tables. However, for ready reference, these are given below in tabular form.

As long as $\overline{X}$ and $R$ values for each sample are within the control limits, the process is said to be in statistical control.

**Summary of Formula used in $\overline{X}$ and *R* Charts**

| *Chart* | *Centre line* | *3 Sigma Control limits* |
|---|---|---|
| $\overline{X}$, Average | $\overline{X}$ | $\overline{X} \pm A_2R$ |
| $R$, Range | $R$ | $D_3\overline{R}$ and $D_4R$ |

| Estimated spread of individual measurement | | $= \overline{X} \pm \frac{3R}{d_2}$ |
|---|---|---|

where $d_2$ is a factor, whose value depends on number of units in a sample. Its value is seen from S.Q.C. Table below.

**Table 14.1.**

| *No. of units in a sample* | $A_2$ | $D_3$ | $D_4$ | $d_2$ |
|---|---|---|---|---|
| 2 | 1.88 | 0 | 3.27 | 1.13 |
| 3 | 1.02 | 0 | 2.57 | 1.69 |
| 4 | 0.73 | 0 | 2.28 | 2.06 |
| 5 | 0.58 | 0 | 2.11 | 2.33 |
| 6 | 0.48 | 0 | 2.00 | 2.53 |
| 7 | 0.42 | 0.08 | 1.92 | 2.70 |
| 8 | 0.37 | 0.14 | 1.86 | 2.85 |
| 9 | 0.38 | 0.18 | 1.82 | 2.97 |
| 10 | 0.31 | 0.22 | 1.78 | 3.08 |
| 11 | 0.29 | 0.26 | 1.74 | 3.17 |
| 12 | 0.27 | 0.28 | 1.72 | 3.26 |
| 13 | 0.25 | 0.31 | 1.69 | 3.34 |
| 14 | 0.24 | 0.33 | 1.67 | 3.41 |
| 15 | 0.22 | 0.35 | 1.65 | 3.47 |

## Process Out–of–Control

After computing the control limits, the next step is to determine whether the process is in statistical control or not. If not, it means there is external causes that throws the process out of control. This cause must be traced and removed so that the process may return to operate under stable statistical conditions.

The various reasons for the process being out of control may be :

(*i*) Faulty tools, (*ii*) Sudden significant change in properties of new materials in a new consignment, (*iii*) Breakdown of lubrication system, (*iv*) Faults in timing of speed mechanism etc.

Tracing of these causes is sometimes simple and straight forward, but when the process is subject to the combined effect of several external causes simultaneously, then it may be lengthy and complicated business.

## Process in–Control

If the process is found to be in statistical control, a comparison between the required specifications and the process capability may be carried out to determine whether the two are compatible. Should the specified tolerances prove to be too tight for the process capability ?

There are three possible alternatives :

(*a*) Re-evaluate the specifications. Whether the tight tolerances are actually needed or they can be relaxed without affecting quality?

(*b*) If relaxation in specifications is not allowed, then a more accurate process is required to be selected.

(*c*) If both the above alternatives are not acceptable, then 100% inspection is carried out to trace out the defectives.

*Conclusions.* When the process is not in control, then the points fall outside the control limits on either $\overline{X}$ or $R$ charts. It means assignable causes (human controlled causes) are present in the process. When all the points are inside the control limits, even then we cannot definitely say that no assignable cause is present but it is not economical to trace the cause. No statistical test can be applied. Even in the best manufacturing process, certain errors may develop and that constitute the assignable causes but no statistical action can be taken. This leads to many practical difficulties regarding what relationship show satisfactory control.

One of the most common causes of lack of control is shift in the mean $\overline{X}$. $\overline{X}$ chart is also useful for the purpose of detecting shift in production. Tool wear and re-setting of machines often account for such a shift. It is necessary to find out when machine re-setting becomes desirable, bearing in mind that too frequent adjustments are a serious setback to production output.

Figure 14.5 shows few examples of $\overline{X}$ charts. The charts *a*, *b* and *c* shows the relation between the process variability and the specifications. The chart *d* illustrates that there is an adequate process from the point of view of the specifications, but there is constant shift in $\overline{X}$. It means periodic resetting of machine is needed to bring down the value of $\overline{X}$ to the control limits, if the original conditions are to be regained.

Therefore, it can be said that the problem of re-setting is closely associated with the relationship between process capability and the specifications. Case (*a*) in Fig. 14.5 would require a smaller number of machine re-sets than case (*b*).

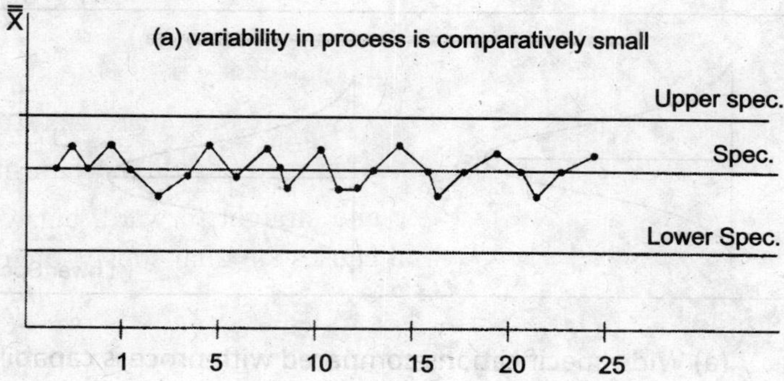

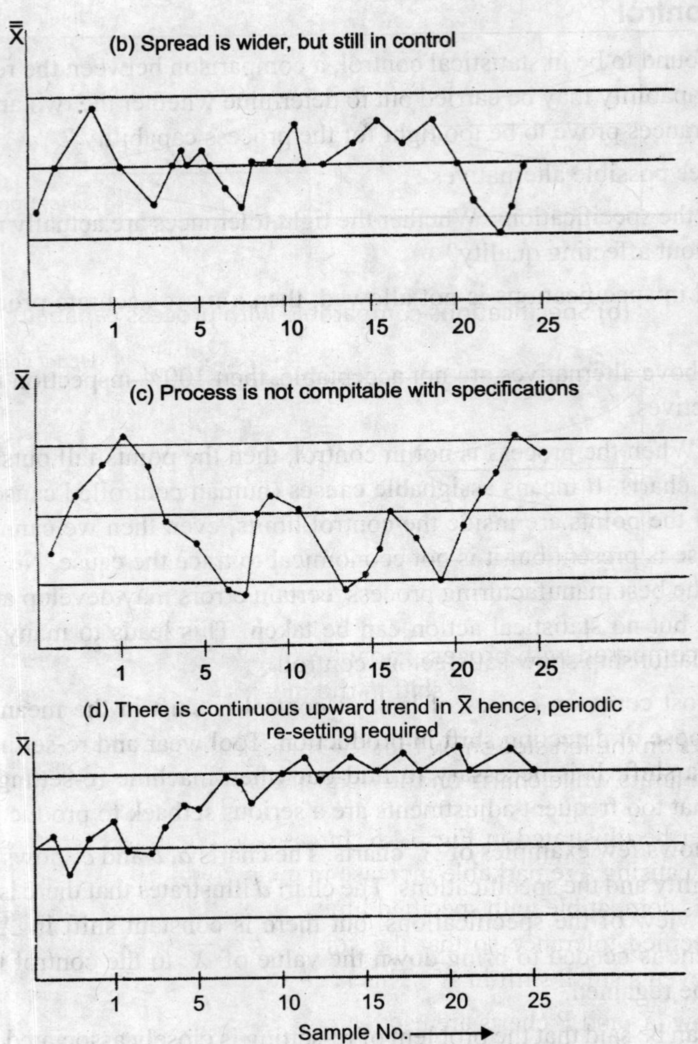


**Fig. 14.5.** Examples of X chart



(a) Wide specifications compared with process capability

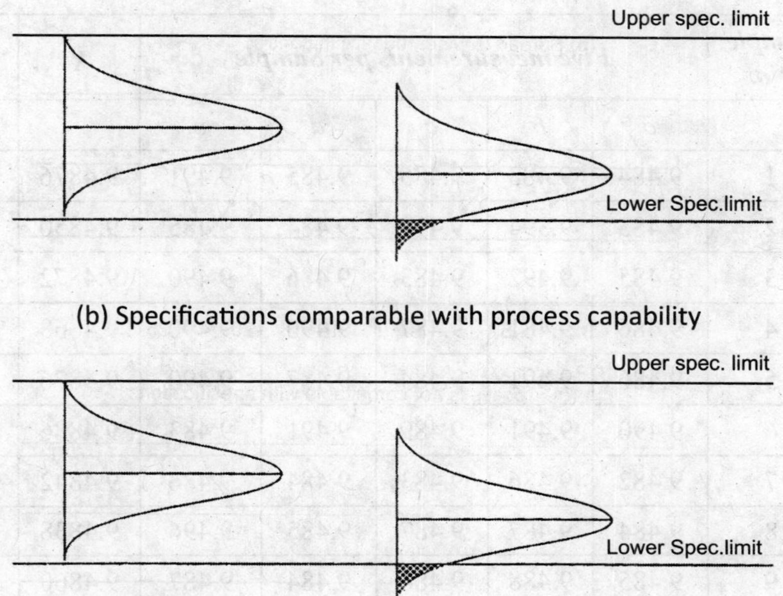


(b) Specifications comparable with process capability

(c) Tolerances compared with process capability, resulting in large scrap especially in case of shift in the mean

**Fig. 14.6.** Charts on the left side show that the mean is half way between the upper and lower specification limits while charts on the right side show downward shift of the mean.

This can further be illustrated in Fig. 14.6. In case (*a*) the mean $\overline{X}$ can shift a great deal on either side without causing a remarkable increase in the amount of defective items. In case (*b*) the process capability is compatible with specified limits. In case (*c*) the process spread $\pm 3\sigma$ is slightly wider than the specified tolerance so that the amount of defectives (scrap) become quite large, whenever there is even a small shift in $\overline{X}$. This needs frequent adjustments.

To illustrate how $\overline{X}$ and *R* charts are used in process control, few examples are worked out as under :

**Example 14.1.** The following table gives record of 5 measurements per sample from lot size of 50 for the critical dimension of jeep valve stem diameter taken every hour, (*i*) Compare the control limits, make plot and explain plotting procedure, (*ii*) Interpret plot, make decision regarding quality of product, process control and cost of inspection.

It is given that specifications are (9.4920 + 0.00 – 0.02 mm).

$$\text{UCL}\overline{X} = \overline{X} + A_2\overline{R}$$

$$\text{LCL}\overline{X} = \overline{X} - A_2\overline{R}$$

| Sample No. | Five measurements per Sample | | | | | $\overline{X}$ | R |
|---|---|---|---|---|---|---|---|
| | a | b | c | d | e | | |
| 1 | 9.484 | 9.483 | 9.485 | 9.485 | 9.491 | 9.4876 | 0.009 |
| 2 | 9.483 | 9.394 | 9.490 | 9.484 | 9.485 | 9.4850 | 0.007 |
| 3 | 9.485 | 9.492 | 9.483 | 9.486 | 9.490 | 9.4872 | 0.009 |
| 4 | 9.486 | 9.481 | 9.487 | 9.490 | 9.490 | 9.4868 | 0.009 |
| 5 | 9.486 | 9.491 | 9.484 | 9.487 | 9.490 | 9.4876 | 0.007 |
| 6 | 9.490 | 9.491 | 9.489 | 9.491 | 9.483 | 9.4886 | 0.008 |
| 7 | 9.482 | 9.486 | 9.483 | 9.484 | 9.486 | 9.4842 | 0.004 |
| 8 | 9.484 | 9.487 | 9.487 | 9.485 | 9.496 | 9.4838 | 0.004 |
| 9 | 9.485 | 9.488 | 9.486 | 9.484 | 9.487 | 9.4860 | 0.003 |
| 10 | 9.484 | 9.481 | 9.482 | 9.485 | 9.483 | 9.4830 | 0.002 |
| 11 | 9.435 | 9.482 | 9.490 | 9.487 | 9.484 | 9.4856 | 0.008 |
| 12 | 9.485 | 9.487 | 9.481 | 9.482 | 9.478 | 9.4826 | 0.009 |
| 13 | 9.488 | 9.477 | 9.482 | 9.485 | 9.484 | 9.4832 | 0.011 |
| 14 | 9.485 | 9.491 | 9.477 | 9.490 | 9.487 | 9.4860 | 0.014 |
| 15 | 9.4748 | 9.483 | 9.487 | 9.488 | 9.490 | 9.4844 | 0.016 |

$$UCL_R = D_4 \overline{R}$$

$$LCL_R = D_3 \overline{R}$$

Here, $$\overline{\overline{X}} = \frac{\text{Sum of all } \overline{X}}{\text{Total no. of samples}} = 9.485$$

$$\overline{R} = \frac{\text{Sum of all R}}{\text{Total no. of samples}} = 0.008$$

From S.Q.C. table 14.1, the values of $A_2$, $D_4$ and $D_3$ can be recorded from the 5 measuremen sample column.

$\therefore$ $$A_2 = 0.58$$

$$D_3 = 0$$

and $$D_4 = 2.11$$

$\therefore$ UCL = $\overline{\overline{X}} + A_2 \overline{R}$ = 9.485 + 0.58 × 0.008 = 9.4896 say = 9.490

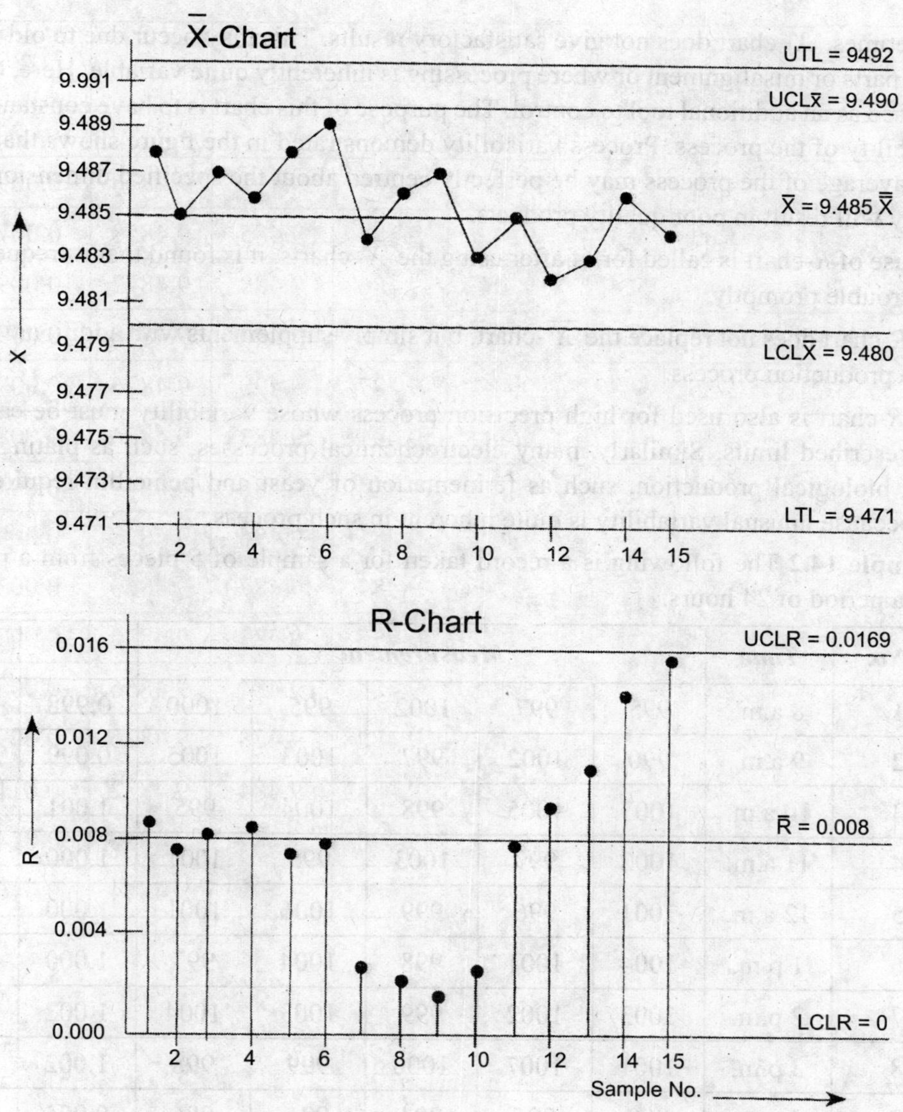


**Fig. 14.7**

$$LCL = \overline{X} - A_2\overline{R} = 9.485 - 0.58 \times 0.008 = 9.480$$

$$\text{UCL}_R = \text{D}_4\overline{R} = 2.11 \times 0.008 = 0.0169$$

$$\text{LCR}_R = D_3\text{R}\overline{R} = 0 \times 0.008 = 0$$

Now charts for $\overline{X}$ and $R$ are plotted as shown in Fig. 17.7 taking abscissa, as sample number nd ordinate as $\overline{X}$ and $R$. $\overline{X}$ and $R$ charts must be drawn one over the other as shown, *i.e.* $R$ chart ıust be exactly under $\overline{X}$ chart.

**What the $\overline{X}$ and $R$ charts tell ?**

Sometimes, $\overline{X}$ chart does not give satisfactory results. This may occur due to old machine, or worn out parts or misalignment or where processing is inherently quite variable. Here, the "Range" chart is used as an additional tool to control. The purpose of this chart is to have constant check over the variability of the process. Process variability demonstrated in the figure shows that though the mean or average of the process may be perfectly centred about the specified dimension, excessive variability will result in poor quality products.

The use of *R*-chart is called for, if after using the $\overline{X}$ charts, it is found that it frequently fails to indicate trouble promptly.

The *R*-chart does not replace the $\overline{X}$-chart, but simply supplements with additional information about the production process.

The *R*-chart is also used for high precision process whose variability must be carefully held within prescribed limits. Similarly, many electrochemical processes, such as plating, and micro chemical biological production, such as fermentation of yeast and penicillin require the use of *R*-chart because unusual variability is quite inherent in such process.

**Example 14.2** The following is a record taken for a sample of 5 pieces from a process each hour for a period of 24 hours.

| ***S.No.*** | ***Time*** | ***Measurement*** | | | | | $\overline{X}$ | ***R*** |
|---|---|---|---|---|---|---|---|---|
| 1 | 8 a.m. | 995 | 997 | 1002 | 995 | 1000 | 0.998 | 0.007 |
| 2 | 9 a.m. | 990 | 1002 | 997 | 1003 | 1005 | 0.099 | 0.015 |
| 3 | 10 a.m. | 1003 | 1005 | 998 | 1004 | 995 | 1.001 | 0.005 |
| 4 | 11 a.m. | 1002 | 999 | 1003 | 995 | 1001 | 1.000 | 0.006 |
| 5 | 12 a.m. | 1001 | 996 | 999 | 1006 | 1001 | 1.000 | 0.010 |
| 6 | 1 p.m. | 1004 | 1001 | 998 | 1004 | 997 | 1.000 | 0.007 |
| 7 | 2 p.m. | 1003 | 1002 | 999 | 1003 | 1004 | 1.002 | 0.006 |
| 8 | 3 p.m. | 1001 | 1007 | 1006 | 999 | 998 | 1.002 | 0.009 |
| 9 | 4 p.m. | 999 | 995 | 994 | 991 | 996 | 0.995 | 0.008 |
| 10 | 5 p.m. | 994 | 993 | 991 | 993 | 996 | 0.993 | 0.005 |
| 11 | 6 p.m. | 994 | 996 | 995 | 994 | 991 | 0.994 | 0.005 |
| 12 | 7 p.m. | 994 | 995 | 998 | 999 | 1001 | 0.097 | 0.007 |
| 13 | 8 p.m. | 1002 | 1004 | 1000 | 994 | 1000 | 1.000 | 0.010 |
| 14 | 9 p.m. | 1003 | 1000 | 996 | 1000 | 1005 | 1.000 | 0.009 |
| 15 | 10 p.m. | 996 | 1001 | 1006 | 1001 | 1008 | 1.103 | 0.012 |
| 16 | 11 p.m. | 995 | 1003 | 1004 | 1006 | 1008 | 1.003 | 0.003 |

| | | | | | | | | |
|---|---|---|---|---|---|---|---|---|
| 17 | 12 p.m. | 1096 | 1005 | 1006 | 1009 | 1008 | 1.006 | 0.004 |
| 18 | 1 a.m. | 996 | 999 | 1001 | 1008 | 996 | 0.999 | 0.012 |
| 19 | 2 a.m. | 1001 | 1004 | 995 | 1001 | 1008 | 1.002 | 0.013 |
| 20 | 3 a.m. | 1003 | 995 | 1002 | 991 | 996 | 0.997 | 0.012 |
| 21 | 4 a.m. | 1004 | 991 | 993 | 997 | 1008 | 0.997 | 0.013 |
| 22 | 5 a.m. | 1003 | 997 | 998 | 1000 | 1001 | 0.999 | 0.006 |
| 23 | 6 a.m. | 1006 | 1001 | 999 | 996 | 997 | 0.999 | 0.010 |
| 24 | 7 a.m. | 1005 | 1000 | 1001 | 998 | 1000 | 1.001 | 0.007 |
| **Total** | | | | | | | **23.976** | **0.216** |
| **Average** | | | | | | | **0.999** | **0.009** |

Here, $\overline{X} = 0.999$

$\overline{R} = 0.009$

From SQC tables, for sample size 5 (see table 14.1)

$$A_2 = 0.58, D_4 = 2.11, \text{ and } D_3 = 0$$

$$\text{UCL}\overline{x} = \overline{X} + A_2\overline{R} = 0.999 + (0.58) \times 0.009 = \mathbf{1.004}$$

$$\text{LCL}\overline{x} = \overline{X} + A_2\overline{R}$$

$$= 0.999 - (0.58) \times 0.009 = 0.999 - 0.00522$$

$$= \mathbf{0.994 \text{ (approx.)}}$$

$$UCL_R = D_4\overline{R} = (2.11) \times (0.009)$$

$$= \mathbf{0.019}$$

$$LCL_R = D_3\overline{R} = 0 \times 0.009 = 0$$

Now $\overline{X}$ and $R$ charts are plotted on the plot, as shown in Fig. 14.8, taking abscissa, as sample number and ordinates $\overline{X}$ and $R$.

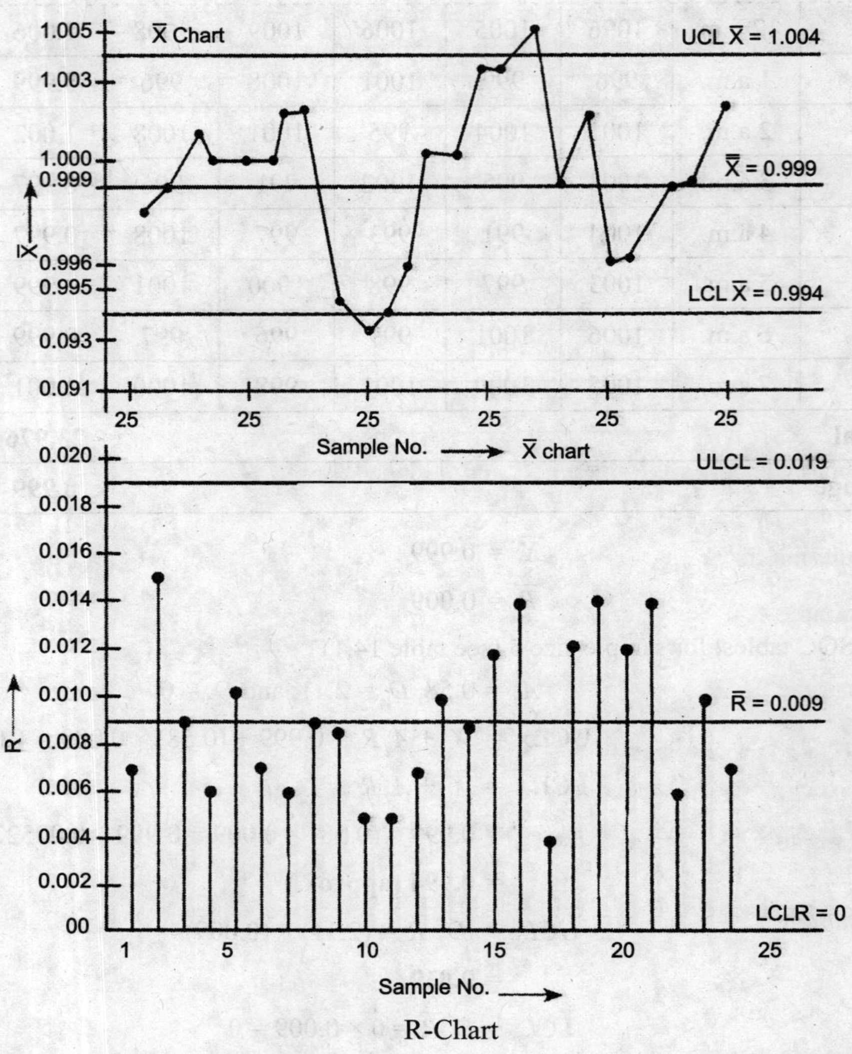

R-Chart

**Fig. 14.8.**

**Inference**

In the $\overline{X}$ chart, most of the time the plotted points, representing average, are well within the control limits but in sample 10 and 17, the plotted points fall outside the control limits. It means something has probably gone wrong or is about to go wrong with the process and a check is needed to prevent the appearance of defective products.

If the cause has been eliminated, the succeeding plotted points will stay well within the control limits, but if more points fall outside the control limits, then a very thorough investigation should be made, even if it is necessary to shut down the production temporarily until everything is adjusted again and no more points fall outside.

**Example 14.3.** Five samples were taken randomly from the manufactured lot of an item and 3 measurements were taken on each sample. The readings are shown in the table given below:

| ***Sample No.*** | ***Three measurements per sample*** | | |
|---|---|---|---|
| | I | II | III |
| 1 | 0.488 | 0.489 | 0.505 |
| 2 | 0.494 | 0.495 | 0.499 |
| 3 | 0.498 | 0.515 | 0.487 |
| 4 | 0.492 | 0.509 | 0.514 |
| 5 | 0.490 | 0.508 | 0.499 |

Calculate the control limits on $\overline{X}$ and $R$ charts and draw the charts.

**Solution.**

Calculation for $\overline{X}$:

For sample 1, $\overline{X_1} = \dfrac{0.488 + 0.489 + 0.505}{3} = 0.494$

For sample 2, $\overline{X_2} = \dfrac{0.494 + 0.495 + 0.499}{3} = 0.496$

For sample 3, $\overline{X_3} = \dfrac{0.498 + 0.515 + 0.487}{3} = 0.500$

For sample 4, $\overline{X_4} = \dfrac{0.492 + 0.509 + 0.514}{3} = 0.505$

For sample 5, $\overline{X_5} = \dfrac{0.490 + 0.508 + 0.499}{3} = 0.499$

$\therefore$ $\overline{X} = \dfrac{\Sigma\overline{X}}{5} = \dfrac{2.494}{5} = 0.499$

**Calculation of Range**

For sample 1, $R_1 = X_{max} - X_{min} - 0.505 - 0.488 = 0.017$

For sample 2, $R_2 = 0.499 - 0.494 = 0.005$

For sample 3, $R_3 = 0.515 - 0.487 = 0.028$

For sample 4, $R_4 = 0.514 - 0.492 = 0.022$

For sample 5, $R_5 = 0.508 - 0.490 = 0.018$

$\therefore$ $\overline{R} = \dfrac{\Sigma R}{5} = \mathbf{0.018.}$

Control limits for $\overline{X}$ chart:

As, $UCL_{\overline{x}} = \overline{X} + A_2\overline{R}$

$$LCL_{\bar{x}} = \overline{X} - A_2\overline{R}$$

where, $\overline{X} = 0.499$

$\overline{R} = 0.018$

$A_2 = 1.02$ ... (using SQC table)

$\therefore$ $U.C.L_{\bar{x}} = 0.499 + (1.02) \times (0.018) = \mathbf{0.5174}$

$L.CL._{\bar{x}} = 0.499 - (1.02) \times (0.018) = \mathbf{0.4807}$

**Control limits for *R* chart**

As, $U.CL._R = D_4\overline{R}$

$L.CL._R = D_3\overline{R}$

where, $D_4 = 2.57$ (From SQC table).

$D_3 = 0.00$ (From SQC table),

and $\overline{R} = 0.018$

$\therefore$ $U.CL._R = D_4\overline{R} = 2.57 \times 0.018 = \mathbf{0.0463}$

$L.CL._R = D_3\overline{R} = 0.00 \times 0.018 = \mathbf{0.00}$

From above, it is clear that all values of $\overline{X}$ and $R$ fall within the respective control limits, which is clear from the figure below :

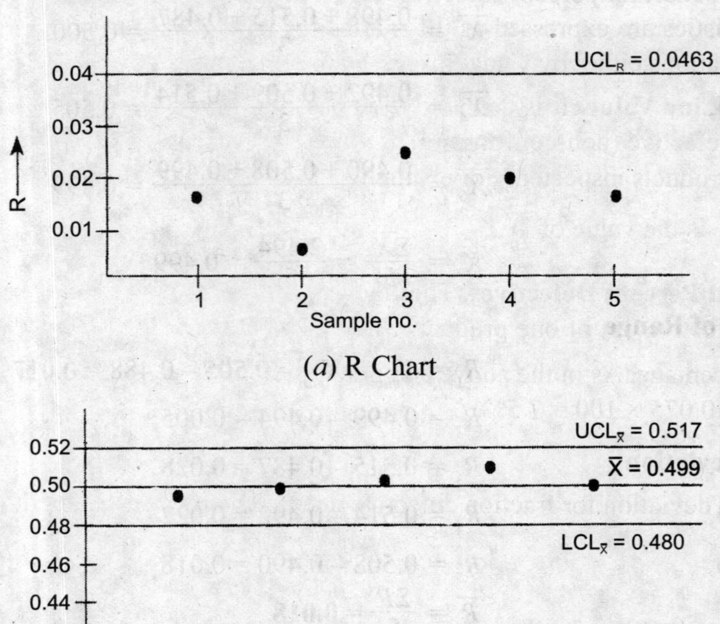


(*a*) R Chart

**Fig. 14.9** (b) $\overline{X}$ Chart

## 14.6. CONTROL CHARTS FOR ATTRIBUTES

The $\overline{X}$ and $R$ control charts are applicable for quality characteristics which are measured directly, *i.e.* for variables. There are instances in industrial practice, where direct measurements are not required or possible. Under such circumstances, the inspection results are based on the classification of products as being defective or not defective, acceptable as good or bad accordingly as that product confirms or fails to conform the specified specification.

In manufacturing, sometimes it is required to control burrs, cracks, voids, dents, scratches, missing and wrong components, rust etc. Here, we inspect products only as good or bad not how much good or how much bad. Furthermore, there are many quality characteristics that come under the category of measurable variables but direct measurement is not taken for reasons of economy. These products are inspected with GO and NOT GO gauges. Again under this type also, our aim is to tell that whether product confirms or does not confirm to the specified values. Quality characteristics expressed in this way are known as attributes.

The various control charts for attributes are explained as under :

### 14.6.1 Attribute Charts for Defective Items

#### The P-Chart

This is the control chart for percent defectives or for fraction defectives. This is used, whenever the quality characteristics are expressed as the number of units conforming or not conforming to the specified specifications either by visual inspection or by GO and 'NOT GO' gauges.

**The Centre Line Value.** It is denoted $\overline{p}$ ($p$ bar) and may be defined as the ratio between the total number of defective (non-conforming) products observed in all the samples combined and the total number of products inspected. For example, 15 products are found to be defective in a sample of 200, then $\frac{15}{200}$ is the value of $\overline{p}$.

**Fraction and Percent Defectives.** The fraction defective value is represented in a decimal as proportion of defective out of one product, while percent defective is the fraction defective value expressed as percentage. As in the above example, fraction defective of $\frac{15}{200} = 0.075$, and percent defective will be $0.075 \times 100 = 7.5\%$.

**Standard Deviation**

The standard deviation for fraction defective denoted by $\sigma P$ is calculated by using the formula,

$$\sigma p = \sqrt{\frac{\overline{p}(1-\overline{p})}{n}}$$

where, $n$ = sample size

$\overline{p}$ = fraction defective.

**Trial Control Limits**

Just as the control limits, for the $\overline{X}$ and $R$ - charts are obtained as ± 3σ values above the average. The two control limits, upper and lower for this chart are also calculated by simply adding or subtracting ±3σ values from control line value. These trial limits are computed to determine whether a process is in statistical control or not.

So, $$\text{UCL}_p = \overline{p} + 3\sigma p = \overline{p} + 3\sqrt{\frac{\overline{p}(1-\overline{p})}{n}}$$

Similarly, $$\text{LCL}_p = \overline{p} - 3\sqrt{\frac{\overline{p}(1-\overline{p})}{n}}$$

Mostly the control limits are obtained on the basis of about 20-25 samples to pick up the problem and standard deviation from the samples is calculated for further production control.

**Example 14.4.** The table shows that successive lots of spindle are coming out of the machine. The spindles are subject to inspection for burrs. The spindles are inspected in samples of 100 each.

Presence of a single or more burrs discriminates the value to be as defective. Compute and construct the chart.

| *Sample No.* | *Sample Size* | *Defectives* | *Percentage* |
|---|---|---|---|
| 1 | 100 | 1 | 1 |
| 2 | 100 | 1 | 1 |
| 3 | 100 | 2 | 2 |
| 4 | 100 | 1 | 1 |
| 5 | 100 | 1 | 1 |
| 6 | 100 | 0 | 0 |
| 7 | 100 | 1 | 1 |
| 8 | 100 | 0 | 0 |
| 9 | 100 | 1 | 1 |
| 10 | 100 | 2 | 2 |
| 11 | 100 | 3 | 3 |
| 12 | 100 | 2 | 2 |
| 13 | 100 | 1 | 1 |
| 14 | 100 | 2 | 2 |
| 15 | 100 | 0 | 0 |
| 16 | 100 | 2 | 2 |
| 17 | 100 | 7 | 7 |
| 18 | 100 | 1 | 1 |

| 19 | 100 | 2 | 2 |
|---|---|---|---|
| 20 | 100 | 0 | 0 |

## Computation and Construction

Here, the maximum percent defective is 7% and the total number of samples inspected are 20. On graph paper, make abscissa for samples number 1, 2, 3, up to 20. Make ordinate as percent defective so as to accommodate 7%. Next go on marking various points, as shown by the table as sample number *vs*. percent defective.

Draw three firm horizontal lines, one each for central line value, upper limit and lower limit after obtaining by calculations.

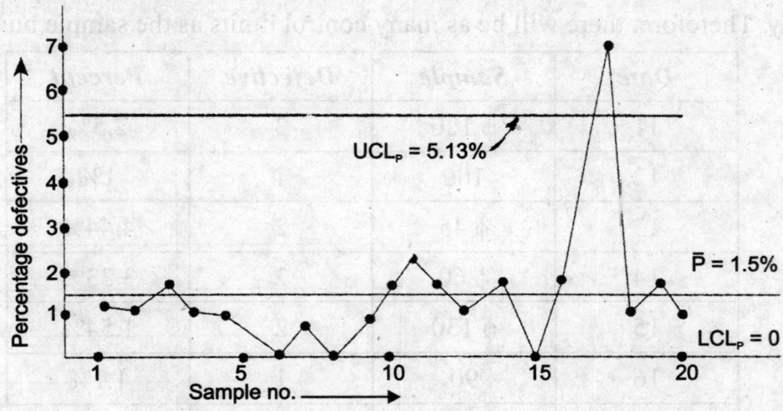


**Fig. 14.10.** *P-chart.*

Estimated fraction defective,

$$\bar{p} = \frac{\text{Sum of defective values}}{\text{Total number of products inspected}}$$

$$= \frac{30}{20 \times 100} = 0.015$$

Percent defective of $\bar{p}$ = 100 × 0.015 = 1.5%

Standard deviation = $= \sigma p = \sqrt{\frac{\bar{p}(1-\bar{p})}{n}}$

$$= \sqrt{\frac{0.015(1-0.015)}{100}} = 0.0121$$

Then, upper control limit

$$= \bar{p} + 3\sigma p$$

$$\therefore \quad UCL_p = 0.015 + 3 \times 0.0121 = 0.0513$$

Lower control limit

$$= \overline{p} - 3\sigma p = 0.015 - 3 \times 0.0121 = 0.015 - 0.0363$$

= – ve value, but – ve value is not possible

Therefore, $LCL_p = 0.$

**Variable Sample Size**

Now consider an example of a p-chart for variable sample size. This is because hourly, daily or weekly production somewhat varies. Therefore, it is always feasible to take the samples of constant sizes, such problems can be solved as under :

(*i*) If the maximum and minimum values of *n* are within 25% of the average of *n*, then calculate average *n* and find the control limits as done in case of *n* constant.

(*ii*) If the variation in *n* is more than 25%, then control limits for each sample size is calculated separately. Therefore, there will be as many control limits as the sample number.

| ***Date*** | ***Sample*** | ***Defective*** | ***Percent*** |
|---|---|---|---|
| 11 | ϕ 120 | 3 | 2.5% |
| 12 | 100 | 1 | 1% |
| 13 | ϕ 45 | 2 | 4.44% |
| 14 | ϕ 60 | 2 | 3.33% |
| 15 | ϕ 130 | 2 | 1.54% |
| 16 | 90 | 1 | 1.1% |
| 17 | 105 | 4 | 3.8% |
| 18 | 80 | 3 | 3.75% |
| 19 | 75 | 1 | 1.33% |
| 20 | 105 | 2 | 1.9% |
| **Total** | **900** | **21** | **2.33%** |

Here, the average sample size will be $\frac{900}{10} = 90$

It is a common practice to apply control limits as long as sample size varies ± 25% of the average sample size, *i.e.* ± 25% of 90 will be 68 and 112. Therefore, mark the samples with ϕ which are below 68 and above 112.

$\overline{p}$ the fraction defective

$$= \frac{21}{900} = 0.023$$

As the samples on dates 12,16,17,18,19 and 20 are covered within ± 25% of the averages, we have now the following sample sizes for which control limits are to be calculated separately.

| 1 | 2 | 3 | 4 | 5 |
|---|---|---|---|---|
| 90 | 120 | 45 | 60 | 130 |

For. this purpose, let us frame a table as follows : go on calculating and filling the values.

| *Sample Size* | $\sigma P$ | $3\ \sigma p$ | $UCL_p(\overline{P}+3\sigma p)$ | $LCLP\ (\overline{P}-3\sigma P)$ |
|---|---|---|---|---|
| 90 | 0.011 | 0.033 | 0.056 | 0 |
| 120 | 0.013 | 0.039 | 0.062 | 0 |
| 45 | 0.022 | 0.066 | 0.089 | 0 |
| 60 | 0.019 | 0.057 | 0.080 | 0 |
| 130 | 0.013 | 0.039 | 0.062 | 0 |

### 14.6.2. Attribute Charts for Number of Defects per unit

#### (A) The C - Chart

This is a method of plotting attribute characteristics. In this case, the sample taken is a single unit, such as length, breadth and area or a fixed time etc. In some cases, it is required to find the number of defects per unit rather than the percent defective. For example, take a case in which a large number of small components form a large unit, say a car or transistor. The transistor set may have defects at various points. In this case, it seems natural to count the number of defects per set, rather than to determine all points at which the unit is defective. Such a condition warrants the necessity for the use of a C-chart.

#### (B) np-Chart

The np-chart is similar to a *p*-chart. In this case, the sample size is constant, and the data values plotted are the actual number of defective items per sample represented by *np* rather than the proportion *p*. In this case, control limits are represented by $n\overline{p} \pm 3\sigma\ np$.

where, $n\overline{p}$ = grand average of all defectives

$$= \frac{\text{Total number of defective}}{\text{Number of samples inspected}}$$

and
$$\sigma np = \sqrt{n\overline{p}(1-\overline{p})}$$

The distribution of the variables in *C*-chart very closely follows the Poisson's distribution. The examples given below, show some of representative types of defects where *C*-chart technique can be effectively applied:

(*i*) Number of blemishes per 100 square metres.

(*ii*) Typing mistakes on the part of a typist.

(*iii*) Number of spots on a distempered wall.

(*iv*) Air gap between two maching parts of a joint.

(*v*) Welding defects in a trunk.

(*vi*) Unweaven points on a piece of a textile cloth.

(*vii*) Leakage in water tight joints of radiator.

**(*i*) The Average Number of Defects**

It is denoted by $\overline{C}$ ($C$ bar) and is the ratio between the total number of defects found in all samples and the total number of samples inspected.

**(2) Standard Deviation**

The sigma of standard deviation for number of defects per unit production is calculated from the formula $\sigma_c = \sqrt{\overline{C}}$.

**Trial Control Limits**

The control limits can be calculated as $\pm 3\sigma_c$ from the central line value $\overline{C}$.

*i.e.*

$$UCL_C = \overline{C} + 3\sqrt{\overline{C}}$$

$$LCL_C = \overline{C} - 3\sqrt{\overline{C}}$$

## (C) U-Chart

As discussed earlier, C-charts are used when sub-group (or sample) consists of a single unit. U-charts are drawn, when sub-group consists of *n* units. In this case :

Central line is drawn at,

$$\overline{u} = \frac{\Sigma C}{\Sigma n}$$

$$= \frac{\text{total number of defects in all units}}{\text{total number of items inspected}}$$

and

$$UCL = \overline{u} + 3\sqrt{\frac{\overline{u}}{n}}$$

$$LCL = \overline{u} - 3\sqrt{\frac{\overline{u}}{n}}$$

When the size of the unit is varying, separate limits are calculated for each sub-group, using the above formula.

**Quality Rating in C-charts and U-charts**

Since all types of defects are not of equal importance and plotting the sum of all defects regardless of type on one chart is rather misleading. Therefore, defects are classified as :

(*i*) critical, major and minor ; or as

(*ii*) very serious, serious, moderately serious, and not serious. These defects are assigned weightage e.g., 10 points to critical, 5 points to major and 1 point to minor defect. The charts are then drawn with this weightage to assess the quality.

**Example. 14.5.** The following table shows the number of defects on the surface of surface bodies in a bus depot, on 21 Sept., 2010

| *Dated* | *Body No.* | *No. of defects* |
|---|---|---|
| 21/9/10 | 1 | 2 |
| | 2 | 2 |
| | 3 | 4 |
| | 4 | 7 |
| | 5 | 5 |
| | 6 | 6 |
| | 7 | 7 |
| | 8 | 14 |
| | 9 | 2 |
| | 10 | 9 |
| | 11 | 3 |
| | 12 | 0 |
| | 13 | 5 |
| | 14 | 4 |
| | 15 | 3 |
| | 16 | 10 |
| | 17 | 4 |
| | 18 | 3 |
| | 19 | 12 |
| | 20 | 6 |
| **Total** | **20** | **110** |

**Computation**

(*i*) Compute the average number of defects $\overline{C}$.

$$\overline{C} = \frac{110}{20} = 5.5.$$

(*ii*) Compute the trial control limits

$$UCL_C = 5.5 + 3\sqrt{5.5} = 12.54$$

$$LCL_C = 5.5 - 3\sqrt{5.5} = -1.54 = 0$$

as –ve defects are not possible.

**Construction**

1. Mark abscissa as the body number to a suitable scale (1 to 20).
2. Mark ordinate as number of defects, say upto 15. Looking to the table, the maximum number of 14 defects are in body No. 8.
3. Mark various points for the body number and the number of defects in that body.

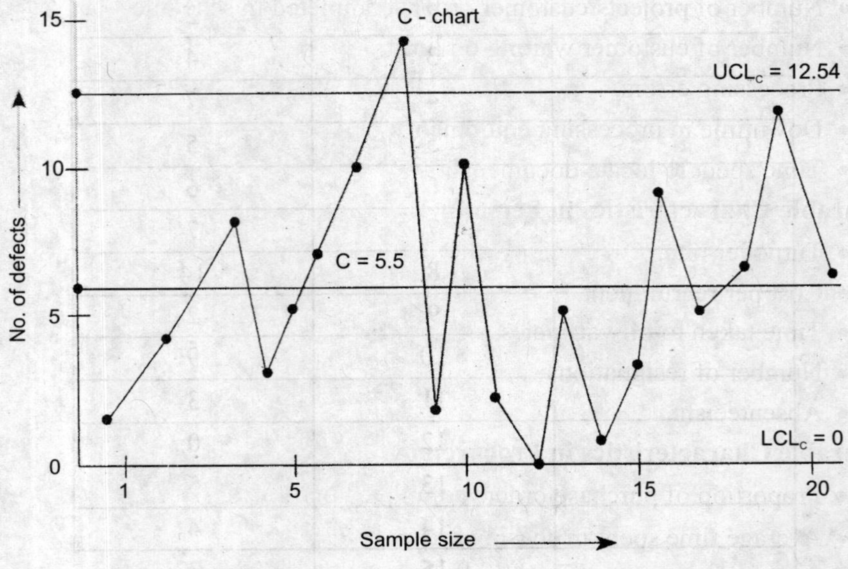


**Fig. 14.11**

4. Join all the 20 points with straight lines and also, draw one line each for average control line value, upper control limit and lower control limit, *i.e.* 5.5, 12.54, and 0 respectively.

**Interpretation.** As shown in the chart, one point No. 8 having 14 defects fall outside the upper control limit. The data relate to the production on 21/9/10, then $\overline{C}$ value require re-calculation which will be $\dfrac{110-14}{19} = 5.03$. The value 5.03 will be the standard value of $\overline{C}$ for next day's production. Consequently, the control limits are also revised, if it decided to apply the data in next day's production, *i.e.* 22/9/10.

## 14.7. MEASURABLE CHARACTERISTICS IN SERVICE SECTOR

As discussed earlier, SPC is applicable to both, manufacturing and service sectors. In both the areas, it is necessary to establish appropriate characteristic which is measurable. It is convenient for the manufacturing sector, where the production process is much more clearly measurable. In manufacturing sector, areas related to personnel, administration, procurement, material handling design, safety, security etc. are actually service areas. Therefore, it is essential to define measurable characteristics, appropriate to service areas. Some of the measurable characteristics in service area are :

**1. Measurable Characteristics in Administration.**

- Average number of typing errors per document.
- Proportion of reports delivered in schedule time.
- Customers complaint rate.
- Number of projects/customer orders completed in schedule.
- Number of customer waiting on line.
- Processing errors.
- Downtime in processing equipment.
- Time spent to locate documents.

**2. Measurable Characteristics in Personnel.**

- Turnover rate.
- Cost per recruitment.
- Time taken to fill vacancies.
- Number of resignations
- Absenteeism

**3. Measurable Characteristics in Procurement.**

- Proportion of purchase orders completed on time.
- Average time spent in chasing orders.
- Supplier quality performance.
- Number of items returned to supplier.
- Average time to complete the order by supplier.
- Number of stock items not used on time

**4. Measurable Characteristics in Material Handling.**

- Average time of stock-out periods.
- Ratio of stock-out to demand.
- Proportion of internal orders concluded on time.
- Response time to customer requests.

**5. Measurement Characteristics in Design**

- Number of mistakes found during checking.
- Number of drawing errors.
- Proportion of drawings not available on schedule.
- Timeliness of design error resolution.

## QUESTIONS

1. (*a*) What are the objectives of quality control in factories?

   (*b*) Define—attribute and variable inspections.

2. State the advantages of using statistical methods of quality control.
3. Define statistical quality control. Discuss how it is used to control the quality?
4. Discuss frequency distribution charts used as a tool of quality control.
5. Write short notes on the following :

   (*a*) Sampling inspection

   (*b*) Statistical techniques used for process control

   (*c*) Statistical quality control

   (*d*) Limits of control charts

   (*e*) Schewhart control chart.

6. Describe the methods of statistical quality control and state their advantages in relation to inspection.
7. State the objectives of quality control and show how statistical quality control helps in achieving them?
8. (*a*) Describe statistical quality control as a technique of management.

   (*b*) Show by illustrative example, range of application of statistical quality control techniques in manufacturing concern.

9. (*a*) What is meant by assignable cause ? When is a process said to be under control ?

   (*b*) Explain how to introduce statistical quality control in a manufacturing concern?

10. Name and describe the purposes of the following methods:

    (*a*) Least squares.

    (*b*) Correlation.

    (*c*) Analysis of Variance

11. What are chance causes ? What are assignable causes ? What are the advantages of statistical methods ?
12. When sampling is desired in place of 100 percent inspection? Name the three classes of sampling plans and compare cost and difficulty of each.
13. Explain clearly the difference between the random or chance causes of variation and the assignable causes of variation.
14. (*a*) Define control charts. How many types of control charts are in use?

    (*b*) Define control limits and write the formulae for central line and upper and lower control limits of various types of charts.

**15.** Write short notes on :

   (*a*) Statistical process control

   (*b*) Process capability

   (*c*) Statistical quality control

**16.** What is the task of Statistical Quality Control ? What are the statistical quality tools available?

**17.** Explain the difference between:

   (*a*) SQC and SPC ; and

   (*b*) SQC and sampling inspection.

**18.** (*a*) When a process can be said to be in statistical control ?

   (*b*) What is the function of SQC.

**19.** (*a*) How the lack of control is indicated on control charts ?

   (*b*) Where it is desirable to use following charts:

      (*i*) Average charts ($\overline{X}$ -charts)

      (*ii*) Defective charts (p-charts)

      (*iii*) Range charts (R-charts)

**20.** (*a*) What is the difference betweeen c-chart and np-chart?

   (*b*) How the process charts check the working of machines and put down the number of rejected parts ?

**21.** Write short notes on :

   (*a*) Principles of control charts for variables.

   (*b*) Producer's risk and consumer's risk

   (*c*) Process variability.

**22.** Explain through diagrams, how will you interpret the patterns of variation on $\overline{X}$ and $R$ charts?

**23.** Discuss the different types of control charts for attributes.

15

# Probability Theory

## 15.1. INTRODUCTION

The word ***'probability'*** or ***'chance'*** is most commonly used in day-to-day conversation. This shows that the event is not certain to take place and certain amount of uncertainty about happening of the event is there. In statistics, attempts are made to present such conditions by which we can make sensible numerical statements regarding uncertainties. For example, we all are quite familiar with the event of tossing a coin. Now, what is the chance that when we toss a coin, it will show a head? More precisely, we say what is the probability of a head in a single toss of a coin?

A head or a tail is equally likely, if the coin is perfectly symmetrical and unbiased. This means than there is one chance in two that it will show a head. In other words, the probability of head or of a tail in a single toss of the coin is 1/2 in each case. But in reality a perfect symmetrical coin does not easily found and if we go on tossing the same coin again and again, we can find out the relative frequency of a head in the long run. Thus this gives a measure of its probability.

As mentioned in the chapter on "Acceptance Sampling and O.C. Curves", probably concept states that certain mass phenomenon have a tendency towards regularity in behaviour *i.e.,* if sample is drawn from the mass of universe (population without any bias that sample is quite likely to display those characteristics that are found in the whole mass. Therefore, inferences drawn from the study such a sample can be relied upon as being representative of the "whole mass".

Probability concept is popularly used in quality control.

## 15.2. TERMS USED IN PROBABILITY

1. **Equally Likely Events :** The events are said to be likely when one event does not occur more often than the other. For example, if an unbiased coin is thrown, each face is expected to be observed approximately the same number of times in the long run.

2. **Simple and Compound Events :** In simple events, the probability of happening or not happening of single event, is considered. If it is asked to find out the probability of drawing one white ball from a bag containing 8 white and 16 red balls, is a case of "simple events". But when joint occurrence of two or more events is considered, we say, we are dealing with a "Compound events". If from the above bag containing 8 white and 16 red balls, two successive draws of 6 white and 6 red balls, are made, we have to find out the probability of getting 6 white balls in the first draw and 6 red ballls in the second draw. This is an example of "Compound event".

3. **Independent Event :** The two events are said to be independent when the occurrence (or non-occurrence) of one, in no way affects the occurrence of the other. If a coin is tossed twice, the result of the first toss in no way would affect the result of the second toss. Similarly, suppose a bag contains 20 homogenous balls and one ball is drawn from it and replaced, then a second ball is drawn and replaced and so on. Thus, if the ball is replaced after each draw, each such draw will be independent because the chances of drawing a ball each time are then equal, *i.e.* 1/20 in this case.

4. **Dependent Events :** When the occurrence of one event affects the occurrence of another event, it is called "Dependent event", such as in the above example, if a ball is drawn and it is not replaced then the probability of the second draw is not the same as that of first draw :

$$\text{Probability of first draw} = \frac{1}{20}$$

$$\text{Probability of second draw} = \frac{1}{19}$$

In this case the second event is dependent on the first because here the result of the first affects the probability of the second.

5. **Mutually Exclusive Events :** If the occurrence of one event prevents the occurrence of the other, the events are said to be "mutually exclusive". These events cannot occur at the same time. For example, when a coin is tossed, if it does not stand on its edge, either the head can be up or the tail can be up. Therefore, when the coin comes to rest, one and only one face shall be upper most *i.e.* it will held at one face at a time. Both the faces cannot be up at the same time.

   To mutually exclusive events $A$ and $B$ cannot happen at the same time and, therefore, the probability of simultaneous happening of the two events $P$ ($A$ and $B$) = 0

   If $A$ occurs for every trail, then $P(A) = 1$.

6. **Scale of Probability :** The probability of an event is a number between 0 and 1. If the event cannot occur, its probability is zero. If it must occur, *i.e.* if its occurrence is certain, its probability is 1. Thus, the scale of probability extends from zero to unity. These are two extreme examples on the scale of probability. In actual practice the value of $P$ usually lies between 0 and 1.

## 15.3. PROBABILITY AND ITS MEASURE

According to Laplace, probability is the ratio of the number of favourable cases to the total number of equally likely cases.

Probability, $P = \dfrac{\text{No. of favourable cases}}{\text{Total No. of equally likely cases}}$

Hence, to find probability, two things are required to be calculated,

(*i*) the number of favourable cases,

(*ii*) the total number of equally likely cases.

In discussing events which can have either of two possible results, it will be convenient to refer to these events as success and failure are usually denoted by $P$ and $q$ respectively.

If an event can result in $n$ different ways, all equally likely (and mutually exclusive) of which $a$ are success and $b$ are failure, then :

$$P = \frac{a}{n} = \frac{a}{a+b}$$

Similarly, $$q = \frac{b}{n} = \frac{b}{a+b}$$

$$\therefore \quad P + q = \frac{a}{a+b} + \frac{b}{a+b} = \frac{a+b}{a+b} = 1.$$

Hence, $P = 1 - q$ and $q = 1 - P$.

Thus $P$ is a positive number and it never exceeds unity. If $P$ is the probability that an event will occur, the odds in favour of its happening are $P : q$ and the odds against its happening are $q : P$.

In cases of coin-toss, dice rolling, drawing a card from deck of cards, we can state the answer in advance without even performing the event. In such cases (known as classical probability cases),

$$\text{Probability of an event} = \frac{\text{number of outcomes where the event occurs}}{\text{total number of possible outcomes}}$$

(*a*) In case of tossing of coin :

$$P\text{ (head)} = \frac{1}{2}$$

(*b*) In case of dice-rolling :

$$P = \frac{1}{6}$$

(*c*) In case of drawing a card (say an ace)

$$P = \frac{4}{52}$$

(*i*) If ace is replaced, chance in next trial, $P = \dfrac{4}{52}$.

(*ii*) If drawn card is not replaced, and first card is not an ace, $P = \dfrac{4}{51}$.

If drawn card is not replaced, and first card is an ace, $P = \dfrac{3}{51}$.

**Example 15.1.** *In a lottery there are 4 prizes and 96 blanks. If a person holds one ticket, what are the chances of (i) getting a prize (ii) not getting a prize.*

**Solution :** Total number of tickets $= 4 + 96 = 100$.

*(i)* Probability of getting a prize.

$$P = \frac{\text{Favourable cases}}{\text{Total equally likely cases}}$$

$$= \frac{a}{a+b} = \frac{4}{4+96} = \mathbf{0.04.\ Ans.}$$

*(ii)* Probability of not getting a prize.

$$q = \frac{b}{a+b} = \frac{96}{100} = \mathbf{0.96.\ Ans.}$$

Check : $P + q = 0.04 + 0.96 = 1$.

**Example 15.2.** *There are 40 white and 60 black balls in a bag. What is the probability that blind person obtains (i) a white ball in that first draw and (ii) a black ball in the second draw, the first ball drawn being not replaced.*

**Solution :** Total balls $= 40 + 60 = 100$.

*(i)* ∴ Probability of getting white ball in the first draw

$$= \frac{a}{a+b} = \frac{40}{100} = \mathbf{0.4.\ Ans.}$$

*(ii)* Total balls now in bag $= 39 + 60 = 99$

∴ Probability of getting black ball in the second draw

$$= \frac{60}{99} = \frac{20}{33}\ \textbf{Ans.}$$

**Example 15.3.** *According to the life tables out of 100,000 children living at 10 years age, 82,200 survive to age 40 of which 1000 die in a year. What is the probability for a man of 40 to survive one more year.*

**Solution :** Total number of survivors at the age of 40 years = 82,200

Out of this 1000 persons die in a year. This means

(82,200 – 1000 = 81,200 persons aged 40 survive one year more

$$\therefore \quad P = \frac{\text{No. of favourable cases}}{\text{Total No. of equally likely cases}} = \frac{81{,}200}{82{,}200} = 0.9878.$$

Hence, the probability that a person aged 40 years, would survive a year more is **0.9878. Ans.**

## 15.4. BASIC LAWS OF PROBABILITY

Following are the 3 laws of probability :

1. The probability that 2 events will both occur can never be greater than the probability that each will occur individually.

2. If two possible events, $A$ and $B$ are independent, then the probability that both $A$ and $B$ will occur is equal to the product of their individual probabilities.
3. If an event can have a number of different and distinct possible outcomes, $A$, $B$, $C$ and so on, then the probability that either $A$ or $B$ will occur is equal to the sum of the individual probabilities of $A$ and $B$ and the sum of the probabilities of all the possible outcomes ($A$, $B$, $C$ and so on) is 1 (that is, 100%).

## 15.5. ADDITION THEOREM

**(*a*) When Events are Mutually Exclusive**

If two events $A$ and $B$ are mutually exclusive (*i.e.*, cannot happen together) the probability of the occurrence of either $A$ or $B$ is equal to the sum of two individual probabilities of $A$ and $B$. This is also called "Theorem of total Probability".

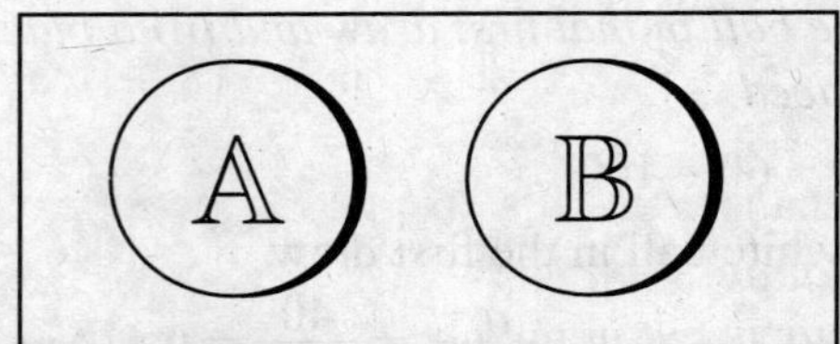


**Fig 15.1.** Two mutually exclusive events.

$$P(A \text{ or } B) = P(A) + (B)$$

It can be extended to three or more mutually exclusive events. Thus:

$$P(A \text{ or } B \text{ or } C) = P(A) + P(B) + P(C).$$

In this addition rule (or theorem),

$P(A \text{ or } B)$ = the probability of either $A$ or $B$ happening.

$P(A)$ = the probability of event $A$ happening.

$P(B)$ = the probability of event $B$ happening.

and can be represented as shown in Fig. 15.1.

**Example 15.4.** *One card is drawn from a standard pack of 52 cards. What is the chance that it is either a king or a queen?*

**Solution :** In a pack of 52 cards, there are 4 kings and 4 queens.

$\therefore$ Probability to draw a king,

$$P_1 = \frac{a}{n} = \frac{4}{52} = \frac{1}{13}.$$

Similarly, Probability to draw a queen,

$$P_2 = \frac{a}{n} = \frac{4}{52} = \frac{1}{13}.$$

As the events are mutually exclusive, the probability that the card drawn is either a king or a queen

$$= \frac{1}{13} + \frac{1}{13} = \frac{2}{13} = \mathbf{0.154\ Ans.}$$

**Example 15.5.** *12 Hindus, 6 Sikhs, 5 Ceylonese, 6 Burmese and 3 Pakistanis apply for a certain job in an embassy where only one candidate has to be selected. If every applicant has an equal chance of being selected or rejected by the committee, what is the probability of the post going to an Indian?*

**Solution :** Total candidates = 12 + 6 + 5 + 6 + 3 = 32

Probability of the post going to a Hindu, $P_1 = \frac{12}{32}$

Probability of the post going to a Sikh, $P_2 = \frac{6}{32}$

∴ Probability of the post going to an Indian

$$P = \frac{12}{32} + \frac{6}{32} = \frac{18}{32} = 0.5625.$$

Thus, there are **56.25%** chances that the post may go to an Indian.

**Example 15.6.** *A box contains 3 red and 7 white balls, one ball is drawn at random and in its place a ball of the other colour is put in the box. Now one ball is drawn at random from the box. Find the probability that it is red.*

**Solution :** At the second draw red ball can be drawn in two ways :

(*i*) When the first ball drawn is red.

(*ii*) When the first ball drawn is white.

(*i*) When the first ball drawn is red :

Probability of drawing a red ball $= \frac{3}{3+7} = \frac{3}{10}$

Now a white ball is put in the box in place of the red ball drawn.

Hence, now there are 2 red and 8 white balls in the box.

∴ Probability of drawing a red ball again $= \frac{2}{2+8} = \frac{2}{10}$

(*ii*) When the first ball drawn is white :

The probability of drawing a white ball $= \frac{7}{3+7} = \frac{7}{10}$

Now a red ball is put in the box in place of the white ball drawn. Hence now there are 4 red and 6 white balls in the box.

∴ Probability of drawing a red ball $= \frac{4}{4+6} = \frac{4}{10}$

The two events are mutually exclusive.

∴ Probability of drawing a red ball $= \frac{2}{10} + \frac{4}{10} = \frac{6}{10} = \mathbf{0.6.\ Ans.}$

### (b) When Events are not Mutually Exclusive

The addition theorem described above is not applicable when the events are not mutually exclusive. For example, if the probability of person's purchasing a shirt is 0.7 and of purchasing a pair of socks is 0.2, we cannot determine the probability of his purchasing either a shirt or socks by adding the two probabilities. The events are not mutually exclusive, he can very well buy a shirt as well as socks.

When events are not mutually exclusive, the addition theorem has to be modified. The probability that atleast one of the two events $A$ and $B$ (not mutually exclusive) will occur, is $P(A \text{ or } B) = P(A) + P(B) - P(A \text{ and } B)$. We subtract $P(A \text{ and } B)$ which stands for the proportion of cases, that are counted twice in $P(A) + P(B)$. The addition theorem, when events are not mutually exclusive is thus reconstructed so as to render $A$ and $B$ mutually exclusive by subtracting the cases in which $A$ and $B$ occur together, *i.e.* simultaneously. Addition rule for events that are not mutually exclusive can be expressed as shown in Fig. 15.2.

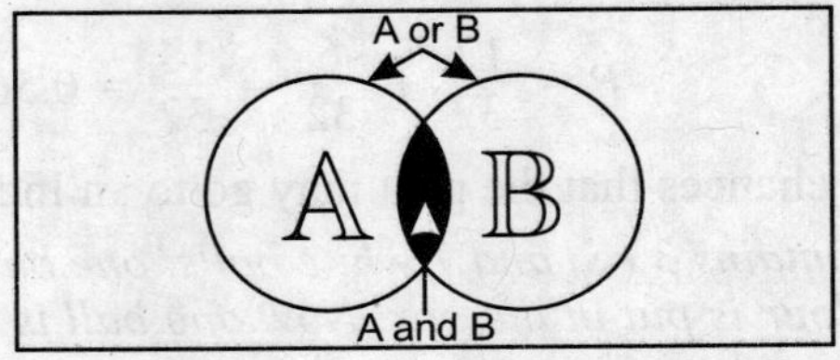


**Fig. 15.2.**

The equation of this rule can be explained as shown below :

$$P(A \text{ or } B) = P(A) + P(B) - P(AB)$$

where, $P(A \text{ or } B)$ = the probability of $A$ or $B$ happening when $A$ and $B$ are not mutually exclusive.

$P(A)$ = the probability of $A$ happening

$P(B)$ = the probability of $B$ happening

$P(AB)$ = the probability of $A$ and $B$ happening together.

**Example 15.7.** *A gunman can hit the target in 3 out of 4 shots whereas another gunman can hit the target in 2 out of 3 shots. Find the probability of the targets being hit at all when they both try.*

**Solution :**

Probability that first gunman can hit the target = $\frac{3}{4}$

Probability that second gunman can hit the target = $\frac{2}{3}$

As both may hit the target, the events are not mutually exclusive.

$$\therefore \quad P(A \text{ or } B) = P(A) + P(B) - P(A \text{ and } B)$$

$$= \left(\frac{3}{4} + \frac{2}{3}\right) - \left(\frac{3}{4} \times \frac{2}{3}\right) = \frac{17}{12} - \frac{6}{12} = \frac{11}{12} \textbf{ Ans.}$$

## 15.6. MULTIPLICATION THEOREM

"If two events $A$ and $B$ are independent, the probability that they will both occur together on any one occasion, is equal to the product of individual probabilities of $A$ and $B$ happening separately, *i.e.*

$$P(A \text{ and } B) = P(A) \times P(B).$$

This is the compound probability of the events and therefore this theorem is also known as the Theorem of Compound Probability of Multiplication of Probability. It can also be extended to three or more independent events.

Thus, $$P(A, B \text{ and } C) = P(A) \times P(B) \times P(C)$$

Multiplication rule for joint, independent events. The probability of two or more independent events occurring together or in succession is the product of their probabilities, and can be expressed as :

$$P(AB) = P(A) \times P(B)$$

where

P ($AB$) = the probability of events $A$ and $B$ occurring together or in succession. This is known as joint probability.

P ($A$) = the probability of event $A$ occurring.

P ($B$) = the probability of event $B$ occurring.

**Example 15.8.** *The probability that a man aged 55 will survive 10 years is 2/5 and a woman aged 45 surviving 10 years is 3/5. What are the chances that they will both survive 10 years.*

**Solution.** Surviving of a man does not affect the surviving of a woman. Hence, the two events are independent. The Probability that they will both survive 10 years.

$$P(A \text{ and } B) = P(A) \times P(B)$$

$$\frac{2}{5} \times \frac{3}{5} = \frac{6}{25} \textbf{ Ans.}$$

**Example 15.9.** *It is 8 : 5 against a person who is now 40 years old, living till he is 70 and 4 : 3 against a person now 50, living till he is 80. What is the probability that one atleast of these will be alive 30 years.*

**Solution.** Probability against a person (now 40 years old), living till he is 70,

$$P_1 = \frac{8}{8+5} = \frac{8}{13}$$

Probability of death in case of second person,

$$P_2 = \frac{4}{4 \times 3} = \frac{4}{7}$$

∴ Probability of the compound event

$$= P_1 \times P_2 = \frac{8}{13} \times \frac{4}{7} = \frac{32}{91}$$

∴ Probability that atleast one of these persons would be alive 30 years,

$$P = 1 - \frac{32}{91} = \frac{59}{91} \text{ Ans.}$$

**Example 15.10.** *A class contains 21 boys and 15 girls, all assumed to be equal in performances. What is the probability that*

(*i*) *a boy will take first prize and a girl second prize.*

(*ii*) *a girl will take first prive and a boy second prize.*

**Solution.** (*i*) In a class of (21 + 15) students, the probability that a boy will take first prize is $\frac{21}{36}$.

Out of the remaining 35 students the probability of one of the 15 girls, taking second prize = $\frac{15}{35}$.

∴ Probability of the double event = $\frac{21}{36} \times \frac{15}{35} = \frac{1}{4} = 0.25$

(*ii*) Here, the probability that a girl will take first prize is $\frac{15}{36}$. Then the probability of one of the 21 boys taking second prize is $\frac{21}{35}$

∴ Probability of the double event = $\frac{15}{36} \times \frac{21}{35} = \frac{1}{4} = 0.25$

Thus boys and girls both winning a prize have equal chances. **Ans.**

**Example 15.11.** *Dr. X expects to marry a girl of the following qualities :*

(*a*) *Pretty appearance : The odds in favour of getting this type of girl are 2 to 5.*

(*b*) *Charming manners : The odds in favour of such a girl are 5 : 5.*

(*c*) *Good education : The odds against getting this girl are 4 to 7.*

(*d*) *No dowry : The odds in her favour, are 6 to 0.*

*The above four attributes are independent. What are the odds against Dr. X to marry a girl of his choice?*

**Solution.** (*a*) The probability of a girl with pretty appearance,

$$p^1 = \frac{2}{2+5} = \frac{2}{7}$$

(*b*) The probability of a girl with charming manners

$$p^2 = \frac{5}{5+5} = \frac{5}{10} = \frac{1}{2}$$

(*c*) The probability of a girl with good education

$$p^3 = \frac{7}{4+7} = \frac{7}{11}$$

(*d*) The probability of a girl with no dowry

$$p^4 = \frac{6}{6+0} = \frac{6}{6} = 1.$$

Since all the attributes are independent, the probability of simultaneous occurrence of all the four qualities

$$P = p^1 \times p^2 \times p^3 \times p^4$$

$$\frac{2}{7} \times \frac{1}{2} \times \frac{7}{11} \times 1 = \frac{1}{11} = \frac{1}{10+1}$$

$\therefore$ The odds against Dr. X getting a girl with all the above four qualities are 10 to 1. **Ans.**

## 15.7. CONDITIONAL PROBABILITY

The multiplication theorem discussed above is not applicable in case of dependent events. Two events $A$ and $B$ are said to be dependent, if $A$ occurs when $B$ is known to have occurred and vice versa. The probability attached to such an event is called "Conditional Probability" and is denoted by $P(A/B)$, *i.e.* probability of $A$ given that $B$ has occurred. Thus

$$P(A/B) = P(AB)/P(B).$$

If two events, $A$ and $B$ are dependent, then conditional probability of $B$, given that $A$ has occurred is denoted by $P(B/A)$.

$$P(B/A) = P(AB)/P(A).$$

**Example 15.12.** A box contains 6 white balls and 24 black balls. Two balls are drawn at random one after the other without replacement. What is the probability that both the balls drawn are white?

**Solution.** The probability of drawing a white ball in the first attempt or

$$P(A) = \frac{6}{6+24} = \frac{6}{30}$$

The probability of drawing the second white ball, given that the first ball drawn is also white and not replaced, or

$$P(B/A) = \frac{5}{5+24} = \frac{5}{29}$$

$\therefore$ Probability that both balls drawn are white

$$P(AB) = \frac{6}{30} \times \frac{5}{29} = \frac{1}{29}.$$

**Example 15.13.** Four cards are drawn without replacement. What is the probability that they are all kings.

**Solution.** The cards not being replaced the probability of getting four kings would be,

$$= \frac{4}{52} \times \frac{3}{51} \times \frac{2}{50} \times \frac{1}{49} = \frac{1}{270{,}725} \textbf{ Ans.}$$

**Example 15.14.** Four cards are drawn without replacement. What is the probability that they all have the same value?

**Solution.** The first card can be any one of the 52 cards. This card not being replaced, the second card may be any one of the remaining 3 cards of the same value as the first card, and so on.

$$\therefore \quad \text{Required probability} = 1 \times \frac{3}{51} \times \frac{2}{50} \times \frac{1}{49} = \frac{1}{20{,}825} \textbf{ Ans.}$$

## 15.8 PERMUTATIONS AND COMBINATIONS

In calculations of probabilities, application of the theory of permutation and combination is essential. We cannot calculate the probability of happening or non-happening of an event without calculating the number of favourable ways and the total number of ways in which an event can happen. Therefore, it is necessary to know some of the important rules of Permutations and Combinations.

### Permutation

Permutation an arrangement of a certain number of distinguishable things, elements of objects in a specified order is called "Permutation". For example, the word "Sum" is a special arrangement of 3 letters S, U and M. Other possible arrangements of these three letters are UMS, MSU, MUS, USM and SMU. In all there are 6 possible arrangements and these arrangements are known as permutations. Thus each of the arrangement containing $r$ things out of $n$ things, giving due attention to the order of arrangement, is called "Permutation". It is represented by ${}^nP_r$

$$\therefore \quad {}^nP_r = \frac{n!}{(n-r)!}$$

If $\quad n = 4, r = 2$

Then $\quad {}^4P_r = \frac{4!}{(4-2)!} = \frac{4 \times 3 \times 2 \times 1}{2 \times 1} = \textbf{12 Ans.}$

### Combination

A "Combination" is not the same thing as permutation. A group of, say, 5 letters constitute a combination of these 5 letters, but this combination can be arranged in 5! ways as has been discussed while dealing with permutations. Therefore, it is possible to have 5 (or n!) permutations of single combination of 5 (or $n$) things.

Although a group of $n$ things form a single combination, the groups can be picked out in such a manner so as to constitute different combinations. Suppose we have to set up a committee of 3 out of 10 scientists. The different ways in which such a committee can be formed, is a problem not of permutations but combinations because here we want to know in how many ways we can pick out a number of scientists (or things) from a group of 10, without any attention to the order in which things are arranged.

Therefore, by combination, we mean any one possible arrangements of $r$ things, out of $n$ different things or elements with no attention given to the order or arrangement.

The number of ways of picking out r things, *i.e.* the number of combinations of $n$ objects when $r$ objects are taken at a time, is denoted by ${}^nC_r$ and is given by

$${}^nC_r = \frac{n(n-1)(n-2)(n-3)......(n-r+1)}{r(r-1)(r-2)......1}$$

$$= \frac{n!}{r!(n-r)!} = \frac{{}^nP_r}{n!}$$

**Example 15.15.** *In how many different ways can a committee of three be formed out of 10 scientists?*

**Solution.** Applying formula

$$^nC_r = \frac{n!}{r!(n-r)!}$$

or $$^{10}C_3 = \frac{10!}{3!(10-3)!} = \frac{10\times 9\times 8\times 7!}{3\times 2\times 7!} = \textbf{120 Ans.}$$

**Example 15.16.** *Find out the number of combinations of 20 balls of different colours, taken 15 balls at a time.*

**Solution.** Using the relation

$$^nC_r = \frac{n!}{r!(n-r)!}$$

$$^{20}C_{15} = \frac{20!}{15!(20-15)!}$$

$$= \frac{20\times 19\times 18\times 16\times 15!}{15!\times 5\times 4\times 3\times 2\times 1}$$

$$= \textbf{912 Ans.}$$

**Example 15.17.** *Five students in a group of 20 are graduate. If 3 students are picked out of 20 in a random manner, what is the probability that they are all graduates? What is the probability that atleast one is graduate?*

**Solution.** The total number of ways in which 3 students can be picked out of 20 = $^{20}C_3$.

The number of ways in which 3 students (all graduates) are picked out of 5 graduates = $^5C_3$.

∴ Probability of selecting 3 students (all graduates) out of 20

$$\frac{^5C_3}{^{20}C_3} = \frac{\dfrac{5\times 4\times 3!}{3!\times 2\times 1}}{\dfrac{20\times 19\times 18\times 17!}{3\times 2\times 1\times 17!}} = \frac{10}{1140} = \frac{1}{114}$$

(*ii*) Now atleast one graduate, means either 1 graduate, or 2 graduates or 3 graduates to be selected.

The number of ways of selecting 1 graduate out of 5 graduates = $^5C_1$.

The number of ways of selecting 2 non-graduates out of remaining 15 = $^{15}C_2$

∴ Probability of selecting 3 students (including one graduate) out of 20

$$= \frac{^5C_1\times {}^{15}C_2}{^{20}C_3}$$

$$= \frac{\dfrac{5!}{1\times(5-1)!}\times\dfrac{15!}{2!(15-2)!}}{\dfrac{20!}{3!(20-3)!}}$$

$$= \frac{\dfrac{5\times 4!}{4}!\times\dfrac{15\times 14\times 13!}{2\times 13!}}{\dfrac{20\times 19\times 18\times 17!}{3\times 2\times 17!}} = \frac{5\times 105}{20\times 19\times 3} = \frac{35}{76}$$

The number of ways of selecting 2 graduates out of 5 graduates = ${}^5C_2$.

The number of ways of selecting one non-graduate out of the remaining 15 = ${}^{15}C_1$.

∴ Probability of selecting 3 students (including 2 graduates) out of 20

$$= \frac{{}^5C_2 \times {}^{15}C_1}{{}^{20}C_3} = \frac{\frac{5\times4}{2}\times 15}{\frac{20\times19\times18}{3\times2}} = \frac{5}{38}$$

The number of ways of selecting 3 graduates out of 5 graduates = ${}^5C_3$.

∴ Probability of selecting 3 students (all graduates) out of 20

$$= \frac{{}^5C_3}{{}^{20}C_3} = \frac{5\times4\times3}{20\times19\times18} = \frac{1}{114}.$$

∴ Probability of selecting 3 students (atleast one being graduate) out of 20

$$= \frac{35}{76} + \frac{5}{38} + \frac{1}{114} = \frac{137}{228} = \mathbf{0.60\ Ans.}$$

**Example 15.18.** Three coins are tosses simultaneously. What is the chance that they will fall with two heads and one tail.

**Solution.** Let $P$ = Changes of a coin fall head = $\frac{1}{2}$

$q$ = chance of a coin not to fall head = $1 - \frac{1}{2} = \frac{1}{2}$

Thus, the probability that out of 3 coins, 2 falls head and one tail

$${}^nC_rP^rq^{n-r} = {}^3C_2P^2q^{3-2}$$

$$= \frac{3\times2\times1}{2\times1} \times \frac{1}{2} \times \frac{1}{2} \times \frac{1}{2}$$

$$= \frac{3}{8} = \mathbf{0.375\ Ans.}$$

**Example 15.19.** *A factory manufacturing electric bulbs has a average output of 1 million bulbs every year. Over a period of one year, the inspection department has rejected 5000 bulbs.*

(*a*) *What is the probability that any of the bulbs being checked by the inspection department will be rejected?*

(*b*) *If the inspection department detects only 95 percent of all sub-standard bulbs, what is the probability that any bulb bought by a customer will be defective?*

**Solution.** (*a*) Probability that bulb being defective is

$$p^1 = \frac{5000}{1000000} = 0.005.$$

This means that 5 bulbs in every 1000 bulbs are defective.

(*b*) As, 5000 bulbs rejected by inspection department constitute 95 percent of all sub-standard bulbs, the total number of sub-standard bulbs is :

$$\frac{5000}{0.95} = 5263 \text{ (approximately)}.$$

Thus the number of defective bulbs which escaped the notice of inspection department and are likely to reach the customer is 263.

Hence, the probability that a customer will get a defective bulb is

$$= \frac{263}{1000000 - 5000} = \frac{263}{995000}$$

$= .0002643$ or **2.6 chances in 10,000. Ans.**

**Example 15.20.** (*a*) *Find the probability of getting the sum of 7 in a single toss of a pair of a dice.*

(*b*) *It the pair of dice is tossed twice, find the probability of scoring 7 points (a) once, (b) at least once (c) twice.*

**Solution.** (*a*) The sum of 7 can be obtained as follows :

(1, 6) (6, 1) (2, 5) (5, 2) (3, 4) (4, 3)

Thus the number of successful ways = 6.

Total number of ways in which the pair of dice can be tossed = 6 × 6 = 36 ways.

$\therefore$ Probability of getting 7 $= \frac{6}{36} = \mathbf{\frac{1}{6}}$ **Ans.**

(*b*) Probability of not getting 7 $= \frac{5}{6}$

Therefore, probability of getting 7 in the first toss and not getting 7 in the second toss

$$= \frac{1}{6} \times \frac{5}{6} = \frac{5}{36}.$$

Similarly, the probability of not getting 7 in first toss and getting 7 in second toss

$$= \frac{1}{6} \times \frac{5}{6} = \frac{5}{36}.$$

Hence the required probability of scoring 7 points once with twice tossing

$$= \frac{5}{36} + \frac{5}{36} = \mathbf{\frac{5}{18}} \textbf{ Ans.}$$

(*b*) The probability of not getting 7 in either toss

$$= \frac{5}{6} \times \frac{5}{6} = \frac{25}{36}.$$

Therefore probability of getting 7 atleast once

$$= 1 - \frac{25}{36} = \mathbf{\frac{11}{36}} \textbf{ Ans.}$$

(*c*) Probability of getting 7 twice $= \frac{1}{6} \times \frac{1}{6} = \mathbf{\frac{1}{36}}$ **Ans.**

**Example 15.21.** *A salesman has a 60 percent chance of making a sale to each customer. The behaviour of successive customers is independent. If two customers A and B enter, what is the probability that he will make sale to A or B?*

**Solution.** As we know that when events are not mutually exclusive,

$$P(A \text{ or } B) = P(A) + P(B) - P(A \text{ and } B).$$

Here, $P(A) = 0.6$

$P(B) = 0.6$

and $P(A \text{ and } B) = 0.6 \times 0.6 = 0.36$

$\therefore$ $P(A \text{ or } B) = 0.60 + 0.60 - 0.36 =$ **0.84 or 84% Ans.**

**Example 15.22.** *A problem of statistics is given to three students, who can solve it with a probability of* $\frac{3}{5}$, $\frac{4}{5}$, *and* $\frac{1}{3}$. *Find the probability that problem shall he solved.*

**Solution.** If *A*, *B* and *C* represent the problem cannot be solved by the three students respectively, we have,

$$P(A) = 1 - \frac{3}{5} = \frac{2}{5}$$

$$P(B) = 1 - \frac{4}{5} = \frac{1}{5}$$

$$P(C) = 1 - \frac{1}{3} = \frac{2}{3}$$

$\therefore$ $P(\text{the problem is not solved}) = \frac{2}{5} \times \frac{1}{5} \times \frac{2}{3} = \frac{4}{75}$.

$\therefore$ Probability that problem is solved $= 1 - \frac{4}{75} = \mathbf{\frac{71}{75}}$ **Ans.**

## QUESTIONS

1. Define the probability of occurrence of an event *E*. State and prove the addition theorem of probability.
2. Define probability and explain the Multiplication law of probability.
3. What are the concepts of independent and mutually exclusive events in probability. State the theorems of total and compound probability.
4. Explain the term "Mutually exclusive" and "Independent events". Give two examples of each.
5. A coin is tossed four times. What is the chance of getting all heads?
6. A chain is made of 15 links. The tensile strength of each link is equally likely to have any value between 70 and 80 kg. What is the probability that the chain will break under a load of 75 kg.
7. In a group of equal number of men and women, 10% men and 45% women are unemployed, what is the probability that a person selected at random is employed?
8. A pot contains 4 white and 6 red balls. Two drawings of 3 balls are made. Find the probability that the first drawings will give all the three white balls and the second all the three red balls if the balls are replaced before the trial.
9. (*i*) A has four shares in a lottery in which there are 4 prizes and 5 blanks. *B* has three shares in a lottery in which there are 3 prizes and 4 blanks. Who has the better chance to win exactly one prize?

   (*ii*) Who has the better chance of winning two prizes?

10. Find the probability that out of 6 coins tossed, exactly 2 will be "heads".

11. Determine the probabilities that of the following events in drawing a card from a standard deck of 52 cards :

(*a*) A seven.

(*b*) A black card.

(*c*) An ace or a king.

(*d*) A black two or a black three

(*e*) A red face card (king, queen, or jack).

What type of probability estimates are these? $\left(\textbf{Ans. } \frac{1}{13}, \frac{1}{2}, \frac{2}{13}, \frac{1}{13}, \frac{3}{26}, \text{Classical}\right)$

12. What is the probability that in selecting two cards one at a time from a deck with replacement, the second card is

(*a*) A face card, given that the first card was red?

(*b*) An ace, given that the first card was a face card? $\left(\textbf{Ans. } \frac{3}{13}, \frac{1}{13}\right)$

13. Given that $P(A) = 3/14$, $P(B) = 1/6$, $P(C) = 1/3$, $P(A \text{ and } C) = 1/7$, and $P(B/C) = 5/21$, find the following probabilities :

(*a*) $P(A/C)$,

(*b*) $P(C/A)$,

(*c*) $P(B \text{ and } C)$, and

(*d*) $P(C/B)$ **(Ans.** 3/7, 2/3, 5/63, 10/21)

14. Determine the probability that

(*a*) Both engines on a small airplane fail, given that each engine fails with probability 0.05 and that an engine is twice as likely to fail when it is the only engine working.

(*b*) An automobile is recalled for brake failures and has steering problems, given that 15 percent of that model were recalled for brake failure and 2 percent had steering problems.

**(Ans.** (*a*) 0.005, (*b*) 0.003.)

# 16

# Correlation and Regression Analysis

## 16.1. CORRELATION-ANALYSIS

The correlation analysis is used to measure the degree of relationship between two or more sets of variables under consideration. Correlation analysis shows whether or not and the extent to which two variables appear to be associated with each other either directly or inversely as corresponding values of each other are selected for analysis or correlation gives a picture of the movement of the two variables.

If there exists some casual relationship between two sets of variables they are said to be correlated to each other. For example, price of cotton and the demand for it are correlated. But if the production of cotton in India increases and the population in Canada also increases, we cannot say that phenomena are related to each other in a strict technical sense in which the term correlation is used. Correlation analysis attempts to determine the degree of relationship between variables.

Suppose we paint small metal parts by immersing them in the paint and then spinning them in a centrifuge to remove excess paint. Surface paint defects occur. Is there a relation between the occurrence of these defects and paint viscosity, time in the centrifuge or lead content in the paint etc.? The answer to such problems can be predicted with the aid of correlation analysis.

Similarly correlation analysis may be used as a means of testing quality of products, thus possibly avoiding the necessity of tests which would result in destruction of items to be tested. Numerous applications may be made in the field of finance where the relationships among stock, prices, dividends, earning money rates and other items are of much interest.This may also be applied in market analysis to estimate the sale potential in new areas.

**Usefulness**

1. Correlation is useful to economists to study the relationship between variables, like prices and quantity demanded. It helps to estimate costs, sales, price and other related variables.
2. It helps in measuring the degree of relationship between the variables, like supply and demand, price and supply, income and expenditure etc.
3. The correlation is helpful in reducing the range of uncertainty of predictions.
4. It helps in calculating sampling error.

## 16.2. TYPES OF CORRELATION

Important types of correlation are :

1. Positive and Negative.
2. Simple and Multiple.
3. Partial and Total.
4. Linear and Non-linear.

1. **Positive and Negative Correlation :** If two variables tend to move together in the same direction *i.e.* an increase in one variable is accompanied by increase in other variable, or a decrease of one variable is accompanied by decrease in other variable, the correlation is called positive or direct correlation. Height and weight, rainfall and yield of crops, price and demand are the some examples of the positive correlation.

   If and increase or decrease in the values of one variable is accompanied by a decrease or increase in the value of other variable respectively, the correlation is called negative or inverse correlation. Price and supply, yield of crops and price etc. are examples or negative correlation.

2. **Simple and Multiple Correlation :** In simple correlation, only two variables are studied and their relationship is determined, for example, quantity of money and price level, demand and price etc.

   In multiple correlation we study more than two variables simultaneously, for example, the relationship of price, demand and supply of a commodity.

3. **Partial and Total Correlation :** The study of two variables excluding some other variables is called partial correlation. For example, study the price and demand neglecting the supply aspects.

4. **Linear and non-linear-Correlation :** In linear correlation, the ratio of change between two variables is uniform. It these variables are plotted on a graph,we get a straight line. These may be direct linear or inverse linear.

In a curvilinear or non-linear correlation the ratio of change between the variables is not constant. The graph obtained in such cases form a curve.

Different types of correlation are shown in Fig. 16.1

## 16.3. METHODS OF MEASURING CORRELATION

The following three methods are used to measure the correlation :

1. Graphic Correlation
2. The Scatter Diagram
3. Co-efficient of Correlation.

1. **Graphic Correlation :** The two sets of variables are plotted on a graph paper and the movement of the two curves may be observed to see if there is any relationship between the two. If the curves tend to move in the same direction, the correlation is positive or negative.

2. **The Scatter Diagram :** This method consists in plotting the two series on a graph and fitting a 'line of best fit' free hand. The line is as close to the points as possible. Its direction shows the extent of correlation. If the line goes upward from left to right it means correlation is positive. Similarly, if the line goes downward from left to right it means correlation is negative. If the points on the plot are scattered largely, it shows little or no correlation. The following figures show some types of correlations.

   These above mentioned two methods show only the relationship and do not give a measure of correlation. The measure of correlation can be co-efficient of correlation.

3. **Co-efficient of Correlation :** Karl Pearson's co-efficient of correlation is commonly used to measure the extent of relationship between two variables by finding out the co-efficient of correlation. According to him, if correlation is perfect Karl Pearson's co-efficient is 1, if there is no correlation at all, the coefficient of correlation will be zero. Limited correlation occurs between 0 and 1. This may be negative or positive according to the nature of correlation.

This co-efficient is represented by symbol '$r$' and is calculated by the following way :

If $x$ and $y$ are two variables, taking $n$ values $x_1, x_2, x_3, ......... x_n$ and $y_1, y_2, y_3, ......... y_n$

Then
$$r = \frac{[n\sum xy - (\sum x)(\sum y)]}{\sqrt{[n\sum x^2] - [(\sum x)^2][n\sum y^2 - (\sum y)^2]}}$$

Here $\Sigma$ = usual sign of summation

Multiple correlation represents the relationship among more than two variables.

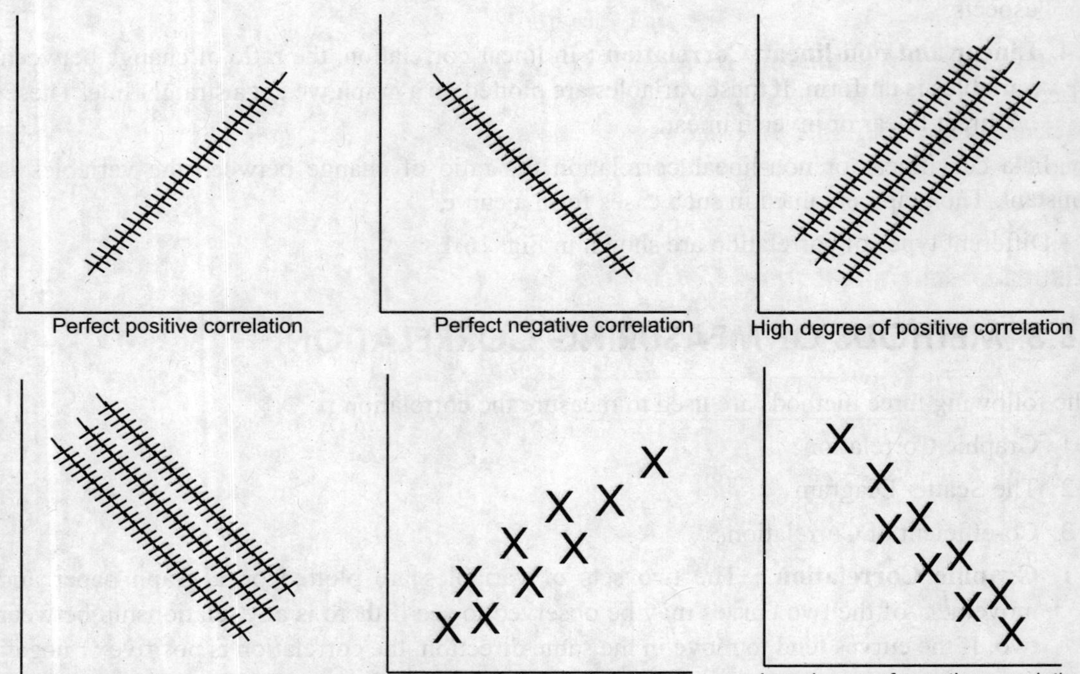

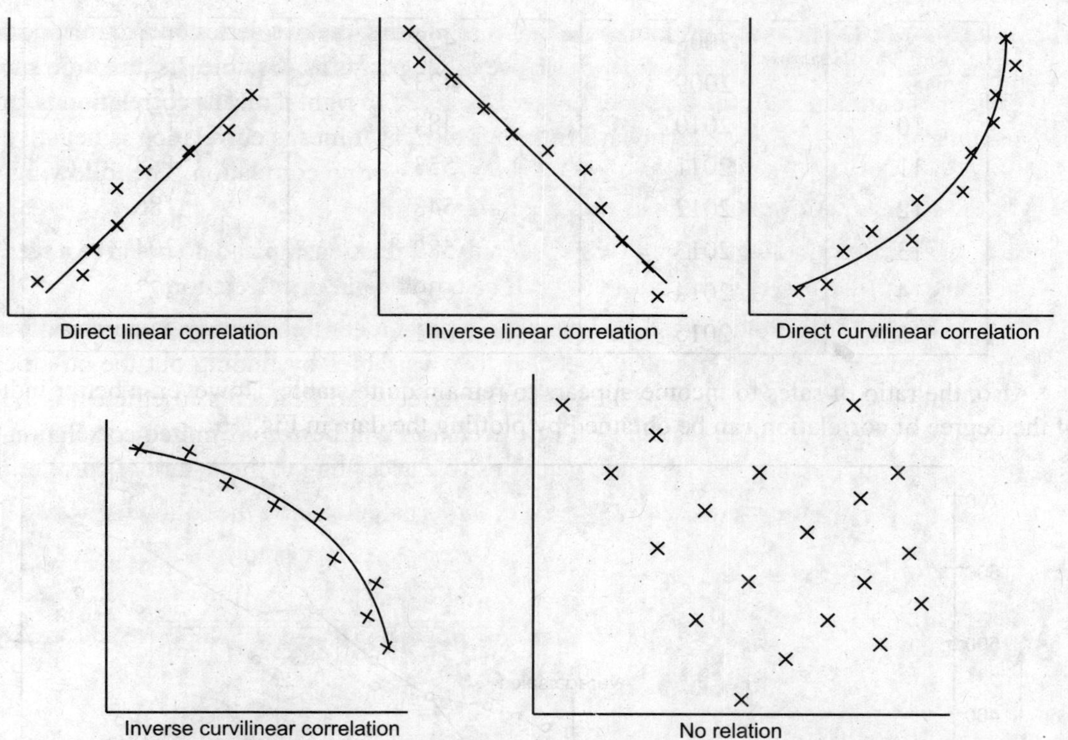


**Fig. 16.1.** Different types of correlation.

**Example for estimating the degree of correlationship.** A rough estimation of the degree of correlation may be obtained by visual inspection of two sets of data arranged in tabular form. A casual glance at Table 16.1 shows somewhat parallel increase in average sales and personal income. On scrutiny, it is observed that the only decrease in each set occurred in 2012, a year of mild recession.

## Visual Determination of Correlation

**Table 16.1. Sales and Personal Income (in lacs of Rs.) 2001-2015**

| *S. No.* | *Year* | *Average Sales (units)* | *Personal Income* |
|---|---|---|---|
| 1. | 2001 | 168 | 66 |
| 2. | 2002 | 182 | 70 |
| 3. | 2003 | 192 | 76 |
| 4. | 2004 | 235 | 92 |
| 5. | 2005 | 304 | 117 |
| 6. | 2006 | 304 | 132 |
| 7. | 2007 | 333 | 147 |

| | | | |
|---|---|---|---|
| 8. | 2008 | 423 | 151 |
| 9. | 2009 | 423 | 159 |
| 10. | 2010 | 484 | 170 |
| 11. | 2011 | 553 | 188 |
| 12. | 2012 | 548 | 186 |
| 13. | 2013 | 589 | 204 |
| 14. | 2014 | 639 | 223 |
| 15. | 2015 | 661 | 234 |

Also, the ratio of sales to income appears to remain quite stable. However, a better indication of the degree of correlation can be obtained by plotting the data in Fig. 16.2

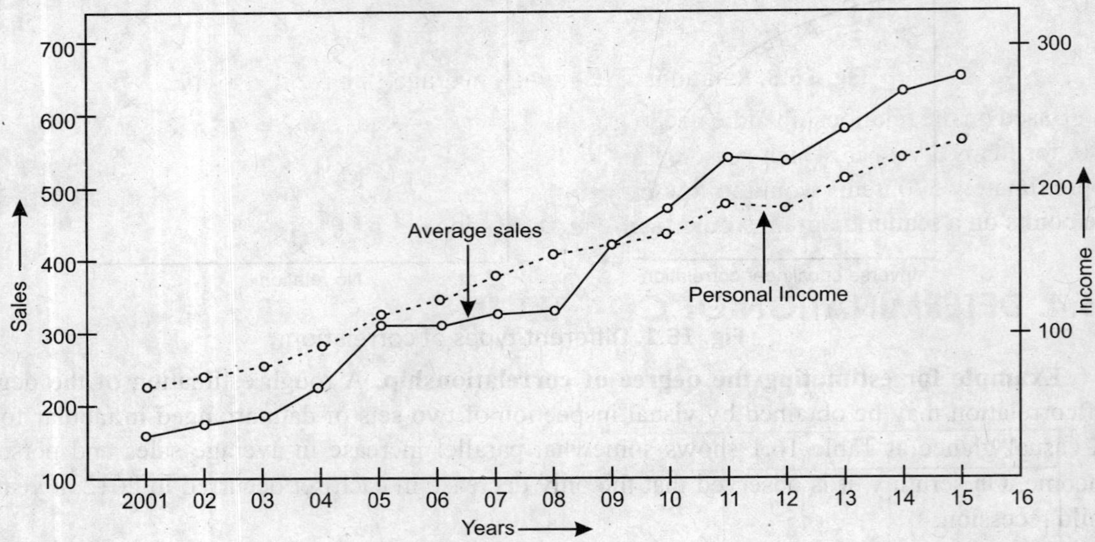


**Fig. 16.2.** Graph showing the Relation between Average Sales and Personal Income.

**Line Chart :** Tendency towards parallel movement of sales and income is more clearly shown in Fig. 16.2. Sales have been plotted against the scale on the left and incomes have been plotted on the scale at the right. These charts are valuable aid in sales forecasting. Forecasts of income by government and private companies can be used as a basis for forecasting company sales.

**Scatter Diagram :** This is the most valuable graphic device for indicating correlation. Here sale and income are plotted as a single point for each year from 2001 through 2015 in Fig. 16.3. A total of 15 points appears in Fig. 16.3. Sales are measured by the vertical axis on the left and income by the horizontal axis. The lowest points at the left represents sales of 168 items and income of 66, which occurred in 2001. The straight line relationship between sales and income is at once apparent.

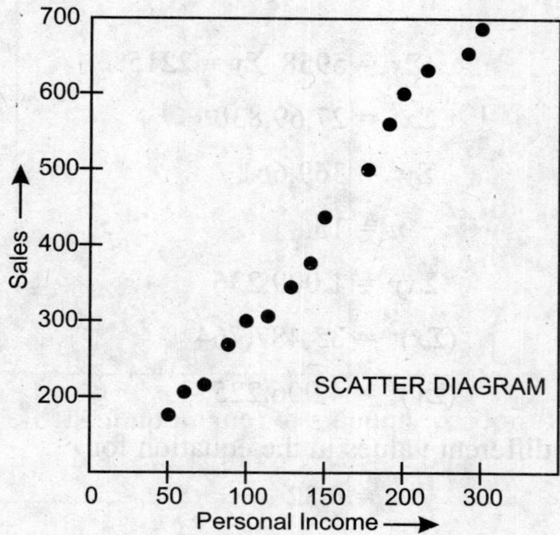


**Fig. 16.3.** Relationship between Average Sales and Income.

Based on the relationship indicated in Fig. 16.3 company would forecast average sales of about 700, for items a year in which personal income of 250 units has been forecast; a sales forecast of approximately 570 items would follow from a personal income of 200 units. A line drawn through the points on a scatter diagram would facilitate forecasting.

# 16.4. DETERMINATION OF CO-EFFICIENT OF CORRELATION

$$r = \frac{[n\sum xy - (\sum x)(\sum y)]}{\sqrt{[n\sum x^2 - (\sum x^2)][n\sum y^2 - (\sum y^2)]}}$$

| *S.No.* | *x* | *y* | *xy* | *$x^2$ (in tens)* | *$y^2$* |
|---|---|---|---|---|---|
| 1. | 168 | 66 | 11,088 | 2,812 | 4,356 |
| 2. | 182 | 70 | 12,740 | 3,301 | 4,900 |
| 3. | 192 | 76 | 14,592 | 3,680 | 5,878 |
| 4. | 235 | 92 | 21,620 | 5,520 | 8,467 |
| 5. | 304 | 117 | 35,568 | 9,240 | 13,700 |
| 6. | 304 | 132 | 40,951 | 9,240 | 17,560 |
| 7. | 333 | 147 | 48,951 | 11,100 | 21,600 |
| 8. | 343 | 151 | 51,793 | 11,800 | 22,560 |
| 9. | 423 | 159 | 67,257 | 17,800 | 25,230 |
| 10. | 484 | 170 | 82,280 | 22,500 | 28,900 |
| 11. | 553 | 188 | 103,964 | 30,600 | 35,450 |
| 12. | 548 | 186 | 101,928 | 30,100 | 34,600 |
| 13. | 589 | 204 | 120,156 | 34,700 | 41,600 |
| 14. | 639 | 223 | 142,497 | 40,800 | 49,780 |
| 15. | 661 | 234 | 154,674 | 43,700 | 54,780 |

From the table

$$\Sigma x = 5958, \Sigma y = 2215$$

$$\Sigma x^2 = 27{,}69{,}830$$

$$\Sigma y^2 = 369{,}661$$

$$n = 15.$$

$$\Sigma xy = 1{,}009{,}236$$

$$(\Sigma x)^2 = 35{,}487{,}764$$

$$(\Sigma y)^2 = 4{,}906{,}225$$

Hence substituting the different values in the equation for $r$.

$$r = 0.32$$

It means the relationship between two variable is 0.32.

## 16.5. REGRESSION-ANALYSIS

With the help of regression, we can estimate the value of one variable from the given value of other variable Regression can be defined as the measure of the average relationship between two or more variables in terms of the original units of the data. According to Ya-Lun Chow, with the help of the regression analysis, we can estimate or predict the unknown values of one variable from the known values of another variable. In the regression analysis, the independent variable is also known as the "regressor" or "predictor" and the dependent variable is known as "regressed" or explained" variable.

Regression analysis is used in local sciences like economics, natural and physical sciences. It is also helpful in business predictions.

## 16.6. METHODS OF REGRESSION-ANALYSIS

1. **Graphic Method :** The points representing pairs of values of concerned variables are plotted on a graph paper, taking the independent variables on horizontal axis, and dependent variables on vertical axis. These points give a scatter diagram, a regression line is the drawn between the points. Such line can be a straight line or a curved line depending upon scatter of points.
2. **Algebraic Method :** It is an algebraic expression of the regression line. Regression equations are algebraic expressions of the regression lines. As there are two regression lines, there are two regression equations :
   (*i*) $X$ on $Y$ is used to describe the variations in the values of $X$ for given changes in $Y$. The regression of $X$ on $Y$ is expressed as

$$X = a + by$$

(*ii*) *Y* on *X* is used to describe the variations in the values of *Y* for given changes in *X*. The regression equation of *Y* on *X* is expressed as

$$Y = a + bx$$

In these equations *a* and *b* are constants which determine the position of line.

When there is perfectly positive correlation (+1) or perfectly negative correlation (–1), the two regression lines will coincide with each other, *i.e.* in that case, there will be only one line.

### Regression line

The dots on the scatter diagram follow a path, this path may be described by a line. Since the dots by themselves do not form a line, this line describes only the average path of the dots. In our example, it wold not describe the relationship of sales to income but rather the average relationship between the two variables for the whole series. Thus, it is a line describing the relationship between the two variables on the average may be called 'the line of average relationship'.

## 16.7. CONCEPT OF REGRESSION ANALYSIS

The concept of the line of average relationship was first used by Sir Francis Galton. He found that if a number of pairs of tall fathers and their sons are observed it will be found that the average height of fathers will not be equal to the average height of sons and the latter average will tend towards the average will tend to regress towards the general average. If the co-efficient of correlation between the heights of fathers and sons is, say 0.6 it means that if a group of fathers had an average height of *x* cm. above the general average the average height of their sons would be only 0.6 *x* cm. above the general average. This trend towards the average is called 'Regression.

The major practical use of the regression line is as 'Estimating line'. The estimating line is fitted by means of an 'estimating equation, $y_e = a + bx$. The equation is also known as 'Regression equation'. For any given value of x, the dependent variable can be determined, by use of estimating equation.

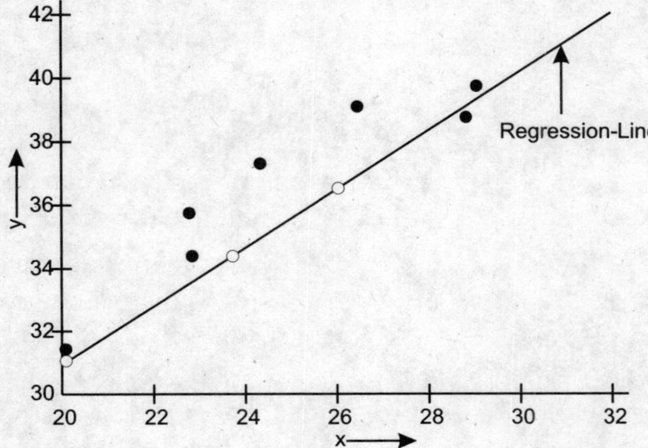


**Fig. 16.4.** Chart showing relationship between two variables. Original plot without characteristics line is called a Scatter Diagram.

A scatter diagram shown in Fig. 16.4, is drawn to represent the relationship between the two different variables. For plotting this chart 10 pairs of readings are taken for 10 different samples in which $x$ and $y$ are related quality characteristics.

Information desired is whether there is any shift in the value of $y$ as the value of $x$ increases. Since $y$ test is destructive and it would be desirable to substitute the non-destructive $x$ test, if it will show the same shift of result.

## QUESTIONS

1. Explain what is meant by the term 'correlation'. Distinguish between positive and negative correlation. What are the properties of the co-efficient of correlation?
2. Explain the meaning of all symbols in the Regression Equation.
3. What is scatter diagram? How does it help us in studying the correlation between two variables in respect of both their nature and extent?
4. Define Karl Pearson's co-efficient of correlation. What is it intended to measure?
5. Distinguish between :
   (*a*) Positive and Negative correlation.
   (*b*) Linear and Non-linear correlation.
   (*c*) Simple, partial and multiple correlation.
6. Explain the concepts of correlation and regression, bringing out the inter-relationship between them.
7. Explain, why there are usually two lines of regression. Point out the case when there is one line of regression.
8. What is regression? How is this concept useful to business forecasting?

# 17 Process Capabilities

## 17.1. INTRODUCTION

Every production engineer knows that repetitive production cycles result in products that are not identical in their characteristics. The reason for this is simply that the production cycles are not really identical in every respect. The causes for variations in the production process may be :

(*i*) The raw materials vary slightly in their properties from batch-to-batch and these variations may affect the properties of the final product.

(*ii*) Operators are different from each other in their skill, performance, aptitude and interest in work.

(*iii*) The parameter of the operations may change from cycle-to-cycle as may be the speeds, the motions of the operators and the characteristics of the tools and machines.

(*iv*) The external conditions, such as temperature, pressure, light and humidity may vary.

## DEFINITION OF PROCESS CAPABILITY

*Process capability* provides a quantified prediction of process adequacy. This ability to predict quantitatively has resulted in widespread adoption of the process capability concept as a major element of quality planning.

*Process capability* can be defined as the measured, inherent variation of the product turned out by a process. Each of the keywords of this definition are clearly defined hereunder :

*Process* refers to some unique combination of machine, tools, methods, materials and people engaged in production. It is generally possible to separate out and quantify the effect of variables entering this combination. Here, the word *Capability* is used in the sense of an ability, based on tested performance, to achieve measurable results. *Measured capability* refers to the fact that process capability is quantified from data which in turn are the results of measurement of work performed by the process. *Inherent Capability* refers to the product uniformity resulting from a process which is in a state of statistical control.

Process capability can also be defined as the measure of the variation under stable or controlled process conditions and is equal to 6σ. The word "process" here includes materials, machines, tools, method and men. Actual variation is more than that expected due to inferior batch of material, change in machine setting, tool wear, change of operator etc. This change in variation is controlled and brought as close to process capability as possible. This process capability for a process is estimated after collecting sufficient number of observations under stable conditions.

Process capability is a measure of the variation of a process and its ability to produce components consistently within specifications. The process capability can be defined only when process is in statistical control. The process is in statistical control when only chance variations (or common causes) are available, and special causes (*i.e.* assignable causes) are eliminated. Special causes can be corrected during the process itself, for example, by changing the worn tool or changing the machine setting or a change in raw materials or the mistakes committed by in experienced operator.

Common cause is a source of inherent variation always present in the process itself. These causes can be corrected only by management, for example, poor lighting, bad layout, old and obsolete machines.

The process when is in statistical control, is predictable with benefits in consistency of quality, productivity and cost. For bringing the process in statistical control, first step should be to detect and eliminate special causes of variation. For detecting special causes, help of control charts is taken which will be discussed in detail in following chapters. Once process performance is predictable, its capability to meet customer requirements can be determined.

Variations (non-uniformity) in all operating systems necessitate quality analysis and quality control. This is necessary because of the following facts:

(*a*) Variation is inevitable in every operating system and no two units of output are alike.

(*b*) The production and use of products and services are most economical, when those products and services are of uniform quality.

The variation cannot be eliminated but by controlling it, we can increase the number of products from the operating system that conform to user requirements.

## USES (PURPOSES) OF PROCESS CAPABILITY INFORMATION

Process capability information serves following purposes :

1. Help designers by providing important information about extent of variability in setting realistic specification limits.
2. Help in selecting most appropriate tolerances which is to be met.
3. In establishing a schedule of periodic process control checks and re-adjustments.
4. The causes of defects detected during the process capability help in designing quality improvement programme.
5. Helps in specifying the quality performance requirements for purchased machines.
6. Assigning machines to classes of work for which they are best suited.

**Advantages**

1. The process capability or machine operating accuracy studies have been used to assure proper maintenance of machines.
2. These are used to provide a basis for equipment replacement programmes.
3. Produce quality product.
4. Reduce rejects by timely detection of problems, as it keeps an eye on the trend of tolerances.

## 17.2. VARIATION IN A PROCESS

While specifying the specifications, an ideal quantity of physical dimensions, such as strength, density, composition etc. are indicated but it is also pointed out that deviation from this ideal figure will be allowed, provided they remain within predetermined limits. One of the functions of quality control is to decide whether these tolerances are compatible with the inherent variabilities of the process or not. In short, there are following two types of causes which are the source of variations in a process :

1. Chance cause variation.
2. Assignable cause variation.

**1. Chance Cause Variation**

This is also known as usual variations. There is always a constant cause system which is operating in a production cycle. As long as constant cause system continues to operate, some percentage of the varying results continue to fall between any given pair of limits. This distribution of results is suitable and constant. The deviation is expected in the system.

**2. Assignable Cause Variation**

This is also known as unusual variation. It is the amount of deviation greater than the specified specification limits. This deviation may be due to the difference in operators, difference in materials or difference in working conditions etc. It has already been explained above that variation is inevitable in any production cycle and there are definite reasons for it. It is found that some of the reasons can be investigated easily and economically, while others require thorough investigation and hence, are uneconomical. Uneconomical causes are designated as chance variation while economical causes as assignable cause variation. Hence, the aim is to put demarcation lines between economical and uneconomical causes. These demarcation lines are known as control lines.

## TYPES OF VARIATIONS

**1. With-in-piece Variation**

These are the variations within the part itself. For example, surface is rough on one portion than another or dimension of one end varies from other end.

**2. Piece-to-piece Variation**

These are the variations among parts produced during the same period of time. This type of variation occurs among pieces produced at the sametime. For example, light intensity of light bulbs produced in the same lot from a machine is different.

**3. Time-to-time Variation**

These are the variations among parts produced at different period of time. This type of variation is illustrated by the difference in products produced at different time of the day. This may be due to the cutting tool wear which changes the cutting characteristics.

Factors contributing to any or all of the above mentioned variations are many, but common are tool wear, loosen bearings, machine vibrations, faulty jigs and fixtures, careless or untrained operators, poor raw-materials, changes in weather etc. These factors result in variations *i.e.* deviation from standard shape, size, colour, strength etc.

Statisticians and engineers have developed methods of describing pattern of variation. These methods may be frequency distribution, measure of central tendency of distribution, dispersion or spread of the distribution etc. These tools (or methods) have already been discussed in previous chapters. Control charts to test for stability of the pattern of variation shall be discussed later on in a separate chapter.

## FACTORS CONTRIBUTING VARIATIONS

The factors contributing to the variations can be classified into following categories:

1. Processes
2. Materials
3. Operators
4. Miscellaneous.

**1. Process**

Variations in this source include tool wear, machine variation, workholding device positioning and electrical fluctuations. When all these variations are put together, there is a certain capability or accuracy within which the process operates. Even supposedly identical machines will have different capabilities.

**2. Materials**

Variations in raw material (which is someone else's finished product) also results variation in the finished product. Such variations are due to quality characteristics, like tensile strength, ductility, porosity, thickness, moisture contents.

**3. Operators**

This is the greatest source of variation. This source of variation includes the method by which the operator performs the operation. It also depends on whether the instruction sheet is being followed exactly the same each cycle. The operator's physical and emotional well-being also contribute to the variation. His personal problem, changed posture or a headache can make an operator's quality performance quite erratic. An operator's lack of understanding of process may also lead to frequent machine adjustment.

4. **Miscellaneous**

   This includes environmental factors, such as heat, light, humidity. Inspection process also causes variations. Faulty inspection equipment or the incorrect application of a quality standard, or too heavy a process on a micrometer can be the cause of the incorrect reporting of variation.

Till these above mentioned four sources of variation fluctuate in a normal or expected manner, a stable pattern of many chance causes of variation develops. These chance causes of variation are inevitable and since they are very small in magnitude, they are difficult to identify. Control charts are used to judge whether or not a constant system of chance causes is present.

## 17.3. ANALYSIS OF PROCESS CAPABILITY

Analysis of process capability consists of following:

1. Elements specifying the tolerances.
2. Determination of whether the process average is centered midway between the tolerance limits.
3. Measurement of the inherent (piece-to-piece) variability of the process.
4. Measurement of the actual variability over a period of time.
5. Causes of the difference between inherent and actual variability. Effective way of making the analysis is by means of control charts and frequency distribution. These will be discussed in the subsequent chapters.

## 17.4. PROCESS CAPABILITY FORMULA

Most common formula for process capability is :

**Process capability** = $\pm 3\sigma$ (a total of 6 $\sigma$), where a (Sigma) is known as the standard deviation of the process under a state of statistical control, which means no drift and no sudden changes. Therefore, if the process is centred at the nominal specification and follows a normal probability distribution, 99.73 percent of production will fall within $\pm 3\sigma$ of the nominal specification.

- If the process is *stable*, the capability will be equal to spread $6\sigma$.
- If the process is *unstable*, the spread will be greater than the capability.

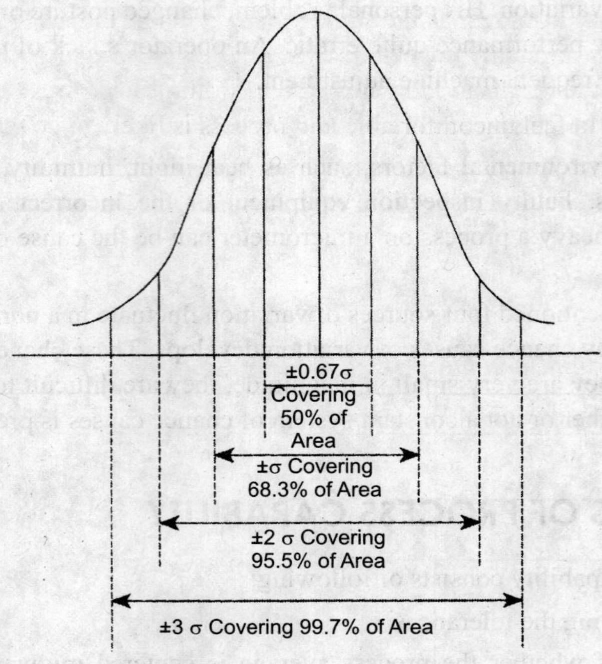


**Fig. 17.1.** The normal curve.

## 17.5. NORMAL CURVE

**It is a frequency curve obtained with the help of a very large number of observations. It observes the normal law and is also called a Probability Curve, Gaussian Curve or Laplacian Curve. Its shape is like a bell symmetrical about F-axis and extends from minus infinity to plus infinity.**

**Table 17.1.**

| ***Points*** | ***% of total area*** |
|---|---|
| $\overline{X} \pm 0.6745\ \sigma$ | 50 |
| $\overline{X} \pm \sigma$ | 68.27 |
| $\overline{X} \pm 2\sigma$ | 95.45 |
| $\overline{X} \pm 3\sigma$ | 99.73 |

**Most of the area under the curve is included within the limits $X \pm 3\ \sigma$. An idea about the distribution of area under the normal curve corresponding to different limits can be obtained from the table 17.1.**

The term σ (Sigma) is known as the standard deviation of the distribution. This, in fact is the basis for control charts in quality control in which ± 3σ limits are usually adopted, which means, we expect 99.73 % of the results to fall within the ± 3σ limits and if results begin to appear beyond these limits, we begin to feel uncomfortable and process is likely to go out of control.

**Example 17.1.** *An industry produces springs of certain quality and the results of inspection of one of its critical dimension (length) is given in the table below. What interpretations can be derived regarding :*

1. *Its central tendency?*
2. *Dispersion?*
3. *Amount of rejects and suitability of the process ?*

| ***Dimension*** | ***Tally*** | ***Frequency*** |
|---|---|---|
| 0.97 | \|\| | 2 |
| 0.98 | 𝍸 𝍸 \|\| | 12 |
| 0.99 | 𝍸 𝍸 \|\|\|\| | 14 |
| 1.00 | 𝍸 𝍸 𝍸 𝍸 | 20 |
| 1.01 | 𝍸 𝍸 𝍸 𝍸 \|\|\|\| | 24 |
| 1.02 | 𝍸 𝍸 𝍸 \|\|\| | 18 |
| 1.03 | 𝍸 𝍸 | 10 |

**Solution.**

(*a*) From the given data histogram and frequency distribution diagrams are drawn as shown in Figs. 17.2 and 17.3.

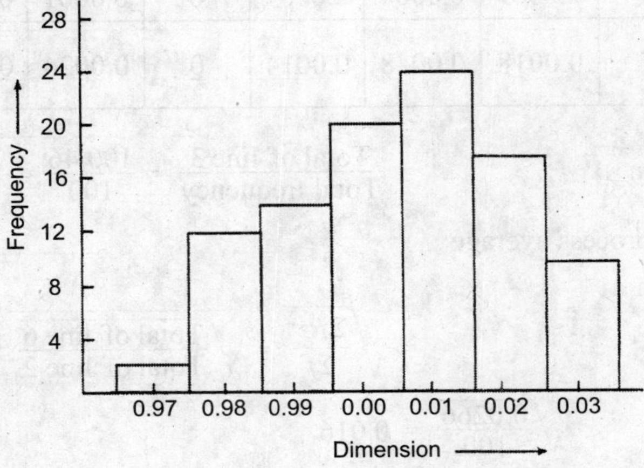


**Fig. 17.2.** Histogram.

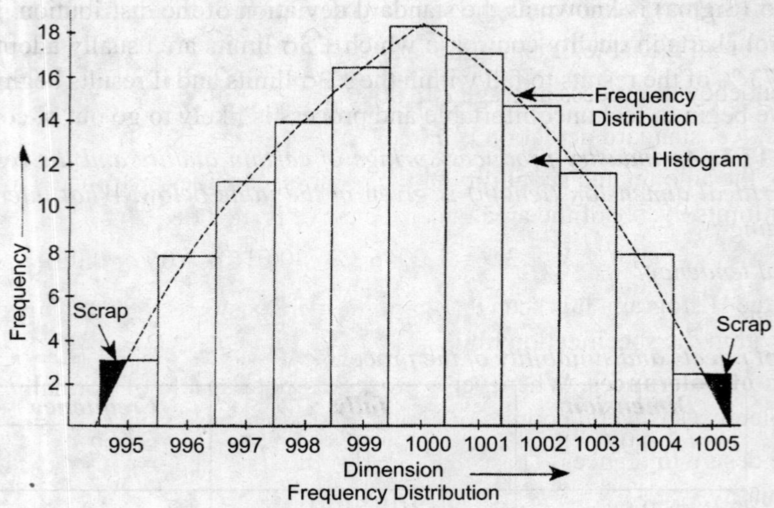


**Fig. 17.3.** Frequency Pattern

(*b*) The calculations of central tendency values, *i.e.* mean and dispersion, *i.e.* standard deviation are made in the tabular form as given below :

| | | | | | | | | | ***Total*** |
|---|---|---|---|---|---|---|---|---|---|
| 1. | Dimension | 0.97 | 0.98 | 0.99 | 1.00 | 1.01 | 1.02 | 1.03 | |
| 2. | Frequency | 2 | 12 | 14 | 20 | 24 | 18 | 10 | 100 |
| 3. | Frequency X Dimension | 1.94 | 11.76 | 13.86 | 20.00 | 24.24 | 18.36 | 10.30 | 100.46 |
| 4. | Deviation from Average 1.00 | 0.03 | 0.02 | 0.01 | 0 | 0.01 | 0.02 | 0.030 | |
| 5. | $(\text{Deviation})^2$ | 0.0009 | 0.0004 | 0.0001 | 0 | 0.0001 | 0.0004 | 0.0009 | |
| 6. | Frequency X $\text{Deviation}^2$ | 0.0018 | 0.0048 | 0.0014 | 0 | 0.0024 | 0.0072 | 0.0090 | 0.0266 |

Average dimension $= \dfrac{\text{Total of line 3}}{\text{Total frequency}} = \dfrac{100.46}{100} = 1.0046$

This is known as process average

Standard deviation

$$= \sqrt{\frac{\Sigma f\sigma^2}{\Sigma f}} = \sqrt{\frac{\text{Total of line 6}}{\text{Total of line 2}}}$$

$$\sqrt{\frac{0.0266}{100}} = 0.016$$

$\therefore$ $\sigma = 0.016.$

The symbol σ(sigma) is conventional abbreviation for the term standard deviation.

**Inferences.** From the table, it is found that:

(*i*) Central tendency or process average is 1.0046.

(*ii*) Dispersion, *i.e.* standard deviation is 0.016.

(*iii*) Regarding the amount and suitability of the process, consider the process to be in ± 3σ limits, as in ± 3σ limits 99.7% of the area under the curve is included :

Therefore, $\overline{X} \pm 3\sigma = 1.0046 \pm 3 \times 0.016 = 1.05$ or $0.96$.

Now from the Histogram, it is seen that minimum dimension is 0.97 and maximum is 1.03. So, the process is within the specification limits.

**Correction of Tolerances.** Whenever a process is not capable of normally producing within the specified tolerances, several courses of action may be adopted. Such as :

(*a*) Check the design tolerances. These may be too close and can be widened without harming the product quality.

(*b*) Make engineering improvement on the process. These may possibly require new equipment.

(*c*) Screen each lot and decide defective allowable.

Frequency distribution diagram shows the bulk of production within the specification limits. Only small and insignificant percentage falls outside.

**Example 15.2.** *Frequency tally sheet for the Rockwell hardness test in shovel blades is as under. Compare the quality of the two lots.*

| *Lot 1* | | *Lot 2* | |
|---|---|---|---|
| ***Hardness No.*** | ***Frequency*** | ***Hardness No.*** | ***Frequency*** |
| 48 | 1 | | |
| 47 | 2 | | |
| 46 | 3 | 46 | 1 |
| 45 | 4 | 45 | 6 |
| 44 | 5 | 44 | 11 |
| 43 | 4 | 43 | 6 |
| 42 | 3 | 42 | 1 |
| 41 | 2 | | |
| 40 | 1 | | |

**Solution.**

$$\text{Mean of lot 1} = \frac{48 + 47 + 46 + 45 + 44 + 43 + 42 + 41 + 40}{9}$$

$$= 44.$$

$$\text{Mean of lot 2} = \frac{46 + 45 + 44 + 43 + 42}{5}$$

$$= 44.$$

Mean in both the lots is same = 44.

Next step is to draw the Histogram for both the lots as shown in Figs. 17.4 and 1.

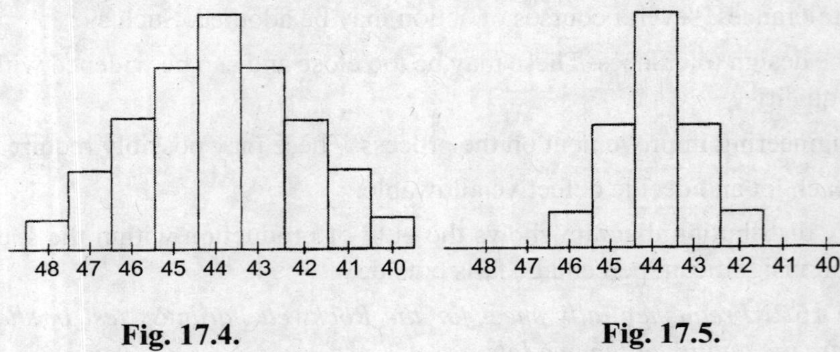


**Fig. 17.4.** **Fig. 17.5.**

Lot 1 and lot 2 have the same value for mean that is 44, but they differ in quality. Lot 2 is superior to lot 1 because it has less variability or spread.

## 17.6. FREQUENCY CURVES COMPARISON

Fig. 17.6 shows the variability in the processes.

**Curve 1.** Variability is considerably small and mean is well-centred. Hence, no problems.

**Curve 2.** Variability is again small but mean is shifted towards right. Hence, possibility of defectives.

**Curve 3.** The danger foreseen in 2, has remained unchecked, resulting in defective products.

**Curve 4.** Dangerously high variability. As a result distribution is 'crowding', both minimum and maximum limits. Investigation should be made as to whether: (*a*) Process variability can be narrowed or (*b*) Consumer's requirements permit widening of the tolerances.

**Curve 5.** The type of distribution in 3 has deteriorated into actual occurrence of defectives due to slight shift in mean towards maximum limit.

**Curve 6.** Here, the type distribution, in 4 has remained well-centred but a slight increase in variability has occurred, resulting in defectives. For remedy, see plot 4 above.

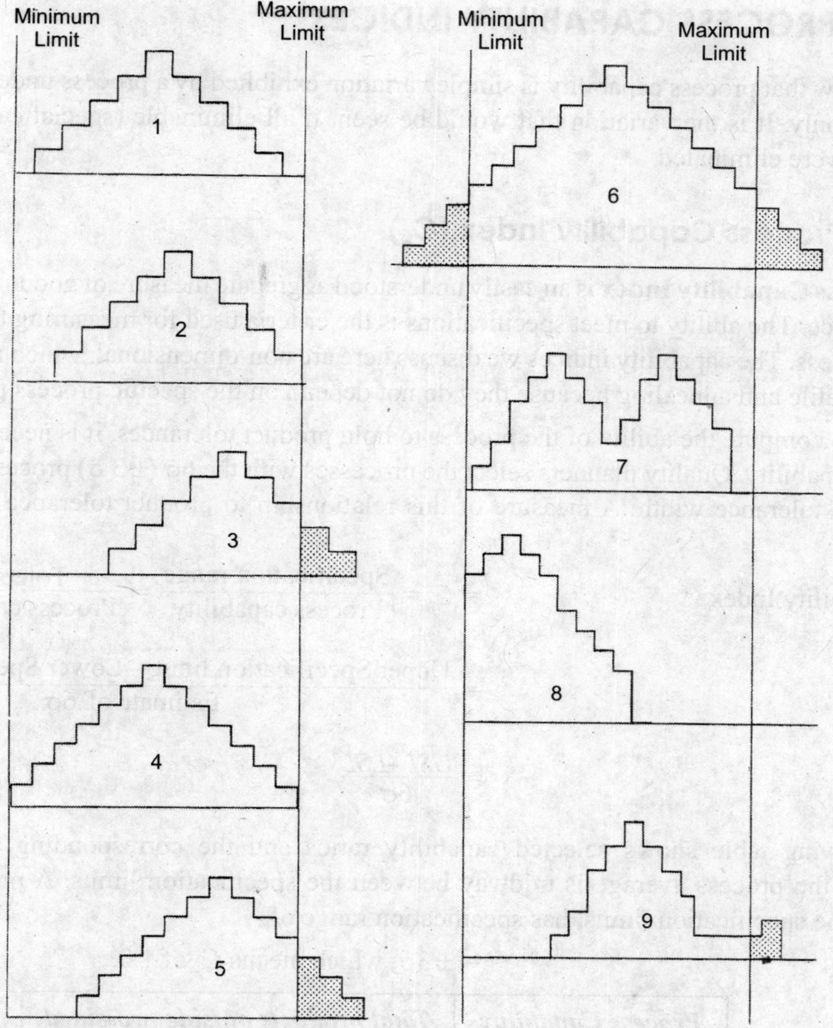


**Fig. 17.6.** Graph showing the relation between average sales and personal income.

**Curve 7.** Double distribution, probably two sets of too many changes in process or material during running of a lot are responsible.

**Curve 8.** Distribution is 'cut off' at the minimum limit. A typical sign that purchaser has screened out defective below minimum limit prior to shipment. If distribution has been properly centred, the cost of screening and losses of product could have avoided.

**Curve 9.** The small distribution outside the maximum limit may represent parts from tool and set-up tryouts not set aside. By proper training, this stage should be corrected.

## 17.7. PROCESS CAPABILITY INDICES

As we know that process capability is simple variation exhibited by a process under common cause influence only. It is the variation that would be seen, if all eliminable (special causes) sources of variation were eliminated.

### 17.7.1. Process Capability Index ($C_p$)

**Process Capability Index** is an easily understood aggregate measure of goodness of the process performance. The ability to meet specifications is the criteria used for measuring the attractiveness of the process. The capability indices we discuss here are non-dimensional, which makes them even more versatile and appealing because they do not depend on the specific process parameter units.

In order to compute the ability of the process to hold product tolerances, it is necessary to quantify process capability. Quality planners select the processes with the 6σ (± 3 σ) process capability well within the tolerance width. A measure of this relationship to product tolerance is the capability index.

$$\text{Capability Index} = C_p = \frac{\text{Specification range}}{\text{Process capability}} = \frac{\text{Tolerance}}{\text{Process capability}}$$

$$= \frac{\text{Upper Specification limit} - \text{Lower Specification limit}}{\text{Estimate of } 6\sigma}$$

$$= \frac{USL - LSL}{6\sigma}$$

Following table shows selected capability ratios and the corresponding level of defects, assuming the process average is midway between the specification limits. A process that is just meeting the specification limits, has specification range of

= ± 3σ, which means $C_p$ of 1.0.

| ***Process Capability index*** $C_p$ | ***Total products outside two-sided specification limits*** |
|---|---|
| 0.5 | 13.36% |
| 0.67 | 4.55% |
| 1.00 | 0.3% |
| 1.33 | 64 PPM |
| 1.63 | 1PPM |
| 2.00 | 0 |

Above table indicates that if specification limits are within 12σ(± 6σ) *i.e.* when $C_p$ is equal t 2, defects are almost zero.

If the capability index is greater than 1.00, the process is capable of meeting the specifications, whereas, if the index is less than 1.00, the process is not capable of meeting the specifications. Because processes are continually shifting back and forth, a $C_p$ value of 1.33. has become a de facto standard. The larger the capability index, the better the quality, therefore, we should strive to make the capability index as large as possible.

## Assumptions Made in Process Capability Study

Interpretation of $C_p$ is based on several assumptions, some of the main assumptions are :

1. The process is in a state of statistical control.
2. Sufficient data are collected during the study to minimize the sampling error.
3. The data are collected over a sufficient period of time to ensure that the process conditions present during the study are representative of current and future conditions.
4. The parameter analyzed in the study follows a normal probability distribution.

## 17.7.2. The $C_{pk}$ Capability Index

As seen above, the process capability, as measured by $C_p$, refers to the variation in a process about the average value. The $C_p$ index, therefore, measures potential capability, assuming that the process average is equal to the midpoint of the specification limits and the process is operating in statistical control. As the average is generally not at the midpoint, it is useful to have a capability index that reflects both variation and the location of the process average. Such an index is $C_{pk}$.

$C_{pk}$ reflects the current process means proximity to either the upper specification limit (USL) or Lower specification limit (LSL). $C_{pk}$ is estimated by:

$$C_{pk} = \frac{Minimum\,(USL - \overline{X})\; or\; (\overline{X} - LSL))}{3\sigma}$$

$C_{pk}$ value of 1.00 is the de facto standard, with some organisations use a value of 1.33.

Comments about $C_p$ and $C_{pk}$ are as follows:

1. $C_p$ value does not change as the process center changes.
2. $C_p = C_{pk}$ when the process is centred.
3. $C_{pk}$ is always equal to or less than $c_p$.
4. A $C_{pk}$ value greater than 1.00 indicates the process conforms to specifications.
5. A $C_{pk}$ value less than 1.00 indicates that the process does not conform to specifications.
6. A $C_{pk}$ value less than 1.00 indicates that the process is not capable.
7. A $C_{pk}$ value of zero indicates the average is equal to one of the specification limits.
8. A negative $C_{pk}$ value indicates that the average is outside the specification.

The above eight points help quality professionals in improving the process. For example, if a $_p$ value is less than one, then corrective action is required to be taken. Initially 100 inspection is necessary to eliminate non-conformance. For corrective action, there are two methods, either to increase the tolerance of the specifications or work on the process to reduce the standard deviation or variability.

### 17.7.3. Capability Ratio (CR)

The capability ratio is defined as,

$$C.R. = \frac{6\sigma}{USL - LSL} = \frac{1}{C_p}$$

$$C.R. \leq 1 \text{ is desirable}$$

## 17.8. MACHINE CAPABILITIES

As repeated runs do not always give exactly the same results, machine capabilities change with time, and the change can take place in a relatively short time period. This aspect is always kept in mind. Machine wear, tool wear, lubrication and coolant conditions, the operators and the machine ability of the material affects the machine capability, sometimes to marked degree. Therefore, the machine capability determined at one time may or may not be an indication later on of the inherent ability to hold to a tolerance.

Machine capability is the variation obtained under stable and controlled conditions, and is equal to 6 times the standard deviation (σ). Actual variation from a machine is expected to be larger than the machine capability due to instabilities and other causes that may creep into from time-to-time.

For estimating the machine capability, standard deviation is determined by collecting sufficient number of observations under stable conditions.

While selecting a machine for purchase, one should know whether the machine he is buying is adequate to hold, the design to tolerance (assuming normal operation and maintenance).

## QUESTIONS

1. (*a*) What are the reasons for variations in tolerances in the production process?
   (*b*) Explain the different types of variations in a production process.
2. (*a*) Define process capability.
   (*b*) Explain the causes which are the source of variation.
3. Explain various factors contributing to the variation.
4. What are the uses of process capability information?
5. What are the elements of analysis of process capability?
6. (*a*) Write down the process capability formula, explain it.
   (*b*) Explain the process capability ratio. Enumerate the assumptions made.

7. Explain the normal curve for frequency distribution, indicating standard deviation and percentage area covered under it.
8. Draw different types of frequency distribution curves indicating the variability in the production processes.
9. Explain the term machine capability.
10. Discuss process capability indices in detail.
11. What is $C_{pk}$ capability index? How it is calculated?
12. What is $C_p$ capability index? Discuss in detail.

    What are the assumptions made in process capability study?
13. What is the difference between $C_p$ and $C_{pk}$? Explain in detail.

18

# Reliability

## 18.1. INTRODUCTION

Customer always wants that the products which he purchases must be reliable. Reliable means that these products should meet requirements without failure for a considerable time. It is also the desire of the manufacturer that whatever he produces, it should be reliable. For this purpose, manufacturers continually re-design their products to rectify defects and discrepancies.

Today the word 'reliability' has acquired a highly specialized technical meaning in relation to the control of quality of manufactured product. BAZCY SKY states the modern concept of reliability in simple language as: "Reliability is the capability of an equipment works, well and works whenever called upon to do the job for which it was designed, such equipment is said to be reliable".

The generally accepted definition of reliability is as under :

"*Reliability* is the probability of a device performing its purpose adequately for the period (time) intended under the given operating conditions encountered".

This definition brings following 4 factors into focus :

1. the reliability is expressed as a probability,
2. the device is required to give adequate performance,
3. the duration of adequate performance is specified, and
4. the operating (environmental) conditions prescribed.

The keywords are now explained hereunder for better understanding of the definition :

***Adequacy.*** As per definition, system must work adequately. This concept of adequacy is different for different purposes. The motor is required to stop, start and to run perhaps for years without failure, while missile system requires to be operated just once, but without fail.

***Period of time intended* (*Duration of Adequate Performance*).** One cannot expect a device or a system to work for ever and that too in the same condition. The device or system wears-out with time and hence, the capability of the system to perform its task adequately depends upon the age of the system. In other words, we can say that reliability is the study of failure rate. Failure characteristics have been discussed earlier in this chapter.

***Operating (environmental) Conditions.*** Operating conditions in which a device is expected to function adequately could be with regard to temperature, humidity, vibration, shock etc. For example, an automobile shock absorber may be satisfactory, if it is used mainly on highways, while its life span will be very short, if it is generally used on uneven and rough roads.

Thus, in simple words we can say that the reliability refers to the ability of a product to function effectively over a certain period of time. Reliability is related to the concept of quality of performance. To ensue customer satisfaction in the performance phase, we address measures to improve reliability in the design phase.

**Difference between Reliability and Quality**

Quality and reliability must be distinguished from one another. Quality is denned as the degree to which a device meets various standards specified for it. Quality standards include efficiency, accuracy, aesthetic standards in addition to the reliability. Whereas, reliability means, "able to be trusted" or " not to breakdown in operation" . This shows that reliability factor is an important factor amongst the quality factors.

**Other Definitions of Reliability**

Reliability may be defined in several ways:

- The idea that something is fit for a purpose with respect to time.
- The capacity of a device or system to perform, as designed.
- The resistance to failure of a device or system
- The ability of a device or system to perform a required function under stated conditions for a specified period of time.
- The probability that a functional unit will perform its required function for a specified interval under stated conditions.

Generally accepted definition of reliability is as under :

**"Reliability is the probability of a device performing its purpose adequately for the period (time) intended under the given operating conditions encountered."**

According to this definition, reliability engineering is concerned with following four key **elements:**

1. **Reliability is a probability.** This means that failure is regarded as a random phenomenon, it is a recurring event, and we do not express any information on individual failures, the causes of failures, or relationship between failures, except that the likelihood for failures to occur varies over time according to the given probability function.
2. **Reliability is predicted on "intended function".** Generally, this is taken to mean operation without failure. However, even if no individual part of the system fails, but the system as a whole does not do what was intended, then it is still charged against the system reliability.
3. **Reliability applies to a specified period of time.** This means that a system has a specified chance that it will operate without failure before specified time. Reliability engineering ensures that components and materials will meet the requirements during the specified time. A piece of mechanical equipment may have a reliability rating value in terms of cycles of use.

4. **Reliability is restricted to operation under stated (or explicitly defined) conditions.** This constraints is necessary because it is impossible to design a system for unlimited conditions. The operating environment must be addressed during design and testing. Also, the same system may be required to operate in varying conditions requiring additional scrutiny.

### 18.1.1. Importance of Reliability

In today's highly competitive and technologically complex environment reliability is very essential. Following are the important product attributes :

1. Reputation of the company.
2. Customer satisfaction.
3. Warranty costs, as replacement and repair costs affect profits.
4. Repeat Business, as improved reliability has a positive impact on future business.

## 18.2. RELIABILITY REQUIREMENTS

Reliability engineering must also address requirements for various reliability tasks and documentation during system development, test, production, and operation. Reliability tasks include various analyses, planning, and failure reporting.

For any system, one of the tasks of reliability engineering is to adequately specify the reliability and maintainability requirements, as defined by the stakeholders in terms of their overall availability needs. Setting only availability targets is not appropriate. Reliability requirements address the system itself, including test and assessment requirements, and associated tasks and documentation. Reliability requirements are included in the appropriate system/subsystem requirements specifications, test plans and contract statements.

The maintainability requirements address the costs of repairs as well as repair time. Testability requirements provide the link between reliability and maintainability and should address detectability of failure modes (on a particular system level).

Originally, reliability quantification consisted of a probability and a mission time alongwith a definition of performance and usage conditions.

With the passage of time as experience is gained in quantifying reliability, many companies are using different indexes which best suits to them in meeting the needs of internal technical personnel, marketing personnel and the users of the product.

Setting overall reliability requirements (goal) means: (*a*) reliability as a number (*e.g.*, 90 per cent of the engines produced should pass through the warranty period without generating a claim), (*b*) the environmental conditions to which the numbers apply, and (*c*) a definition of successful product performance. The designers should be able to define and understand these requirements in terms of the design in greater depth.

Some of the **common terms used in reliability** requirements are:

- Mean time between failures (MTBF)
- Mean time to failure (MTTF). This means mean time to first failure of the product.
- Failure rate (*i.e.*, number of failures per unit time).
- Mean life.
- Mean time between maintenance (MTBM). This means mean time between a specified type of maintenance action.
- Longevity (*i.e.*, wear-out time for a product).
- Availability (*i.e.*, operating time expressed as a percentage of operating and repair time).
- **System effectiveness.** This means the extent to which a product/device achieves the requirements of the user.
- Probability of success, (used for non-time oriented products).

MTTF, MTBF, MTTR, Reliability, maintainability and availability have been discussed in detail in the chapter on "Life-testing and Reliability".

## 18.3. DESIGNING FOR RELIABILITY

Design engineers should ensure that a product should have a long service life with a minimum failures. As products become more complex, failures increase with operating time.

Reliability design begins with the development of a (system) model. Reliability models use block diagram and fault trees to provide a graphical means of evaluating the relationship between the different parts of the system. These models may incorporate predictions based on failure rates taken from historical data. Important fundamental failure mechanisms are identified and analyszed and practical requirements are provided to designers to generate low-stressed designs and products that are protected against damage and too much wear over time.

One of the most important design techniques is redundancy. This means that if one part of the system fails, there is an alternate success path, such as a backup system.

Another design technique to prevent failure in the first place is "physics of failure", relies on understanding the physical process of stress, strength and failure at a very detailed level, possible with use of handling mechanisms like creep, stress relaxation, fatigue, crack growth and probabilistic design. The material or component can then be re-designed to reduce the probability of failure and to make it more robust against variation.

Another effective way to deal with unreliability issues is to perform analysis to be able to predict degradation and being able to prevent unscheduled down events/failures from occurring. RCM (Reliability Centred Maintenance) programmes can be used for this purpose.

### 18.3.1. Factors Affecting Product Design

Following factors which affect the product design, need consideration while designing a product:

**(A) Technical Factors**

1. Operating conditions : Type of workers available and conditions of noise, heat, vibrations etc., generated during manufacturing.
2. Performance : Turning speed, feed etc., of material used, accuracy, type of material required.
3. Maintenance aspects.
4. Experience of the company.

**(B) Industrial Engineering Factors**

1. Economy in production : Materials, workstudy, layout, tooling etc.
2. Appearance *i.e.* aesthetic look.
3. Ergonomics *i.e.* whether the use of the product is comfortable.

**(C) Production Engineering Factors**

1. Standardisation
2. Simplification
3. Tolerance
4. Finish
5. Safety
6. Tolerance.

These have been discussed separately in the chapter.

**(D) Customer Needs Expectations**

The needs of the user are translated into a set of product design and development or research and development requirements for manufacturing. For overall design effectiveness, it is essential to provide these inputs at an early stage so as to address functional performance, reliability, maintainability, safety, manufacturability and other attributes.

Product development translates customer expectations for functional requirements into specific engineering and quality characteristics. For traditional products, this process is simple, and can be achieved by experienced design engineers without using any special techniques. For new and modern products, the desired product attributes are decided based on the customer expectation/need and then steps are taken for identifying the necessary characteristics for raw materials, components, sub-assemblies and process steps.

For the purpose of ensuring that customer needs are translated into both, the design of the product and the design of the process, technique known as **quality function deployment (QFD)** is used. QFD is a technique consisting of a series of interlocking matrixes that translates customer needs into product and process characteristics.

**(E) Design Parameters**

As we know, the most basic product feature is performance *i.e.*, the output, which is created by engineers using engineering principles to combine inputs of materials, parts, sub-assemblies, liquids etc. For each of these inputs, the design engineer identifies parameters and specifies the numerical values so as to achieve the required output of the final product. For each of these parameters, the specifications state a target value and a tolerance range around the target. This process is known as parameter and tolerance design. While selecting these target values, it is necessary to set values so that the performance of the product during use is not affected by variability.

Requirements are specified using reliability parameters. The most common reliability parameter is the mean time to failure (MTTF), which can also be specified as the failure rate (this is expressed as a frequency or the number of failures during a given period. These parameters are very useful for systems that are operated frequently, such as motor vehicles, machinery, and electronic equipment. Reliability increases, as the MTTF increases. The MTTF is usually specified in hours, but can also be used with other units of measurement, such as kilometers or cycles.

In other cases, reliability is specified as the probability of mission success. For example, reliability of a scheduled aircraft flight can be specified as a dimensionless probability or a percentage, as in system safety engineering. These are devices or systems that remain relatively dormant and only operate once. Examples include automobile airbags, thermal batteries and missiles. Single-shot reliability is specified as a probability of one-time success. Single-shot missile reliability may be specified as requirement for the probability of a hit. For such systems, the probability of failure on demand (PFD) is the reliability measure— which actually is an unavailability number. This PFD derived from failure rate and mission time for non-repairable systems.

**(F) Manufacturability**

Decisions made during the design of product and process has great influence on product costs, ability to meet specifications and the time required to bring a new product to the market. The cost of changes in the design, afterwords say during pilot production can be huge.

Similarly, the selection of tolerances affects the economy of quality (cost of manufacture and quality) and also on the fitness of use and hence, the salability of the product.

Design for manufacturability focuses on simplifying a design to make it more producible. In this, emphasis is on reducing the total number of parts, the total number manufacturing operations and design simplification. These aspects have been discussed in detail in the chapter on "Value Engineering". Such design simplifications also reduces the assembly errors and other sources of quality problems during the manufacture.

From the above, it is clear that design for manufacturability is a technique which aims to simplify a product/process design to facilitate manufacture. The producibility and minimum possible production cost of a product are established by the product designer. His first responsibility is to create something that meets the functional requirements, then his efforts should be to design for manufacturability (or producibility) and low manufacturing costs (referred to as "production design").

**(G) Cost and Product Performance**

Designing for performance which includes reliability, maintainability, safety and other perameters must be done with a simultaneous objective of minimizing cost. Formal tehniques of achieving an optimum balance between performance and cost include both, quantitative and qualitative approaches. Quantitative approach uses a ratio relating to performance and cost, for example, "what we get for each unit of money spent". The ratio is very useful in comparing alternative design approaches to accomplish a desired function.

"Value Engineering" is a commonly used technique for evaluating the design of a product to assure that the essential functions are provided at minimal overall cost.

**(H) Selection of Tolerances**

This is an important decision which is required to be taken by the designer regarding selection of tolerances for product as its characteristics to be controlled during manufacture. The "tolerance limits" specify the allowable limits of variability above and below the nominal value set by the designer. The selection of these tolerances effects the economics of quality in two ways, viz. (*a*) fitness for use and thereby the saleability of the product, and (*b*) cost of manufacture (which includes facilities, tooling, productivity etc.) and cost of quality (which includes inspection, scrap, rework etc). As setting tight tolerances might inevitably lead to additional costs, it is considered by the designer at this stage to avoid additional cost by relaxing the tolerance specifications of the less crucial components.

## 18.4. EVALUATING DESIGN BY TESTING

Following are the main type of tests generally used for evaluating a design:

| *S.N.* | *Type of test* | *Performance test* |
|---|---|---|
| 1. | Performance | - To determine ability of product to meet basic performance requirements. |
| 2. | Stress | - To determine levels of stress that a product can withstand. |
| 3. | Reliability test | - To determine product reliability and compare to requirements. To monitor for trends. |
| 4. | Maintainability | - To determine time required to make repaires and compare to requirements. |
| 5. | Life test | - To determine wear-out time for a product and failure modes associated with time. |

All the above mentioned tests though provide some degree of design assurance, but they also involve some risk, especially in respect of following principal sources:

1. The designer aims to attain fitness for intended use, but actual use/misuse by the user can differ.
2. Models (or products manufactured during pilot-run) are usually built by skilled specialists under the direct supervision of the designer, but actual production is carried out by less skilled workers under normal supervisors.
3. Specification may vary, when production in full swing takes place from that of models which are built in small numbers.

For details about testing refer chapter on "Life-testing and Reliability".

## 18.5. PREDICTING RELIABILITY DURING DESIGN

As we know that prediction of reliability requires the use of prior performance data, and probability theory to calculate the expected failure rates for various circuits, configurations etc. Though the reliability prediction is not accurate, following steps help in assessing the approximate prediction of reliability:

1. The product (the system, subsystems and units) must be precisely defined in terms of their configurations, boundaries, inter-relationships and the interfaces with other systems. The functional requirements of the product, and the conditions that constitute failure or unsatisfactory performance must also be defined.
2. For systems in which there are redundancies or other inter-relationships among parts, a reliability block diagram should be prepared.
3. Then a probability model for predicting reliability is developed which considers redundancies and other conditions.
4. Next step is to collect the informations relevant to the parts reliability, which includes parts function, parts stresses, parts ratings, internal and external environments and operating time.
5. Parts reliability data are then selected, which include information on catastrophic failures, tolerance variance. These and other related informations should be collected and designer should build up a data bank from variety of sources, such as field performance studies, data from parts manufacturers, specified life-tests, data available from industry or other research organisations.
6. Above informations are then used to obtain reliability predictions.

Other prediction methods are based on various statistical distributions like exponential distribution, reliable distribution.

Some, recognized authors on reliability engineering have aruged that too much emphasis is often given to the prediction of reliability parameters, whereas more effort should be devoted to the prevention of failure (reliability improvement). Failures can and should be prevented in the first place for most cases. The emphasis on quantification and target setting in terms of (*e.g.*) MTBF might provide the idea that there is a limit to the amount of reliability that can be achieved.

## 18.6. LIFE-TESTING

Life-testing of products is the most essential requirement in certain industries especially those manufacturing electric tubes, razor blades etc. Life-testing is performed so as to ensure whether the product is as per specifications or not. While manufacturing, it is essential to test the components as well as operations.

Life-test ensures the manufacturer that the product shall give good performance during its guaranteed life. As explained earlier control of the quality of a product is performed by means of check applied at certain stages in the manufacturing line and at final stage. Similarly, 'life-test' must also be performed throughout the production period so that good life performance can be ensured.

However, life-testing involves extra expenditure but the informations obtained from these tests are very important so as to take guarantee of the life of the product by the manufacturer.

**Objectives of Life–Tests.**

Main objects of life-tests are as follows :

1. To make sure that user will get a reliable life of the product.
2. To show, if there is any manufacturing defect so that the same can be rectified in future lots.

**Classification of Life–Tests.**

Life-tests are classified as follows :

(*a*) ***Quality Control Life-Tests.*** These tests are for checking the quality.

(*b*) ***Pilot-run Life-Tests.*** The life-tests are performed, when any change in the production is proposed, that is, these are to check the proposed production.

(*c*) ***Establishment Life-Tests.*** These life-tests are performed, whenever a new type of product is introduced.

(*d*) ***Application Life-Tests.*** When conditions for the use of product are different than that for which it is generally used, then these life-tests are performed.

**Sample or Individual Life–Testing**

Whether a product is to be tested for life-test individually or by sampling depends upon their importance. For very important products, such as radar, transmitting tubes where high reliability, greater stability and long life is required, individual product must be tested for life-tests. Products of less importance, such as electric bulbs, fans, electric press, radio receiving tubes etc. are put to sample testing for life-tests.

In sample testing percentage of products put to life-tests are decided on the basis of their relative importance.

**Life-Testing Procedure**

Life-testing is performed by putting the maximum stresses, load vibration, frequency or voltage for which it has been designed. If a product works satisfactory under its maximum loading and its performance is nice at extreme conditions, then the life-test is said to have been satisfactory.

Main difficulty in life-testing is that there is no reliable techniques for life-testing and hence, there is necessity of evolving a satisfactory method. However, the method given above is being employed to give relative reliability.

## 18.7. TESTS FOR EVALUATING A DESIGN

Since field experience comes too late, therefore, it is desired to have various forms of testing the product to simulate field use. Reliability prediction, design review and other techniques are though valuable as early-warning devices, they cannot be a substitute for the ultimate proof (*i.e.* use of the product by the customer).

Earlier when reliability engineering was not developed, different tests like performance, environmental, stress, life were made to evaluate a design. Therefore, reliability, maintainability and other parameters also included in the list of tests.

Following is the list of tests used to evaluate a design for different purposes:

| | |
|---|---|
| 1. Performance test | 1. To determine ability to meet basic performance requirements. |
| 2. Environmental test | 2. To evaluate ability to withstand defined environmental levels. |
| 3. Stress test | 3. To determine level of stress that a product can withstand so as to determine safety margins inherent in the design. |
| 4. Reliability test | 4. To determine reliability of the product and compare with its requirements. |
| 5. Maintainability test | 5. To determine time required for repairs and compare with requirements. |
| 6. Life test | 6. To determine wear-out time and failure modes associated with time. |
| 7. Pilot run | 7. To determine capability of meeting design requirements. |

The tests should also cover the risks due to the following principal sources :

1. **Intended use versus actual use.** There is variation in actual use from the designer's concept.
2. **Model construction versus subsequent (actual) production.** Actual production is carried out by less skilled factory workers as compared to models built by skilled specialists under the supervision of designers.

**Reliability Test Requirements**

Reliability test requirements can follow from any analysis for which the first estimate of failure probability, failure mode or effect needs to be justified. Evidence can be generated with some level of confidence by testing. Testing reliability requirements is problematic for several reasons. A single test is in most cases insufficient to generate enough statistical data. Multiple tests or long-duration tests are usually very expensive. Some tests are simply impractical, and environmental conditions can be hard to predict over a system's life-cycle.

Reliability engineering is used to design a realistic and affordable test program that provides empirical evidence that the system meets its reliability requirements. Statistical confidence levels are used to address some of these concerns. A certain parameter is expressed alongwith a corresponding confidence level; for example, an MTBF of 1000 hours at 90% confidence level.

The combination of reliability parameter value and confidence level greatly affects the development cost and the risk to both, the customer and producer. Care is needed to select the best combination of requirement - *e.g.* cost-effectiveness. Reliability testing may be performed at various levels, such as component, subsystem and system. Also, many factors must be addressed during testing and operation, such as extreme temperature and humidity, shock, vibration or other environmental factors.

Reliability engineering must assess the root causes of failures and device corrective actions. Reliability engineering determines an effective test strategy so that all parts are exercised in relevant environments in order to assure the best possible reliability under understood conditions. For systems that must last many years, reliability engineering may be used to design accelerated life tests.

## 18.8. FAILURE RATES AND PRODUCT LIFE–CYCLE

One cannot expect a product or device or a system to work for ever and that too in the same condition. The product or device wears out with time and hence, the capability of the device is to perform its task adequately depends upon its age. Experience has shown that failure characteristics of most of the products (or devices or systems), follow a definite pattern, known as 'bath tub curve' and is indicated in the figure 18.1. To understand clearly, we can divide the product life in following three periods :

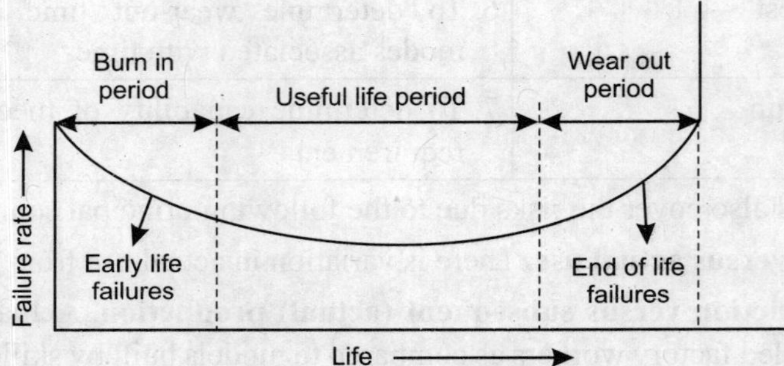


**Fig. 18.1.** Curve to indicate failure rate and product life-cycle.

(*a*) **Burn-in-period (Infant mortality period).** When system is given a trail run during initial period, there may be rapid failures known as initial failures.

These failures are concerned with malfunctioning due to poor design, poor workmanship and poor quality. The sub-standard components are located and then replaced. This will improve the reliability.

(*b*) **Useful life period.** After the burn-in period, actual useful life of normal use starts. During this period, failure rate is low but occurs unexpectedly and at random intervals such failures are known as 'Normal failures' or 'Chance failures'.

(*c*) **Wear-out Period.** Beyond its useful life period, failure rate increases very much. This is due to excessive wear after the expected useful design life of the device or system has been exceeded. The failures during this period are known as 'Ageing failure' or 'Wearout failures'.

The curve shown in Fig. 18.1 is sometimes referred as the 'Bath Tub' characteristics.

## 18.9. MEAN TIME TO FAILURE (MTTF)

As all the specimens do not fail at the sametime, they have different times to failure. Hence, we are required to calculate the mean time to failure of all the specimens. If $t_1$ is the time to failure for the first, and $t_2$ is the time for the second specimen, and $t_N$ is the time to failure for the Nth specimen, the MTTF for $N$ specimens will be:

$$\text{MTTF} = \left(\frac{t_1 + t_2 + \ldots\ldots t_N}{N}\right) = \frac{1}{N}\sum_{i=1}^{N} t_i$$

Since it is difficult to record the time to failure for each component, when the number of specimens tested are very large. Therefore, in such a case we record the number which fail during specific interval of time. If $n_1$ is the specimens that failed during the first hour, $n_2$ in second hour, and $n_k$ in *Kth* hour, then MTTF for $N$ specimens will be:

$$\text{MTTF} = \left(\frac{n_1 + 2n_2 + 3n_3 \ldots. + kn_k}{N}\right)$$

**Some Other Related Terms**

1. **Mean Time Between Failures (M.T.B.F.).** It is the average value of time intervals between successive failures of a product or an equipment.

Thus,
$$\text{M.T.B.F.} = \frac{\text{Equipment operating time}}{\text{No. of observed failures}}$$

2. **Failure Rate.** It is the number of failures per min.

∴ Failure Rate,
$$F = \frac{1}{\text{M.T.B.F}}$$

3. **Probability of failures.** It is defined as one minus the reliability of a system.

*i.e.*
$$P_f = 1 - r = 1 - e^{-nt/T}$$

or
$$P_f = \frac{nt}{T}$$

where, $n$ = No. of elements in a device

$t$ = cumulative time

$T$ = M.T.B.F.

4. **Mean Time to Re-store (M.T.T.R.).** It is time required to locate a failure and to repair it.
5. **Reliability Improvement Factor.** It is the ratio of probability of failure of present system to that of improved system.
6. **Availability.** It is the ratio of satisfactory operating time to the total operating time of the system, *i.e.*

$$\text{Availability} = \frac{\text{M.T.B.F}}{\text{M.T.B.F} + \text{M.T.T.R}}$$

## 18.10. RELIABILITY AND UNRELIABILITY

The reliability is the percentage of healthy items passed the given test. If out of total $N$ items, $n$ number pass the test and $m$ do not pass the test, then:

(*i*) Reliability will be,

$$R = \frac{n}{N}$$

(*ii*) Unreliability will be,

$$F = \frac{m}{N}$$

Here, $R + F = 1.$

**Example 18.1.** If we test 100 lamps, out of which 80 pass the test. Calculate reliability and unreliability.

**Solution.** Here,

$$n = 80;\ m = 20.$$

Reliability, $R = \frac{n}{N} = \frac{n}{n+m} = \frac{80}{n+m} = \frac{80}{100} = \mathbf{0.8\ Ans.}$

Unreliability, $F = \frac{m}{N} = \frac{m}{n+m} = \frac{20}{100} = \mathbf{0.2\ \ Ans.}$

**Check:** $R + F = 0.8 + 0.2 = 1.0$

**Causes of Unreliability**

(*i*) Increased complexity of the product,

(*ii*) Many assemblies with large number of parts.

In respective reliabilities of various components of a complex equipment depend on:

(*a*) The technologies of their production,

(*b*) The quality of materials used in their manufacture,

(*c*) The condition (or environment) in which they operate, etc.

Thus, the reliability of an equipment is closely related to several uncertainty factors. As uncertainties are dealt by probability theory, the reliability is, therefore, dealt by the probability.

**Factors Affecting Reliability**

As reliability depends on the following factors, attention should, therefore, be given on these factors so as to make the product reliable:

1. Product or process design.
2. Material quality.
3. Manufacturing process.
4. Testing and inspection.
5. Maintenance system.
6. Working environment.
7. Product complexity.
8. Number of sub-assemblies and their standardization.

Out of the above factors, the design is the main cause of unreliability and therefore, designing for reliability is being discussed in detail.

## 18.11. RELIABILITY DURING DESIGNING

While designing, it should be remembered that error rate is directly proportional to complexity, and the greater the number of components, the greater the chance of failure. Value engineering technique for analysing functions versus cost should be conducted while designing for reliability.

Parts should be designed with fail safe principle in mind, for which it is important to consider that how the part/component fails.

If possible, failure should occur in non-catastrophic manner and should be of no harm to operator, *e.g.*, allowing safety valve in pressure vessels.

Redundancy is another way of achieving reliability. Similarly, for increasing the reliability, the item may be protected from extremes of environmental conditions, *e.g.*, heat, cold, vibrations or excessive load. Avoid using unproven parts to be used.

Maintainability and serviceability are important conditions in designing for reliability. Ease of maintenance and servicing contributes to higher field reliability, as this will enable field staff to maintain the item in a better manner. The items should, therefore, be designed keeping these characteristics in mind. Specify replacement schedules to remove and replace low reliability parts before they reach the wear-out stage.

While designing for higher reliability, the cost of obtaining the desired reliability must be considered. The improvement in reliability may not have been worth the higher cost. This means that there is a trade-off between reliability and cost, therefore, it would be of interest to compare the increase with the improvement in the reliability. Excluding the situations where safety of human being is involved, in the design of systems, an objective evaluation of the cost-reliability trade-off will make decision-making more realistic.

**Example 18.2.** *In a test of electric fuses, 100 fuses fail in 5 hours. The failure was recorded as follows:*

| ***Hrs.*** | 1 | 2 | 3 | 4 | 5 |
|---|---|---|---|---|---|
| ***No. failed*** | 20 | 15 | 25 | 20 | 20 |

Calculate failure rate λ, and hazard rate *Z* for this test.

**Solution:** As failure rate is number of failures per unit time.

$$\therefore \qquad \text{failure rate } \lambda = \frac{100 \text{ failures}}{5 \text{ hrs.}} = \textbf{20 fuses/hr. Ans.}$$

Hazard rate $Z_1$ (for first hour) = 20 fuses/hr.

$Z_2$ (for second hour) = 15 fuses/hr.

$Z_3$ (for third hour) = 25 fuses/hr.

$Z_4$ (for fourth hour) = 20 fuses/hr.

$Z_5$ (for fifth hour) = **20 fuses/hr. Ans.**

**Example 18.3.** *An electronic system has a M.T.B.F. of 1000 hours and a M.T.T.R. of 40 hours, what is availability ?*

**Solution.**

Given that M.T.B.F = 1000 hours

and M.T.T.R. = 40 hours

As we know that,

$$\text{Availability} = \frac{\text{M.T.B.F.}}{\text{M.T.B.F} + \text{M.T.T.R}} = \frac{1000}{1000 + 40} = \frac{1000}{1040}$$

$$= \mathbf{0.961.\ Ans.}$$

**Example 18.4.** *System is composed of 1000 elements, each having a M.T.B.F. of 100,000 hours. What is the probability of failure of the system, if its cumulative operating time is 10 hours?*

**Solution.** Since, probability of failures = 1 -- Reliability

*i.e.* $p_f = 1 - R = 1 - e^{-nt/T}$

where, $n$ = Cumulative operating time = 10 hours

$T$ = M.T.B.F. = 100,000 hours.

$\therefore$ $$pf = 1 - e\frac{10 \times 1000}{100,000}$$

$$= 1 - e^{0.1} = 1 - 0.905 = \mathbf{0.095\ Ans.}$$

**Alternative Method.** Since, probability of failure.

$$pf = 1 - e^{\frac{-nt}{T}}$$

$\therefore$ $$pf = \frac{nt}{T} = 10 \times \frac{1000}{100,000} = \mathbf{0.1.\ Ans.}$$

**Example 18.5.** *If the reliability of a system is increased from 0.9 to 0.95, find out the Reliability Improvement Factor.*

**Solution.** Probability of failure in I Case

$$= 1 - r_1 = 1 - 0.9 = 0.1$$

and probability of failure in II case $= 1 - r_2 = 1 - 0.95 = 0.05$

$\therefore$ Reliability Improvement Factor

$$= \frac{\text{Probability of failure in I case}}{\text{Probability of failure II case}}$$

$$= \frac{0.1}{0.05} = \mathbf{2\ Ans.}$$

**Conclusion.** Thus, by increasing the reliability of the system from 0.9 to 0.95 probability of failure has been reduced to half, hence system is twice as reliable as first system.

**Example 18.6.** (*a*) *An electronic device can be designed utilising either vacuum tubes or transistors. If a device having 5 tubes of M.T.B.F. of 10,000 hours, each is transistorised with 20 transistors having M.T.B.F. of 80,000 hours. Does it pay to transistorise from the reliability point of view?*

(*b*) If 40 transistors are employed in above example, what conclusion can you reach from the results?

**Solution.** (*a*) probability of failure in I case (*i.e.*, with 5 tubes)

$$Pf_1 = \frac{n_1\, t}{T_1} = \frac{5t}{10,000} = \frac{t}{2000}$$

Similarly, probability of failure in II Case *i.e.*, with transistors,

$$pf_2 = \frac{n_2 t}{T_2} = \frac{20t}{80,000} = \frac{t}{4000}$$

This shows that probability of failure is reduced with transistors, thus, it increases the reliability. Hence, it is useful to transistorize. In this case, Reliability Improvement Factor,

$$Q = \frac{pf_1}{pf_2} = \frac{t/2000}{t/4000} = 2$$

with 20 transistors reliability becomes twice.

(*b*) Probability for failures with 40 transistors,

$$pf_3 = n_3\, \frac{t}{T_3} = \frac{40t}{80,000} = \frac{t}{2000}$$

∴ Reliability Improve Factor

$$= \frac{pf_1}{pf_2} = \frac{t/2000}{t/2000} = 1.$$

Thus, we conclude that by increasing the number of elements reliability decreases. Hence, to get maximum reliability, number of elements must be kept minimum.

## 18.12. EQUIPMENT RELIABILITY PROCESS

Equipment reliability process includes the integration and co-ordination of a broad range of equipment reliability activities, such as developing and implementing long-term equipment health plans, monitoring equipment performance and condition, and make continuing adjustments to preventive maintenance tasks and frequencies based on equipment operating experience.

Equipment reliability process includes activities like.

1. Performance monitoring. It includes system performance component performance, operation monitoring, testing and inspection results etc.
2. Scoping and identification of critical components.
3. Review existing project management and other maintenance strategies/systems.
4. Define reliability requirements of plants and industries and take steps to satisfy them.
5. Continue equipment reliability improvements.
6. Life Cycle Management, including long term system and component health prioritization of improvement activities and integration of long term plans into management's long term activities.

7. Reliability Growth Analysis. It is helpful for the improvement in a reliability parameter over a period of time due to changes in product design or the manufacturing process. Reliability growth management is the systematic planning for reliability achievement as a function of time and other resources, and controlling the ongoing rate of achievement by reallocation of these resources based on comparisons between planned and assessed reliability values.
8. Monitoring the reliability the Mean Time Between Failures (MTBF), and the failure rate of the system, equipment or product also establishes a trend in the increase in the reliability.
9. Reliability can be improved considerably by adopting "Redundancy" in the system, as discussed in the later part of this chapter. Redundancy means duplication (or triplication or more) of electronic, electrical mechanical components or back up systems that are used to keep equipment working if their counter parts fail.

## 18.13. RELIABILITY AND MAINTENANCE

Machines, buildings and other service facilities are subject to deterioration due to their use and exposure to environmental conditions. If this process of deterioration is not checked, it may render them unserviceable. It is, therefore, necessary to attend to them from time-to-time to repair and recondition so as to enhance their life economically.

Maintenance aspect is more important in the case of machines due to their non-uniform pattern of wear and tear which depends on large number of factors, hence proper attention should be given to protect the machine and its components from under wear so as to protect them from failures. A proper attention means lubrication, cleaning, timely inspection and systematic maintenance.

The old concept of maintenance was "maintenance is for preserving physical asset". However, the new concept is that "maintenance is for preserving the function of asset". The **latest concept of maintenance** lead to maintenance which leads to preserving the inherent reliability or built in capability of any asset.

With the growth of industrialization. The complexity and sophistication of the machine they started creating problems for the operating personnel and the concept of maintenance as a separate identity and separate discipline started. Recently in many organisation, maintenance engineering has been taken as a composite discipline, including all types of repairs, overhauling, inventory management, root cause analysis, reliability and performance monitoring etc.

The maintenance avoids production hold-ups, interruptions or loss of standard efficiency of operation. Increased availability of well maintained plants is the matter of considerable importance as it directly affects plant capacity, productivity and profit-ability. In general, operation and maintenance is synonymous with high level of availability, reliability and assets' operability linking directly with production capacity, productivity and business profits.

Earlier the objective of maintenance function was considered to optimize plant availability at minimum cost. Today, it is being considered as, "maintenance affects all aspects of business effectiveness and risk (risk includes safety, environmental integrity, energy efficiency, product quality, and customer service, not just plant availability and cost.)

### 18.13.1. Maintenance Functions

**(*A*) Basic Functions**

1. **Replace unserviceable item.**
2. **Repair.**
3. **Overhaul.**
4. **Rebuild/Reconditioning.**
5. **Servicing/Lubrication.**
6. **Inspection** (comparing the characteristics with established standards through examinations.
7. **Test** (Verify the serviceability by measuring the characteristics of an item and compare with prescribed standards.
8. **Adjust** (*i.e.* setting the operating characteristics to specified parameter.

**(*B*) Composite Functions**

1. Reducing downtimes and increasing the equipment availability and equipment utilization.
2. Analyze repetitive failure and arrange their elimination.
3. Forecast maintenance spares, tools and consumables and help their procurement and inventory management.
4. Economy in maintenance department.
5. Maximizing the utilization of available resources.
6. Ensuring safety and reducing environmental pollution.
7. Cost reduction and cost control.

## 18.14. DESIGNING A MAINTENANCE SYSTEM

Maintenance system is a methodology and strategy for establishing a good maintenance management principles and providing a framework for identifying, mapping and controlling the elements of maintenance functions.

Presently many maintenance systems/strategies are in use in industries and selection has to be made depending the need, complexity and reliability needed and also considering techno-economics. Maintenance systems may be planned (preventive and predictive maintenance), unplanned (breakdown or corrective maintenance).

Following are the main reasons for evaluating/considering maintenance systems/strategies :

1. Which set of operations that should be performed and their frequency?
2. With aging of the plant a different sets of tasks is needed to maintain reliability.
3. Efforts needed to reduce maintenance expenditure without increasing risk or reducing reliability etc.
4. It the equipment regularly available to perform planned/routine maintenance activities?

5. Will the cost to shut down the equipment be less than the cost of breakdown?

The resulting strategy must strike a balance between maintenance cost and plant reliability. This evaluation develops tools and techniques for determining the best mix of maintenance tasks.

For the purpose of designing the maintenance system/strategies, historical and statistical records of the maintenance work are maintained and compiled to assess the results and to provide guidelines for future. The maintenance system should also decide the following in advance :

1. The form, method and details of doing the maintenance of each individual item of the plant, equipment and other machines.
2. The tools, spares, number of workmen, and time required to carry out this maintenance.
3. The frequency of carrying out this maintenance operation.
4. The method of analyzing the results.

## 18.15. RELIABILITY CENTRED MAINTENANCE (RCM)

RCM is a procedure for determining maintenance strategies based on reliability techniques and encompasses monitoring and well known analysis methods, such as failure mode Effects and Criticality Analysis (FMECA). The primary objective of the RCM process is to identify ways to avoid or reduce the consequences of failures which, if allowed to occur,will adversely impact personnel safety, environmental health or economics.

RCM is a process used to determine the maintenance requirement of any physical asset in its operating context. Today, RCM is an advanced maintenance strategy for increasing asset availability by minimizing downtime caused by failure, reducing an asset's total cost of ownership and increasing overall. Equipment Effectiveness (OEE). RCM is the optimum mix of reactive, preventive, predictive and proactive maintenance practices. It also involves some design/redesign and redundancy.

In short, RCM is a methodology to balance the resources being used with the required in inherent reliability.

**Objectives of RCM**

- Maintenance strategy optimization,
- Extension of equipment life span,
- Elimination of chronic problems of machine,
- Root cause analysis,
- Justified preventive maintenance tasks.

**What RCM Achieves?**

- Greater safety and environmental integrity.
- Improved operation performance (output, product quality, Customer satisfaction).
- Greater maintenance cost effectiveness.

- Longer useful life of expensive items.
- To build a comprehensive data base.
- Greater motivation of individuals.

## 18.16. OTHER CONCEPTS OF MAINTENANCE SYSTEMS/STRATEGIES

This article deals with modern maintenance practices with need based improvements and innovations. These have come up because of increased competition and the concept of lower cost per unit of production. This helps in improved availability and reliability of equipments, which are needed for substantive for improving maintenance performance and optimization of maintenance.

### 18.16.1. Condition Monitoring

Condition monitoring is the condition based maintenance and is concerned with extracting information from machine, to indicate its condition and enable them to be operated and maintained with safety and economy. The use of condition monitoring and non-destructive testing is the part of maintenance strategy with the aim to maximise the availability of the equipment.

### 18.16.2. Monitoring the Failures

With the advancement that has taken place in recent past in the field of predictive or diagnostic maintenance system, it is possible to predict the failure of machine much before they occur, so that maintenance staff can prepare themselves and arrange necessary parts required and skilled manpower for repairs to put the machine back on work. In order to study the failure we must understand the types of failure, which can be classified as follows :

(*a*) *Mechanical failure* due to vibration, mis-alignment, unbalance fatigues, bad or worn out bearings, high temperature etc.

(*b*) *Thermal failure* due to over-heating, resulting from lack of lubrication or adequate cooling or electrical failure.

(*c*) *Chemical failure* due to high corrosin, abrasive particles in the fluids.

Above mentioned failures can be avoided if proper monitoring is done. For monitoring, various devices employed are :

**(*A*) Monitoring Mechanical Failures**

1. **Shock pulse meter :** It detects in rolling elements, like ball and rolling bearings well in advance.
2. **Vibration meter :** It measures vibration level to assess whether it is within the safe limits.
3. **Vibration analysis :** It measures amplitude of vibration at different frequencies so as to know the reason for undue high vibration.
4. **Ultrasonic flow detectors :** It detects minor cracks.

5. **Mechanical or electrical strain gauge :** It measures deflection of foundations, columns, etc.

**(*B*) Monitoring Thermal Failures**

1. **Infra-red thermometer :** It detect hot spots for bearing and other parts of the machinery by the remote sensing.
2. **Thermovision :** This displays the hot spot detected by above device on the video screen.

### 18.16.3. Techniues for Corrective Maintenance

Latest techniques adopted by the engineers for corrective maintenance.

(*a*) **Plasma spraying of metal/alloys :** It helps in restoring wornout parts to original dimensions and make them corrosion and erosion resistance.

(*b*) **Metalock system** of repairing cracks and prevent its spreading further.

(*c*) **Eutectic welding** techniques, for depositing hard surfacing materials on worn-out parts, which can be later on machined to required dimensions and tolerances.

(*d*) **Heavy chromium plating** techniques, for restoring worn-out shafts, bearings etc.

### 18.16.4. Reclamation of Worn-Out Parts

In preventive maintenance, maintenance operations are scheduled and initiated prior to the occurrence of failure, thereby preventing the machines from failing during operation cycle. Meantime between failure (MTBF) for most of the components are identified and replacement are arranged accordingly. The success of the system depends upon availability of spares at proper time. Certain items which cannot be reclaimed or salvaged are to be purchased and kept in store for replacing at proper time. But due to latest technology most items can be reclaimed or salvaged resulting in cost effectiveness.

Most equipment and machineries are subjected to impact, adrasion and heat as main wear factors. The vital parts which wear-off very fast need replacement. The parts which have high costs, high inventory holding costs and poor availability, reclamation is done with the object to restore a worn area to its original dimensions and improve its wear-resistance. Following are the main types of wears :

(1) **Corrosion :** It is deterioration of material due to chemical action of liquids or gases.

(2) **Erosion :** It is wasting away of materials by prolonged contact with an unfriendly environment like acid, heat etc.

(3) **Friction :** It is the rubbing of one surface against the other. In extreme cases it leads to freezing or seizing.

(4) **Impact :** It is sudden shock loads causing localised compression or deformation.

(5) **Abrasion :** It is the grinding action by a soiled sliding or rubbing against a surface.

### 18.16.5. Six Sigma Maintenance

Six Sigma Maintenance is the application of six sigma principles in maintenance. It focuses on reducing the variation in production process. By reducing variation a business can achieve higher control over its operational systems, increases their cost effectiveness and encouraging productivity.

The Term Six Sigma refers to a measure of process variation (six standard deviations) that translates into an error or defect rate of 3.4 parts per million, six sigma methodology improves any existing business process by constantly reviewing and returning the process. To achieve this, six sigma uses a mythology known as DMAIC (Define opportunities, Measure performance, Analyze opportunity, Improve performance, control performance).

Six Sigma relies on statistical techniques to reduce defects/failures and it incorporates the basic principles and techniques used in Business, Statistics and Engineering.

Six Sigma concept have been discussed in detail in the chapters on "TQM concepts" and "TQM tools and techniques" in the book.

### 18.16.6. Five S (5-S) Concept in Maintenance

This concept (developed in Japan) assume that no effective and quality job can be performed without clean and safe working environment and without behavioural rules. The 5-S are five action verbs, all starting will and S in Japanese **(Seiri, Seiso, Seiton, Seiketsu and Shitsuke)**. In English these are : **Sort, Clean, Set in Order, Standardize and Sustain**. The meaning of these terms are explained hereunder :

1. **Seiri (Sort) :** This means sort-out and organise items as critical, important, frequently used, not need at present or useless. For sorting, different techniques such or ABC sorting, VED (Vital, Essential, Desirable).
2. **Seiso (Clean) :** It involves cleaning the work. place *i.e.* free of burrs, grease,oil, waste, scarp etc. There should be no loosely hanging wires or oil leakage from machines.
3. **Seiton (Set in Order) :** This concept is that "Each item has a place, and only one place." The items should always be placed back after use at the same place.
4. **Seiketsu (Standardize) :** This means, to decided on standards for keeping the work place, machine and pathways neat and clean. These standards are implemented for whole organisation and tested/inspected randomly.
5. **Shitsuke (Sustain) :** The 5-S concept is considered as a "way of life" and bring about **self-discipline** among the employees of the organisation self-discipline includes punctuality, wearing uniform and badges, following work procedures, dedication to the organisation etc.

5-S concept is effective in all the departments in the organisation including maintenance, production, offices etc.

Following are the **main benefits of 5-S concept**.

1. It helps in timely delivery by timely completion of job.
2. It improves quality and reduces defects/failures.

3. It helps in reduction of waste in materials, space and time.
4. Reduces inventory and storage costs.
5. Reduces equipment downtime.
6. It helps in increasing the safety, profitability etc.

## 18.16.7. Five Zero (5-Zero) Maintenance Concept

The five zero (5-Zero) concept was also introduced in Japan. This include five zeros as **0-Breakdown, 0-Fault, 0-Delays, 0-Stock, and 0-Paper work**. These "Zeros" represent "ideals" or "aims" to be achieved. These individual zero concepts are discussed hereunder :

1. **Zero Breakdown Concept**

   As breakdowns occur due to equipment disorders/defects which remain invisible for one or the other reason and remain unattended. If these defects are corrected in time, breakdowns can be reduced to zero. This is the principle behind the zero defect concept.

This implies a very high degree of reliability, combined with very good maintenance capability. For zero breakdown following actions are necessary :

1. Maintain equipment in good condition by cleaning, lubrication, bolt tightening and carrying out other adjustments.
2. Adhere to good operating conditions.
3. Correct the design weaknesses.
4. Restore deterioration.
5. Improve operating and maintenance skills.

In the breakdown concept the equipment operator is given more responsibilities, such as :

(*a*) Maintain equipment in good condition through cleaning lubrication, bolt tightening and carrying out timely adjustments.

(*b*) Detect deterioration through visual inspection, sound and other abnormalities noticed during operations.

(*c*) Enhancing skills for operation, adjustment etc.

However, maintenance staff must be assigned with the following functions :

1. Providing technical support to operation staff.
2. Restore deterioration thoroughly and accurately by adopting inspection techniques, condition based monitoring and over-hauling if required.
3. Doing corrective maintenance, if any design weakness is noticed.
4. Enhancing maintenance techniques of condition monitoring, inspections and overhauling.

Thus, both production as well as maintenance personnel, should associate aim for zero breakdown. As productivity improves progressively, suitable training and dialogue should be a continuous process so that breakdowns are nearly eliminated.

**2. Zero Fault**

Zero fault means that fault should not be allowed to occur, if it occurs, that should be detected at an early stage and corrected at the initial stage. Zero fault policy is a maintenance policy with a high technical ability using facilities like most suitable vibration and lubrication monitoring gadgets and other elements for diagnosis of equipment behaviour. Action should be taken so that wear and tear are not induced and operational speed should be sufficiently below the maximum speed.

**3. Zero Delay**

This concept require planned and rapid response to equipment outage. Exact points which require attention should be correctly known so that no time is lose for fault diagnosis and/ or repair. For this purpose operation and maintenance manual, standard operating and maintenance practices, timely interpretation of condition monitoring data and alarm and effective communication are essential to reduce any possible delay. Proper planning and scheduling is essential in maintenance jobs with available scheduled shout downs so that actual delay is almost nil and no separate shutdown is needed for maintenance.

**4. Zero Stock**

Zero stock concept means that spares and other materials are procured in such a way that these are received only when they are actually required for consumption. In this way, the materials are not unnecessary stocked in the store and therefore the inventory carrying cost is negligible.

For adopting 'zero stock' concept, it is essential to adopt 'zero fault' concept. Further availability of spare parts must be assured at known locations of manufacturer (specifically involving zero delay concept).

**5. Zero Paper Work**

The concept of 'zero paper work' tries to eliminate paper work, or atleast reduce to barest minimum. This concept involves extensive use of computers and other handheld devices and integrates the same with system computers with customized software.

## 18.17. SPARE PARTS MANAGEMENT

Production machines and other equipment worth crores of rupees remain idle for want of spares, while on the other hand huge stores lying which perhaps may not be used at all. This emphasize the need for paying more attention on management of spares. Improvement in capacity utilization, cost reduction, and reliability can be achieved by better spare parts management. The objective of spare parts management is to provide right parts in right quantity, at right place at right time and at the right cost. "A spare part can be defined as, part identical to the part of a machine which needs replacement due to wear and tear during the operating life of equipment."

**Factors Governing Spare Parts Planning**

(*i*) Usage rate and equipment life.

(*ii*) Service level.

(*iii*) Type of maintenance system adopted and extent of preventive maintenance.

(*iv*) Lead time for procurement.

(*v*) Category of spare parts *i.e.* moving or non-moving, overhaul spares, irregularly used, insurance or maintenance spares.

(*vi*) After sales service of equipment by its manufacturer.

(*vii*) Cost of the item.

**Procurement of Spares**

Following are the main parameters of purchasing.

(*i*) Right Time. (*ii*) Right Source (*iii*) Right Price (*iv*) Right Quality

(*v*) Right Contract (*vi*) Right Procedure. (*vii*) Right Quantity.

**Spare Parts Problems**

- Requirement of spares are uncertain in quantity and in time.
- It is uneconomical to manufacture the parts in small numbers.
- Range of spare parts is very large.
- Cost of spares becoming obsolete is very high.
- Due to large range of spare parts, their identification is a real problem.
- Lead time for procurement of spares very too much. This problem is major in the cases of imported equipments

## 18.17.1. Selective Control Techniques

Selective Control Techniques are based on the principle that it is impossible to manage and control every item of spares inventory. Selective control management, therefore concentrates time and attention on those items where it is justified either due to essentiality or amount of money involved. Various selective control techniques are mentioned in table given below :

| *S. No.* | *Title of Techniques* | *Basis* | *Application* |
|---|---|---|---|
| 1. | ABC (Always Better Control) | Annual Consumption Value in Rupees. | Inventory Control |
| 2. | HML (High, Medium, Low) | Unit price of material | Delegation of purchase powers |
| 3. | VED (Vital, Essential, Desirable) | Operational characteristics | Storage point |
| 4. | SDE (Scaree, Difficult, Easy) | Availability of items | Purchase strategy |
| 5. | XYZ | Annual inventory valuation | To control non-moving items |
| 6. | F.S.N. (Fast, Slow, Non-moving) | Issues from stores | Obsolescence control |
| 7. | H.M.L. (High, Medium, Low) | Unit price of material | To delegate purchasing powers |
| 8. | Essential, Important Normal) | Equipment criticality | Maintenance |

## 18.18. SWOT ANALYSIS

SWOT analysis is a strategic planning technique used to help a person or organisation to identify strength, weaknesses, opportunities, and threats (SWOT) related to business competition or project planning.

SWOT analysis aims to identify the key internal and external factors seen as important for achieving and objective.

SWOT analysis is used in any decision making situation when a desired and state (objective) is defined.

**Strength :** Strength is a characteristics of the business or project that give it an advantage over others.

**Weaknesses :** These are the characteristics of the business that place the business or project at a disadvantage relative to others.

**Opportunities :** These are the elements in the environment that the business or the project could exploit to its advantage.

**Threats :** These are the elements in the environment that could cause trouble for the business or the project.

The strengths and weaknesses are the factors internal to the organisation, while opportunities and threats presented by the environment are the factors external to the organisation.

**Internal Factors (Strengths and Weaknesses)**

(*a*) Human resources.

(*b*) Physical resources (location, building, equipment etc.)

(*c*) Financial resources.

(*d*) Activities and processes including programmes and systems of the organisation.

(*e*) Past experiences.

**External Factors (Opportunities and Threats)**

(*a*) Future trends in the concerned field.

(*b*) The economy (Local, national or international)

(*c*) Funding sources.

(*d*) Demographics (Changes in age)

(*e*) Physical environment.

(*f*) Legislation (whether new legal requirement make the job difficult easier).

(*g*) Local, national or international events.

**Applications of SWOT Analysis**

1. Explore new solutions to the problems.

2. Identify the barriers that will limit the goals (objectives).
3. Decide the most effective direction.
4. Reveal possibilities and limitations for change.
5. To revise plans to give best results.
6. To enhance credibility.

## 18.19. RELIABILITY ECONOMICS

The costs and economics play a major role in the application of reliability and its attainment. The objective is not merely to produce a system of highest reliability as it requires higher cost in manufacture, research and development. The main objective is to evolve a system which reflects optimum total cost, optimum cost aspect for reliability is shown in Fig. 18.2.

The Fig. 18.2 indicates that for increasing the reliability, production cost and cost of research and development also increases. On the other hand, the cost of maintenance (including cost of spares) reduces with the increase in reliability factor. The curve of total cost when plotted against reliability will be similar in shape as shown in Fig. 18.2.

This cost curve will have minimum cost, known as optimum cost $C_o$ corresponding to optimum reliability $R_o$.

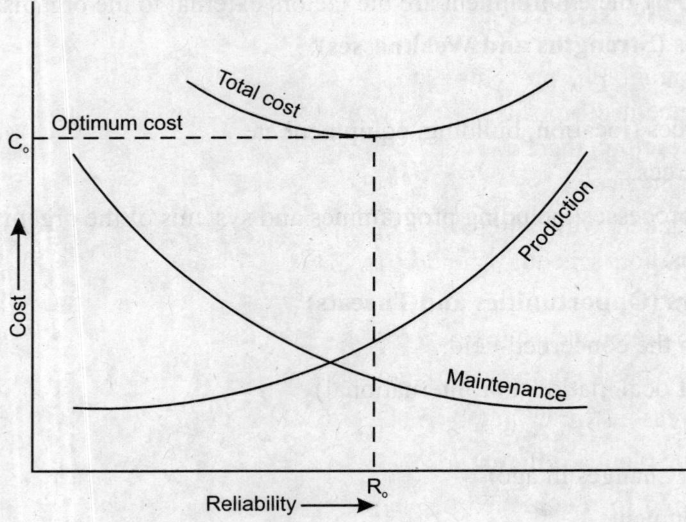


**Fig. 18.2.** Optimization of Reliability.

In the process of designing a system, be its electrical, mechanical or electronic the reliability of the system depends on a large number of parameters which directly affect the behaviour of the system. Any improvement in the reliability (quality) of the system will be accompanied by increased cost. In such a situation, it would be of interest to compare the increase cost with the improvement in the reliability factor of the system or the instruments involved. In such cases it is essential to decide whether it is worth investigating in auxiliary devices or using higher quality materials.

Reliability depends on the following factors. Therefore, attention should be given on these factors so as to make the product or system reliable.

1. Product or system design.
2. Material quality.
3. Manufacturing process.
4. Testing and inspection.
5. Maintenance system.
6. Working environment.
7. Product complexity.
8. Number of sub-assemblies and their standardization.

The curves in Fig. 18.2 show that the investment cost will generally increase with higher reliability. On the other hand, the user cost (maintenance cost including cost of spares) associated with failures will decrease as the reliability increases. The total life cycle costs will, therefore, be the sum of these two individual costs.

## 18.20. DECISION SUPPORT SYSTEM FOR MAINTENANCE

As seen in above paragraph, preventive maintenance reduce the number of breakdowns, but preventive maintenance itself means downtime of machine, although it is a planned downtime, it also requires cost. Therefore, there is a trade off (strike a balance) between, preventive maintenance and breakdown maintenance.

Care should be taken while preparing maintenance programme so that as far as possible inspection and lubrication schedule should coincide, so that machine idle time and production disruption may be less.

Presently many maintenance systems/strategies are in use in industries and selection has to be made depending on the need, complexity reliability needed and also considering technoeconomics.

There are many reasons for evaluating/selecting maintenance strategies, such as :

– With aging of the plant a different mix of tasks is required to maintain reliability.
– When it is desired to reduce maintenance expenditure without increasing risk or reducing reliability.

A good maintenance system must have an integrated information system for interacting with various areas, such as :

– Work procedures (operation and maintenance etc.)
– Reports regarding problems, defects and faults
– Work schedules, job orders.

– Work history

– Close liaison with purchasing inventory, finance, contractors etc.

Other set of informations/conditions which help in determining the strategy are :

(*a*) Is the equipment regularly available to perform planned/routine maintenance activities?

(*b*) Will the cost to shout-down the equipment be less than the cost of failure (breakdown)/

(*c*) Is equipment downtime a problem?

The resulting strategy (decision making about maintenance) must strike a balance between maintenance cost and plant reliability. The evaluation develops tools and techniques for determining the best mix of maintenance tasks.

Following strategies/systems are available for maintenance. A decision is required to be taken out of these, considering the circumstances.

– Breakdown and emergency maintenance
– Corrective maintenance
– Opportunistic maintenance
– Routine maintenance
– Scheduled/Fixed time maintenance (Preventive maintenance)
– Condition based maintenance (Predictive maintenance)
– Proactive maintenance.

## 18.21. RELIABILITY, AVAILABILITY AND MAINTAINABILITY (RAM)

Reliability and maintainability are the two important parameters which decide the performance or effectiveness of an equipment, and directly contribute to the availability of that particular equipment or product. Reliability and maintainability jointly affect availability. RAM is a new concept in maintenance management. With proper consideration of reliability, availability and maintainability (RAM) in the design, manufacturing and installation phases, the number of failures can be reduced and their consequences minimized.

### 18.21.1. Reliability

1. **Definition:** Reliability can be defined as, "the probability of an equipment performing its purpose adequately, for the period intended, under the given operating conditions".
2. **M.T.B.F. (Mean Time Between Failure) :** This is the most common reliability measurement parameter, and is defined as, "mean value of the durations of operating time between consecutive failures, under given conditions."
3. **Cause of Failure :** The main cause of failure in any equipment is that stress induced in a given component during the service life overcomes the inherent strength of the component. Therefore, in order to minimise failure, all efforts should be made to ensure that stress induced

in the equipment does not approach the limits, where permanent distortion of any of the components is likely to set in.

4. **Bath-Tub Curve :** If failure rate is plotted against time for a particular class of equipment, the curve obtained is similar to Bath-Tub as shown in Fig 18.3 below, and is normally termed as 'Bath-Tub Curve'.

5. **How to Improve Reliability:** Reliability can be improved:

   (*a*) by improving the strength of the components of the equipment.

   (*b*) by ensuring that the stress levels are contained within the normal limits.

   (*c*) by strict adherence to preventive maintenance schedule and immediate attention to even the most minor faults. This helps in retarding the ageing process resulting in increased economical serve life.

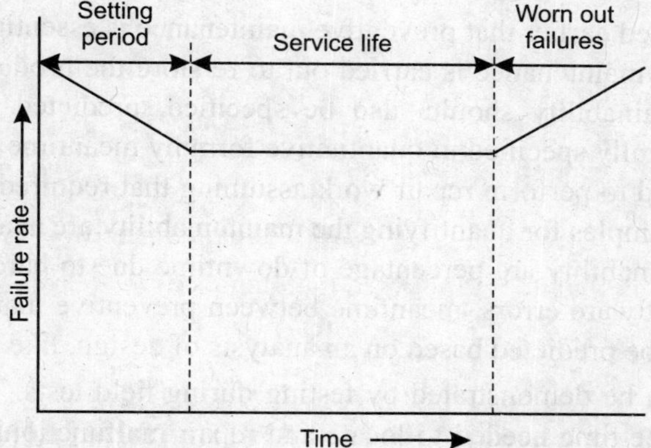


**Fig. 18.3.** Bath-Tub Curve

## 18.21.2. Maintainability

1. **Definition :** Maintainability can be defined as, "the probability that a unit, equipment or system will be re-stored to certain specified conditions within a given period, when maintenance is done with prescribed procedure and resources".

Therefore, the aim of maintainability is to reduce the down time of the equipment, which includes:

(*a*) time to carry out preventive maintenance, and

(*b*) time taken in fault analysis, and repair.

From the above, it is clear that for improving the maintainability, we have to lay down systematic procedure, and must ensure that resources required for re-storation of the equipment are provided timely.

2. **Quantity Measures for Maintainability.** These are :

   (*a*) Mean Time To Repair (M.T.T.R.). It is the mean time required for repair of an equipment. It does not include waiting.

(*b*) Mean Time Between Maintenance (M.T.B.M.). This shows the frequency of preventive maintenance.

**3. Factors Affecting the Maintainability:**

- Accessibility.
- Standardisation.
- Safety aspects.
- Availability of literature.
- Training of operators and maintenance crew.
- Maintenance procedure.
- Maintenance monitoring.

**Designing for Maintainability**

As we have discussed earlier that preventive maintenance is essential to reduce the number of failures, and corrective maintenance is carried out to re-store the product to operable conditions. Like reliability, maintainability should also be specified, predicted, analyzed and measured. Maintainability is generally specified in quantitative form by meantime to repair (MTTR). MTTR is the mean time needed to perform repair work assuming that required spare part and technician are available. Other examples for quantifying the maintainability are available. Other examples for quantifying the maintainability are percentage of downtime due to hardware failures, percentage of downtime due to software errors, meantime between preventive maintenance actions etc. The maintainability should be predicted based on an analysis of design, like reliability.

Maintainability can be demonstrated by testing during field tests. The demonstration should consist of measuring the time needed to locate and repair malfunctioning or to perform selected maintenance tasks.

**Reliability and Maintainability Trade-off**

From the discussions we had till now, notice that availability of a system is a complex function of reliability, maintainability and supply effectiveness.

This can be expressed as ;

$$A_S = f(R_S, M_S, S_S)$$

where,

$A_S$ = System availability,

$R_S$ = System reliability,

$M_S$ = System maintainability, and

$S_S$ = Supply effectiveness.

We have also discussed earlier that,

Availability, $$A = \frac{MTBF}{MTBF + MTTR} = \frac{1/\lambda}{\left(\frac{1}{\lambda}\right) + \left(\frac{1}{\mu}\right)}$$

where,

$\lambda$ = constant hazard rate,

$\therefore$ $1/\lambda$ = Mean time between failure (MTBF)

and $\dfrac{1}{\mu}$ = Mean time to repair (MTTR)

Let the ratio,

$$\frac{\text{mean downtime}}{\text{mean time to failure}} = \frac{\left(\frac{1}{\mu}\right)}{\left(\frac{1}{\lambda}\right)}$$

$$= \frac{\lambda}{\mu} = P$$

Then, $$A = \frac{1}{1+P}$$

From the above, it is clear that reliability, maintainability, and supply effectiveness are the inputs and the availability is the output. But the designer is required to achieve a balance between performance, which includes reliability and maintainability, and cost. In view of this, he is required to decide whether to opt for achieving maximum availability for a given cost or to achieve a required availability atleast cost.

### 18.21.3. Availability

Availability of an equipment is the proportion of time that the equipment is functional. Theoretically, this can be indicated as (Fig. 18.4 be referred),

$$\text{Availability} = \frac{\text{M.T.B.F.}}{\text{M.T.B.F.} + \text{M.T.T.R.}}$$

where, M.T.T.R. is Mean Time To Repair

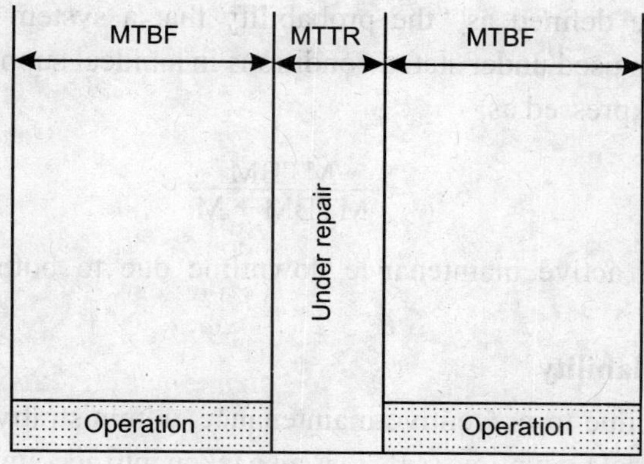


**Fig. 18.4.** A concept of availability.

When a system is unavailable due to breakdowns and is put back into operation after each breakdown with proper repairs, the mean time between breakdown is defined as the mean time between failure (MTBF). Frequently, system is unavailable on account of periodic inspections or preventive maintenance and not because of breakdowns. The time spent for this is termed as preventive maintenance downtime. When preventive-maintenance downtime is zero or is not considered, MTBM is the same as MTBF. System downtime is the total time for which a system is down for active maintenance, and varies from one type of failure to another.

Considering above, "Availability" can be classified in three ways, namely: (*a*) Inherent availability, (*b*) Achieved availability, and (*c*) Operational availability. Each of these are discussed hereunder :

**(*A*) Inherent Availability**

This is "the probability that a system or equipment shall operate satisfactorily, when used under stated conditions in an ideal support environment, without consideration for any preventive maintenance at any given time.":

This definition excludes:

(*a*) time required for preparation,

(*b*) preventive maintenance downtime,

(*c*) downtime due to non-availability of supplies, and

(*d*) downtime due to administrative reasons.

$$\text{Inherent Availability} = A_i = \frac{\text{MTBF}}{\text{MTBF} + \text{MTTR}}$$

In this definition "ideal support environment" means the ready availability of tools, parts, manpower etc.

**(*B*) Achieved Availability**

In this, downtime due to preventive maintenance is also taken into account. The achieved availability can be defined as "the probability that a system or equipment shall operate satisfactorily, when used under stated conditions in an ideal support environment at any given time." It may be expressed as,

$$A_a = \frac{\text{MTBM}}{\text{MTBM} + \text{M}}$$

where, $M$ = Mean active maintenance downtime due to both, preventive and corrective maintenance.

**(*C*) Operational Availability**

In this, downtime due to preventive maintenance, administrative reasons and due to supply known as Managerial Downtime (MDT) is also taken into account. The operational availability can be defined as "probability that a system or equipment shall operate satisfactorily, when used under stated conditions and in an actual supply environment at any given time". It may be expressed as,

$$A_o = \frac{\text{MTBM}}{\text{MTBM} + \text{MDT}}$$

**Example 18.7.** *An equipment has a MTBF as 1000 hours. The time to manage spare parts is 1 hour. Repair consumed a time of 5 hours. The mean time required for record keeping and other administrative work is 1 hour. Determine the availability of the equipment.*

**Solution.** Availability $= \dfrac{1000}{1000 + 1 + 5 + 1}$

$= \dfrac{1000}{1007}$ 0.99 or **99% Ans.**

## 18.22. SYSTEM RELIABILITY

Till now, we have discussed reliability and probability of failure for components or elements of a system. Calculation of reliability or probability of failure of a system is very difficult, therefore, the system is generally broken down to subsystems and elements. The reliability factors then can be estimated. Here, we shall discuss the methods for determining system reliability from the reliability factors of the subsystems and elements.

Different elements/components or subsystems of a product or device can be connected basically in following 3 ways :

(*i*) Series.

(*ii*) Parallel.

(*iii*) Combined (*i.e.* series and parallel system together).

## 18.23. SYSTEMS CONNECTED IN SERIES

This is a simplest combination of units that form a system. This is shown where the system consists of *n* units which are connected in series.

1 ---- 2 ---- 3 ---------- n →

Let the successful operation of these individual units be represented by $X_1, X_2 .........X_n$ and their respective probabilities by,

$P(X_1), P(X_2)..........P(X_n)$.

For the successful operation of the system, it is necessary that all the *n* units function satisfactorily. Utilising the probability concept,

(*i*) *Probability of system* (with dependent dissimilar units),

$$P(S) = P(X_1 \text{ and } X_2 \text{ and.......and } X_n)$$

$$= P(X_1) \times P(X_2/X_1 \text{ and } X_2) \times .......... \times P(X_n/X_1 \text{ and } X_2 \text{ and.......and } X_n - 1).$$

Here, $P(X_2/X_1)$ represents the probability of the successful operation of unit 2 under the condition that unit 1 operates successfully.

(*ii*) Probability of system (with independent identical units),

$P(S)=P(X_1) \times P(X_2) \times .........\times P(X_n)$.

This shows that the system fails, if any of the unit fail *i.e.*

$$P(S) = 0, \text{ if } P(X_1) \text{ or } P(X_2) \text{ or } P(X_3) \text{ or } P(X_n) = 0.$$

Conversely, this also shows that if even one element's probability of functioning is improved, the whole system's reliability is improved.

**Example 18.8.** *Consider a series system, in which the probability of each element is given below :*

*Determine the system's reliability.*

**Solution.** Since the probabilities of the elements are :

$$p_1 = 0.8$$
$$p_2 = 0.7$$
$$p_3 = 0.9$$
$$p_4 = 0.6$$

∴ System's Reliability $R_s = 0.8 \times 0.7 \times 0.9 \times 0.6$

$= \mathbf{0.3024.}$ **Ans.**

**Note :** From this example, we observe the following :

(*i*) The system's reliability in the series system is lower than the least reliability of the elements.

(*ii*) If the probability of the element having least probability is improved from 0.6 to 0.8, the system reliability improves from 0.3024 to 0.4032 only, *i.e.* it is not appreciably improved. Therefore, it is difficult to achieve high reliability with the series system.

**Example 18.9.** *At an electric generating system, the reliability and failure rate of each of the units in the system is given below :*

| ***Unit*** | ***Reliability*** | ***Failure rate*** |
|---|---|---|
| Furnace | 0.6 | $8 \times 10^{-3}$ |
| Boiler | 0.8 | $12 \times 10^{-3}$ |
| Chimney | 0.9 | $12 \times 10^{-3}$ |
| Super heater | 0.9 | $4 \times 10^{-3}$ |
| Turbine | 0.85 | $3 \times 10^{-3}$ |
| Generator | 0.89 | $15 \times 10^{-3}$ |

*Find the total reliability of the power station, and its failure rate.*

**Solution:** Reliability of the system,

$$R_s = P_1 \times p_2 \times P_3 \times P_4 \times P_5 \times P_6$$

$$= 0.6 \times 0.8 \times 0.9 \times 0.9 \times 0.85 \times 0.89$$

$$= \mathbf{0.3} \quad \textbf{Ans.}$$

Failure rate,

$$\lambda = 10^{-3}(8 + 12 + 12 + 4 + 3 + 15) = 54 \times 10^{-3}$$

$$= \mathbf{0.54} \quad \textbf{Ans.}$$

**Example 18.10.** *In an hydraulic system, following three elements are connected in series with independent reliability factors as given below. What is the reliability of the control system ?*

| | |
|---|---|
| Element 1 | 0.98 |
| Element 2 | 0.92 |
| Element 3 | 0.90 |

**Solution.** Since the elements are connected in series and have independent performance characteristics, the system reliability,

$$R_s = 0.98 \times 0.92 \times 0.9$$

$$= \mathbf{0.811} \quad \textbf{Ans.}$$

**System's Reliability in terms of Probability of Failure**

If the system consists of $n$ identical elements in series, and if each element has a reliability factor $p$, and probability of failure as $q$. The systems reliability for independently functioning elements,

$$R_s = p \times p \times p \times ........ \times p = \boldsymbol{p^n}$$

or considering failure rate,

$$R_s = (1 - q) \times (1 - q) \times ......... \times (1 - q) = \mathbf{(1 - q)^n}$$

If reliability factor is very high, $q$ is very small, and in such case,

$R_s = (1 - q)^n @ \mathbf{1 - nq}$.

**Example 18.11.** *If the probability of each of the 10 components connected in series is 0.99, determine the reliability of the system considering the approximation method.*

**Solution.** Reliability of the system,

$$R_s = p^n = (1 - q)^n$$

using approximation method,

$$R_s = 1 - nq, \text{ here } q = (1 - p) = 1 - 10 \times 0.01$$

$$= 1 - 0.1 = \mathbf{0.9} \quad \textbf{Ans.}$$

**Note :** While calculating with original formula, it gives $R_s = (0.99)^{10} = 0.9044$.

Thus, approximation formula gives almost the same value.

**Example 18.12.** *A system has ten identical components connected in series. It is desired that the system should have the reliability of 0.95. Determine how good the performance of each component should be?*

**Solution.** Since the components are in series, the system reliability,

$$R_s = p^{10}$$

where, $p$ = component reliability

Therefore, $R_s = 0.95 = p^{10}$

or $p = 0.9949.$

Hence, in order to get system reliability of 0.95, each component must have a reliability factor of **0.9949 Ans.**

**Alterative Method**

Using approximation method,

$$R_s = 0.95 = (1-q)^n = 1 - nq = 1 - 10q$$

$$\therefore \quad q = \frac{1-0.95}{10} = 0.005$$

$$\therefore \quad p = 1 - q = 1 - 0.005 = 0.995$$

Hence, reliability factor of each component = **0.995 Ans.**

## 18.24. SYSTEMS CONNECTED IN PARALLEL

A parallel system is shown below, which has *N* number of elements connected together in Fig 16.1.

In a parallel system if any one element fails, the system still continue to function. Unless all the elements (components) fail simultaneously, the system does function. The reliability of the system can be calculated very easily by considering the conditions for system failure.

Let $P_k$ = Probability of any element $k$ functioning at a given time, $t$.

Then,

$(1 - p_k) = q_k$ = Probability of element $k$ failing in the system.

$\therefore$ The probability of all the elements failing together.

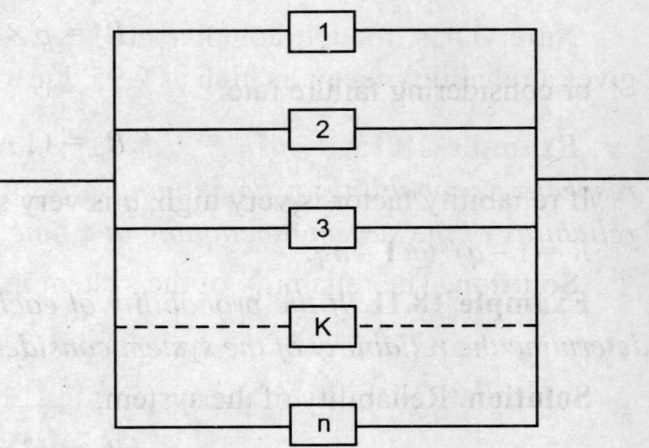

**Fig. 18.5**

$$= q_1 \times q_2 \times q_3 \times \ldots\ldots. \times q_k \times \ldots. \times q_n$$
$$= (1-p_1) \times (1-p_2) \times (1-p_3) \times \ldots \times (1-p_k) \times \ldots. (1-p_n).$$

Therefore, the probability of a parallel of system functions at a given time $t$ is,

$$R_p = 1 - q_1 \times q_2 \times q_3 \times \ldots. \times q_k \times \ldots. \times q_n,$$

$$1 - \{(1-p_1) \times (1-p_2) \times (1-p_3) \times \ldots \times (1-p_k) \ldots\ldots \times (1-p_n)\}$$

**Example 18.13.** *A system consisting of 3 components in parallel, has the component reliability of 0.90 and are independent of each other.*

*Determine the system reliability.*

**Solution.** As we know that,

$$R_p = 1 - \{(1 - p_1) \times (1 - p_2) \times (1 - p_3)\}$$

Here, $p_1 = p_2 = P_3 = 0.90$

$\therefore$ $R_p = 1 - (1 - 0.90)^3 = 1 - (0.10)^3 = 0.999$

Hence, systems reliability = **0.999 Ans.**

**Note :** This reveals that a parallel system greatly increases the system reliability.

**Example 18.14.** *A parallel system composed of ten identical independent components, has a system reliability as 0.95. What is the reliability factor of the components ?*

**Solution.**

As $R_p = 1 - (1 - p)^{10}$

or $0.95 = 1 - (1 - p)^{10}$

$\therefore$ $(1 - p)^{10} = 0.05$

$\therefore$ $1 - p = 0.7419$

or $p = 0.2581$ **Ans.**

**Note:** Thus, though components have very low reliability factor of 0.2581, still the system gives a reliability factor as high as 0.95 due to composition of ten identical components in parallel.

**Example 18.15.** *Consider a system having two elements connected in parallel with their respective probability of functioning at any time t, are : $p_1 = 0.9$ and $p_2 = 0.8$. Calculate the reliability of the system functioning at a time t.*

**Solution.** The reliability of the system in parallel,

$$R_p = 1 - \{(1 - p_1) \times (1 - p_2)\}$$

1

2

where, $p_1 = 0.9$

$P_2 = 0.8$

$\therefore$ $R_p = 1 - \{(1 - 0.9) \times (1 - 0.8)\} = 1 - (0.1 \times 0.2)$

$= 1 - 0.02 =$ **0.98 Ans.**

**Example 18.16.** *Three lamps are connected in parallel to produce light in a hall. The reliabilities of the lamps are 0.92,0.95 and 0.96. Find the reliability of the total lamp system.*

*If these lamps are connected in series, determine the reliability of the system.*

**Solution.**

(*A*) When the lamps are in parallel.

$$R_p = \{(1 - p_1) \times (1 - p_2) \times (1 - p_3)\}$$

where, $p_1 = 0.92$

$p_2 = 0.95$

$p_3 = 0.96$

$$\therefore \quad R_p = 1 - 1\{(1 - 0.92) \times (1 - 0.95) \times (1 - 0.96)\}$$

$$= 1 - (0.08 \times 0.05 \times 0.04) = 1 - 0.00016$$

$$\therefore \quad R_p = 0.99984 \text{ or } \mathbf{99.984\%\ Ans.}$$

(*B*) When the lamps are in series :

$$R_s = p_1 \times p_2 \times p_3 = 0.92 \times 0.95 \times 0.96$$

$$\therefore \quad R_s = \mathbf{0.82 \text{ or } 82\%\ Ans.}$$

**Example 18.17.** *Two electrical resistance having their failure rates* $\lambda_2 = 0.1$ *and* $\lambda_1 = 0.2$ *per hour. Calculate their reliability after 10 hours, if they are: (a) in parallel system, and (b) in series system.*

**Solution.**

(*A*) If the system is having parallel connections :

$$R_p = 1 - \{(1 - e^{-\lambda 1t})\,(1 - e^{-\lambda 2t})\}$$

Since $p_1 = e^{\lambda 1t}$ and $p_2 = e^{\lambda 2t}$

$$\therefore \quad R_p = e^{-\lambda 1t} + e^{-\lambda 2t} - e^{-(\lambda 1 + \lambda 2)t}$$

where, $\lambda_1 = 0.1$ and $\lambda_2 = 0.2$ and $t = 10$

$$R_p = e^{-0.1 \times 10} + e^{-0.2 \times 10} - e^{-(0.1 + 0.2)10}$$

$$R_p = e^{-1} + e^{-2} - e^{-3} = 0.3679 + 0.1353 - 0.0498$$

$$= 0.4534.$$

$$= \mathbf{45.34\%\ \ Ans.}$$

(*B*) If the system is having series connections :

$$R_s = e^{-\lambda 2t} \times e^{-\lambda 2t} = e^{-(\lambda 1 + \lambda 2)t} = e^{-(0.1 + 0.2)10} = e^{-3}$$

$$= \mathbf{0.0498 \text{ or } 4.98\%\ \ Ans.}$$

**Note :** This shows that with the resistances reliability is about 10 times with parallel connections as compared to that of series connections.

**Example 18.18.** Reliability of one single path of a circuit is 0.4. Calculate the number of parallel paths to obtain the reliability of the system as 0.8.

**Solution.**

As, $$R_p = 1 - (1 - p)^n$$

where, $$R_p = 0.8$$

$$p = 0.4$$

$$n = \text{number of paths in parallel} = ?$$

∴ By putting the values, we get,

$$0.8 = 1 - (1 - 0.4)^n$$

or $$(1 - 0.4)^n = 0.2$$

or $$(0.6)^n = 0.2$$

∴ $$n \log 0.6 = \log 0.2$$

∴ $$n = \frac{1.6094}{0.5108} = \textbf{3 paths Ans.}$$

## 18.25. SYSTEMS CONNECTED IN SERIES AND PARALLEL COMBINED

Upto now, we have discussed the reliability of the systems having either elements connected in series or in parallel only. Now we shall discuss the systems which have both, series or parallel connections. Systems with such combined connections can be of following two types:

**1. General Series-Parallel Connections**

This type of system consists of stage 1, stage 2 .....stage $K$ connected in series, while each stage is having a number of parallel elements. Such a configuration is shown in the Fig. 18.5 given below:

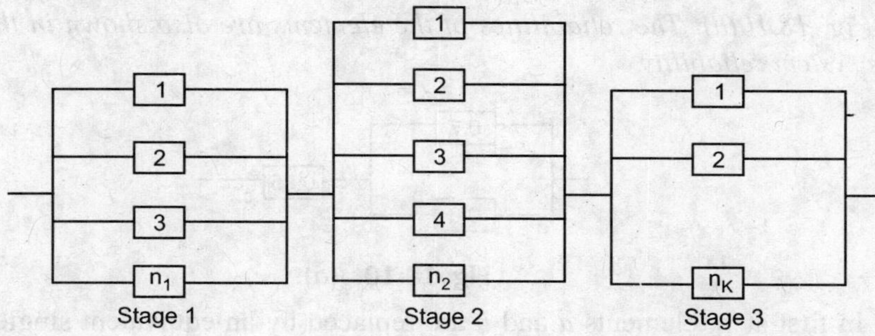


**Fig. 18.6.** General Series-Parallel Connections.

Such problems can be solved in two phases. In first phase, all the stages are individually solved to know their reliability as a subsystem, thus making the system as composed of K sub-system in series as shown in Fig 18.7. In second phase, this series system is solved to give the combined reliability of the entire system.

Stage 1 — Stage 2 — Stage K

**Fig. 18.7.**

**2. General Parallel-Series Connections**

This type of systems consist of $K$ parallel branches, each branch containing a number of elements connected in series. Such a configuration is shown in Fig. 18.8.

Such problems are also solved in two phases. In first phase, reliability of individual branches, which are having elements in series, are calculated. This reduces the system to a simple parallel system as shown in Fig. 18.8, and the reliability of this can be calculated in second phase.

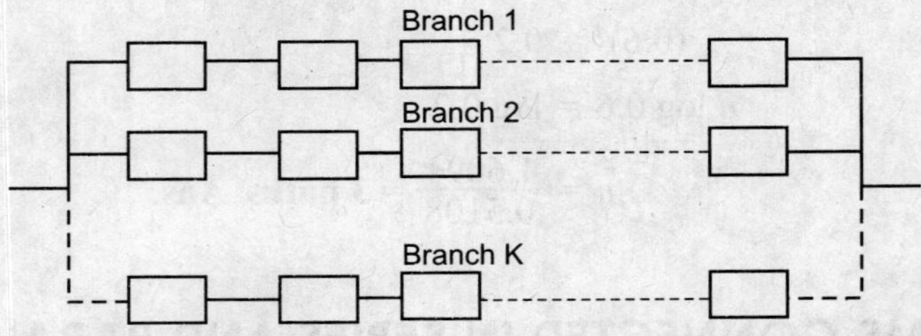


**Fig. 18.8.** General parallel-series connections.

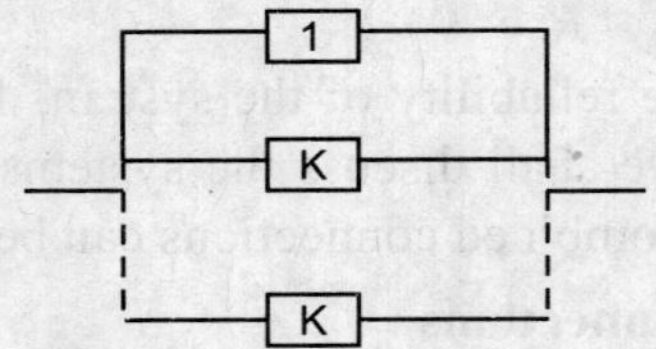


**Fig. 18.9.**

**Example 18.19.** *A system consisting of three elements a, b and c is having a configuration as shown in the Fig. 18.10(a). The reliabilities of the elements are also shown in the Fig. 18.10(b). Determine the system reliability.*

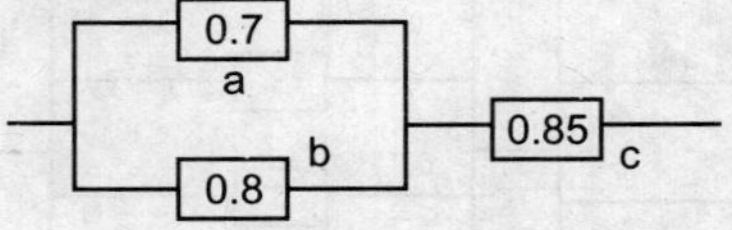


**Fig. 18.10.** (*a*).

**Solution.** In first step, elements $a$ and $b$ are replaced by an equivalent single element $d$. The reliability of which should be equal to the combine reliability of $a$ and $b$.

$$\therefore \quad R_d = \{(1 - 0.7)(1 - 0.8)\}$$

$$= 1 - 3 \times .2$$

$= 1 - 0.06$

$= 0.94.$

The given configuration, is, thus, modified to that shown in Fig. 18.10 (*b*).

d c

0.94 0.85

**Fig. 18.10.** (b).

Therefore, the reliability of the system is,

$$R = 0.94 \times 0.85$$

$$= \mathbf{0.799 \text{ or } 79.9\%.\ Ans.}$$

**Example 18. 20.** *Calculate the system reliability for the units connected as shown in Fig 18.11 (a).*

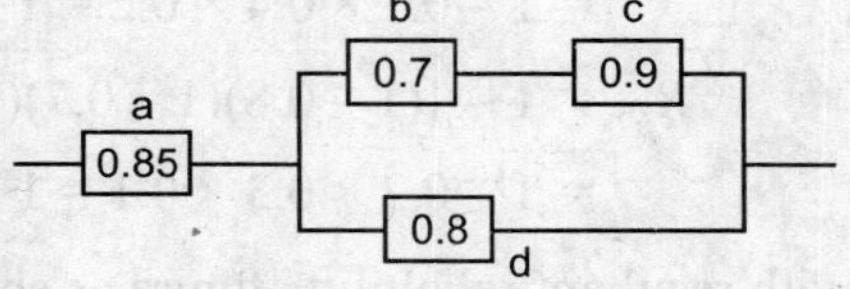


**Fig. 18.11** (*a*).

**Solution.**

**1st Step :** In this system units *b* and *c* are first replaced by unit *e*.

$$R_e = 0.7 \times 0.9 = 0.63.$$

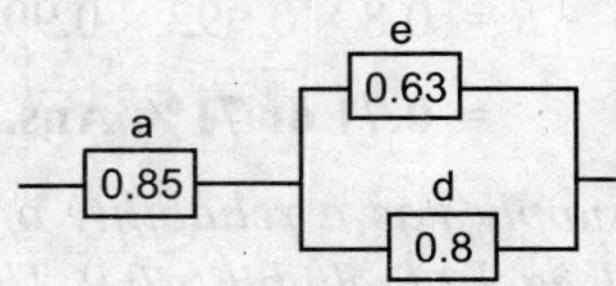


**Fig. 18.11** (*b*).

**II Step :** *d* and *e* units are then replaced with unit *f*.

$$R_f = 1 - \{(1 - 0.63) \times (1 - 0.8)\}$$

$$= 1 - 0.37 \times 0.2 = 1 - 0.074$$

$$= 0.926.$$

a f

0.85 0.926

**Fig. 18.11** (*c*).

**III Step :** The system now reduces to simple series system, the reliability of which is,

$$R = 0.85 \times 0.926$$

$$= \mathbf{0.7871 \text{ or } 78.71\%\ Ans.}$$

**Example 18.21.** *Consider a system with series and parallel connections as shown in the Fig. 18.12 (a). The probabilities of functioning of each of the elements is given in figure itself. Find the reliability of the whole system.*

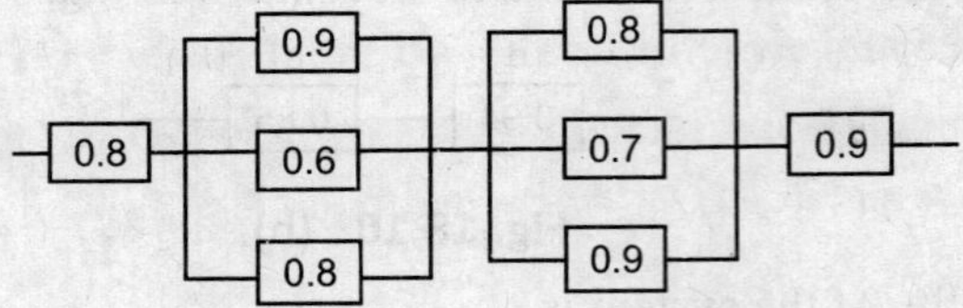


**Fig. 18.12** (*a*).

**Solution. Step I:** Reducing parallel system to single units :

$$R_{p1} = 1 - \{(1 - 0.9)(1 - 0.6)(1 - 0.8)\}$$
$$= 1 - 0.1 \times 0.4 \times 0.2 = 1 - 0.008 = 0.992.$$

and
$$R_{p2} = 1 - \{(1 - 0.8)(1 - 0.7)(1 - 0.9)\}$$
$$= 1 - 0.2 \times 0.3 \times 0.1 = 1 - 0.006 = 0.994.$$

**Step II:** Replacing units with resultant reliability, figure as shown in Fig. 16.11(*b*)

0.80 — 0.992 — 0.994 — 0.9

**Fig. 18.12** (*b*)

The reliability of the system can then be calculated as follows :

$$R = 0.8 \times 0.992 \times 0.994 \times 0.9$$
$$= \mathbf{0.71 \text{ or } 71\% \text{ Ans.}}$$

**Example 18.22.** *An electric supply has a reliability of 0.9, A house wiring connects three lamps of reliability 0.9 with a switch each of reliability 0.9. There are two fans of reliability 0.8 with switches of reliability 0.9. One heater is also used with a reliability of 0.7 with a switch of reliability 0.8. Calculate the total reliability of the house wiring system.*

**Solution.** Figure for the wiring system indicating reliability of each is shown at Fig. 18.13.

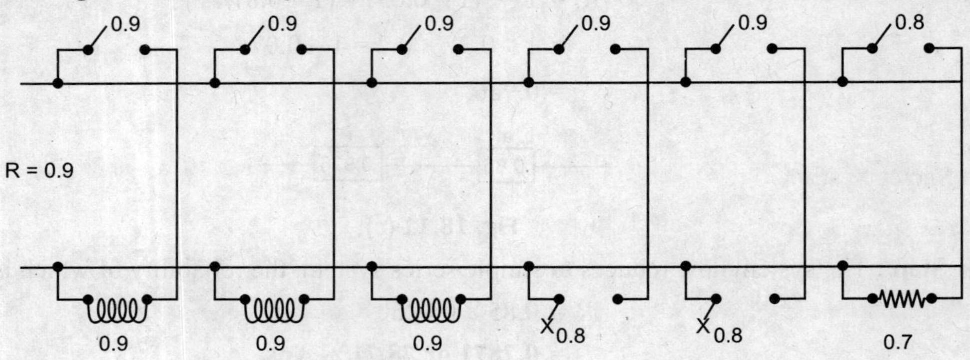


**Fig. 18.13** House wiring system connected to supply of $R = 0.9$.

Reliability of supply = $R_1$ = 0.9

Reliability of lamp and switch $R_2 = R_3 = R_4 = 0.9 \times 0.9 = 0.81$

Reliability of fan and switch $R_5 = R_3 = 0.9 \times 0.8 = 0.72$

Reliability of resistance and switch $R_7 = 0.8 \times 0.7 = 0.56$.

Since all these seven connections, including the supply system are in parallel, the total reliability,

$$R = 1 - \{(1 - R_1)(1 - R_2)(1 - R_3)(1 - R_4)(1 - R_5)(1 - R_6)(1 - R_7)\}$$

$$= 1 - \{(1 - 0.9)(1 - 0.81)(1 - 0.81)(1 - 0.81)(1 - 0.72)(1 - 0.72)[(1 - 0.56)\}$$

$$= 1 - 0.1 \times 0.19 \times 0.19 \times 0.19 \times 0.28 \times 0.28 \times 0.44$$

$$= 1 - 0.0000236$$

$$= 1 - 0.9999764 \text{ or } \mathbf{99.99764\%} \quad \textbf{Ans.}$$

## 18.26. MEAN TIME BETWEEN FAILURE OF THE SYSTEM

This is sometimes known Mean Time To Failure (MTTF)

**1. In Parallel System,**

$$\text{MTBF} = m = \frac{1}{\lambda} + \frac{1}{2\lambda} + \frac{1}{3\lambda} + \ldots\ldots \frac{1}{n\lambda}$$

where, $\lambda$ = failure rate

and $n$ = number of components in parallel.

**2. In series system,**

$$\text{MTBF} = m = \frac{1}{\lambda_1 + \lambda_2 + \ldots \lambda_n} = \frac{1}{n\,\lambda}$$

**Example 18.23.** *Three electric lamps are connected in parallel. The failure rate of each lamp is $\lambda = 0.001$ per hour. Find the Mean Time Between Failures.*

*If the same lamps are connected in series, calculate MTBF.*

**Solution.**

**(*A*) In Parallel System:**

$$\text{MTBF} = m = \frac{1}{\lambda} + \frac{1}{2\lambda} + \frac{1}{3\lambda} = \frac{1}{0.001} + \frac{1}{2 \times 0.001} + \frac{1}{3 \times 0.001}$$

$$= 1000 + 500 + 333$$

$$= \textbf{1833 hrs. Ans.}$$

**(*B*) In Series System**

$$\text{MTBF} = m = \frac{1}{\lambda_1 + \lambda_2 + \lambda_3}$$

$$= \frac{1}{3\lambda}$$

$$= \frac{1}{3 \times 0.001} = \textbf{333 Ans.}$$

## 18.27. RELIABILITY IMPROVEMENT

The basic means of improving the reliability is to: (*a*) reduce chances of break down, and (*b*) increase the strength of the component of the product or equipment, while ensuring that the stress levels are either contained or reduced.

Some of the means for achieving this are :

**1. Means for Improving the Strength**

(*i*) Taking greater care in the quality control in selecting the materials and in manufacturing processes involved.

(*ii*) Adherence of the manufacturers recommendations strictly during the initial running of the product or equipment. This reduces overall wear.

(*iii*) Following standardisation and simplification techniques.

(*iv*) Adopting built-in redundancy.

(*v*) Recommending the economic life of the product or equipment and timely discard to prevent adverse effects.

**2. Improvement Through Reduction of Stress**

(*i*) Avoid over-use/over-loading.

(*ii*) Ensure prevention of 'misuse' by training the operator for improvement in his performance which would lead to significant reduction is stress. Operator continuity results in the building up of operators pride in equipment performance and prevent its 'misuse', 'over-use' and 'over-loading'.

(*iii*) Increase in automation, so as reduce the effects of operator failures.

## 18.28. IMPROVING RELIABILITY DURING DESIGN

It should be remembered that if the reliability of the equipment or product is to be improved, cost of its design and development increases, while cost of repair and maintenance decreases.

Reliability engineer helps the design engineer by defining areas needing improvement and by assisting in the development of alternatives. Following are some approaches used in improving a design :

(*i*) Review the user's needs to see, if the unreliable parts are really necessary. If not required eliminate such parts. If they are required, examine if their reliability and availability can be improved either through changes in the design or by improving the maintenance programme.

(*ii*) Use redundancy.

(*iii*) Use standard parts whose reliability has been proven by actual field usage.

(*iv*) Use derating to ensure that the parts are applied lesser stresses than those which they can withstand.

(*v*) Use 'robust' design, so that product can handle unexpected environment.

(*vi*) Control the operating environment to reduce failure rates. For example, electronic components are required to be protected against the climate, shocks and higher temperature.

(*vii*) Recommending specified replacement schedules so as to remove and replace low-reliability parts before they reach the wear-out stage.

(*viii*) Tests are regularly performed during 'burn-in' period and detect 'infant mortality' failures so as to eliminate sub-standard components.

(*ix*) Conduct research and development of those components which contribute most of the unreliability.

## Use of Pareto Principle in Reliability Improvement

Pareto principle when applied to reliability states that a majority of the failures may be attributed to only a small proportion of the many possible causes. These 'vital few' out of several causes are identified for tackling the problem to show significant result. The Fig. 18.14 given below, also known as 'Pareto Chart' or 'Pareto analysis' indicates that factors leading to a majority of the defects may be relatively few.

Pareto analysis have also been discussed in the chapter on "Total Quality Management".

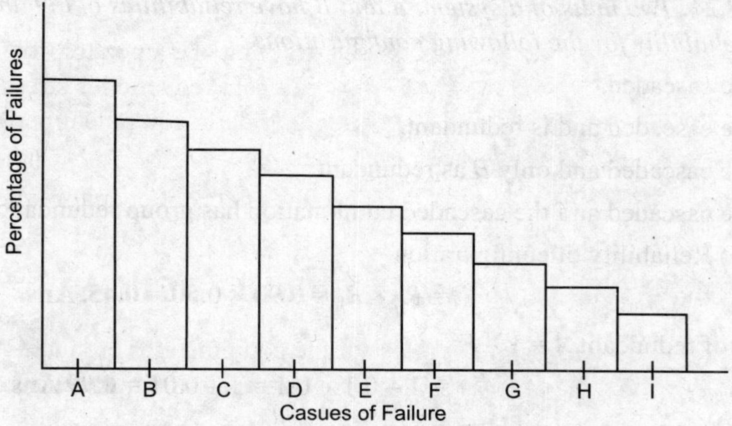


**Fig. 18.14.** Pareto analysis in reliability improvement.

# 18.29. FACTORS AFFECTING RELIABILITY

Reliability depends on the following factors. Therefore, attention should be given on these factors so as to make the product or system reliable:

1. Product or system design.
2. Material quality.
3. Manufacturing process.
4. Testing and inspection.
5. Maintenance system.
6. Working environment.
7. Product complexity.
8. Number of sub-assemblies and their standardization.

## 18.30. REDUNDANCY

When either it is not possible to manufacture highly reliable components or the cost of manufacturing, such components is very high, the system reliability can be improved by of introducing redundancies. This involves the creation of additional parallel paths in the system. In parallel redundancy, two or more elements operate at the sametime to accomplish the task, although any single element is capable of handling the job independently in case of failure of the other elements.

Redundancy technique utilise two parallel elements to reduce the probability of failure.

$$\text{Reliability} = 1 - (p_f)^2 = 1 - F^2$$

### Group Redundancy

In practical approach, the purpose of group redundancy is to provide each channel of elements^ which perform a function, with another duplicate channel. Thus, we have a normal channel or a redundant (standby) channel.

The probability of failure of a system containing a total number of $N$ elements, $n$ elements in each group and having separate redundant groups, is given by $p_f = N.\ nt/T$.

**Example 18.24.** *Two units of a system, A and B have reliabilities of 0.9 and 0.50 respectively. Determine the reliability for the following configurations* :

- *A* and *B* are cascaded.
- *A* and *B* are cascaded and is redundant.
- *A* and *B* are cascaded and only *B* as redundant.
- *A* and *B* are cascaded and the cascaded combination has group redundancy.

**Solution.** (*a*) Reliability of configuration

$$= R_a \times R_b = 0.90 \times 0.50 = \mathbf{0.45.\ Ans.}$$

(*b*) Reliability of redundant $A = 1 - F^2$

$$= 1 - 0.1 \times 0.1 = 1 - 0.01 = \mathbf{0.99\ Ans.}$$

Similarly, reliability of redundant $B$

$$= 1 - F^2 = 1 - 0.5 \times 0.5 = 1 - 0.25 = 0.75$$

∴ Reliability of configuration

$$= 0.99 \times 0.75 = \mathbf{0.74}\quad \mathbf{Ans.}$$

(c) Reliability of $A = 0.9$

Reliability of redundant

$$B = 1 - F^2 = 1 - 0.5 \times 0.5 = 0.75$$

∴ Reliability of cascaded combination

$$= 0.9 \times 0.50 = 0.45$$

∴ Reliability of group redundancy

$$= 1 - F^2 = 1 - (1 - 0.45)^2,$$

$$= 1 - 0.55 \times 0.55 = 1 - 0.28. = \mathbf{0.72} \quad \textbf{Ans.}$$

**Example 18.25.** *A system consists of 1000 elements, each having a M.T.B.F. of 100,000 hours. Its cumulative uprooting time is one hour,*

(*a*) What is the probability of failure ?

(*b*) What is the probability of failure, if it is designed in a group redundant manner each group consisting of 10 elements ?

(*c*) What is the Reliability Improvement Factor ?

**Solution.**

(*a*) Since, $n = 1000$ elements

$t = 1$ hour

$T = 100,000$ hours

Probability of failure,

$$pf_1 = \frac{nt}{T} = \frac{1000 \times 1}{100,000} = \mathbf{0.01} \textbf{ Ans.}$$

(*b*) In group redundancy,

$$pf_2 = N.n. \left(\frac{t}{T}\right)^2$$

where, $N = 10$ elements

$$= 1000 \times 10 \times \left(\frac{1}{10^5}\right)^2 = \frac{10^4}{10^{10}} = \mathbf{10^{-6}} \textbf{ Ans.}$$

(*c*) Reliability Improvement Factor,

$$Q = \frac{Pf_1}{Pf_2} = \frac{0.01}{10^{-6}} = 10^4 = \mathbf{10,000} \textbf{ Ans.}$$

**Example 18.26:** *If two identical units each having a reliability of 99.0 percent for specified mission time, are used in parallel redundancy, what overall reliability will be obtained ? Also, find reliability improvement factor.*

**Solution.** Overall reliability

$$R = 1 - q_1.q_2 = 1 - \{(1 - 0.99)(1 - 0.99)\}$$

$$= 0.9999 \text{ or } \mathbf{99.99\%} \quad \textbf{Ans.}$$

Reliability Improvement Factor,

$$Q = \frac{pf_1}{pf_2} = \frac{1 - 0.99}{1 - 0.9999} = \frac{0.01}{0.0001} = \mathbf{100} \textbf{ Ans.}$$

**Example 18.27.** *The reliability factor of a unit has been increased from 0.8 to 0.9. Determine reliability improvement factor.*

**Solution.**

Since, the probability of failure in first case,

$$pf_1 = 1 - 0.8 = 0.2.$$

and, the probability of failure in second case,

$$pf_2 = 1 - 0.9 = 0.1$$

Therefore, Reliability Improvement Factor,

$$Q = \frac{pf_1}{pf_2} = \frac{0.2}{0.1} = 2 \textbf{ Ans.}$$

**Note :** Here, we observe that if the reliability of the system is increased from 80% to 90%, the probability of failure is reduced to half and consequently the system has become twice as reliable as the first system.

**Example. 18.28.** *A complex electronic system has four vacuum tubes for operation whose M.T.B.F. is 10,000 hours, (a) If the system is changed by replacing vacuum tubes with 16 transistors, the MTBF increases to 80,000 hours, find the usefulness of the transistors for reliability, (b) If the number of transistors provided are 32, determine its effect on overall reliability of the system.*

**Solution.**

(*a*) (*i*) Probability of failure with vacuum tubes,

$$pf_1 = n_1 \times \frac{t}{T_1} = 4 \times \frac{t}{10,000} = \frac{t}{2500}$$

(*ii*) Probability of failure with 16 transistors,

$$pf_2 = n_2 \times \frac{t}{T_2} = 16 \times \frac{t}{80,000} = \frac{t}{5000.}$$

Reliability Improvement Factor,

$$Q_1 = \frac{pf_1}{pf_2} = \frac{t/2500}{t/5000} = 2 \textbf{ Ans.}$$

This shows that application of transistors is useful, as it has improved the reliability of the system.

(*b*) The probability of failure with 32 transistors,

$$pf_3 = \frac{t}{T_3} = 32 \times \frac{t}{80,000} = \frac{t}{2,500}$$

$\therefore$ Reliability Improvement factor, $Q_2 = \frac{pf_1}{pf_2} = \frac{t/2500}{t/5000} = 1.$

Thus, by increasing the number of transistors from 16 to 32 (the principle is applicable for all the components) the reliability of the system has reduced. Therefore, for higher reliability, number of components or parts should be as less as possible.

## 18.31. STANDBY REDUNDANCY

Standby redundancy is another type of redundancy that can be introduced in a system. Comparison of parallel system and standby system is shown in the Fig. 18.15 (*a*) and (*b*). In parallel system, all the paths are active from the beginning of the operation of the system till both of its elements fail. In this system, all the paths are not in operation since beginning, but will be operating when first system fails.

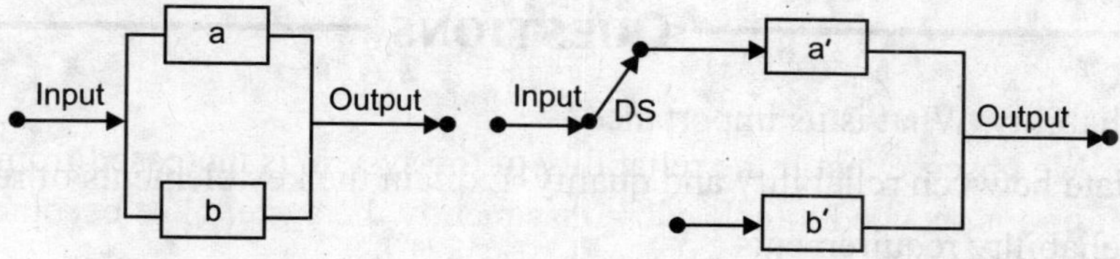


**Fig. 18.15.**

In a standby system, all the paths are not active at the sametime. Initially, when the system is put to operation 'Decision Switch' (D.S.) connects the input end to element $a'$ while the other element $b'$ is kept in reserve in a turned off condition. In case, element $a'$ fails, the decision switch senses this by a built-in mechanism, and the connection is made to the standby element $b'$. It is assumed in the analysis that time taken in changing the connections and in warm-up is negligible.

In this example, the reliability of parallel system,

$$P_p = 1 - \{(1-p)(1-p)\}$$

$$= 2p - p^2$$

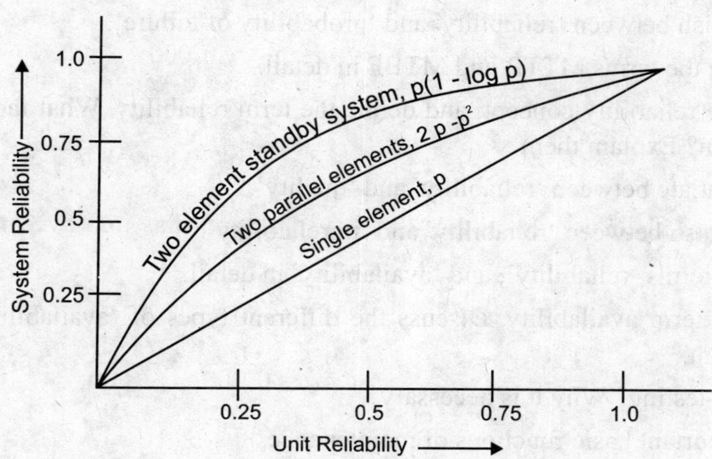


**Fig. 18.16.** Reliability with different configurations.

and reliability *i.e.* probability of success for the standby system,

$$P_s = 1 - p(a') \times p\left(\frac{b1}{a1}\right)$$

If both the elements are identical, and reliability of each being $p$, the reliability of the standby system is,

$$P_s = p(1 - \log_e p)$$

Comparison of the reliabilities of three configurations namely, for a single element, for two active identical elements in parallel, and for a two-element standby system with identical elements are shown in Fig. 18.16.

## QUESTIONS

1. Define reliability. What is its importance?
2. Differentiate between reliability and quality. Explain the key elements of reliability.
3. Explain reliability requirements.
4. Explain 'designing for reliability' in detail.
5. Discuss the various factors considered while designing a product.
6. Mention the steps used in assessing the approximate prediction of reliability.
7. How will you predict reliability during design?
8. List main types of tests 'with their purpose' generally used for evaluating a design.
9. What is life-testing? Why it is necessary?
10. Explain the term 'Life-Testings'. Describe the objects of life-tests. How will you classify various life-tests?
11. Describe failure characteristics with the help of sketch.
12. (*a*) Distinguish between 'reliability' and 'probability of failure'.

    (*b*) Describe the terms MTTR and MTBF in detail.
13. Describe the reliability concept, and define the term reliability. What factors are included in the definition? Explain them.
14. (*a*) Differentiate between 'reliability' and 'quality'.

    (*b*) Distinguish between 'reliability' and 'unreliability'.
15. Explain the terms 'reliability', and 'availability' in detail.
16. Explain the term availability. Discuss the different types of 'availability' and differentiate between them.
17. What is life-testing? Why it is necessary?
18. Name 5 important basic functions of maintenance.
19. Write an essay on "importance of maintenance" Mention important functions of maintenance
20. How will you evaluate maintenance performance?
21. How will you plan for maintenance system?
22. Describe planned maintenance strategy.

**23.** Discuss "reliability centered maintenance."

**24.** What are the different types of maintenance systems?

**25.** What is the difference between quality and reliability in maintenance?

**26.** What is the difference between maintainability and reliability of equipments?

**27.** Discuss RAM (Reliability Availability and Maintainability).

**28.** What is RCM (Reliability Centered Maintenance)? Explain its working.

**29.** What is 'six sigma' and 'six sigma maintenance.'

**30.** Explain briefly '5-zero maintenance concept.'

**31.** What is "5-S concept? How it is used in maintenance?

**32.** What do you understand by maintenance strategy/system? Name common maintenance strategies and explain the basis of their selection.

**33.** Explain the following in brief :

(*a*) Maintenance functions.

(*b*) Designing a maintenance system.

(*c*) Condition monitoring.

(*d*) Monitoring the failure.

(*e*) Corrective maintenance.

**34.** Discuss 'Spare Parts Management' in detail. Explain the selective control techniques.

**35.** What is SWOT Analysis? Explain the internal and external factors in the organisation. Mention common applications of SWOT analysis.

**36.** Explain the reliability economics. What is optimization of reliability?

**37.** Explain the term 'system reliability'.

**38.** Describe a system connected in series. What is the system's reliability in terms of probability of failure ?

**39.** Describe a system connected in parallel. What is its probability of failure ?

**40.** Justify the statement, "more failures occur in series as compared to parallel systems".

**41.** How will you find out reliability of systems connected in series and parallel combined ? Explain with the help of sketches.

**42.** Explain the terms :

(*a*) Mean Time Between Failure

(*b*) Mean Time To Repair.

**43.** (*a*) Define the terms 'redundancy' and 'group redundancy'.

(*b*) How will you improve the reliability through strength improvement?

(*c*) How will you improve the reliability through reduction in stress?

**44.** Explain the methods for improving reliability during design.

45. What is 'Pareto Curve'? How will you use it in reliability improvement?
46. Enumerate various factors affecting reliability.
47. What is redundancy? How it improves the reliability? Differentiate standby redundancy with parallel redundancy.
48. Define and explain reliability.
49. How a designer is expected to design for: (*a*) Reliability, and (*b*) Maintainability? How a designer should trade off between reliability and maintainability on one side cost on the other?
50. Explain the terms Guarantee, Warrantee and Claims.
51. Explain the term 'reliability improvement'.
52. What is 'Pareto Curve'? How will you use it in reliability improvement?
53. Enumerate various factors affecting reliability.
54. What is redundancy? How it improves the reliability?

# 19 Quality Management System

## 19.1. INTRODUCTION

A quality management system organises overall activities of the company in such a way that the technical, administrative and human factors affecting the quality of products or services are kept under control. The quality management system guides the co-operated actions of the people, machines and information to achieve the quality objectives.

**1. Activities**

Activities of quality management system are :

(*i*) Marketing to evaluate customer needs and use requirements.

(*ii*) Design and engineering to translate the customer needs into product, process and material specifications.

(*iii*) Purchasing to select the vendors who can supply materials, components, sub-assemblies as per specifications.

(*iv*) Production to ensure that product is produced under controlled conditions in conformance to standards.

(*v*) Quality assurance to identify appropriate test methods and exercise quality control techniques.

(*vi*) Shipping to ensure proper packaging, transportation and distribution of material.

(*vii*) Documentation to maintain system and progress documents at each stage of operation.

(*viii*) Product development for innovation and improvement based on customer's feed-back.

(*ix*) Auditing to identify the non-conforming of the system and product, and follow up the corrective actions.

**2. Benefits**

(*i*) To meet the customer requirements by providing quality products or services to satisfy the customer needs.

(*ii*) Good reputation helps in better marketability of the company's products and services.
(*iii*) Confidence is created
(*iv*) Consistivity in quality
(*v*) Productivity improvement
(*vi*) Better financial performance
(*vii*) Brings clarity in working
(*viii*) Better documentation
(*ix*) Better monitoring
(*x*) Increases export potential
(*xi*) Human resource development.

**3. Quality Function**

(*i*) Marketing and market research
(*ii*) Design and product development
(*iii*) Procurement
(*iv*) Process planning and development
(*v*) Production
(*vi*) Inspection, testing and examination
(*vii*) Packaging and storage
(*viii*) Sales and distribution
(*ix*) Installation and operation
(*x*) Technical assistance and maintenance
(*xi*) Disposal after use.

**4. Quality and Top Management**

Responsibility for and commitment to quality always belong to the highest level of management. Following action points are necessary to be adopted by top management to achieve quality objectives of the company :

(*i*) Define and state quality policy
(*ii*) Appoint a management representative
(*iii*) Define responsibility and authority
(*iv*) Establish an internal verification system
(*v*) Establish a quality system
(*vi*) Review the functioning of quality system at regular intervals.

**5. Installing the Quality System**

**(*A*) Preparations**

(*i*) Analyse the existing status and identify what needs to be done. Prepare an action-plan.

(*ii*) Develop an organisation structure.

(*iii*) Develop quality system documentation.

(*iv*) Prepare the material and machinery resources.

**(*B*) Implementation**

(*i*) Implement the documented quality system.

(*ii*) Establish internal quality audit system.

(*iii*) Monitor, control and stabilise the quality system.

(*vi*) Harmonise the practices with the standards.

## 19.2. ISO–9000–A QUALITY MANAGEMENT SYSTEM

ISO is the **International Organisation for Standardization**. It is located is Switzerland and was established in 1947 to develop common international standards in many areas. Its members come from over 130 national standards bodies. ISO first published its quality standards in 1987, revised then in 1994, and then re-published an updated version in 2000. Standards presently applicable are known as **"ISO-9000 : 2008 Standards"**, and facilitate international trade by providing a single set of standards that people everywhere would recognise and respect.

ISO-9000 refers to a set of standards and is the only available internationally accepted standard for quality management system in the world. It is rapidly becoming the most important quality standard and hundreds of thousands companies in over 100 countries have already adopted it. ISO-9000 is applicable to all types of organisations in manufacturing or service sectors. It is a documentation-oriented system which allows complete freedom on selection and use of process and framing of operating procedures and work instructions. This is a widely recognised quality management tool and meet the quality requirements of every kind of products or services. Production of consistently good quality product or service is very important for customer confidence and higher positioning of buyer perception. Every conscious company who wants to survive and grow, have either adopted this standard or in the process of adopting it.

A properly established quality management system will help to reduce cost, improve quality, develop confidence and a good image in the minds of customers and public. This requires consistent implementation, careful auditing and total commitment of the whole organisation.

The second revision of ISO-9000 series, known as ISO-9000 : 2000 does not include the term 'Quality Assurance'. This reflects the fact that the quality management system requirements specified in this edition, in addition to quality assurance of product, also aim to enhance customer satisfaction.

The ISO-9000:2000 have been adopted as Indian standard without deviations by the Bureau of Indian Standards (BIS)., and this is referred as "IS/ISO. 9000 : 2000 Quality management systems". BIS has now adopted the latest version ISO-9000:2008 (discussed in the end of this chapter).

The adoption of quality management system by any organisation should be a strategic decision. The design and implementation of an organisation's quality management system is influenced by varying needs. The quality management principles stated in ISO-9000 and ISO-9004 of 1994 have been taken into consideration during the development of this International standard.

This International standard promotes the adoption of a process approach when developing, implementing, and improving the effectiveness of a quality management system, to enhance customer satisfaction by meeting customer requirements.

An activity using resources, and managed in order to enable the transformation of inputs into outputs, can be considered as a process. Often the output from one process directly forms the input to the next. The application of a system of processes within an organisation, together with the identification and interactions of these processes, and their management, can be referred to as the "process approach".

ISO-9000 set of standards are **"generic management system standards".** This means that the same standards can be applied:

- to any organisation, large or small, whatever its product;
- including whether its "product" is actually a service;
- in any sector of activity; and
- whether it is a business enterprise, a public administration, or a government department.

The "ISO-9000 quality management system" adopting organisations fulfill:

- the customer's quality requirements ;
- applicable regulatory requirements ;
- enhance customer satisfaction ; and
- achieve continual improvement of its performance.

Many companies require their suppliers to adopt ISO-9000 and get registered. Registered companies find that their market opportunities have increased, as it ensures a sound quality management system. Registered companies had reduction in customer complaints, significant reductions in operating costs and increased demand for their products and services. Other benefits can include better working conditions, increased market share, and increased profits.

**Aims of ISO - 9000**

To provide for development of quality system to achieve:

(*a*) Quality for products or services, and

(*b*) Customer satisfaction.

**Areas of Application**

1. Marketing
2. Design and development
3. Procurement
4. Production
5. Quality Assurance
6. Packaging and storage
7. Sales and distribution
8. Servicing

**Who Can Adopt ISO-9000?**

1. Manufacturing organisations:
   (*a*) Product manufacturing industries
   (*b*) Processing industries.
2. Service Organisations :
   (*a*) Technical - Consultancy, design, engineering, testing etc.
   (*b*) Professional - Legal, security, training, management etc.
   (*c*) Hospitability - Catering, hotels, tourism etc.
   (*d*) Banking - Insurance, banking, portfolio management etc.
   (*e*) Transportation - Airlines, rail, road, sea travels.
   (*f*) Health - Hospitals, nursing homes, laboratories etc.
   (*g*) Communication - Postal, Telecommunication.
   (*h*) Government - Police, Taxation, public administration, public services etc.

## 19.3. HISTORY AND ORIGIN OF ISO-9000

After issuing several inspection system documents in the 1950's, the U.S military later integrated them into a set of requirements documents and issued them in December, 1963 with the names of *Inspection System Requirements and Quality Programme Requirements.* Thereafter, documents issued were on standard clauses in procurement, contracts, required control over final inspection and testing; and then on *Calibration System Requirements*. Similarly, Canadian series of standards were issued in four levels in the mid 1970's ; and the British standard was issued in three levels in 1979 as quality management systems.

In the meantime, in December, 1979, the United States issued Generic Guidelines for quality systems. This was a menu of quality management elements, and each organisation could choose the elements they felt were helpful, allowing them for almost infinite degree of tailoring.

Since different standards for different countries were creating problems to international trade, necessity was felt for developing internationally recognised quality management standards. The ISO Technical Committee (TC -176) was, therefore, constituted, which had its first meeting in 1980, and issued its first standard ISO 8402 regarding "Quality System - Vocabulary". Thereafter, in 1987, they issued ISO-9001, 9002 9003 and 9004. These standards were later on revised in 1994, and then extensively revised in the year 2000. This was then modified in 2008.

Before going into the details of ISO-9000 series of standards, we shall first discuss the term "standard" and "standardisation".

**Standard.** A standard is defined as a document, established by consensus and approved by a recognised body, that provides ; for common and repeated use, rules, guidelines or characteristics for activities or their results, aimed at the achievement of the optimum degree of order in a given context.

**Standardization.** A standardization is an activity consisting of the process of formulating, issuing and implementing standards.

## 19.4. ADVANTAGES (NEEDS) OF ISO-9000-REGISTRATION

It is widely acknowledged that proper quality management improves business, often having a positive effect on investment, market share, sales, sales growth, sales margins, competitive advantage, and avoidance of litigation. The quality principles in ISO 9000:2000 are also sound,and ISO 9000 guidelines provide a comprehensive model for quality management systems that can make any company competitive. Implementing ISO often gives the following advantages:

1. Creates a more efficient, effective operation.
2. Increase customer satisfaction and relation.
3. Reduces audits.
4. Improves marketing.
5. Improves employee motivation, awareness, and morale.
6. Promotes international trade.
7. Increases profit.
8. Reduces waste and increases productivity.
9. Common tools for standardization.
10. Reduction in Scrap, re-work, and non-conformities.
11. Reduction in breakdowns and downtimes.
12. Reduction in claims of non-conforming product, and returned product.
13. Improvements in on-time deliveries.

Against above benefits, there is only one negative side, *i.e.*, increase in the prevention and appraisal costs.

## 19.5. ISO-9000 : 1994–QUALITY SYSTEM STANDARDS

With increased focus on quality issues worldwide, the International Organisation for Standardization (ISO) brought out 6 standards. One on standards terminology (ISO 8402) and 5 standards (known as ISO 9000 series.). This series of standards establish requirements with which company's Quality Management System can be installed, operated and also evaluated both, in-house and independently by third parties. The ISO 9000 series of standards serve as a basis for ensuring quality to all providers of goods and services. These six standards are:

ISO 8402 -- Quality systems - Vocabulary

ISO 9000 - Quality systems - Guidelines for selection and use of standards on quality systems.

ISO 9001 -- Quality systems - Models for quality assurance in design/development, production, installation and servicing.

ISO 9002 -- Quality systems - Model for quality assurance in production and installation.

ISO 9003 -- Quality systems - Models for quality assurance in final inspection and test.

ISO 9004 -- Quality Management and quality system elements.

**Certification**

It is the mechanism by which a customer can have confidence in a company and is most effective, when carried out by a national certification body. In Europe, already both, large and small purchasing organisations place great importance upon the ability of their suppliers to demonstrate that they are operating effective quality system which meet the fact that the company operates a quality system complying with the standard, allows the purchaser to have increased confidence in the quality of the product concerned with the supply of product. Assessment and registration of a quality management system to ISO 9000 series is done by the reputed authorised firms.

**What is ISO - 9000 Standards ?**

1. It is a system standard for quality management. These standards are generic, and not specific to any particular product and can be used in manufacturing and service industries alike.
2. It defines the basic disciplines and specifies the procedure and criteria to ensure that the output of the organisation consistently meets the customer's requirements.
3. It guides to establish, operate, document and maintain an effective, economic quality system which will demonstrate that the organisation is committed to quality and is capable to meet the specified quality requirements.

## I.S.O. 9000: 1994 Series

The standards are based on the consolidated result of science, technology and experience and aimed to promote optimum community benefits. These standards can be formulated and issued for all kinds of products, processes and services, which includes equipment, material, component, system, interface, procedure, function, methods, etc.

I.S.O. started the work on quality standardization through their technical committees and issued six standards related to quality.

I.S.O. 8402 in the year 1986, followed by I.S.O. 9000, I.S.O. 9001 I.S.O. 9002, I.S.O. 9003, and I.S.O. 9004 in the year 1987. The latter five of these are popularly known as I.S.O. 9000, series. When we refer to I.S.O. 9000, we mean the whole series or a particular standard belonging to the series.

This helped in avoiding confusion, because different terms like quality control, quality assurance, quality management, quality policy, quality plan, quality system etc. have acquired different or conflicting meaning in different countries.

Since most international firms in their tender notices now clearly mention that only I.S.O. 9000 certified firms only need apply, therefore, Indian companies expanding their overseas base, have to obtain this certificate.

While the use of most sophisticated machinery, high technological inputs and trained man power are essential, they are not themselves adequate, greater importance is given to the well documented systems, which guide each one of business processes to precisely tell what to do, when and how. The degree of standardisation extends towards systemisation at all levels of operations of the enterprise.

I.S.O. 9000 series promote standardised management of quality systems in order to achieve commonly established global quality standards. These standards primarily provide assurance to the buyer that the supplier has in fact well-documented, well-maintained and practiced quality systems covering all his operations, thereby ensuring consistency in quality of his processes, products and services. I.S.O. 9000 series of standards reflect refinements in all practical and generally applicable principles of quality systems. Implementation of I.S.O. 9000 standards by an organisation provides opportunity to move from a state of disorganized systems into high degree of system standardization.

I.S.O. 9000 insists on existence and adoption of internal quality audits which help in identification of non-conformities from the set procedures, if any and for taking necessary corrective steps, well in time.

In order to evolve and implement appropriate procedure, documents and records, the company has to train every single employee towards these quality system. I.S.O. 9000 standards involve all employees, workmen upwards to the level of directors. All these need to be trained to understand and appreciate both, implicit and explicit requirements of the I.S.O. 9000 standards.

I.S.O. 9000 also necessitate the periodic review of implementation. The review may be in the form of market feedback, customer complaints, and improvement in methods are systematically planned and executed.

Following steps should be taken to attain the I.S.O. registered status :

(*i*) Management commitment

(*ii*) I.S.O. education

(*iii*) Organisation to work on systems

(*iv*) Documentation

(*v*) Study of existing systems

(*vi*) Align existing systems towards I.S.O. standards

(*vii*) Audits and accreditation.

## Characteristics of I.S.O. -- 9000

- I.S.O. 9000 is the only available internationally accepted standard for quality management system.
- It does not replace, but complements the product standards.
- I.S.O. 9000 is applicable to all types of industries or organisation in manufacturing or service sector.
- It stands for systematic standardization and certification rather than product standardization and certification.

– I.S.O. 9000 is a documentation-oriented system which allows complete freedom on selection and use of processes and framing of operating procedures and work instructions.

– A mistake made in selection of proper product standard can never be compensated by I.S.O. 9000 implementation.

**Areas Covered in I.S.O. -- 9000 : 1994 Series**

1. **ISO. 9000** provides the guidelines for selection and use of the quality standards.
2. **ISO. 9001** is a quality system model for quality assurance in design/development, production, installation and servicing. This is the most exhaustive standard. The engineering organisations, where the manufacturing capabilities are based on in-house design have to work for ISO. 9001 certification. Manufacturers of: (*a*) household goods like TV, refrigerator etc. (*b*) perishable consumer goods like tooth-paste etc. which have both, servicing and design/development have to work towards ISO. 9001.
3. **ISO. 9002** provides a model or quality assurance only in production and installation. This does not cover areas of design/development and servicing. ISO. 9002 also looks at internal quality audits. Steel plants, departmental stores, hospitals, chemical plants etc., where the designing and servicing do not constitute the key activities, may prefer ISO. 9002.
4. **ISO. 9003** deals only with quality systems related to final inspection and testing.
5. **ISO. 9004** provides guideline for quality management and quality system elements.

In addition to the ISO. 9000 series, ISO. 8402 deals with quality vocabulary used in the ISO. 9000 series.

## 19.6. ISO-9000 : 2000 SET OF STANDARDS

ISO-9000 currently includes three quantity standards : ISO-9000 : 2000, ISO-9001 : 2000 and ISO-9004: 2000. In these standards ISO-9001 : 2000 presents requirements, while ISO-9000 : 2000 and ISO-9004 : 2000 presents guidelines. All of these are process standards (not product standards). The certificate is awarded to an organisation in respect of compliance of standards ISO-9001 : 2000.

**Following standards currently make up the ISO-9000 family :**

| ***Standards and Guidelines*** | ***Purpose*** |
|---|---|
| ISO-9000 : 2000, Quality Management Systems – Fundamentals and Vocabulary. | For understanding the standards and defines the fundamental terms and definitions used in the ISO-9000 family. |
| ISO-9001 : 2000, Quality Management Systems – Requirements | This is the requirement standard used to assess the ability to meet the customer and applicable regulatory requirements and thereby, address customer satisfaction. It is now the only standard in the ISO-9000 family against which third-party certification can be granted. |

| | |
|---|---|
| ISO-9004 : 2000, Quality Management Systems - Guidelines for performance improvements | This guideline standard provides guidance for continual improvement of quality management system to benefit all parties through sustained customer satisfaction. |

From the above, it is clear that in order to develop a quality management system, you are required to only meet the requirements specified by ISO - 9001:2000. You can consult the ISO-9000 : 2000 and ISO - 9004 : 2000 guidelines only when you need clarification. Your quality management system must simply meet requirements, as specified in ISO-9001: 2000. When your quality system has been fully developed and implemented, you carry out an internal assessment to ensure that you have met every single ISO-9001 : 2000 requirement. When you are ready, you ask an external auditor to audit the effectiveness of your quality management system. If your auditors find that you have introduced and implemented the ISO-9001: 2000 standard, they will certify that your quality system has met ISO's requirements, will then issue an official certificate to you and will record your achievement in their registry. You can then announce to the world that the quality of your products and services is managed, controlled, and assured by a registered ISO-9001: 2000 Quality Management System.

## 19.7. QUALITY MANAGEMENT PRINCIPLES–ISO - 9000 : 2000

ISO - 9000:2000 standards are based on eight quality management principles. ISO choose these principle because they can be used to improve organisational performance and achieve success. These principles can be used by senior management as a framework to guide their organisation towards improved performance. The eight quality management principles, as given in the ISO -9000: 2000, Quality management systems – Fundamentals and Vocabulary; and in ISO -9004: 2000, Quality management systems – Guidelines for performance improvements are:

**Principle 1 : Focus on your Customers**

Organisations depend on their customers. Therefore:

- Organisations must understand customer needs.
- Organisations must meet customer requirements.
- Organisations must exceed customer expectations.

**Principle 2 : Provide Leadership**

Organisations rely on leaders. Therefore :

- Leaders must establish a unity of purpose and set the direction the organisation should take.
- Leaders must create an environmental that encourages people to achieve the organisation's objectives.

**Principle 3 : Involvement of People**

People at all levels are the essence of an organisation and therefore:

- Organisations must encourage the involvement of people at all levels.

- Organisations must help people to develop and use their abilities.

**Principle 4 : Use a Process Approach**

Organisations are more efficient and effective, when they use a process. Therefore:

- Organisations must use a process approach to manage activities and related resources.

**Principle 5 : Take a System Approach**

Organisations are more efficient and effective, when they use a systems approach. Therefore:

- Organisations must identify inter-related processes and treat them as a system.
- Organisations must use a systems approach to manage their inter-related processes.

**Principle 6 : Encourage Continual Improvement**

Organisations are more efficient and effective, when they continually try to improve. Therefore:

- Organisations must make a permanent commitment to continually improve their overall performance.

**Principle 7 : Get the Facts Before taking a Decision**

Organisations perform better, when their decisions are based on facts. Therefore :

- Organisations must base decisions on the analysis of factual information and data.

**Principle 8 : Mutually Beneficial Supplier Relationship**

Organisations depend on their suppliers to help them create value. Therefore:

- Organisations must maintain a mutually beneficial relationship with their suppliers.

## 19.8. ISO-9001 : 2000 - REQUIREMENTS

ISO - 9001: 2000 is the standard intended for quality management system assessment and registration. This apply uniformly to organisations of any size or description. ISO presents its requirements in section 4 to 8 of ISO - 9001 : 2000 standard. Broad features of these sections and requirement thereof, which have to be built in the documentation and then implemented, are given hereunder :

### Section 4 : System Requirements

#### 4.1. Establish your quality system

Your organisation needs to document and use a quality system. Then, there is a need to continually improve it. For this, the organisation must:

- Identify key processes to meet customer requirements.
- Establish the order of these processed and how they fit together.
- Establish how you will control these processes.
- Make resources available to support these processes.

- Measure these processes to not only ensure that they do what you wanted to put that you plan for them to improve.
- Where any process has been outsourced, it must be ensured that control over them is retained.
- Implement your quality management system.
- Manage and monitor process performance.
- Improve the quality management system.

## 4.2. Documentation Requirements

- Develop documents that reflect what organisation does.
- Develop documents to implement quality system including quality policy and objectives.
- Document procedures.
- Describe as to how processes interact.
- Prepare Quality Manual including the scope of quality system.
- Approve documents before their distribution.
- Provide the correct version of documents at points of use.
- Review and re-approve documents, whenever they are updated.
- Monitor documents that come from external sources.
- Quality records (working forms/registers or other records) are used and kept to prove the system is functioning properly.
- Develop a procedure to control records.

## Section 5 : Management Requirements

## 5.1. Management Commitment

Top management should support the Quality Management System and should involve in its continual improvement:

- Promote the importance of quality.
- Promote the need to meet customer requirements, regulatory requirements, and satisfactory requirements.
- Develop a quality management system.
- Establish quality policies.
- Ensure quality objectives are established.
- Provide quality resources.
- Implement quality management systems.
- Perform quality management reviews.
- Improve quality management system.

## 5.2. Customer Focus

- Understand and identify customer requirements.
- Meet customers requirements.
- Enhance customer satisfaction.

## 5.3. Establish a Quality Policy

- Define the organisation's quality policy and ensure that it serves the organisations purpose.
- Ensure that it emphasises the need to meet requirements.
- Ensure that it facilitates the development of quality objectives.
- Ensure that it makes a commitment to continuous improvement.
- Review the policy to ensure that it is still suitable.

## 5.4. Quality Planning

- Formulate quality objectives by ensuring that objectives are set for functional areas.
- Ensure that objectives support the quality policy.
- Ensure that objectives are measurable.
- Plan the development and implementation of quality management system.
- Plan the improvement of quality management system.

## 5.5. Authority and Responsibility of Quality System

- Define and communicate responsibilities and authorities.
- Appoint management representative who should oversee the quality management system and report the status regularly.
- Ensure sufficient communication processes are established.
- Ensure responsibilities and authorities are defined and communicated within the organisation.

## 5.6. Management Review

- Evaluate the performance of quality system and whether it should be improved.
- Inputs to management review shall include: results of audits, customer feedback, process performance and product conformity; any preventive and corrective actions; previous actions and their outcomes and recommendations for improvement.
- Generate actions to improve quality system and products.

## Section 6. Resource Management Requirements

### 6.1. Provision of Resources

- Provide resources needed for implementing the quality management system (QMS) and make sure that customer requirements are being met.

### 6.2. Providing Human Resources

- Provide competent personnel for which ensure that they have the right experience, education, training and skills.
- Maintain a record of competence.

### 6.3. Providing Infrastructure

- Provide and maintain the infrastructure needed to achieve product/service conformity to requirements.

### 6.4. Providing Work Environment

- Identify needed work environment.
- Manage needed work environment.

## Section 7. Realisation Requirements

### 7.1. Planning of Product Realisation

- Plan and develop processes needed to realise (make/generate) the product in line with QMS.
- Develop methods to control quality during product realisation.

### 7.2. Customer Related Processes

- Identify customer requirements and other requirements imposed by external agencies (including statutory requirements) and the requirements that organisation wishes to meet.
- Review customers' product requirement before you agree to sell it.
- Handle any changed requirements.
- Communicate with customers by developing a process to control communications with customers and implement it.

### 7.3. Product Design and Development

- Define your product design and development stages.

- Clarify design and development responsibilities and authorities.
- Manage interaction between design and development groups.
- Update design and development plans, as changes occur.
- Define design and development inputs.
- Create product design and development outputs.
- Approve design and development outputs prior to release.
- Use design and development outputs to control product quality.
- Carry out design and development reviews.
- Perform design and development verifications.
- Conduct design and development validations.
- Manage design and development changes.

## 7.4. Control Purchasing Function

- Control purchasing process - For this ensure that suppliers as well as purchased product meet requirements.
- Describe the products which are being purchased.
- Specify the requirements that must be met.
- Verify purchased products at suppliers premises and also at your own premises.

## 7.5. Control Production and Service Provisions

- Control production and service provisions *i.e.* processes informations, instructions, equipment, measurements and other activities.
- Validate production and service provision *i.e.*, prove that processes, personnel and equipment can produce planned outputs.
- Identify and track the products *i.e.* establish and maintain the indentity of the products and their status.
- Protect the property (drawings, data, personnel, environment etc.) supplied by the customers.
- Preserve the products and components during internal processing as well as during final delivery.

## 7.6. Control of Monitoring and Measuring Devices

- Calibrate the equipment and verify them at specified intervals or prior to use against any relevant standards.
- Caliberation must be adjusted, as necessary.
- It must be identified to establish, when the equipment will require re-calibration.
- Calibrated equipment must be stored and used in such a way as to prevent its mis-alignment.

## Section 8. Remedial Requirements (Measure, Analysis and Improvement)

### 8.1. Perform Remedial Processes

- Plan and implement remedial processes to demonstrate that a process is capable of producing desired results.
- Use remedial processes to improve QMS.

### 8.2. Monitor and Measure Quality

- Monitor and measure customer satisfaction.
- Plan and perform regular internal audits.
- Monitor and measure quality processes.
- Take action, when processes fail to achieve planned results.
- Monitor and measure product/service characteristics.
- Keep a record of product/service monitoring and measuring activities.

### 8.3. Control Non-Conforming Products

- Ensure that products/services/processes not conforming to requirements/plans are suitably identified and controlled to prevent misuse.
- Controls and responsibilities must be identified within a documented procedure.
- Re-verify non-conforming products that were corrected, meet the requirements.
- Maintain records of such products and describe the actions taken to deal with non-conformities.

### 8.4. Analyse Quality Information/Data

- Demonstrate the effectiveness of the quality system and then evaluate where continual improvement can be achieved. Standard indicators are usually ; customer satisfaction ; conformance to requirements ; characteristics and trends of processes and products ; and supplier performance.

### 8.5. Make Quality Improvements

- Improve quality management system through the use of quality policy, objectives, audits, analysis of data, corrective and preventive actions and management review.
- Corrective action be taken after analysing cause of problems and a documented procedure be written to this effect.
- Record the results that corrective actions achieve.
- Examine the effectiveness of corrective actions.
- Develop preventive actions to eliminate potential problems. For this, a documented procedure should be established.

## 19.9. ISO-9000:2008 VERSION

ISO-9001:2008 basically re-narrates ISO-9000:2000. The 2008 version only introduced clarifications to the requirements of ISO-9001:2000 and some changes intended to improve consistency with ISO-14001: 2004. There were no new requirements.

This fourth edition (first edition ISO-9000:1987 version, second edition ISO-9000:1994 version; third edition ISO-9000:2000 version, and fourth edition ISO-9000:2008 version) cancels and replaces the third editions, which has been **amended** to clarify points in the text and to enhance compatibility with ISO-14001: 2004.

This version states that the design and implementation of an organisation's quality management system is influenced by:

(*a*) its organisational environment, changes in that environment, and the risks associated with that environment,

(*b*) its verying needs,

(*c*) its particular objectives,

(*d*) the products provided,

(*e*) the process employed,

(*f*) its size and organisational structure.

It is not the idea of this standard to imply uniformity in the structure of quality management systems or uniformity of documentation.

This International Standard promotes the adoption of a process approach when developing, implementing, and improving the effectiveness of a quality management system, to enhance customer satisfaction by meeting customer requirements. According to this new version, ensuring control over outscourced processes does not absolve the organisation of the responsibility of conformity to all customer, statutory and regulatory requirements. The type and extent of control to be applied to the outsourced processes shall be defined within the quality management system.

This new version also defines the term 'work environment' which relates to those conditions under which work is performed including physical, environmental and other factors (such as noise, temperature, humidity, lighting or weather).

This version also include the post-delivery activities under the heading "customer-related processes" which include actions under warranty provisions, contractual obligations, such as maintenance services, and supplementary services, such as re-cycling or final disposal.

## 19.10. CRITICISMS OF ISO-9000

1. A common criticism of ISO-9000 and 9001 is the amount of money, time, and paper work required for registration.
2. Some believes that ISO standards elevate inspection of the correct procedures over broader aspects of quality, and, therefore, the workplace becomes opressive and quality is not improved.

3. Some others believe that it is effective only as a guideline, but mislead companies to think that certification means better quality.
4. Certifications are often based on customer contractual requirements rather than a desire to actually improve quality.

The quality has a positive effect on return on investment, market share, sales growth, better sales margins and competitive advantage; but taking a quality approach is unrelated to ISO-9000 registration. In fact, ISO itself advises that ISO-9001 can be implemented without certification, simply for the quality benefits that can be achieved.

## 19.11. EFFECTIVENESS OF ISO-9000

Effectiveness of the ISO system being implemented depends on a number of factors, the most significant of which are:

1. **Commitment of senior management to monitor, control and improve quality.** Organisations that implement an ISO system without this desire and commitment often take the cheapest road to get a certificate and ignore problem areas uncovered in the audits.
2. **How well the ISO system integrates into current business practices.** Many organisations that implement ISO try to make their system fit into a readymade quality manual instead of creating a manual that documents existing practices and only adds new processes to meet the ISO standard, when necessary.
3. **How well the ISO system focuses on improving the customer experience.** The broadest definition of quality is "Whatever the customer perceives good quality to be." This means that a company doesn't necessarily have to make a product that never fails; some customers will have a higher tolerance for product failures, if they always receive shipments on-time or have a positive experience in some other dimension of customer service. An ISO system should take into account all areas of the customer experience and the industry expectations, and seek to improve them on a continual basis. This means taking into account all processes that deal with the three stakeholders (customers, suppliers, and organisation); only then will a company be able to sustain improvements in the customer's experience.
4. **How well the auditor finds and communicates areas of improvement.** Many auditors simply rely on submitting reports that indicate compliance or non-compliance with the appropriate section of the standard. Auditors that can clearly identify and communicate areas of improvement in language and terms executive management understands facilitate action on improvement initiatives by the companies, they audit. When management doesn't understand why they were non-compliance and the business implications associated with non-compliance, they simply ignore the reports and focus on what they do understand.

## 19.12. STANDARDS FOR SERVICE ORGANISATIONS

Service organisations have organised system of special skills and facilities. Before understanding service quality, we must first know the characteristics of service organisations. Service organisation have following characteristics:

1. Direct sale to the customer.
2. Direct contact with the user.
3. Service provided on demand.
4. Time schedule is important.
5. Service can not be stored or transported like a physical product.

Quality in service can be achieved by defining and controlling the quality characteristics of service and service delivery.

ISO-9004 part -2 : 1994, provides guidelines for establishment of quality management system for providing a service, which is "fit for use" and meets the customer's expectations.

**Service Quality**

Like a product quality, service quality is also based on 'fitness for use.' The service must respond to the needs of customer in price, delivery schedule and suitability to meet the purpose. 'Fitness for use' is the extent to which the service successfully satisfies the customer's needs, as it rendered.'Fitness of use' is determined by those features of service that customer recognises as beneficial to him, like timeliness, consistency, disturbance/trouble free, cleanliness, accuracy etc.

### 19.12.1. Developing Service Quality System

A quality management system for service organisation can be developed, established and maintained with the help of ISO- 8402, ISO-9000, ISO-9004 and ISO-9004-Part 2. An overview of ISO-9000 series of standards for service organisations is shown in the following diagram :

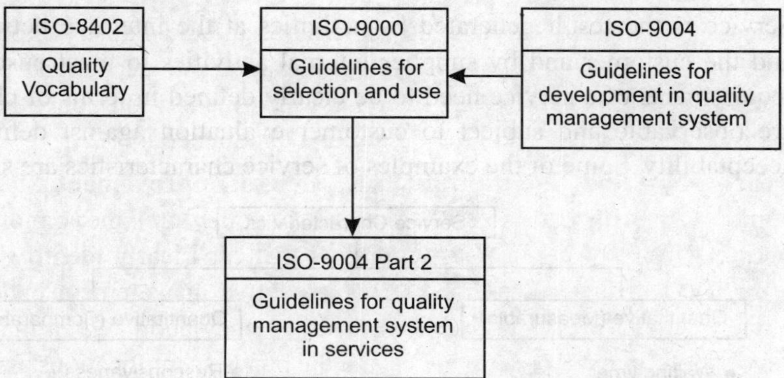


**Fig. 19.1** An overview of ISO-9000 standards for services.

### 19.12.2. ISO - 9004-Part 2 : 1994

**(Guidelines for Quality Management System for Services)**

**1. Introduction**

Following are essential for the service organisation to achieve the quality :

(*a*) Customer needs are properly understood and met.

(*b*) Commitment to quality at all levels of organisation.

(*c*) A quality management system is established for continuous review and improvement of quality based on customer's feedback and their perception of the service provided.

**The benefits of application of this system are :**

(*a*) Improved service performance and customer satisfaction.

(*b*) Improved productivity, efficiency and cost reduction.

(*c*) Improved market share.

In order to achieve above benefits, quality system for service should also respond to human aspects by:

(*a*) managing the social process,

(*b*) regarding human interaction as an important aspect,

(*c*) recognising the importance of customer's perceptions of the organisation's image, culture and performance,

(*d*) developing the skills and capability of personnel, and

(*e*) motivating personnel to improve quality and to meet customer expectation.

**2. Quality in Service**

**(*A*) Service:**

Service is the result generated by activities at the interface between the supplier and the customer and by supplier internal activities to meet customer needs. The requirements of a service need to be clearly defined in terms of characteristics that are observable and subject to customer evaluation against defined standards of acceptability. Some of the examples of service characteristics are shown below :

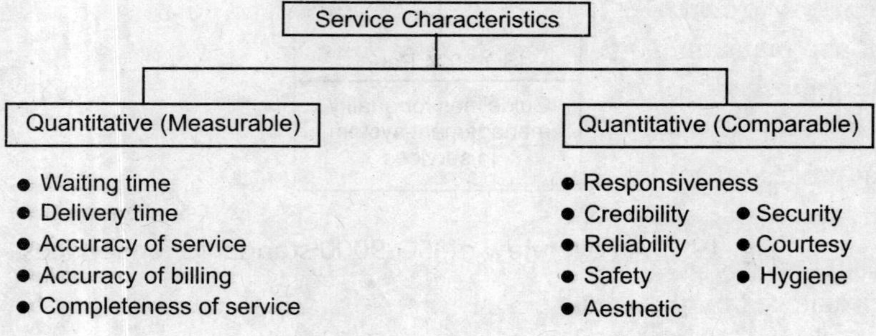


**Fig. 19.2.** Service characteristics.

**(B) *Service Delivery***

In order to exercise control over the quality of the services, the processes that deliver a service also need to be defined in terms of characteristics, as they directly affect service performance. Some examples of service delivery characteristics are indicated hereunder :

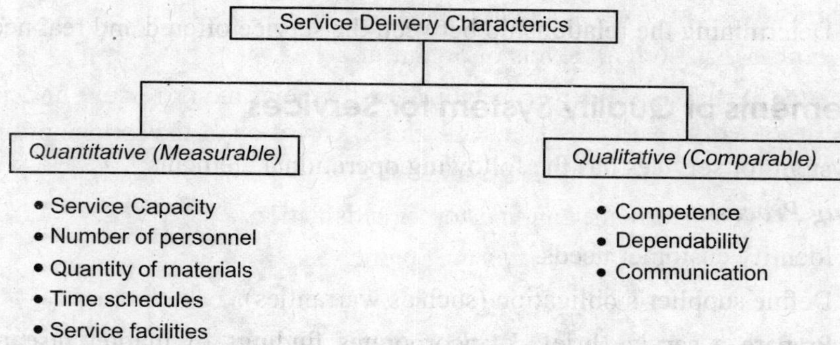


**Fig. 19.3.** Service delivery characteristics.

The service and service delivery quality are measured and compared with that of objectives laid down and desired service quality can be maintained continuously through the control of process.

**3. Quality System Principles**

(*A*) ***Management Responsibility:*** Management is responsible for:

(*i*) stating a quality policy,

(*ii*) defining quality objectives,

(*iii*) assigning quality responsibilities,

(*iv*) providing personnel and material resources, and

(*v*) conducting periodical review.

(*B*) ***Personnel and Material Resources :*** Management should provide sufficient and appropriate manpower and material resources to implement the quality system and achieve the quality objectives.

(*C*) ***Quality System Structure :*** The service organisation should develop, establish, document, implement and maintain a quality system as a means by which stated policies and objectives may be accomplished.

The quality system elements should be structured to establish adequate control and assurance over operational process affecting service quality.

(*D*) ***Interface with Customers :*** Management should establish effective interaction between customers and service organisation personnel. Methods for improvement of customer contacts should be reviewed by the management. An effective communication with customer having following features is very essential :

(*i*) Describing the service, its scope, availability and delivery schedule.

(*ii*) Stating the cost of service, and explaining the inter-relationship between service, delivery and cost.

(*iii*) Explaining the procedure to resolve the problem, if any.

(*iv*) Providing adequate and readily accessible facilities for effective communication.

(*v*) Determining the relationship between the service offered and real need of customer.

### 19.12.3. Elements of Quality System for Services

The quality system for services has the following operational elements:

**1. *Marketing Process:***

(*a*) Identify customer needs.

(*b*) Define supplier's obligation (such as warranties).

(*c*) Prepare a service brief. It incorporates findings of market research, and agreed supplier obligations.

(*d*) ***Service Management.*** Management should establish procedures for planning, organising, implementing the launch of service. Necessary resources, facilities and technical support should be provided.

(*e*) ***Quality in advertising.*** Advertisement to promote the business should reflect the specification and should take account of customer's perception of the quality of service provided.

**2. *Design Process:***

The designing process involves translating the service brief into :

(*a*) Service specifications, which defines the service to be provided.

(*b*) Service delivery specifications, which define the methods used to deliver the service, and

(*c*) Quality control specifications, which defines the procedure for evaluation and control of service and service delivery characteristics.

**3. *Service Delivery Process :***

Provision of a service to customer entails:

(*a*) adherence to prescribed service delivery specifications,

(*b*) monitoring that service specification is met, and

(*c*) adjusting the process when deviations occur.

Service quality is assessed by the supplier as well as customer. Elements of service delivery process are :

(*a*) Assign the responsibilities for service delivery.

(*b*) Assess the service quality,

(*c*) Find out the customer assessment.

(*d*) Record service status,

(*e*) Take corrective actions for non conformities.

4. ***Service Performance Analysis and Improvement:***

Operations of service process should be evaluated on continuous basis, and opportunities should be identified for improvements in service quality. For the purpose of service performance analysis, following steps should be taken :

(*a*) Establish continuous system for appraisal.

(*b*) Develop customer feedback system.

(*c*) Obtain supplier's assessment.

(*d*) Analyse customer reactions and complaints.

(*e*) Conduct regular audits.

(*f*) Take appropriate improvement action.

## 19.13. INSTALLATION OF QUALITY SYSTEM

The installation process of a quality system can be broadly divided into following three phases :

1. Preparations for ISO-9000 quality system.
2. Implementation of ISO-9000 quality system.
3. Registration and Certification of quality system.

Time required for installing the quality system may vary from 6 months to even 5 to 7 years, depending upon the following factors :

(*i*) Existing level of quality management.

(*ii*) The will of management and personnel to adopt the quality system.

(*iii*) Complexity of the process.

(*iv*) Characteristics of product.

(*v*) Competence and skill of the employees.

(*vi*) Size of the organisation.

(*vii*) Promptness in taking corrective actions.

### 1. Preparations for Quality System

Preparations for ISO-9000 quality system is done in following steps:

**Step 1 :** *Management's commitment to ISO -9000*. It can be demonstrated by:

(*a*) Making the organisation's people to understand and implement the quality policy.

(*b*) Taking appropriate action for establishment and implementation of a quality system.

(*c*) Not permitting any deviation in quality activities.

(*d*) Involvement of top management in planning implementation and review activities of quality system.

**Step 2:** *Set up an implementation committee.* This committee may have 4 to 6 members selected from various disciplines. One ISO-9000 co-ordinator is also appointed to co-ordinate all quality system activities under the leadership of top management.

**Step 3 :** *Start ISO-awareness campaign.* Awareness programmes are conducted to communicate the employees of all levels to make them understand the purpose of introduction of ISO-9000 quality system, its advantages to the employees and customers.

**Step 4 :** *Conduct Status Review and prepare an Action Plan.* This includes the following:

(*a*) List out as to what is needed to install the quality system ?

(*b*) Review the existing set up against, what is needed,

(*c*) What actions are to be taken to meet the requirements of quality system ? It should be clarified :

What is to be done ?

Who will do it ?

By what time it shall be done ?

**Step 5:** *Develop an organisation structure for quality management.* This aspect have already been discussed in detail in the chapter on 'organising the quality'.

**Step 6:** *Develop Quality System Documentation.* Quality system is normally documented by means of:

Quality Manuals.

Quality Procedures.

Work instructions, and

Quality records.

**Step 7 :** *Prepare the resource system to meet the requirements of standards.* For design, development, production and supply of the products or services, various resources, such as machineries, facilities, know-how, testing and measuring equipments, material handling equipments etc. are required. Right type of process technology, and right type of processing and control equipments are required for effective implementation of quality system.

## 2. Implementation of ISO-9000 Quality System

ISO-9000 quality system can be implemented only after preparation phase, as explained above, is complete. Main steps involved in the implementation phase are:

**Step 8 :** *Implement the documented quality system*: In this step, quality related activities are performed as per the quality policies, procedures, work instructions, as defined in quality manual and other quality system documentation.

**Step 9 :** *Establish internal quality audit system.* An internal auditors team is formed, who are trained with professional agency. They should conduct a planned and documented periodical audit of all quality related activities of the quality system. In initial stages, it helps various departments to continuously improve their performance.

**Step 10:** *Monitor and stabilize the quality system*. Implementation of quality system should be continuously monitored to ensure that all activities are being performed as planned, any deviation found is corrected. The observations of monitoring should be reported to the management and concerned persons.

**Step 11:** *Conduct Pre-registration internal audit*. After stabilization of the system, an internal audit should be conducted to determine whether all the requirements are being met to qualify for certification. For this purpose, a detailed check list is prepared and then used during pre-registration assessment of quality system. Only when the system is found satisfactory, certification body should be approached for registration.

## 3. Registration and Certification

The organisation after having established and operating the quality system, now it need to be verified and certified by an independent certification body to meet the contractual requirements with their customers.

**Step 12 :** *Apply for registration*. Registration process starts with the submission of an application in the prescribed proforma alongwith a questionnaire, quality system documentation, and registration fees, to the nationally/internationally recognised and accredited certification agencies. Every country has one or more recognised certification agencies. In India Bureau of Indian Standards (BIS) is a qualified certification body. In addition to BIS, some other international accredited certification bodies are also operating in India.

**Step 13:** *Adequacy audit by certification body*. This is basically an office exercise by the auditors to determine the extent to which the documented quality system is meeting the requirements of the quality system standards with quality manual, quality procedures and other quality documents. The adequacy audit is done in two phases : (*a*) examination of quality system documentation, and (*b*) preaudit visit of the organisation.

**Step 14 :** *Compliance audit by the certification body*. This audit is carried out to determine the extent to which the documented quality system is implemented and observed by the personnel of the organisation. In this audit, data gathering and collection of evidences is done through interviews, discussions, examination of records and physical observation of the processes. The non-conformities identified during the audit are substantiated by evidences. These non-conformities (if any) are to be corrected by the organisation within a specific time frame, and got to be re-verified from the auditors.

Afterall, the corrective actions are taken, and requirements of ISO quality standards are met, the auditors recommend the certification body for quality system certification.

**Step 15:** *Certification*. Based on the final recommendations of the auditors, ISO-9000 quality system certificate is issued by the certification agency. This certificate is valid for specific period, generally three years. During this validity period, the certification body conducts unannounced surveillance visits to verify the effective implementation and maintenance of the quality system established by the firm. If the firm fails to maintain the quality system, the certificate may be withdrawn or suspended.

The licence granted by the certification body automatically expires at the end of the validity period, which is required to be got renewed by the firm. The licence can be renewed, after satisfactory compliance audit of the firm is re-conducted by the certification body.

## 19.14. ISO: 14000 SERIES STANDARDS (ENVIRONMENTAL MANAGEMENT SYSTEM)

ISO (the International Organisation for Standardization) is a worldwide federation of national standards bodies (ISO member bodies). It is located in Switzerland and was established in 1947 to develop common international standards in many areas. Its members come from over 130 national standards bodies. The work of preparing International Standards is normally carried out through ISO technical committees. International Standards are drafted in accordance with the rules given in the ISO directives. The main task of technical committees is to prepare the international standards. Draft International Standards adopted by the technical committees are circulated to the member bodies for voting. Publication, as on International Standard requires approval by atleast 75% of the member bodies casting a vote.

The subjects on which there is no ISO standard, BIS (Bureau of Indian Standards) prepare the standards, based on the experiences gained and make them compatible with other similar ISO standards keeping in mind the interest of users for integrating with other management system.

As we know that the ISO standards are a series of written specifications that describe internationally accepted protocols for the operation, features, performance or management of processes. ISO-14000 series is a group of documents that define and provide guidance for an Environment Management System (EMS). They suggest how an EMS is to be used and evaluated and how it relates to business process and products. Driving the adoption of ISO 14000 increases environmental consciousness around the world in driving companies to react in many ways.

## 19.15. CONCEPTS OF ISO : 14001

The ISO 14001 is the nucleus of the ISO 14000 series of international standards. ISO 14001 'Environmental Management System – Requirements with guidance for use' was first published in 1996 and later revised in 2004. It specifies a framework of control for an Environmental Management System against which an organisation can be certified by a third party.

**This standard (ISO-14001) is applicable** any organisation that wishes to:

(*a*) implement, maintain and improve an environmental management-system;

(*b*) assure itself of its conformance with its own stated environmental policy;

(*c*) demonstrate conformance:

(*d*) ensure compliance with environmental laws and regulations;

(*e*) seek certification of its environmental management' system by an external third party organisation;

(*f*) improve the performance while managing the cost of improvement;

(*g*) continuously improves its environmental performance;

(*h*) enhancing image and market share.

It enables an organisation to develop an environmental policy, establish objectives and processes to achieve the policy commitments, take action, as needed to improve its performance and demonstrate the conformity of the system to the requirements of this International Standard. The overall aim of this standard is to support environmental protection and prevention of pollution in balance with socio-economic needs.

ISO 14001: 2004 is compatible with the provisions of ISO 9001 for the benefits of the user community. ISO : 14001 (EMS) require commitment to the organisation's EMS policy, applicable regulations, and continual improvement.

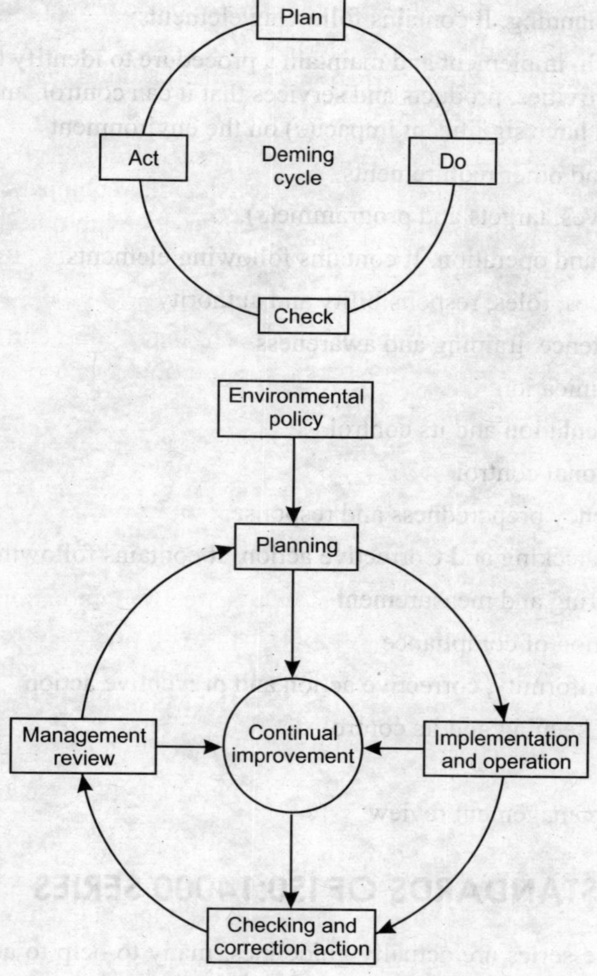


**Fig. 19.4.** EMS (ISO : 14001) and Deming's Cycle.

The basic approach to EMS is shown in Fig. 19.4. It begins with the environmental policy, which is followed by planning, implementation and operation, checking and corrective action, and management review. The EMS approach follows the Deming's PDCA cycle. Thus, there is a logical sequence of events to achieve the continually improvement.

## 19.16. REQUIREMENTS OF ISO: 14001

Various requirements of ISO: 14001 standards are divided into following six groups or clauses:

1. Organisation that shall establish, maintain and continually improve an environmental management system.
2. Environmental policy, which should show management commitment, leadership and direction for the environmental activities.
3. Environmental planning. It contains following elements:
   (*a*) Establish, implement and maintain a procedure to identify the environmental aspects of its activities, products and services that it can control, and determine those aspects that can have significant impact(*s*) on the environment
   (*b*) Legal and other requirements
   (*c*) Objectives, targets and programme(*s*).
4. Implementation and operation. It contains following elements:
   (*a*) Resources, roles, responsibility and authority
   (*b*) Competence, training and awareness
   (*c*) Communication
   (*d*) Documentation and its control
   (*e*) Operational control
   (*f*) Emergency preparedness and response.
5. Environmental checking and Corrective action. It contains following elements:
   (*a*) Monitoring and measurement
   (*b*) Evaluation of compliance
   (*c*) Non-conformity, corrective action and preventive action
   (*d*) Record keeping and its control
   (*e*) Audit.
6. Environmental management review.

## 19.17. OTHER STANDARDS OF ISO:14000 SERIES

Other standards in the series are actually guidelines, many to help to achieve registration to ISO 14001. These include the following:

| | | |
|---|---|---|
| 1. | ISO 14004 | Provides guidance on the development and implementation of environmental management systems. |
| 2. | ISO 14010 | Provides general principles of environmental auditing (now superseded by ISO 19011) |
| 3. | ISO 14011 | Provides specific guidance on audit of an EMS (now superseded by ISO 19011) |
| 4. | ISO 14012 | Provides guidance on qualification criteria for environmental auditors and lead auditors (now superseded by ISO 19011) |
| 5. | ISO 14013 | Provides audit programme review and assessment material |
| 6. | ISO 14020 | Provides environmental labelling under product oriented standards |
| 7. | ISO 14030 | Provides guidance on environmental performance targets and monitoring within an EMS |
| 8. | ISO 14040 | It covers Life-cycle assessment under product-oriented standards. |
| 9. | ISO 14060 | It covers Environmental aspects in product standards under product-oriented standards. |

## 19.18. BENEFITS OF EMS

Benefits of environmental management systems are of following two types:

**1. Global Benefits**

(*i*) Facilitate trade and remove trade barriers.

(*ii*) Improve environment of planet earth.

(*iii*) Build consensus about the need for environmental management and common terminology for EMS.

**2. Organisational Benefits**

Benefits from implementation of EMS are as under:

(*i*) Anticipating and meeting the environmental requirements.

(*ii*) Reducing uncertainty.

(*iii*) Meeting customer requirements.

(*iv*) Improve public image.

(*v*) Improving profitability by minimising waste and reducing energy and resource consumption.

(*vi*) Helps in obtaining insurance at reasonable cost

(*vii*) Increase market share

(*viii*) Reduces incidents that result in liability

(*ix*) Facilitates the attainment of permits and authorization from different agencies.

Implementation of ISO: 14001 leads to "Green consumerism".

## 19.19. OCCUPATIONAL HEALTH AND SAFETY ASSESSMENT SERIES (OHSAS) : 18001

Health and safety is one of the most important aspects of an organisation's smooth and effective functioning, good health and safety performance ensures an accident free industrial environment. In view of this, organisations have started attaching the importance of Occupational Health and Safety (OH&S). The BIS, accordingly formulated IS 18001 in the year 2000 and then revised in the year 2007. While preparing the IS 18001 : 2007 'Occupational health and safety management system - requirements with guidance for use' assistance was taken from BS 8800 : 1996 'Guide to occupational health and safety management system', and AN/ NZS 4804 :1997 'Occupational health and safety management system - General guidance and principles, assessment and supporting techniques'.

While preparing IS 18001, compatibility with following ISO standards have been kept in mind:

(*i*) ISO 14001: 2004 'Environment management systems - requirements with guidance for use'.

(*ii*) ISO 9001: 2000 'Quality management systems-requirements'.

The intention of IS 18001: 2007 is to assist the organisations to develop a systematic approach to management of OH&S in such a way as to protect their employees and others, whose health and safety may be affected by the organizations' activities. This standard also intends to improve OH&S performance of organisations by providing the requirements and guidance for use. The OH&S management systems may be integrated with the management of other aspects of business performance in order to:

(*a*) minimize risk to employees and others,

(*b*) improve business performance, and

(*c*) assist organizations to establish a responsible image at the market place.

In addition, Indian Standards are available on large number of safety codes on various construction activities, construction machineries, PPEs etc. The engineers at site should exercise reasonable and proper safety precautions for the safety of people at all works under their control, in accordance with the instructions contained in the safety manual prepared on the basis of these standards and those given in various acts and safety codes, relating to the works.

### OHSAS-18001 : 2007

In order to that all organisations (Plants-Projects) adopt uniform practices, British Standards Institutions have brought out a standard called OHSAS (Occupational Health and Safety Assessment Series) 18001:1999 dealing with occupational health and safety. As per British Standards, this Occupational Health and Safety Assessment Series (OHSAS) standard and the accompanying OHSAS 18002 'Guidelines for the implementation of OHSAS 18001' have been developed in response to customer demand for a recognizable occupational health and safety management system standard against which their management systems can be assessed and certified. OHSAS

18001 has been developed to be compatible with the ISO 9001:2000 (Quality) and ISO 14001:2004 (environmental) management system standards, in order to facilitate the integration of quality, environmental and occupational health and safety management system by organisations.

IS 18001: 2007, an Indian Standard on Occupational Health and Safety Management System– Requirements with Guidance for use. It gives requirements for occupational health and safety (OH&S) management systems to enable an organisation to control occupational health and safety risks and improve its performance. The main theme of this standard is that the risks to employees and others should be eliminated, or minimised. The organisation should declare its OH&S policy, which should be implemented in a transparent manner. Necessary mechanism should be installed so that OH&S policy is implemented in letter and spirit. The objectives ensured, and continually improved.

It is necessary that such conformance is demonstrated to others for getting certification of OH&S management system from an external independent organisation. All undesired events in a workplace which can give rise to accidents, ill health, death, injury, damage or other loss need to be thoroughly investigated, people to be trained to safeguard against them, and these need to be eliminated. Similarly, all hazards, *i.e.*, source/situation capable of injuring or ill health, damage to property or workplace environment etc. should be identified and action plan drawn for safeguard against them.

**1. Objectives and Benefits**

Objectives and benefits of OH&S management system are:

1. Reduce workplace injuries and illness
2. Reduce costs
3. Reduce staff absence
4. Increase productivity
5. Regulatory compliance
6. Improve insurance liability rating
7. Positive response from customers.

**2. Basic Requirements (Elements) of OHSAS – 18001**

The basic elements on which OHSAS concentrates are:

1. General Requirements
2. OH&S policy
3. Planing:
   (*a*) Hazard identification, Risk assessment and Risk control
   (*b*) Legal and other requirements compliance
   (*c*) Setting of objectives and targets
   (*d*) Management Programme(*s*)

4. Implementation and operation
   (*a*) Organisational structure and responsibility
   (*b*) Training, awareness and competence
   (*c*) Consultation and communication
   (*d*) OHSMS (Occupational Health & Safety Management System) documentation and data control. This includes developing processes and procedures for implementation and achieving
   (*e*) Resourcing
   (*f*) Operation control
   (*g*) Emergency preparedness and response
5. Checking and Corrective action
   (*a*) Monitoring accidents, incidents, non-conformances and corrective and preventive action
   (*b*) Record and record management
   (*c*) Audit
6. Management Review and improving the OH&S management system.

**3. Responsibilities of Employers**

OH&S management system emphasizes the following responsibilities on employers for safety of personnel:

1. To provide a work environment which is free from hazards that are likely to cause death or serious physical harm to employees.
2. To ensure that employees have and use safe tools and equipment and that such equipment is maintained in a proper working condition.
3. To update operating procedures.
4. To train employees so that they follow safety and health requirements.
5. To use labels, signages or other appropriate forms of warning, as are necessary to ensure that employees are aware of all hazards to which they are exposed.
6. To provide suitable PPE.

## 19.19.1. Terms and Definitions

As per IS/ISO standards on occupational health, safety and environment the definitions of some common terms are given hereunder:

1. **Accident.** Undesired event giving rise to death, ill health, injury, damage or other losses to personnel or property.
2. **Audit.** A systematic, independent and a documented process for obtaining evidence and evaluating it objectively to determine the extent to which defined criteria are fulfilled.

3. **Auditor.** A person with the competence to conduct an audit.
4. **Continual Improvement.** Recurring process of enhancing the OH&S (environmental) management system, to achieve improvements in overall OH & S (environmental management) performance.
5. **Corrective action.** Action to eliminate the cause of a detected non-conformity or other undesirable situation. Correction action is taken to prevent recurrence, whereas preventive action is taken to prevent occurrence.
6. **Document.** Information and its supporting medium. The medium can be paper, magnetic, electronic or optical computer disc, photograph or master sample, or a combination thereof.
7. **Environment.** Surroundings in which an organisation operates, including air, water, land, natural resources, flora, fauna, humans, and their interrelation. Surroundings in this context extend from within an organisation to the global system.
8. **Environmental Aspect.** Element of organisation's activities or products or services that can interact with the environment.
9. **Environmental Impact.** Any change to the environment, whether adverse or beneficial, wholly or partially resulting from an organisation's environmental aspects.
10. **Environmental Management System (EMS).** Part of an organisation's management system used to develop and implement its environmental policy and manage its environmental aspects. A management system includes organisational structure, planning activities, responsibilities, practices, procedures, processes and resources,
11. **Environmental Objectives.** Overall environmental goal, consistent with the environmental policy that an organisation sets itself to achieve.
12. **Environmental Performance.** Measurable results of an organisation's management of its environmental aspects.
13. **Environmental Policy.** Overall intentions and direction of an organisation related to its environmental performance as formally expressed by top management. It provides a framework for action and for the setting of environmental objectives and environmental targets.
14. **Environmental Target.** Detailed performance requirement, applicable to the organization or parts thereof that arises from the environmental objectives and that needs to be set and met in order to achieve those objectives.
15. **Hazard.** A source or a situation with a potential to cause harm in terms of human injury or ill health, damage to property, damage to the environment or a combination of these.
16. **Hazard Identification.** The process of recognizing a hazard in existence and defining its characteristics/impact.
17. **Incident.** Event that give rise to an accident or has the potential to lead to an accident. An incident where no ill health, injury, damage or other loss occurs, is also referred to as 'near-miss'. The term incident includes "near-misses".

18. **Internal Audit.** Systematic, independent and documented process for obtaining audit evidence and evaluating it objectively to determine the extent to which the environmental management system audit criteria set by the organization are fulfilled.
19. **Non-conformity.** Non-fulfillment of a requirement.
20. **Objectives.** Goals that an organization sets itself to achieve.
21. **Occupational Health and Safety Management System.** A set of inter-related or interacting elements to establish OH&S policy and objectives, and to achieve those objectives,
22. **Occupational Health and Safety Objectives.** Overall goals in terms of OH&S performance, arising from the OH&S policy that an organisation sets itself to achieve, and which is quantified, where practicable.
23. **Occupational Health and Safety Policy.** Overall intentions and direction of an organization in relation to its overall OH&S performance as formally expressed by top management. The OH&S policy provide a framework for its action and for setting its OH&S objectives and targets.
24. **Occupational Health and Safety Targets.** A detailed performance requirement quantified, wherever practicable pertaining to the organisation that arises from the health and safety objectives and that needs to be met in order to achieve those objectives.
25. **Organisation.** Company, corporation, firm, enterprise, authority or institution, or part or combination thereof, whether incorporated or not, public or private that has its own functions and administration.
26. **Performance.** Measurable results of the OH&S management system, related to the organisation's control of health and safety risks, based on its OH&S policy and objectives.
27. **Preventive Action.** Action to eliminate the cause of a potential non-conformity.
28. **Prevention of Pollution.** Use of processes, practices, techniques, materials, products, services or energy to avoid, reduce or control (separately or in combination) the creation, emission or discharge of any type of pollutant or waste, in order to reduce adverse environmental impacts.
29. **Procedure.** Specified way to carryout an activity or a process.
30. **Record.** Document stating results achieved or providing evidence of activities performed.
31. **Risk.** The combination of frequency, or probability of occurrence and consequence of a specified hazardous event.
32. **Risk Analysis.** A systematic use of available information to determine how often specified events may occur and magnitude of their likely consequences.
33. **Risk Assessment.** The overall process of estimating the magnitude of risk and deciding whether the risk is tolerable,
34. **Safety.** State in which the risk of harm to person or damage to property is limited to a tolerable level. Safety can also be defined as freedom from unacceptable risk of harm.

35. **Standard.** A document, established by consensus and approved by a recognized body that provides; for common and repeated use. Rules, guidelines or characteristics for activities or their results, aimed at the achievement of the optimum degree of order in a given context.

36. **Standardization.** A standardization is an activity consisting of the process of formulating, issuing and implementing standards.

37. **Tolerable Risk.** Risk that has been reduced to a level that can be endured by the organization, having regards to its legal obligations and its own OH & S policy.

38. **Workplace.** Any physical location in which work related activities are performed under the control of the organisation. The organisation should take into account the OH&S effects on personnel who are, for example, travelling or in transit, working at the premises of a client or customer, or working at home.

## 19.20. QS - 9000 AND ISO/TS-16949

**QS-9000 is a sector specific standard developed by the automobile and truck manufacturers for their suppliers.** It was developed initially by a joint efforts of the "Big three' Americal automakers; General motors, Chrysler, and Ford and was introduced in 1994. It has been adopted by several heavy truck manufacturers. This takes ISO-9001: 1994 as the base and adds additional requirements for the automotive industry.

ISO/TS-16949 is an ISO technical specification aimed at the development of a quality management system that provide for continual improvement emphasizing **defect prevention and the reduction of variation and waste in the automotive industry supply chain.** It is based on the ISO-9001 standards and was first published in 1999 and latest edition was published in 2016.

This ISO/TS-16949 has three basic levels: (*i*) ISO-9001, (*ii*) sector specific requiremens, and (*iii*) company - specific requirements. The ISO/TS-16949 : 2009 in conjunction with ISO-9001: 2008 defines the quality management system requirements for design and development, production, and when relevant, installation and service of automotive - related products.

Its aim is to improve the system and process quality to increase customer satisfaction to identify problems and risks in the production process and supply chain to eliminate their causes and to examine and take corrective and preventive measures for their effectiveness. The focus is not on the discovery, but on the avoidance of errors.

## 19.21. ISO-27001 (INFORMATION SECURITY MANAGEMENT SYSTEM)

ISO - 27001 is a specification for an information security management system (ISMS). It is a framework of policies and procedures that includes all legal, physical, and technical controls involved in an organisation's information risk management processes.

ISO/IES - 27001 : 2013 (latest edition) is **an information security standard** that was published in sept., 2013, which supersedes ISO/IEC 27001: 2005 published by the ISO and the International electro–technical commission (IEC) jointly.

This 2013 standards put more emphasis on measuring and evaluating how well an organisation's ISMS is performing and there is a new section on outsourcing, which reflects the fact that many organisations rely on third parties to provide some aspects of information technology. More attention is paid to the organisational context of information security.

## 19.22. QUALITY AUDITS

Quality audits are performed to find whether the end product satisfies the desired quality specifications, proper functioning of all equipment and machinery, and operators are carrying out their duties as per specified quality plans. Special care must be given for auditing of tools, gauges and testing equipments, specifications and drawings. Audits should be carried out by unbiased persons and without prior intimation, it should cover each and every person involved in the process.

'Quality audit' can be defined as "a systematic and independent examination to determine whether quality activities and related results comply with planned arrangements and whether these arrangements are implemented effectively and are suitable to achieve objectives".

The purpose of a quality audit is to evaluate the need for improvement or corrective action. The quality audit is an independent review conducted to compare some aspects of quality performance with a standard for that performance.

The purpose of quality audits is also to provide independent assurance that:

(*i*) plans for attaining quality are such that when followed, intended quality can be attained,

(*ii*) products are fit for use and safe for the user,

(*iii*) standards and regulations defined by government agencies and other bodies are being followed,

(*iv*) there is conformance to specification,

(*v*) the data system provides correct and adequate information on quality to all concerned,

(*vi*) deficiencies are identified and corrective actions are taken in time, and

(*vii*) improvement opportunities are identified and concerned personnel are informed.

The quality audits are scheduled on the basis of the status and importance of the activity to be audited and shall be carried out by personnel independent of those having direct responsibility for the activity being audited. The results of the audits are recorded and brought to the notice of personnel, having responsibility in the area audited. The management personnel responsible for the area shall take timely corrective action on deficiencies found during the audit. The results of these quality audits form an integral part of the input to management review activities. Management needs to establish a system for correcting deficiencies or non-conformities revealed during the audit.

In the initial stages, quality audits should be carried out frequently, say once a quarter. Once the system is well-established, an annual audit may be adequate. Similarly, departments critical to the successful operation of the quality system like manufacturing may be audited more frequently than others like marketing and training.

Follow-up of quality audit activities shall verify and record the implementation of the corrective action taken.

Quality audits are of three kinds; namely: (*a*) first party audit .*i.e.* internal audit, carried out by the organisation itself and used for internal quality management purpose, (*b*) second party audit *i.e.* Customer audit and is carried out by the customer and (*c*) third party audit *i.e.* external audit and is carried out by an independent organisation usually a qualified national or international agency.

### 19.22.1. Types of Audits

1. **System Audit:** It includes evaluation of any activity that can affect final product quality. Quality systems audit, reviews the quality aspects of various segments of the overall quality system, such as marketing, design and development, production, quality assurance, process control, final inspection and testing, internal audit etc.
2. **Product Audit:** It involves the re-inspection of product to verify the adequacy of acceptance or rejection decisions made by inspection and testing department. Product audit is an independent evaluation of product quality to determine its fitness for use and conformance to specification. This takes place after completion of inspection, and is conducted for:
   (*a*) estimating the quality level of the products delivered to the customers,
   (*b*) evaluating the effectiveness of the inspection decisions, and
   (*c*) providing information useful in improving the outgoing product quality level and improving effectiveness of inspection.
3. **Adequacy Audit:** It is a management audit to determine the extent to which the documented system represented by the quality manual and procedures adequately meets the requirements of the applicable standard.

### 19.22.2. Structuring the Audit Programmes

Audit programmes are usually structured *i.e.* they are designed to carry out agreed purposes, and are conducted under agreed rules of conduct. The audit programmes are structured collectively by heads of activities which are to be the subject of audit, heads of auditing department, and upper management.

Audits are generally conducted by full time auditors, who are skilled in both, technical and human relations aspects. Sometimes, auditors relationships with those whose work is being audited become quite strained. Deficiencies found in the audit may be resented because of the implied criticism therein. In order to avoid such a situation, an extensive discussions is warranted with respect to the following :

(*i*) Reasons behind the audit.
(*ii*) Avoiding an atmosphere of blame.
(*iii*) Balance in reporting.
(*iv*) Depersonalising the report.
(*v*) Post audit meeting.

**Steps in Structuring an Audit Programme are:**

1. Discussion on purposes to be achieved by audit.
2. Approach for conducting the audit.
3. Study of policies, procedures and other applicable rules.
4. Scheduling of audit.
5. Conducting the audit.
6. Verification of factual findings.
7. Preparation of report with facts and recommendations.
8. Discussion of reports.
9. Decisions on action to be taken.
10. Follow-up.

**Planning and Performing Audits**

Main steps in performing quality audits are initiation, planning, implementation, reporting and completing. Steps for planning and performing in detail are:

1. Request for audit programme.
2. Determination of scope, objective and timing.
3. Selection of audit team including its leader.
4. Determination of audit elements.
5. Assignment elements to auditors.
6. Preparation of audit plan.
7. Distribution of audit plan and audit notification.
8. Audit commencement meeting.
9. Data/evidence gathering and evaluation.
10. Audit supervision and co-ordination.
11. Post audit meeting.
12. Drafting of report.
13. Review and submit report finding.
14. Finalizing the audit report.
15. Distribution of the audit report.
16. Decision on follow-up of finding.
17. Follow-up.

**Use of Reference Standards in the Audit**

The reference standards normally available include:

1. Policies of the company applicable to quality.

2. Customer and company quality specifications.
3. Pertinent government specification.
4. Company, industry, and other pertinent quality standards on products and processes.
5. Published guides for conduct of quality audits.
6. Pertinent quality departmental instructions.

**Discoveries of Causes and Recommendations of Audit**

In many companies, the auditor is expected to investigate major deficiencies in an effort to determine their causes, This investigation then becomes the basis of the auditor's recommendation.

Auditors are also expected to make recommendations with a view of reducing deficiencies and improving performance.

### 19.22.3. Audit Reporting

Audit results are documented in the audit report, the draft of which should be discussed and reviewed in a post-audit meeting held with the management of the activity that was audited. The report should include the following items :

(*i*) Purpose and scope of the audit.

(*ii*) Details of the audit plan, including audit personnel, dates, activities audited, personnel contacted, material or documents reviewed, number of observations made etc.

(*iii*) Standards, check-list, or other documents used during the audit.

(*iv*) Audit observations, supported with evidences, conclusions, and recommendations.

(*v*) Recommendations about improvement opportunities.

(*vi*) Recommendations for follow-up the proposed corrective actions.

## QUESTIONS

**1.** What is quality management system? What are its benefits?

**2.** Explain the term 'ISO-9000 Quality System' ? Illustrate various ISO-9000 standards.

**3.** What are the aims of ISO-9000 ? Mention their areas of application.

**4.** (*a*) Who can adopt ISO-9000?

(*b*) Explain the benefits of ISO-9000.

**5.** Explain with reference to ISO-9000: 1994 the salient features of:

(*a*) ISO-8402 (*b*) ISO-9000

(*c*) ISO-9001 (*d*) ISO-9002

(*e*) ISO-9003 (*f*) ISO-9004

**6.** Write short notes on:

(*a*) Characteristics of ISO-9000

(*b*) I.S.O. standards for manufacturing organisations.

(*c*) I.S.O. standards for service organisations.

7. How will you develop quality system for a service organisation?
8. Explain the operational element of quality system for services.
9. How will you do planning for installation of quality system?
10. Explain in detail:

    (*A*) ISO-9000 : 1994

    (*B*) ISO-9000 : 2000
11. What is the difference between ISO-9000 : 1994 and ISO-9000 : 2000?
12. Explain the history and origin of ISO-9000.
13. Explain the quality management principles of ISO-9000 : 2000 standards.
14. Explain the various requirements for ISO-9001 : 2000
15. Explain about ISO-9000:2008 version in detail.
16. How does the conceptual approach to ISO : 14001 differ from ISO : 9001?
17. What is the aim of the EMS standard?
18. Which of the elements in ISO 9001 are similar to ISO 14001?
19. Explain in detail about 'quality audit ?
20. Explain different types of quality audits.
21. Explain ISO : 14000 series of standards.
22. Discuss concepts of ISO : 14001.
23. Mention requirements of ISO : 14001.
24. Discuss about Occupational health and safety assessment series : 18001.
25. Explain OHSAS-18001 in detail.
26. Explain basic requirements of OHSAS-18001,
27. Discuss objectives and benefits of OHSAS-18001.

# Index

## A

## K



## L



## M



## N

## P

**T**



**U**



**V**



**X**



**Y**



**Z**

# TOTAL QUALITY MANAGEMENT

## M.P. POONIA|S.C. SHARMA

## FEEDBACK FORM

1. Which topics from your examination point of view are inadequately or not covered in this book?

2. Is there any misprints/ mistakes/ factual inaccuracy in this book? If so, please specify.

3. What is your assessment of this book as regards the presentation of the subject-matter, expression, precision and price in relation to the other recommended books available on this subject?

4. Which competing books you regard as better than this? Please mention their author and publishers.

5. Any further suggestions/comments you would like to make for the improvement of the book?

***PS:** If needed, please attach a separate sheet.*

**Name:** __________

**College:** __________

**Address:** __________

**E-mail:** __________

**Mobile:** __________

*Please mail the feedback form at:*

*KHANNA BOOK PUBLISHING CO. (P) LTD.*

*4C/4344, Ansari Road, Daryaganj, New Delhi-110002*

*You can also email this feedback form at* **contact@khannabooks.com** *or* **Whatsapp** *at +91 – 99109 09320*

**BEST FEEDBACK WILL BE REWARDED SUITABLY.**